Contesting Empires ∾

Contesting Empires ~

Opposition, Promotion, and Slavery

Jonathan Hart

CONTESTING EMPIRES
© Jonathan Hart, 2005.

First published in 2005 by
PALGRAVE MACMILLAN™
175 Fifth Avenue, New York, N.Y. 10010 and
Houndmills, Basingstoke, Hampshire, England RG21 6XS
Companies and representatives throughout the world.

PALGRAVE MACMILLAN is the global academic imprint of the Palgrave Macmillan division of St. Martin's Press, LLC and of Palgrave Macmillan Ltd. Macmillan® is a registered trademark in the United States, United Kingdom and other countries. Palgrave is a registered trademark in the European Union and other countries.

ISBN 1–4039–6453–X

Library of Congress Cataloging-in-Publication Data

Hart, Jonathan Locke, 1956–
    Contesting empires : opposition, promotion, and slavery / Jonathan Hart.
        p.cm.
    Includes bibliographical references and index.
    ISBN 1–4039–6453–X (alk. paper)
        1. Colonies—America. 2. Europe—Territorial expansion. 3. Imperialism. 4. Slavery. I. Title.

JV221.H28 2005
325.7—dc22   2004054413

A catalogue record for this book is available from the British Library.

Design by Newgen Imaging Systems (P) Ltd., Chennai, India.

First edition: February 2005

10 9 8 7 6 5 4 3 2 1

Printed in the United States of America.

For James Locke Marshall Hart

First was the world as one great cymbal made,
Where jarring winds to infant Nature played.

Andrew Marvell, *Music's Empire*

Contents ∾

List of Illustrations   ix

Preface and Acknowledgments   xv

1. Introduction   1

2. After Spain   11

3. Opposition from Within   43

4. Promoting Empire   67

5. Slavery to the American Revolution   91

6. Slavery Since the American Revolution   129

7. Conclusion   195

Notes   203

Index   251

List of Illustrations ⁓

1. *The Somerset House Conference*, 1604. Unknown Artist.
   Courtesy of the National Portrait Gallery, London
2. *The Battle of Princeton*, by James Peale (1749–1831).
   Courtesy of Princeton University Libraries

The Somerset House Conference, 1604. Unknown Artist. Courtesy of the National Portrait Gallery, London

The Battle of Princeton, by James Peale (1749–1831). Courtesy of Princeton University Libraries

Preface and Acknowledgments ⌇

"Contesting empires" can suggest internal strife within an empire or that between empires. The images on the dust jacket of this book and the two plates represent these two kinds of contests. Both involve the English (British), first in their peace with Spain in 1604 after more than twenty years of tension with this great power, and the second in the midst of internal conflict during the 1770s. The cover, the "Battle of Princeton," by James Peale (1749–1831), depicts a key battle in 1777 during a British civil war —the War of Independence or American Revolution.

These two images are about contest and the resolution of that contestation through peace or war. On August 29, 1604, after years of conflict, Spain and England signed a peace treaty at Somerset House, the residence of Anne of Denmark, the Queen Consort and a center of Jacobean culture. In the spring and summer of 2004, in celebration of this conference, Somerset House and King's College, London, have set up a series of events, "Talking Peace 1604," to explore its historical and cultural significance, and to celebrate Anglo-Spanish relations in the Europe of today (http://www.somerset-house.org.uk/1604). When I was viewing one of the paintings of this peace conference of 1604 in the National Portrait Gallery in London in 2002 and 2003 and wanted to have it as a plate or cover in this book, I did not know that there would be events to mark this occasion. One of those events—scheduled from May 20 to July 25, 2004—will bring together the two immense and closely related paintings of the Spanish– Flemish–English peace conference of the summer of 1604, one now housed in the National Maritime Museum in Greenwich and the other in the National Portrait Gallery (Unknown artist, 1604, oil on canvas, 81 in. × 105 1/2 in. [2057 mm × 2680 mm]). The interest in this peace and the events planned for this year are remarkable.

The group portrait from the National Portrait Gallery commemorates the peace treaty between England and Spain. The website of that gallery sets out the seating plan (I have conflated the information on its site (www.npg.org.uk)). "On the left are the members of the Hispano-Flemish delegation (from the window): Juan de Velasco, Duke of Frias, Constable of Castille, who was present only at the signing of the treaty; Juan de Tassis, Count of Villa Mediana; Alessandro Robida, Senator of Milan; Charles de Ligne, Count of Aremberg; Jean Richardot, President of the Council of State; Louis Vereyken, Audencier of Brussels"; on the right (from the window), the English commissioners: Thomas Sackville, first Earl of Dorset and poet and Lord Treasurer (1536–1608); Charles Howard, first Earl of Nottingham (1536–1624); Charles Blount, Earl of Devonshire (1536–1606); Henry Howard, Earl of Northampton (1540–1614); Robert Cecil, Viscount Cranborne (1563–1612). According to the notes the National Portrait Gallery provides, "Between 20 May and 16 July 1604 eighteen conference sessions were held at Somerset House, and the treaty was signed on 16 August. Although it apparently bears the signature of the Spanish painter Juan Pantoja de la Cruz, this painting also bears an impossible date. It is generally thought that both signature and the date are false and that it is by a hitherto unidentified Flemish artist. It may be associated with John De Critz the Elder, paintings by whom were probably the sources for the portraits of Robert Cecil and Thomas Sackville." The triangulation of Spain, the Netherlands, and England was a key to European politics and had implications well beyond from 1568 to 1648.

The Peale brothers, Charles (1741–1827) and James, played important roles in painting the civil strife in British North America that led to the independence of the United States and both were soldiers on the American side during this conflict. Born in Maryland, Charles Willson Peale studied with Benjamin West in London and painted William Pitt and George Washington. The Battle of Princeton itself occurred to the west of Nassau Hall, which is the center of Princeton University. In 1890, Allan Marquand said of that building: "Washington's portrait by the elder Peale is there, telling us also of the fall of General Mercer at the Battle of Princeton. (This picture was give[n] to the college by Washington himself, and occupies the very frame which once held the shot-riddled portrait of George II.) It is cherished also as a memorial of the sessions of the Continental Congress held in the college library in 1783" ("On the Campus: Princeton University," *Grounds & Buildings*; *Cosmopolitan* (NYC), Vol. 8, April 1890; see http://etc.princeton.edu/CampusWWW/Otherdocs/campus.html). The fact of or mythology over Washington taking George II's place in this frame (not to mention that of his son, George III) is a legend or representation of contest within the British Empire. This displacement also expresses of kind of continuity: the picture changes but the frame is the same. Both survive experience. This contest within became a contest between empires even as eventually the British Empire would translate to American power. James Peale's "Battle of Princeton" also represents a shift from British power to

American independence. Although this study involves a discussion of contests in different empires, the role of Britain and the American colonies the United States is central.

When I began specific research on this book in 1993, I could not have predicted the different elaborations of which it would be a part. My various volumes about the New World and empire, which Palgrave Macmillan has been publishing in a series, have taken on different forms and have been published according to what research was completed first rather than the order in which projects were begun or researched. There is a kind of staggered overlap among the complementary but distinct volumes in my series. As I have thanked many people in *Representing the New World, Columbus, Shakespeare and the Interpretation of the New World,* and *Comparing Empires,* I keep the acknowledgments relatively brief here, not due to ingratitude but to avoid too much repetition. I thank those I have mentioned in the acknowledgments section of the aforementioned books. I thank the president, fellows, students, and staff at Clare Hall, Cambridge; the Masters, fellows, students, and staff at Kirkland House, Harvard, and Wilson College, Princeton; the faculty, staff, and students at the Faculties of History and English at Cambridge and at the Departments of English and Comparative Literature at Harvard, at the Departments of History and Comparative Literature, and the Committee of Canadian Studies at Princeton for being generous and marvelous hosts and colleagues. University of Alberta has been supportive of my research and has generously allowed me to take time off to work on this book. Fellowships from the Social Sciences and Humanities Research Council, the British Council, the Fulbright Commission, Camargo Foundation, and Princeton University funded me for this and other projects. I think the directors, trustees, academic committees, and staff of these organizations, without whose support I would have had difficulty completing this and other research.

I thank Peter Burke and Anthony Pagden for encouraging my research on the promotion of empire and related areas and Nicholas Canny for his advice on related research. My gratitude is due to Anne Barton, Philip Ford, Anthony Pagden, Gordon Teskey, and Michael Worton for their support and encouragement of this and other work. Thanks, too, go to Charles Hart, George Hart, and Nicole Mallet for their advice on the translation of Duplessis-mornay. I also thank Alfred and Sally Alcorn, Diane Barrios, E. D. Blodgett, Marisa Bortolussi, Kerri Calvert, Mary Baine Campbell, Ross Chambers, John Charles, Olive Dickason, M. V. Dimić, G. Blakemore Evans, Margaret Ferguson, Stephen Ferguson, Jeannine Green, Judith Hanson, Nat Hardy, Thomas Healy, Shelagh Heffernan, Edward Jarron, Michèle Lamont, Dale Miller, Kenneth Mills, Steven Mobbs, Joyce Pilling-Back Margaret O'Reilly, Donald and Cathlenn Pfister, Ben Primer, Christian

Riegel, Peter Sinclair, Irene Sywenky, Pauline Thomas, Godfrey Waller, Robert Wilson, and others. I would like to remember Edward Said and Thomas M. Greene at the School of Criticism and Theory, Mark Kaplanoff at Cambridge and Lara Moore at Princeton.

I thank my hosts at Harvard, Cambridge, Hull, Madeira, Lisbon, Warwick, and elsewhere since 1992 who have heard me give various related talks in the field and provided me with stimulating suggestions and questions. I also thank the librarians, curators, and archivists at Widener, Houghton, and the other libraries at Harvard, the John Carter Brown, the Firestone and Mudd (Princeton), the Rutherford and Special Collections (Alberta), the Baldwin Room (Metropolitan Toronto), the Royal Ontario Museum (Toronto), the National Portrait Gallery (London), the Fitzwilliam Museum, the Royal Commonwealth Library, and the University Library (Cambridge), the British Library, the Bibliothèque Nationale (Paris), the Archive National in Paris, the Archive d'Outre Mer (Aix), and other museums, libraries, and galleries (too many to note here). I thank Kristi Long then at Garland and later at Palgrave—an earlier version of one of the chapters appeared before: thanks to Routledge: 1996; "Strategies of Promotion in Oviedo and Thevet and Hakluyt," *Imagining Culture: Eassays in Early Modern History* and *Literature*, ed. Jonathan Hart (New York: Garland, 173–92), reproduced by permission of Routledge/Taylor & Francis Books, Inc. Further gratitude to the National Portrait Gallery (particularly Helen Trompeteler) for permission to reproduce on a plate NPG 665, "The Somerset House Conference" by an Unknown Artist, and to Princeton Library (especially to Stephen Ferguson, Charles Greene, AnnaLee Pauls, and Ben Primer) for permission to reproduce one of the plates and the cover James Peale's "The Battle of Princeton" (Oil painting. Philadelphia, n.d., Graphic Arts, Iconography Collection. Department of Rare Books and Special Collections, Princeton University Libraries; Z-GA-GEN-2).

The encouragement and support of my editor at Palgrave Macmillan, Farideh Koohi-Kamali, has been generous and exemplary on this and other projects. Her colleagues, including Melissa Nosal, Roee Raz, Ian Steinberg have also been wonderful over the years. Veena Krishnan has done a fine job in production. I have been fortunate to work with this publisher and those who work there.

Many thanks to friends, family, and my parents, George and Jean, and my wife, Mary, and our children James and Julia. I owe my gratitude to John and Julia Marshall and their family. This book is also in remembrance of John Henry Marshall, who died as it was being completed. I dedicate this book with thanks to my son, James.

Chapter 1 ∾

Introduction

C   *ontesting Empires* focuses on the "contesting of empire," that is the contest or agon of establishing an empire or being first among empires and the contest against, or opposition to, empire. When "empire" is made plural, there is then an even greater sense of empires in a contest one with the other. At the heart of the book is the tension between the promotion of empire and the opposition to empire. The contest can be within an empire as well as between them and contestation can be as much about internal debate and dissent as about conflict and war with external powers. The very intricacy of the story of empire is that the opposition between us and them has never been as set as ideology might delineate.

In the notion of contest there is both comparison and contrast, recognition and misrecognition. A mixture of fear, awe, and wonder seems to have surrounded the language of travel in European accounts before Columbus set sail for the western Atlantic.[1] In the late Middle Ages and early Renaissance the Judeo-Christian and classical inheritance of European culture was there to bolster the expansion of the powers of Western Europe. In fits and starts— or what J. H. Elliott has called "the slow, erratic but nevertheless persistent process by which the Old World adjusted itself to the forces released by its conquest of the New"—the Europeans saw their own realm in a kind of typology with that newly "discovered" world. This typological urge could take on strange forms that reversed expectation in cultural "domination." This conquest was not so linear and certain as it might be construed retrospectively. For instance, the English even reimagined the ancient Picts and Britons through John White's drawings of North American Natives in 1585.[2]

One of the most remarkable aspects of European expansion—even amid promotion, rationalization, and self-justification in the imperial enterprise— was a use of critical thinking and doubt that called into question the very words and actions that underpinned empire. Some of this questioning came from leading figures in the Catholic Church itself. Although the papal donations of the fifteenth century were designed to help Portugal and Spain expand throughout the Atlantic world (including the New World), members of the Church questioned the authority of the pope. Francisco de Vitoria, a Dominican scholar and professor of theology at the University of Salamanca in Spain, gave lectures, beginning in 1532, in which he set out fundamental principles of international law. He addressed the idea of dominion and of the authority of the pope over non-Christians. In number 19 of the Summary to the First Section, Vitoria wrote: "Barbarians are not precluded by the sin of unbelief or by any other mortal sins from being true owners alike in public and in private law."[3] In the first article of the Summary of the Second Section, Vitoria maintained that Emperor Charles V "is not lord of the whole world." Even if he were, Vitoria argued in the second article of that Summary, "that would not entitle him to seize the provinces of the Indian aborigines and to erect new lords and put down the former lords or to levy taxes." After asserting the limits of the power of the emperor, Vitoria, in the third article, set out the constraints on the authority of the pope, who "is not civil or temporal lord of the whole world, in the proper sense of civil lordship and power." In the sixteenth article Vitoria continued to set out those limitations: "Christian princes cannot, even on the authority of the pope, restrain those aborigines from sins against the law of nature or punish them therefore." In the Summary of the Third Section, Vitoria explored lawful titles whereby Spain could have had power over the aboriginal peoples in America. For example, the sixteenth article stated: "The Indian aborigines could have come under the sway of the Spaniards through true and voluntary choice." Vitoria was careful to see the problems of tyranny and to argue that sovereignty was related to the interests of the Natives and not the profit of the Spaniards because, as a professor of theology, he was interested in salvation, for the Spanish as well as the "Indians." The exploration of the different sides of the debate over the nature and the status of the indigenes in relation to the Natives was also something that fellow Dominicans, Antón Montesino, and Bartolomé de Las Casas, also brought into the public eye and called attention to court as well as to the Church. The authority of Aristotle was contested, for instance, over the theory of natural slavery and its application to the Indians of the New World, something epitomized in the debate between Juan Ginés de Sepúlveda and Las Casas.[4]

While this introductory matter frames the debate in this book, chapters 6 and 7 on slavery discuss the greatest "contesting" in both main senses of the word as it is used in this study. These two discussions on holding and trading slaves use the American Revolution as the divide because it was toward the end of this struggle in which Pennsylvania banned the slave trade and set an example for other British American colonies (later new American states). The concluding remarks also gesture toward the significance of internal and external tensions and contests, particularly as they relate to the ambivalent instance of Spain, the promotion of and opposition to empire, and the question of slavery. The culture, ethics, politics, and economics of slavery haunt the whole colonial and imperial enterprise of the Europeans from the Portuguese in Africa in the early fifteenth century to the breakup of the European empires and the assertion of American power in the twentieth century.

The arc of the book is to set out the early contest in the New World, particularly among Spain, France, and England, and then to proceed to the opposition to empire, the promotion of empire, and the question of slavery. Why this progression? After establishing briefly the idea of contesting empire(s) and discussing key terms and the structure of the volume here, the main body of the book begins with the establishment of Spanish leadership in the colonization of the New World. *Contesting Empires* then moves to the subsequent development of French and English texts about colonies in the Americas; to an opposition to expansion, war and colonization that is sometimes forgotten or underplayed in discussions of empire and colonies; to the promotion of empire that helps, with the opposition to empire, to constitute a contradiction; to the question of slavery that widens the discussion both in time and space because it ranges from early Arab, African, and Portuguese practices in Africa and beyond to the legal abolition of slavery in the British Empire, the United States, and elsewhere in the nineteenth century. These chapters on slavery place in context the mainly fifteenth- and sixteenth-century material about the New World of the earlier chapters. They also gesture toward a wider debate on enfranchisement and the widening of human rights, something that is involved in a democratic push, at least in industrialized countries and some key developing states, like India.

This volume also concentrates on how rhetoric was used to persuade others, whether monarchs or courtiers or readers, for or against exploration, expansion, settlement, and empire. In Western Europe a tension developed over the question of overseas empires, so that the different European cultures expressed disjunctive attitudes. The stakes were high because what happened in the New World was often interpreted in relation to Europe, so that coming to terms with the New World was frequently a taking into account of changes in the Old World. The comparative method is integral here because it places each empire in a wider context: while recognizing differences among them, it also reduces extravagant claims for each. The volume draws on little discussed topics and sources, for instance, the work of Philippe de Mornay, seigneur du Plessis-Marly, a Huguenot hostile to Spain and a diplomat serving Henri de Navarre, who was his ambassador in London in 1577–78 and whom Richard Hakluyt the Younger may have known well in France in the 1580s Duplessis-Mornay was a friend of their mutual acquaintance,

Philip Sidney, who translated Duplessis-Mornay's treatise on Christian religion. Other times, I examine the work of well-known figures from an alternative point of view, such as Thomas More's and Erasmus's satire on or opposition to war or expansion. Each of these works, in conjunction with rare archival material, changes the other and creates a different context in which to compare these contesting empires. Well-known critics of warfare and empire, like More, Erasmus, and Montaigne, or promoters of empire, like Oviedo, Thevet, and Hakluyt, all of whom had close ties to Crown and court, find themselves in the company of lesser-known and marginal figures and in the context of documents that are not part of high culture. The way *Contesting Empires* is structured, where the comparisons within the body of the book involve dramatic contrasts, should bring out these tensions, rivalries, and disjunctions. For example, whereas chapter 3 discusses the opponents to empire or conquest in Europe—like More, Erasmus, and Montaigne (one English, the other Dutch and the last French)—chapter 4 examines the rhetorical dimension of how Oviedo, Thevet, and Hakluyt—advisers or historiographers to the rulers of Spain, France, and England respectively—frame the knowledge of the New World and the policies of empire.

II

The body of the book emphasizes important aspects of the internal and external contests of empire. In chapter 2, "After Spain," I maintain that doubleness and disjunction characterized the attitude of the European powers who played catch up with Spain after Columbus's landfall in the Americas: they sought to emulate and displace Spain. Having become the "superpower" of the sixteenth century and being still a great power in the seventeenth and eighteenth centuries in the New World even though its power had waned in Europe, Spain had to contend with England, France, and the Netherlands, who came after Spain in both senses of the expression. Here, I develop a central motif in this study: divided from within, the European countries displayed divisions amongst themselves. With hindsight, it is easier to observe a single purpose in each nation and its expansion or in Western Europe in the exploration and settlement of the Americas. The Spaniards watched their backs even if others looked at Philip II as a threat to the peace of Europe, thought that his riches destabilized the continent, and feared that his power was invulnerable. The other Western European powers were after Spain, which is to come and go after that country. Some of the writers, like Bartolomé de Las Casas, whom the other powers used in their representations of Spain, were Spaniards who, while not opposing colonization, criticized some of its motives and excesses. In promoting their state's imperial expansion, some authors emulated Spanish texts on the New World or used them as a tool of propaganda. In this chapter I seek out visual representations and other material that I have not used before in my comparative discussions of European colonization. I set out various historical and literary representations of Spain, some relatively well-known and some not, to illustrate this emulation and blackening of Spain. The rivalry of the French and English with the Spanish focused on the Revolt in the Netherlands in the late sixteenth and early seventeenth century. A recurring motif in my book is typology: a typological or double image keeps cropping up between Spanish cruelty to the Natives in the New World and that in the Netherlands.

In chapter 3, "Opposition from Within," I observe that there are four principal kinds of opposition to European expansion west. First, during meetings in December 1486 and January 1487, the Columbus commission rejected Columbus's arguments. Key members of the learned and administrative classes in Spain, or Europe, opposed some plans for expansion and empire. Second, some important European clergy and intellectuals in particular opposed European expansion or the exploitation of the peoples of the New World. Third, Columbus's exploration began a great legal debate between Portugal and Spain and later involved the papacy and other European countries. It sometimes happens that discussions slip into making Natives and Europeans into two groups with coherent and opposing interests. To an extent, there is some sense to this view, but conflicts amongst Europeans and amongst Natives as well as rival allies make this kind of opposition too bald. Moreover, later on, in trade blocs different European and Native nations were allied. Another related kind of opposition from within occurred in the ambivalence in European representations of the lands and peoples of the New World: Columbus and Verrazzano display an ambivalence that prepares the way for Las Casas, Montaigne, and others to portray the Natives as critics of Europe. Fourth, the Christian critique of riches and power, which could occur in the Church or at court, also applied to European actions in the New World, for instance, in parts of Thomas More's *Utopia* (1516). European expansion was not as univocal: humanists, such as Erasmus, More, Las Casas, and Montaigne, were not the handmaids of the imperial theme. A typology, or double image, exists between Europe and the New World in the writings of these European nations, implicitly and explicitly expressed in the writings of these figures.

Having first created settlements in the New World, Spain developed knowledge that became useful for other European countries eager to expand overseas. Possession of knowledge might well lead to the possession of the New World. In chapter 4, "Promoting Empire," I focus on a close analysis of three important texts by key figures attached to the courts in Spain, France, and England respectively: Gonzalo Fernández de Oviedo's *Natural History of the West Indies* (1526), André Thevet's *Les Singvlaritez de La France Antarctique, Avtrement nommée Amerique* (1558), and Richard Hakluyt's *The Principall Navigations of the English Nation* (1589). This close attention consists mainly of looking at the rhetoric or art of persuasion of the promotional tracts in encouraging settlement of the New World. As in the study more generally, this chapter emphasizes the relation between rhetoric on the one hand and history, ethnology, and literature on the other through an inductive method, which complements the largely deductive framework of much of the recent work in the area of literary and cultural studies. Evidence and argument should serve as checks to each other. These writers had to sell the idea of American colonies owing to resistance at home and hardships overseas. The utopian descriptions of the Americas, beginning with Columbus, did not convince everyone, so that finding settlers and financial backing for colonies, especially among the French and English, was not an easy task.

Chapter 5, "Slavery to the American Revolution," begins with a brief discussion of the classical inheritance of slavery in Europe as well as of Europe after the fall of Rome. Some of the countries, like England, that became involved in the slave trade themselves had the institution of slavery among them and some of their own compatriots were slaves. Sometimes Europeans were enslaved in war with other cultures long after slavery had withered within the boundaries of their own countries. The chapter makes some distinction between slavery and servitude and concentrates first on the Portuguese involvement in the African slave trade beginning in the fifteenth century. This trade involved exchanges of slaves through Black African and Arab sources as well as direct raids or *razzias*. Although slavery had withered in northern Europe, it was something to which southern Europe, including the Iberian powers, were accustomed. The discussion ranges from Gomes Eannes de Azurara, a Portuguese chronicler in Africa in the fifteenth century, through Bartolomé de Las Casas, who defended Native Americans against slavery but did not extend that defense to Black Africans, to the *Code Noir* (1685), Aphra Behn's *Oroonoko* (1688), and beyond. Behn's text receives close attention in my analysis partly because it raises important questions about slavery in terms of racial, social, and sexual issues. The devastating effects this trade had on Africa is something that has long left its intricate traces.[5] Those for and against had to contend with Aristotle's theory of natural slavery and the varying representations of servitude in the Bible. The Portuguese and Spaniards had also experienced the institution of slavery under the Moors but became actively involved themselves. In the sixteenth century, England, through captains like John Hawkins, had tried to profit from that Spanish slave trade. The Dutch, who had once freed slaves from an Iberian ship in one of their ports and had opposed slavery, became main players in the trade as the seventeenth century wore on. Because slavery made those islands so profitable, the French gave up Canada for Guadeloupe and Martinique. The demand for sugar, whether in Madeira or in the Caribbean, developed slavery on a vast scale. Before Wilberforce and Lincoln, there were opponents to slavery: for instance, some popes came to condemn the practice. There were others who rationalized and naturalized slavery because it had so increased their personal wealth and that of Europe. There was then a "contesting" of slavery in the imperial centers, the colonies, and former colonies that was an aspect of the more general debate over liberty, which was part of the establishment of empire and also characterized the English, American, and French Revolutions.

In chapter 6, "Slavery Since the American Revolution," I discuss some of the founders of the United States and their attitudes toward slavery and how it was involved in their lives. The economics of slavery in Europe, Africa, the Americas, and beyond represents another concern of this chapter. Besides expected figures like Abraham Lincoln, others less obvious, like Jeremy Bentham, inform the debate on slavery. Even Lincoln, who helped to abolish slavery, experienced some of the same dilemmas as "Europeans" in their expansion, colonization, and the coming of independence in some of their colonies: they all faced the contradictions of slavery. Part of what I stress here is how women talked about slavery in their letters and diaries, so that notions of gender and class are made messier and even murkier. The writings of African Americans, men and women, also express the view of those whose people were mistreated and oppressed. A change in economics, politics, and consciousness meant that serfs and slaves were freed in Europe from 1810 to 1861, from Prussia through Austria to Russia, and the institution of slavery (and not just the trade) was abolished (or at least made illegal) from 1834 to 1889 from British North America through the United States to Brazil. Human rights, as expressed through figures like M. K. Gandhi and Martin Luther King, become later phases in a discourse contra slavery and pro liberty. The legacies of slavery and indeed slavery itself (although outlawed, it exists) as well as those of empire are still with us. In Africa, although the Europeans tried to abolish slavery, the institution persists. As late as 1980, although abolished three times, in Mauritania, slavery existed as Arab masters still kept black African slaves much as they had done when the Portuguese first entered Africa in 1441.[6] Slaves persist elsewhere: in recent years slavery has been connected to illegal migration, prostitution, diplomats, charcoal making, and the carpet industry.

III

The interpretation of cultures is contested in the fields of sociology and anthropology and their practice and theory. Pierre Bourdieu has argued for a reflexivity that "does not have much in common with 'textual reflexivity' and with all the falsely sophisticated considerations on the 'hermeneutic process of cultural interpretation' and the construction of reality through ethnographic recording."[7] Bourdieu distinguishes his observer from that in Marcus and Fisher, Rosaldo and Geertz, who, he argues, tend "to substitute the facile delights of self-exploration for the methodical confrontation with the gritty realities of the field."[8] Ethnographic writing need not be reduced to poetics and politics or interpretive skepticism, although I also think it important to call attention, as I have done in my earlier work, to what Mary Louise Pratt calls "contestatory expressions from the site of imperial intervention." In this case there is also in the imperial theme a transcultural translation of knowledge in which marginal groups select and shape the materials given to them by the metropolitan culture, so that appropriation might be as much a colonial matter as an imperial one. Rhetorical analysis, especially as it occurs in chapter 4, is another attempt in my work, in the context of others working in the field, to bring out the comparative and contesting nature of European expansion and contact with other cultures.[9] Over the period of my study, from the early fifteenth century to the present, the shift from natural philosophy to science, "discovery" is a form of recognition and misrecognition. In all this, subjectivity, intersubjectivity, and objectivity contest and mix while doubt and knowledge discipline each other. As an antidote to assuming too great a role for the personal, Bourdieu balances this denial of scientific knowledge in the age of European imperialism. Perhaps, as he suggests, there does not have to be a firm choice in the attempt of understanding, seeing, and knowing:

> In short, one does not have to choose between participant observation, a necessarily fictitious immersion in a foreign milieu, and the objectivism of the "gaze from afar" of an observer who remains as remote from himself as from his object. Participant objectivation undertakes to explore not the "lived experience" of the knowing subject but the social conditions of possibility— and therefore the effects and limits—of that experience and, more precisely, of the act of objectivation itself. It aims at objectivizing the subjective relation to the object which, far from leading to a relativistic and more-or-less anti-scientific subjectivism, is one of the conditions of genuine scientific objectivity.[10]

Bourdieu's paradoxical objectivity in science is suggestive even where I might differ from him. The condition of our knowing and not knowing is contestatory. It is too easy to throw over the natural philosophy, technology, and science that was part of European expansion. Nonetheless, it is also a cautionary tale to occlude the dark side of this economic and political expansion. Paradoxically, it might be that objectivity, if that is entirely possible in the human sciences, allows for a means of calling up short aspects of the imperial and colonial enterprise. It is the very critical distance that allows for satire, irony, and other weapons that expose the abuses of empire. In the contest of empire there is agony, the ambivalent and contradictory expressions in words and actions in the meeting of cultures.

Contesting Empires contributes to various fields—history, literary studies, politics, and ethnology,—that meet in the study of empires and colonies. As in my earlier studies published on the New World and empire, in this book I hope to bring forward new material and contexts to reach students, scholars, and readers generally.[11] For instance, the chapters on slavery will connect this institution in the English-speaking world to earlier practices in other cultures, the slave trade in the Americas to that in Africa and other places, and examine the tension between the opposition to slavery and the promotion of it over a period much wider than the eighteenth- and nineteenth centuries, which have been the main periods of concentration in the field. In this book I continue to use the comparative study of empires, an area that relates well to, and should interest, those who study or write on national literatures, histories, and politics. Perhaps most in slavery, although also in the other institutions used in European colonization, there was much at stake in the "contesting" of empire.

Chapter 2 ⁓

After Spain

The French and English questioned the Spanish imperium, and sometimes their own empires, but no amount of questioning, as intricately ambivalent and as admirable as it might seem to us on the dry side of empire, could halt the push to translate empire. This almost obsession that the English and French had with Spain is a central part of this discussion. It is also important to remember that Jean de Léry and Michel de Montaigne used the St. Bartholomew's Massacre of 1572 as a marker of French barbarity. The Spanish were not alone in condemning themselves. How much the English could express and reveal this self-criticism early on, beyond Thomas More's general satire, is an open question. This discussion leads to that about the opposition from within. Despite opposition to exploration and the expansion, European voyages and settlement in the New World persisted. The tensions between opposition to and promotion of expansion is something the following chapters explore, but for now the question of emulation, rivalry, and displacement is a central concern.

Although the Spanish had achieved the first landfall in the New World since the Norsemen, other European monarchs, like Henry VII of England, ignored their claim to share, with the Portuguese, the world unknown to the Europeans. An ambivalence and contradiction occurred in the attitude of the powers who played catch up with Spain in the Americas: leaders, representatives, or subjects of these states could envy and revile Spain almost in the same breath. Spain became the "superpower" of the sixteenth century and was still a great power in the seventeenth and eighteenth centuries in the New World even if its power had declined in Europe. England, France, and the Netherlands came after Spain in both senses of the expression. Here, I am developing a central motif in this book—the European countries were divided from within and showed divisions amongst themselves, so that it is too easy, *ex post facto*, to see a simple, unopposed, and harmonious impulse to imperialism in each nation let alone a univocal pan-European imperial expansion in the Americas. A rising capitalism, a need for new markets, and greed drove the powers to expand and exploit sometimes well beyond the humane or religious rhetoric of court and Church. Gold, resources, and land often became too tempting for conscience to prevail, something not alien to a market economy then or now.

Here I set out various historical and literary representations of Spain, some relatively well known and some not, to illustrate this emulation and blackening of Spain. One of my unexpected findings is that while circumstances shifted from the late medieval and early modern periods to the Enlightenment, some of the same attitudes remained as persistent tropes and figures in this coming to terms with Spain. Much of this rivalry, amongst the French and English with the Spanish, centered on the Revolt in the Netherlands in the late sixteenth and early seventeenth century, where that Spanish possession split in two and where the northern part gained independence and became a leading Protestant power. France and England had much to do with that long war, which also played out their own internal religious divisions and which helped to create a world power, perhaps the leading commercial, naval, and imperial force in the middle of the seventeenth century. A typology between Spanish cruelty to the Natives in the New World and abuses in the Netherlands became a bitter weapon in a propaganda war with Spain. Even as Spain declined, the ghost of its former glory could still be found in English and French writings into the eighteenth century and beyond. The arc of this pursuit of Spain is the matter of what follows.

I

From Columbus's landfall, the other European powers, most notably England and France, tried to compete with Spain and to circumvent its legal claim, along with Portugal—something the papacy supported—to the New World. In 1589 Richard Hakluyt's *The Principall Navigations* included a map between the "To the Reader" and the dedicatory poems in Greek and Latin, which included an inscription on what is now Western Canada that stated that America was first detected by Columbus in 1492 in the name of the king of Castile.[1] Perhaps to counter the priority of Columbus and Spain in America, Hakluyt tried to build up a translation of empire from classical Rome saved by Britons to "Renaissance" Britain itself:

> Flauius Constantine, syrnamed the great, King of the Britaines after his father, and Emperour of the Romanes, borne in Britainie of *Helena* his mother, and there created Emperour made his natiue countrie partaker of his singular glorie, and renoume.
>
> Hauing conquered and put to flight the Almanes, Spaniards, Frenchmen, and their Kings for a spectacle throwne out to wilde beastes, he held France it

selfe as subiect vnto him: and hauing happily deliuered the Italians from the tyrannie of *Maxentius,* he preferred 3. of his mothers vncles, all Britaines, namely *Leoline, Trahere,* and *Marius,* whom in his actions he had found more faithful vnto him then any others, to be of the order of the Romane Senators.[2]

In creating an English claim in America as well as an assertion of empire or a special status in European history, Hakluyt attempts many ways to circumvent, subvert, or confront Spain and other rivals. The classical past becomes a way of forging an argument for colonization in the present and for imperial power in the future out of, for England, an insecure power in Europe and various disappointments and failures in settling the New World.

North America in the mythology and history of French exploration of the New World was something France came to later than the West Indies and South America. The need to precede the Spanish and Portuguese was a challenge to the French and the English both. The French made claims, not too dissimilar to those of the English, that they in fact had discovered America. Rivalries with Spain had an uneven development: the French seem to have made a more concerted effort than the English did in the exploration of the New World from about 1520 to 1542. In a well-known instance, François Ier (1515–47) asked to be shown Adam's will as evidence of France giving up the right to territory in the New World.[3] He would not accept this "divine" law that underpinned the agreement between Portugal and Spain but, instead, adopted the principle of first possession by Europeans.[4] The Natives were to have no rights of possession of their lands because they did not occupy them as Europeans did, that is in a permanent civil society or a Christian society. The Portuguese themselves had used this principle of *terra nullius* in Africa in the fifteenth century, so that they, and the Spanish, were now going to deny this legal interpretation in the New World. François and Henry VIII had both aspired to being the Holy Roman emperor, but the election of the young Charles I of Spain as emperor Charles V maintained the Habsburg succession and meant that the French king felt that Spain hemmed in France from Flanders through Burgundy and Italy to Spain itself. France claimed Milan and other parts of Italy, and a war with Spain began in 1521.

The French joined the English and Spanish in the search for a northwest passage. Verrazzano was a Florentine living in Rouen and a part of a network of Italian merchants, principally from Florence, who lived in Lyon, Paris, and Rouen, who traded under the French flag.[5] His expedition of 1523–24 raided the Spanish coast and then, reduced to one ship, proceeded to North America at thirty-four degrees of latitude then sailed north to avoid Spanish ships.[6] While sailing from the Carolinas to Nova Scotia, Verrazzano made detailed notes on Natives, vegetation, and rivers, but returned home without having discovered a northwest passage. While the Spanish wrote extensively about their experiences in the New World, the English did not produce narratives about their early voyages. The first book to appear in English about voyages was *Of the newe landes* . . . , which Jan van Doesborch printed in Antwerp about 1511 and which included a description of "Armenica" or America, such as accounts by Vespucci; descriptions of Africa, by Balthasar Springer, an agent of Anton Welser, the German financier; narratives of Eastern Christians, and a version of Prester's John's *Letter.* England lagged behind its rivals in empire.[7] Whereas the English had begun well with the practical knowledge of the voyages of the Cabots, they even more than the French, showed an apathy toward, and ignorance of, cosmography and mathematics, producing the first printed text on basic arithmetic in English or by an Englishman in 1543.[8] The example of Spain and of the Continent generally, which was part of the changes that humanism and the growth of science had wrought, had not always penetrated the insularity of England. In the first few decades following the Columbian landfall, the English did not always pursue their best interests.

An interlude by John Rastell, More's brother-in-law, which he published after his planned voyage to America failed, was the first book in English about the New World printed in England. In *A new interlude of the four elements,* Rastell has Experience describe the New World and successful voyages to its northern parts, represents a call for more English exploration and for an overseas empire, and revisits the question of origins and regret.[9] In some cases it took the Spanish to interpret their rivals in the New World at the time, and it was not until the second half of the sixteenth century that the English, like the French, began to build their own significant archive of narratives and commentary on the Americas. Even in this period, both the English and the French relied heavily on the translation of Spanish works on their colonies to build their own library of empire and to help to establish permanent settlements overseas.

Unlike France, England was closely tied to Spain, when briefly, from 1553 to 1558, Philip of Spain and Mary I, were married. This Spanish match caused anxiety, especially amongst Protestants, in England. For a brief moment, there was, however, the possibility of the union of Spain and England and an heir for Mary and Philip. However much time did not bear out that great imperial theme, and actually embodied a greater split between the Spanish and English nations, some hope of a greater glory affected a writer, like Richard Eden, who in his own career moved ambivalently between support for and suspicion of the idea of union and the imperial marriage itself.

Eden also tried to bring the English up-to-date on geography and exploration: in 1553, *A Treatyse of the newe India,* his translation of a part of the fifth book of Sebastian Münster's cosmography, came out and was dedicated to John Dudley, earl of Warwick and duke of Northumberland, who supported Lady Jane Grey, which later made it hard for Eden to win the firm support of Mary I no matter how much he motivated his later rhetoric to that end. In his epistle to the reader, for instance, Eden addressed the question of the incredible and hopes that when reading of "the great abundance of gold, precious stones and spices, which the Spaniardes and Portugales have brought from the South partes of the worlde, as from the newe founde landes and Ilandes," the reader would think of the wisdom and gold God brought Solomon.[10] Eden was implying that just as God and gold could not be separated, truth, wisdom, and gold were divine gifts.

The prefatory matter of Eden's translation of the *Decades* of Peter Martyr (Pietro Martire d'Anghiera), an Italian humanist working in the service of Spain, described the procession of Philip and Mary in London on August 18, 1554. The translator wanted to celebrate the glory and excellence of Philip's ancestors in the New World.[11] This praise of Spain for the conversion of the Natives followed the papal bull of 1493 in which Alexander VI, who also had Spanish connections, supported the work of the Spanish Crown in this area and presented empire as a good emanating from God.[12]

What I have called "God and gold" as a synecdochic motive for this oxymoronic expansion of Europe to the Americas embodies this coexistence and clash of feudal religion and commercial desire. This was the major tension in Columbus's coming to terms with the Natives in the western Atlantic islands. Eden, who in an earlier passage had proclaimed that "The Spanyardes haue shewed a good exemple to all Chrystian nations to folowe"—justified the gold before, but along with, God.[13] He declared that "although summe wyll obiecte that the desyre of golde was the chiefe cause that moued the Spanyardes and Portugales to searche the newe founde landes, trewly albeit we shulde admitte it to bee the chiefe cause," but Eden said that a man could be a warrior or a merchant and a Christian at the same time.[14] Rather than remain a critical bystander, Eden argued that England should follow Spain on the pursuit of gold and God in the New World. By implication, the best way would be to embrace the marriage of Mary and Philip. This hope would not be pursued for long: Eden was removed from office for heresy, and even before Mary died without an heir, it seemed that Philip, whose father Charles had arranged the marriage, had lost interest. England was neither destined to be Catholic nor to be united with Spain. Instead, a great series of conflicts would brew between England and Spain in Europe and in the New World.

II

The promotion and critique of empire that existed in Spain was transmitted through translations in French and English. In France cosmographies, "collections" that were a mixture of natural history, redaction, and translation of classical and Spanish sources, history, and geography, were often used to promote French aspirations for trade and expansion in the world. In France and England histories and collections, from André Thevet to Samuel Purchas, represented this ambivalence both in the prefatory matter and in the contradictory materials brought together. Writers like Eden, Thevet, and Hakluyt used the relation between European and Native to define their imperial and national identities.[15] Richard Eden's hope of a union of Spain and England in 1555 was a faded dream long before the massacre in 1565 galvanized the French and English Protestants into a concerted anti-Spanish campaign of polemics and propaganda, so often launched in conjunction with translations of books by or about Spaniards.[16] Behind many travel narratives in the English Renaissance, such as Hakluyt's "Prose Epic of the modern English nation" (including Purchas' continuation of it), lay a whole network of Spanish, French, and English sources about mediation and the relation between Europeans and Natives.[17] The coming to terms with the example of Spain also depended on the Revolt of the Netherlands against Spain and the War of the Spanish Succession.[18] How different were the French and British practices from those of the Spanish when we look behind the rhetoric of the Black Legend?

As much as the French had looked at the riches of Spain as an example to be emulated and envied, France made early inroads into the authority of Portugal and Spain in the New World. When François Ier died in 1547, his colonial policy of discovery, conquest, and settlement had influenced the European powers.[19] The French corsairs traded and pirated along the coast of Brazil as far south as Rio de Janeiro, arming the Natives against the Portuguese, who were displacing them with settlers. By 1550, France, not Portugal, controlled the coast from Cape Frio to Rio de Janiero. Trade and religious ideals sometimes clashed among the French as they had among the Spanish. After the failures of Cartier and Roberval to find riches in Canada, Admiral Gaspar de Coligny, a Huguenot and first minister to Henri II, turned his attention to Brazil where Nicolas Durand de Villegagnon was to found a colony. Coligny's aims for the Brazil expedition were to find a base for imperial expansion, to create a Huguenot sanctuary, and to weaken the Catholic powers of Spain and Portugal by loosening their hold on the New World.[20]

During the 1550s and 1560s, Coligny organized voyages to the New World as a place of refuge for French Protestants. The first voyage was to the site of Rio Janeiro in 1555, under the direction of Nicolas Durand, chevalier de Villegagnon and vice admiral of Brittany. In 1556 three ships from Honfleur were sent to reinforce Villegagnon's colony. In 1560, the Portuguese captured the French base but were not able to eliminate the French from

Brazil until 1603, when they were in a political union with Spain.[21] After the failure in Brazil, Coligny then attempted to break the Spanish monopoly by creating a French base in Florida, but internal strife and the Spanish military ended this attempt.[22] France had not had good fortune in establishing a permanent settlement in Canada, Brazil, or Florida.[23] André Thevet and Jean de Léry, who were both in Brazil, represented the strife between French Catholics and Protestants at home and in the Americas.

Even the religious ideals were intricate because in the 1550s Geneva Calvinists in Brazil and in the 1560s French Protestants in Florida had tried to build permanent settlements to rival Spain and attempted to convert the indigenous population but had failed.[24] The Jesuits, on the other hand, had proclaimed missionary success in Africa, Asia, and the Americas. The Church of England was a national Church with the monarch at its head, so that the political rivalry with Catholic Spain was necessarily religious. France, which experienced terrible internal strife between Catholics and Protestants, displayed a two-part rivalry with Spain. The Huguenots opposed the authority of the papacy and Spain while French Catholics often thought of France as the eldest daughter of the Church whose place Spain and Portugal had usurped with the discovery of the New World. This last attitude would later be clearly expressed in Marc Lescarbot's history of New France. France and England needed Spanish knowledge of the New World to dispossess it of that world. The rhetoric of texts about the New World, sometimes by ship captains, sometimes by educated humanists, embodied, refracted, and displaced this economic, political, and religious rivalry.

The French showed anxieties over the relative success of the Spanish to establish permanent colonies and the failure of France to do so. This situation emphasized the French desire to imitate the Spanish and envy and outrage over Spain's advantage. To right this wrong, writers and translators took two primary strategies—to give advice or to denounce Spain—sometimes in the same work. At other times, for the greater glory of the ancients and of France, writers ignored Spain, as if it were not worthy to take up the mantle of Greece and Rome. It is important to realize, even though the focus of this chapter is on French and English uses of Spain, that the trope of the translation of empire through the translation of study continued to be strong and provided a way for France (and England) to circumvent or occlude Spain in order to rival it. The office that André Thevet gained, cosmographer to the king of France, was like the one Oviedo had lobbied for three decades before.[25] Thevet was aware of Spain's greatness but wanted to concentrate on the great power of France. He claimed to provide valuable advice and insisted on his unique ability to combine astute observations of the New World with strong scholarship. Thevet was a controversial figure: whereas Jean de Léry and François de Belleforest ridiculed his scholarship and character, Ronsard and Du Bellay esteemed his work.[26] Cosmography was as much about advancement as it was about the advancement of knowledge.

A crisis in France occurred when the Spanish and French fought over Florida, a conflict that had close connections with the divisions between Protestant and Catholic in France and with the Protestant powers at court in England. The figure of Jean Ribault was a focus for anxiety for Spain and its pro-Spanish allies in France and a figure of hope for Protestants in France and England. In fact, the French original is lost and Thomas Hacket's translation of 1563 is the extant account. At the center of Gaspar de Coligny's policy in France was to ruin Spain by attacking what he thought was its vulnerability—the colonies in the Americas.

After the French experienced problems coexisting with the Portuguese in Brazil, they sought to establish themselves in Florida, which the Spanish claimed but barely occupied. Jean Ribault of Dieppe and René de Goulaine de Laudonnière led the expeditions from 1562 to 1565.[27] Ribault's chronicle is a central document in the French relations with Spain in the Americas and, along with Nicolas Le Challeux's account of the massacre of the Huguenots, represented a turning point in the pursuit of Spain in the New World. Addressing a French official, probably Coligny, at the opening of *The Whole and True Discovery* (1562), Ribault said that the admiral had long wished for the day when France could make new discoveries and find regions full of riches and commodities, which other countries (Portugal and Spain are named though unnamed here) have done to the honor and merit of their princes and for the great profit of their state, provinces, and domains. In a refrain now familiar, Ribault followed this anatomy of riches with the ideal of God. The hand of God would lead these Natives who live bestially to the holy laws of Christ, for God had foreseen their conversion. Ribault moved on to the failures of others, such as Sebastian Cabot, to settle this land and mentioned other voyages by Verrazzano, Cartier, and Roberval, thereby showing an awareness of an archive French experience and possession in the New World. Ribault found a new way to sail to Florida that evaded the Spanish and framed his narrative in a world divided between God and Satan.

When Ribault returned to Normandy, he found it in the middle of a civil war between Catholics and Protestants and so he went to England hoping, perhaps, for the help of Queen Elizabeth I (1558–1603) for his cause. His partner in this Anglo-Huguenot scheme of colonization was Thomas Stukely, who revealed Ribault's plans to the Spanish ambassador. Wanting an entrance into the Caribbean, the queen and John Hawkins were, as John Parker has observed, trying to impress the Spanish with the usefulness of the English in the West Indian slave trade while exploring the possibility of joining the French in Florida against Spain.[28] England was taking a position that was pro-Spanish and anti-Spanish at the same time. In January 1565, in contravention of the king of Spain's laws of trade, Hawkins took a load of Africans from Sierra Leone to the Caribbean and, seeing how profitable that voyage was, stopped in Florida, where his Dieppe pilot led him, and offered the French colonists passage home, but Laudonnière refused the offer. At this point, it seems that Hawkins thought trading with Spain would be better than raiding its ships as the French had planned.[29]

The Spanish destruction of the Huguenots in Florida during Ribault's fourth voyage, had a chronicler in Nicolas Le Challeux, one of the survivors of the slaughter. Le Challeux appealed to the king as the monarch of all the French, and not someone sympathetic to Catholic or Protestant, to seek retribution against Spain. The climax of the terrible tale is the treachery and surrounding the death of Ribault.[30] The broken promises, cowardice, and cruelty of the Spanish that Le Challeux describes here contributed, along with the use of Las Casas's critique of Spanish abuses in the New World, to the Black Legend of Spain. Le Challeux's dramatic style makes personal the suffering and sacrifices of the French in the New World, so that his lament for the death of a hero, while intended to raise the French against the Spanish, did little to promote colonization in the New World.

The death of the martyr, Jean Ribault, actually led Le Challeux to denounce the idea of Huguenot colonization in the Americas, for he took a domestic view of how this sacrifice and the violence at the hands of the Spanish ruptured the lives and families of the French settlers who had been in Florida during the attack: "Let them go to *Florida* who list, for my parte I would not wishe, that that man, that is a housholder, should so leaue his occupation, for to seeke his aduenture in a straunge countrey, & for a greater profite of gaine: what faire promysse so euer is made of his enterprise."[31] Divine providence here has displayed anger over the colony and is not a foundation for the expansion of Christendom, what later became known in the history of the United States as Manifest Destiny. Le Challeux's discourse was a warning, a text that described the negative example of colonization. Love of Christ was best at home with one's family in France. The prayer was for peace and domestic bliss and not for religious communities overseas.[32]

During these years, the question of religious difference tore France apart and left it unable to establish a coherent colonial policy. A terrible time of division and violence in the country surrounded the Massacre of St.Bartholomew's Day at Paris in 1572. Even under these difficult internal circumstances, cosmographies, like those of Belleforest and Thevet, continued to look outward and to encourage French expansion.[33] Their use of Spain often appeared in the contexts of internal strife in France and French failures at colonization in the New World. Belleforest's *L'Histoire Vniverselle dv Monde* (1570, reissued 1572) revealed this friction.[34] The internal strife in

France made it difficult in this Preface to concentrate on cosmography and the rivals of the French in colonization.[35] Thevet's *Universal Cosmography* (1575) was a positive testimony to Villegagnon's expedition to Brazil and represented Spain positively.[36] The Spaniards were the first to discover Peru and to see bestial, uncivil, and cruel "Savages."[37] Thevet mentioned the myths of the Natives expecting the arrival of the Spanish in Mexico and Peru as being like those Natives who awaited the coming of the Portuguese and French.[38] A community of European merchants, including the Spanish and French, traded with the Brazilian Natives.[39] Thevet admired "the Spaniard and Portuguese, who know how to dissimulate and temporize with these Barbarians."[40] In cosmography, it was difficult to separate the factual from the mythical.

In addition to cosmographies, translations continued to play an important role amongst the French and English efforts to build up an archive of the Americas. In a history of discourse, where, as in this case of the historiography of expansion, translation is so central, there is sometimes a lag between event or original textual argument, representation, or record and its transmission into other languages. Latin was available to the elite, but most often the translation into Spanish and then into French and English or some variation on that process (Spanish to French, French to English) meant a greater and more popular dissemination than of the Latin original. Many Spanish authors decided to write in Spanish, and, for some, especially among the captains, adventurers, and settlers, the vernacular was the only option, or what might be called the confident option. Some of the texts on Spain are not French or English translations but are histories and narratives of exploration, encounter, settlement that involve imitation of, allusion to, and commentary on, Spain.

A gap occurred between the mission of the Huguenots in Brazil in 1556 and Jean de Léry's *Histoire d'vn voyage faict en la terre dv Bresil, avtrement dite Anerique* (1st. ed. 1578, 2nd. 1580). In that wide gap of time between the Brazilian colony and Léry's narrative lay Nicolas Le Challeux's account of the Spanish massacre of the French Protestants in Florida in 1565 and the Massacre of St. Bartholomew's Day in 1572, not to mention the siege and famine of Sancerre that Léry survived. Le Challeux's narrative of 1566 was about disturbing events that supplement those Léry described, which occurred about seven to eight years before but about which Léry published about twelve years after Le Challeux did. To complicate matters, the account of Jean Ribault, the central figure (along with the author/narrator) in Le Challeux's work, has a complex textual history because the French original, which does not seem to have been published, is not extant and the English version had to wait for Richard Hakluyt the Younger to give it some light after the Spanish Armada. Moreover, Thomas Hacket's translation of

Le Challeux appeared in 1566, the same year as the original. The textual responses to the events in Brazil and Florida in French and English were staggered over the years and this response to events, as well as intervening events, complicates the representation of the example of Spain. Léry's account of Brazil from 1556 to 1558 came out in 1578. The events Léry described occurred after those Las Casas represented (from Columbus to the debate of 1551). Las Casas was translated into English in 1583: Léry first appeared in English in Purchas (1613–25). An important context for Le Challeux's account were the French and English translations of Francisco López de Gómara, *La istoria de las Indias y Conquista de México* (1552), which appeared in 1578, and Urbain Chauveton's edition of Benzoni's history (which included Le Challeux's account and then proceeded to the representations of Las Casas and Léry). Hakluyt, a collector of narratives of travel, exploration, and settlement about the New World, included a third version of Ribault's experience in Florida. This recursive overlapping demonstrates the primary concern of interpretation in these accounts and histories of past events. History as writing revisited history as event. The end of Chauveton's book was also suggestive of the ambivalence over the Spanish, which was characterized in the translations of opposing and mixed views of Natives in works by Gómara on the one hand and Las Casas and Girolamo Benzoni on the other.[41] Gold, greed, and the abuse of the Indians became themes of French, English, and Dutch Prefaces to translations and books about Spain in the New World.

Even amidst civil strife, France considered, in addition to its own failures at home and abroad, the model of Spain. Although the failure of the Villegagnon's colony in Brazil occurred in 1560, the civil war prevented Jean de Léry from recording his account until much latter: the first edition was printed a year before Chauveton's book and the second edition a year after—it revisited French division in the New World, suggesting all the typology of a divided France in years ahead of the experience but before the date of publication. In Léry's account and experience in Brazil and at home, France was its own worst enemy—even greater than Spain was at this time. The dedication of Léry's *Histoire* was addressed to François de Coligny, the son of Gaspar de Coligny, the admiral of France, who had obtained royal support for Villegagnon's colony in Brazil and who, as the leader of Protestants in France, was killed in the Massacre of St. Bartholomew's Day in 1572. The elder Coligny, having convinced Henri II that the trade in brazilwood was profitable and that it was important to challenge the monopoly of Spain and Portugal in the New World, was able to find the Huguenots a refuge there.[42] Léry's dedication began with the memory of François de Coligny's father.[43] Léry asserted that with this foundation "more than ten thousand persons of the French nation would be there and also in full and sure possession for our

King as the Spaniards and Portuguese are in the name of theirs."[44] Even if Léry advocated religious reform, he did not place that above France and its king. Spain and Portugal were rival nations that had been able to settle where the French should have stayed.

Another revisiting of the past, this time from about 1550 to 1580, was Lancelot Voisin, sieur de La Popelinière's *L'Histoire de France* (1581).[45] La Popelinière stated the charge of Spanish cruelty but not without emphasizing that this view was part of a campaign to turn popular feeling against Spain, particularly in relation to the "cruelty of the Spaniards in Flanders" that moves "the people to a revolt."[46] While negotiations were going on over the marriage of Philip of Spain and Mary of England, some anti-Spanish sentiments surfaced in London. The fourth book began with the marriage of Philip and Mary and included the divisions between the Spanish and the English even in 1558 when they were supposed to be united.[47]

The role of Spain in Europe and the New World led the French to examine their relation with the English as well. In the shifting alliances and balances of power the Native of the Americas was a figure that could be used to make a point about Spanish success or cruelty in Europe and the New World depending on the writer and the context. Neither the French nor the English wrote with consensus about the Spanish, and soon they, too, would move from trade with the Natives to establishing permanent settlements amongst them as the Spanish had. The theory of relations with the Natives would move more squarely into a connection with the realm of practice.

III

A good example of the way France and England shared their concerns, not to mention their archive, about Spain is in their translations of Gómara, Martin Fumée's in 1578, and Thomas Nicholas's in 1578. The French translations went through at least six printings of Part I of *La Historia* (1552) between 1568 and 1580 and a minimum of six more printings of Parts I and II during the next twenty-six years, whereas the English translation appeared much less often: in both languages Gómara was printed much more often than Las Casas. There was often no direct line between Spain and its rivals but refractory and oblique many-sided relations. Despite the divisions within France, the French still focused on the Spanish in works like Fumée's translation of Gómara. The third of five parts focused on the voyage of Magellan and differences between the Spanish and Portuguese colonies.[48]

The English translation, which was launched in a more peaceful situation than its much-printed French predecessor, emphasized the model or precedent that Spain set for England in the New World. Nicholas found Gómara's "delectable and vvorthy Historie" to be "a Mirrour and an excellent president."[49] History as the memory of honor and glory from the ancients through the medieval and Renaissance chronicles, also constituted one of the themes of the Spanish, English, and French history plays from about 1580 to 1690.[50] The hope for triumph was a way of promoting empire rather than dwelling, as Hakluyt the Younger later did, on the tardiness or desultoriness of the English to expand.

Nicholas framed his claim for the English in the Americas between a description of Spanish gold and glory and his own travels in Spain. He related the Spanish and English experience in the New World through the discovery of gold. Martin Frobisher and Michael Lok [Locke] have, according to Nicholas, proved the existence of gold in the northwest, which all of Europe had forsaken except Elizabeth I and her subjects, a region beyond the "hote Zoane," where most learned writers had located gold deposits, so that God has undoubtedly appointed the queen.[51] Nicholas was also explicit in his use of Cortés as an example to the English.[52] England needed such a great man but also patience learned from reading the histories of the experiences of Spain and Portugal in colonization. In this regard Nicholas paid homage to Francis Walsingham's generous promotion of good and profitable attempts, new discoveries, adventures, and his advocacy at court.[53] Although Nicholas had spoken of profit, he had done so in conjunction with honor and not as an end in and of itself. His stance was pro-Spanish, but he was not entirely anti-Indian. His *muthos* was a narrative of redemption: the Indians had been great and cruel sinners but they became so pious, they put the Christians to shame. It is as if in translating Gómara he represented the Natives as moving from Sepúlveda's Aristotelian natural slaves to Las Casas's holy people. The body of the text proceeded to the birth and lineage of the hero of this history of conquest: Cortés.[54] How different would be the advice that Hakluyt was to give Walsingham in 1584 in a text more critical of Spain— "Discourse on Western Planting."

IV

In Paris, Hakluyt may have met with Phillippe de Mornay, seigneur du Plessis-Marly, a Huguenot hostile to Spain, a diplomat, who, as the ambassador of Henri de Navarre in London in 1577–78, knew Walsingham and Lady Stafford. On April 24, 1584, Mornay presented to the French king an unpublished work: "Discours au Roy Henri III. Sur les moyens de diminuer l'Espaignol," which was probably known to Hakluyt.[55] Reflecting the views of Henri de Navarre, Mornay said that Philip II was a tyrant who was undermining France, the Netherlands, and Europe; that France and England should blockade the English Channel from Spanish shipping; that France should attack the Spanish Empire in the New World in order to seize it and to prevent the king of Spain from receiving the bullion that permitted him to tyrannize Europe. Duplessis-Mornay's anti-Spanish themes echoed similar positions in Drake and Coligny and foreshadowed those in Hakluyt the Younger, a central figure in the history of the English (British) empire who helped to create an archive and base for knowledge that aided England in becoming a leading Protestant power and a great nation on the verge of empire. Duplessis-Mornay advocated that the French must, like the Spaniards, follow a path of conquest, but, unlike them, treat the Natives well. He even argued that the indigenous peoples be used against their cruel Spanish conquerors.[56] This theme from Duplessis-Mornay would echo through the work of Hakluyt, Ralegh, and other English writers.

Duplessis-Mornay's work deserves more attention in English. It, too, has its own complicated history that makes its authorship and transmission as problematic as the Columbus *Letter* and *The Broken Spears*. In his letter to Henri III, this Huguenot leader made some perceptive statements about France's security, so that the point of view is more French than Protestant. In this analysis Duplessis-Mornay observed that the House of France and the House of Austria are those powers today "because of their grandeur, in peace or war" that affect whether "Christendom is peaceful or troubled."[57] The Habsburgs ruled Austria and Spain and surrounded France with their possessions in the Netherlands, central Europe, and Spain. Duplessis-Mornay recounted the balance of power between Spain and France:"In the long wars, which had been between the two Crowns of France and Spain, these princes, having gone through diverse tests, recognized that they could not win much one from the other, and so resolved to rest." He then reported that peace followed.[58] The balance of power that Duplessis-Mornay described between Spain and France had been thrown into jeopardy owing to the misfortune ("nostre malheur") of falling into a civil war, so that with the many battles against each other, it was necessary to take into account that the Spanish had thus won against the French "and what is more, without losing anything."[59] According to Duplessis-Mornay's analysis, the Spanish acquired from Portugal rich territories, such as islands and the East Indies and because of the French inability to oppose the Spaniard ("l'Espaignol"), "Here he is with three advantages over us since the peace made with him," namely, "our weak-ening, his augmentation and reputation of arms."[60] Even in the face of the French civil wars, this Protestant leader saw ways to counteract the advantage of Spain. France, although it had losses, was enfeebled not in manpower but in concord and discipline. These internecine wars, "however, engendered an infinite number of soldiers" could be used against the Spaniard and their use "outside the kingdom would render in part the health, tranquility and union of our state."[61] Here is a foreign policy that external wars makes for internal peace, which would temper any notion that the Huguenot leadership was interested in tearing the country apart for the sake of religious scruples. What Duplessis-Mornay declared next echoes in the Netherlands and England as well: "Also, this great growth of the Spaniard has placed all neighboring princes in fear and jealousy."[62] Duplessis-Mornay called for people to rally under the banner of France, "with all their means, against the misproportioned grandeur and immoderate ambition of the House of Austria."[63] He wanted to rally the French—Duplessis-Mornay used "nous" to stress unity and not division—their "spirit, force and courage" against "the reputation that the king of Spain has on us."[64]

Some key members of the French elite, like some in English court circles, perceived Philip II as a threat. The better things get inside the country, the more the French can attend to opposing Spain without "open war" by means of building "a puissant league against this grandeur of Spain" and maintaining "domestic impediments, so that she is constrained and is contained within her borders."[65] Duplessis-Mornay thought that the queen of England would join the league because "Conspiracy has been discovered, incited by the king of Spain and conducted by his ambassador, not only against her state, but against her own person."[66] Elaborating on this enmity between England and Spain, Duplessis-Mornay reported that Elizabeth I gave the Spanish ambassador forty days to leave England and sent an envoy to declare her case to Philip II, who had taken steps in Scotland to encourage a young prince against her and "the Scots already begin to taste the silver of Spain."[67] This silver was something that often came from the Americas and caused suspicion among the rivals of Spain. Duplessis-Mornay was also hopeful that the princes of Germany, whose support would be more difficult to obtain "because they are many, and not yet reunited in one body," would act against the House of Austria, which controlled the Holy Roman Empire.[68] The hope was for an alliance "between most of the Protestant princes and several imperial cities."[69] Duplessis-Mornay also set out how Henri III was supposed to express his support for these princes, through William of Hessen, "longtime friend of this state," and others.[70] Having considered the role of Denmark and Sweden and their relation to the king of Spain, Duplessis-Mornay summed up the main focus of the league: "This alliance was impeded by the means of several men of means, who did not want the ruin of the Low Countries."[71] Henri III was key in ensuring that the king of Spain not "achieve the ruin of those of the Low Countries."[72] The reason this league should grow is "because the Spaniard has given offense to several princes and republics which will be very pleased to be under the protection of and participating in this league; and in the long term, rivers will swell from streams."[73] This writer was promoting with the king an idea that would isolate Spain and marshal all the hope and prospective support he could find for it: Duplessis-Mornay tried to be realistic by discussing some of the difficulties with the states to the east of France, but this is an optimistic position designed to help France find unity within by focusing on an enemy without. Nonetheless, rather curiously, Duplessis-Mornay used what appears to be an unfortunate metaphor—the alliance as a sick man who can be brought back as opposed to the dead man who needs a miracle to be resuscitated—while such an image is used to underscore the theme of *tempus fugit,* that no time should be lost or the patient will be past treatment. As Duplessis-Mornay said, although not as explicitly as I am saying, those who are at war with Spain can help France now if Henri III acts in a timely fashion.[74] They won't always be warring against the Spanish.

What is the threat? "The empire," for Duplessis-Mornay, "is one of the great grandeurs of the House of Austria."[75] As this house usually looks for alliances within, so an emperor marries a daughter of Spain. Thus "by this means the German Empire, and the whole state that belongs to the king of Spain," will "In our days rejoin" into "the largest monarchy" and one "certainly redoubtable to all the princes of Europe."[76] The election of the Holy Roman (German) emperor was a matter of power for some and the balance of power for others like Duplessis-Mornay, so tallying possible votes in the election was not his concern alone. Duplessis-Mornay accused the king of Spain of inciting violence, but countered this propensity with plans for French military action, as violent, to eradicate those leaders who support Philip II.[77] All these plans served a French objective:

> This would be a preparation to recover one day for the House of France the empire, which has continued in the House of Austria these last years, for the one reason, that she possesses the frontiers of the Turks, who are in truth the gateway ["boulevart"] to Germany, which well needs to be defended in the name and with the arm of the empire.[78]

Spanish power would, in Duplessis-Mornay's view, not be necessary because the House of France, having an alliance with Turkey, would be able to exempt Germany and the countries of the House of Austria from this war and "the council of Turkey has resolved to extend its conquests towards milder countries, like Sicily and Italy" rather than countries on the frontier that have a more rigorous climate.[79]

Duplessis-Mornay also shifted to another territory that bordered on France, the Netherlands, a great possession for the Spanish: "The king of Spain in all that he possesses, has nothing more beautiful, more rich, more polished than the Low Countries," something harmful to France and that would be hard to take without open war ("sans guerre ouverte").[80] Burgundy is strategic in the communication between Flanders on the one hand and Italy and Spain on the other and the Swiss are also strategic in this plan against Spanish might: here Duplessis-Mornay sounds like a military as well as political strategist.[81] He provides a prescient discussion of Spanish vulnerability in the rough waters of the English Channel ("la manche d'Angleterre") because owing to the way the currents and geography work, the Spaniards could only approach the coast of France or gain that of Flanders "with extreme danger" and the coast of England, "which has more ports and easier access than ours," is closed to Spain.[82] If, on the other hand, Henri III "wished to help the estates of the Low Countries, in an under-handed way ("sous main") and to allow his subjects to serve in the war, then "there is little doubt that in a little time the provinces that follow the Spanish party, would feel unsafe ("mal secoureues"), would throw themselves into the arms of your majesty rather than endure the yoke of the others who follow the estates."[83] In return for this help, Duplessis-Mornay suggests, the king "will already be able to impose a few conditions."[84] This adviser claimed to the king that "I know for certain that the nobility and the most respectable cities of Artois, Hainault, etc., enter into a great jealousy of the prince of Parma, who, in all the places that he has reconquered from the estates, placed garrisons all devoted to him, and not dependent on the estates of the said provinces."[85] According to Duplessis-Mornay, Parma has gone against his treaties with the said cities and they are as so many citadels in the middle of them [the provinces] and acted without their counsel or consent.[86] The implication is that the French influence or even liberation would be welcomed under the circumstances that the Spanish had imposed on the part of the Netherlands that they controlled.

Various other important spheres of influence preoccupied Duplessis-Mornay's analysis of countermeasures against Spanish power. The strategic location of Spain, which controlled the straits of Gibraltar, allows it to trade from the Atlantic into the Mediterranean, "Through this [strait], all that Spain brings from the Indies, whether oriental or occidental, is transported conveniently in Barbary, in Italy, and inland."[87] Duplessis-Mornay suggested that at little cost to the king a person of quality ("personne de qualité") could carry out a design on Majorca ("Mallorque"), a key fortification that allows Spain sure access to all the Mediterranean, including its own territories such as Naples, Sicily, and Milan, and that such an enterprise could be launched readily from Languedoc or Provence.[88] Part of Duplessis-Mornay's plan would involve subterfuge and deflection: "And for sparing the name of his majesty one could use that of the king of Navarre or of Portugal; and as a last resort ("pis-aller"), he who undertakes it, if well assisted, would do it without going to those pains."[89] Other fronts would also distract the Spanish.

This plan against Spain was not the first that the king would have heard: "Against the Indies and occidental navigations, several fair designs have been, for a long time, proposed to his majesty, and to which, perhaps, it would be awkward ("malaisé") to add anything."[90] Duplessis-Mornay considered that four great vessels could defeat the Spanish fleet from Peru, and he agreed with "several great navigators of diverse nations, who seem to have been well recognized, who have often assured me that four thousand men landing in the place on the isthmus called Darien, between Panama and Nombre de Dios, could easily make themselves masters of it."[91] This plan sounds very much like one of Drake's ventures, so that the Huguenot and English strategies against Spain, as the figure of Jean Ribault and the work of Richard Hakluyt the Younger also suggest, were often intertwined. This proposal, while not calling for a canal, would take advantage of the thin finger of land between the Atlantic and the Pacific, where John Keats's "stout Cortez" found himself unexpectedly displaced, so that the French could find and, with military power, maintain a route that would preclude the sea route round Africa and would allow trade with the Moluccas ("Moluques") near present-day Indonesia.[92] Moreover, "we could mildly trade with the inhabitants of the country, who have retired into the mountains because of the horror and cruelty of the Spaniards and from whom we could obtain much help and commodity ("commodité") against him [the Spaniard]."[93] The cruel Spaniard, a staple of the Black Legend of Spain, makes an appearance in Duplessis-Mornay, as it had in Le Challeux and Benzoni and would, almost at the same time, in Hakluyt.

The East Indies demanded another strategy because many of the viceroys and governors there, presumably in Portuguese possessions that Spain in 1580 had declared theirs as well as Portugal itself, had not yet recognized the king of Spain and could tend, with the help of Henri III, toward "king Don Antonio," the Portuguese claimant to the throne of Portugal.[94] The East Indies, once under Portugal, would need to have another route than the one the king of Spain controlled for their spices, drugs, precious stones, and other commodities if they were to move away from Spain because this trade had greatly enriched Spain and the Low Countries, the staging point for "all the commerce of Christendom."[95] This trade the French could divert across the isthmus between Panama and Darien as Duplessis-Mornay had suggested, or it could follow the ancient route "that this same merchandise took under the grandeur of the Romans, from the Moluccas to the entrance to the Gulf of Arabia "to the port Suez, called by the ancients *Heroum portus*" for distribution to the cities of the Mediterranean.[96] For this second route—the translation of empire could be based on ancient economic models and trade patterns—the king of France could give these viceroys and governors a choice because "The Turk will easily grant to his majesty the surety and liberty of this passage; because of the alliance between them and the riches of these countries."[97] This action will please the Venetian, who lost so much from the diversion of this trade; the Marseillais will be enriched as well as the French merchant more generally; in fact, the whole of France and Christendom will be better: "the Spaniard alone will feel a notable diminution; in the diminution of which resides today the conservation of France and the augmentation of all Christian princes."[98] The lessening of Spanish power is the enlargement of that of France and all the states of Christendom.

According to the "memory of histories," this trade "has changed its route five times, and it was diversified according to the disposition of empires for the convenience or inconvenience of their travel."[99] Duplessis-Mornay then outlined the routes that the Genoese, English, Spanish, and Portuguese had in the trade with East Asia, and he set out a final proposal for French control of this trade. In recapitulating, Duplessis-Mornay summarized the aim of his discourse on ways to diminish Spain: "These are the means that can take hold to weaken and impoverish the Spaniard, and break the course of his prosperity and grandeur, awaiting an overt force."[100] This discourse is like Hakluyt's in the same year and it seems as though the Huguenots influenced the English Protestant position in the "American party" who promoted colonization to the New World at the court of Elizabeth I. The Huguenot leadership understood the importance of the struggle in the Netherlands in the fight against Spain, which was represented as the great threat in Europe. In Duplessis-Mornay's text the success and power of Spain is spelled out almost exclusively in the details of the very plans to wreck them.

Duplessis-Mornay was a friend of Philip Sidney, who died in the war against Spain in the Netherlands in 1586.[101] The English, too, had been split over religion, although the strife never reached the pitch it did in France. According to Christopher Hill, English Catholics were considered to be either "unpatriotic peers and gentlemen" or "ignorant rabble": in Essex in 1591, three years after the defeat of the Armada, rioters wanted the Spanish to liberate them with an invasion.[102] In this chapter and in the study generally, I have tried to provide some reminders of the divisions within the groups, cultures, and nations under discussion, for otherwise it becomes too ready to speak in an undisrupted manner of something unified that was seldom so. The career of Walter Ralegh from hero and goad to Spain to a sacrifice by execution because of his anti-Spanish stance, also shows that the attitudes of the English elite could shift over time. When Elizabeth I died in 1603 and James I ascended the throne, friendship and peace with Spain were pursuits of the English government. With the Stuarts, the conflicted view of Spain could also reach the royal household itself. For instance, Lewis Bayly, chaplain to Prince Henry, who encouraged an aggressive Protestant foreign policy, and later to James I (as well as being Bishop of Bangor in 1621) went to prison for denouncing the proposed Spanish marriage of Prince Charles.[103] Once again the idea of typology enriches the way Spain was viewed, as sometimes it was a typological relation between the country inside and out, in this case of England and Spain. In the early 1680s John Bunyan probably wrote a work that was left unpublished, *Of Antichrist and his Ruin*, where he made the point that civil laws that forcefully regulate worship "as in the Spanish Inquisition" allow to remain in them "the spirit of the Man of Sin."[104] The established church was thereby likened to the zealous court of the Catholic Church in Spain.

It was not simply a double image of the Old World and the New that complicated the use of Spain, but also comparisons within Europe. For now, let us turn back to the conflicts of the 1580s in which Philip Sidney, Duplessis-Mornay, and Richard Hakluyt the Younger and others found themselves. During the 1580s, the English and the French Protestants especially looked to the Netherlands, as well as to America, in seeing the likeness of Spain in the mirror of tyranny. Richard Hakluyt the Younger, long since a staple of English accounts of the colonization of the Americas and much recognized as an editor of travel accounts and voyages, appears here in a context that suggests his affinities to, and perhaps how he was influenced by, leading Huguenots like Duplessis-Mornay. There was a close relation between English and French Protestants of the time that was often mediated through the civil war in the Low Countries.

England, like France, had a strategic interest in the Netherlands. Leicester's papers concerning the Low Countries also show the interest England took in this vital area. On February 1, 1579 a document in French speaks about how the Provinces have banded together "to chase from this country the Spaniards."[105] Texts from the period from about 1579 to 1586, England and the Netherlands show how close England and the Netherlands had become in their fight against Spain. "A mynutte of Instructions for the earle of Leycester" set out that the Netherlanders should have restored to them "their ancient fourme of governement "by removing the king of Spain's power in that country.[106] Elizabeth considered that the English had made a great sacrifice in fighting for the Low Countries against Spain: the Dutch "desire their prosperitie and defense against the crueltie of their enemies, as wee haue not spared at this time to sende to them a great nôbre [nomber] of our people vnder the leadynge of divers gentlemen of speciall name, noble birth, as wee coulde not have made of men of more estimation to have gonne to anie warre," meant, at this point in the civil war, that the English would remind the Netherlands of the depth of their commitment and the Dutch would reaffirm their loyalty and express their gratitude to Elizabeth I.[107] The deputies wanted to thank Elizabeth for her defense of "these countries against the oppression of the Spaniards and their adherents" and expressed their fraternity, love, and obedience but also assert their sovereignty—threading the needle between England and Spain.[108] The Estates-General wished to thank Elizabeth for promulgating peace and freedom of worship and defending them against the tyranny of the king of Spain and the Inquisition but also asserting, as gently as possible, the sovereignty of the Netherlands.[109] This triangle among French, Dutch, and English Protestants would have been on the mind of Richard Hakluyt and Duplessis-Mornay as they looked at the relations of the Old World and the New and the preeminence of Spain in Europe and overseas.

V

The secret advice of Richard Hakluyt the Younger to the crown, which appeared in "Discourse on Western Planting," revealed the importance of Spain to the development of the French and English (later British) Empires. This "private" Hakluyt was much more anti-Spanish than the public collector and editor of travel narratives, but even in this depreciation of Spain, he displayed emulation and admiration. The destruction of the Huguenots in Florida and the Revolt of the Netherlands against Spain helped to urge the English court, including strong Protestants and the "American" party, to challenge Spain. As France was suffering through a civil war in which Catholic and Protestant were killing each other, England was in a better position to dispute Spanish hegemony. From the 1580s until the Peace of Utrecht, which ended the War of the Spanish Succession, and beyond, shifts in the balance of power changed the relations between other European nations and Spain. By 1713 the power of Louis XIV, including the possibility of France and Spain being united under the rule of the House of Bourbon, threatened other nations in the region. This anxiety could also have religious dimensions: for instance, in a dedication signed on October 20, 1713, to *Bibliothecæ Americanæ Primordia* (1713), White Kennett, a bishop, included in his wide-ranging topics, "the Tyranny and Cruelty of the Spaniards in MEXICO and PERV, their Baptizing in Blood, and then teaching a Religion of such outward Pomp and Ceremony, as was very little different from the Pagan Idolatry."[110] The British experienced something quite like the anxiety the French suffered when Mary I and Philip married in the 1550s. France was emerging as the Continental great power, so that it was becoming and would remain the chief rival to Britain in Europe and America during the eighteenth century. This was a situation Hakluyt could only imagine in the 1580s as Spain was the dominant power at the time. Although this chapter embodies these sweeping changes, it also demonstrates that, despite this mutability, the attitudes toward Spain, especially amongst the French and English, had remarkable staying power.

Hakluyt's two principal works in which he discussed Spain were *Divers Voyages* (1582) and "The Discourse on Western Planting" (1584). These texts were part of a network of works in France and England urging their respective nations to catch up with Spain and to establish permanent colonies.

For instance, Humphrey Gilbert's *Discourse of a Discoverie for a Passage to Cataia* (1566, pub. 1576) foreshadowed Hakluyt's work. Before the first voyage of Martin Frobisher, who had met Gilbert in 1572 and who was also associated with Henry Sidney and Michael Lok, the state papers included a document, a kind of brief summa of Hakluyt's *Divers Voyages*, and "Discourse" *avant la lettre,* that set out an English colonial policy that could discover lands that were unoccupied and use the commodities found there and that sought to spread the Christian faith in this territory all without offering "any offence of amitie."[111] In this anonymous document, "A Discovery of Lands Beyond the Equinoctial," the author made an important claim that summarizes the English position on expansion into the New World—in a fashion that is a prolepsis for the carving up of Africa by Europeans during the nineteenth century—that

> The Ffrenche have their portion to the northwarde directlie contrarie to that which we seke. For the places alredie subdued and inhabited by the Spaniard or Portugall we seke no possession nor interest. But if occasion be free frendlie traffique with theim and their subiectes which is as lawfull as muche wythout iniurie as for the Quenes subiectes to traffiques as merchants in Portugall or Spain hit self. [112]

While the figure of Columbus, and later Las Casas, became part of the lexicon and imagery of the French and English archive of the Americas, the revisitation of origins to the right to settle the New World was something that the French and English felt compelled to repeat, perhaps because the Spanish and Portuguese continued to insist on the legitimacy of the papal bulls of the 1490s and first decade of the 1500s and the treaties between Spain and Portugal at that time.

Hakluyt was not alone in his views of Spain in the period from the 1560s to late 1580s: Urbain Chauveton was also critical of Spanish abuses in the New World. He stressed Benzoni's critique of the cruelty of the Spanish in the West Indies—how, for instance, they hunted slaves—as well as asserting that some Spanish historian had taken away the honor of the discovery of the New World by Columbus.[113] Chauveton's summary described Benzoni's judgment "that is to say judgements of God on the head of those who have oppressed this poor people."[114] The French use of Las Casas and Benzoni was as a providential scourge of the Spanish colonists in the New World: Natives became a weapon against Spain. The Spanish crown and the papacy could not always decide on the nature of the Natives and whether they should have liberty or not.[115] This strategy for using the Natives as figures of criticism against Spain and resistance to it intensified in France, the Netherlands, and England.

None the less, Hakluyt made extensive and significant arguments and collections of travel narratives on a scale unparalleled in England. At the opening of the "Epistle Dedicatorie" to Philip Sidney in *Divers Voyages,* Hakluyt expressed the ambivalence to Spain and Portugal: they had come to possess the most temperate lands, but even though the English have missed this opportunity, as the Portuguese were past their prime and "the nakednesse of the Spaniards" was apparent, the English now had hope to share America with the Iberian powers. The "Epistle Dedicatorie" made a direct appeal: "I Maruaile not a little (right worshipfull) that since the first discouerie of America (which is nowe full fourescore and tenne yeeres) after so great conquests and plantings of the Spaniardes and Portingales there, that wee of Englande could neuer haue the grace to set fast footing in such fertill and temperate places, as are left as yet vnpossessed of them."[116] Among other things, Hakluyt stressed the right of possession to North America owing to English discovery.[117] Moreover, Hakluyt reported that English merchants in Spain had said that Philip II had passed a law that forbade Spanish subjects from exploring the lands north of the forty-fifth parallel because he did not want them to find the passage from the south to the north sea and because he did not have enough people to possess the land. In this vacuum the English should pursue God and glory.[118] If these men did not follow this course, God would "turne euen their couetousnes to serue him, as he hath done the pride and auarice of the Spaniardes and Portingales, who pretending in glorious words that they made their discoueries chiefly to conuert Infidelles to our most holy faith, (as they say) in deed and truth sought not them, but their goods and riches."[119] Although Hakluyt had doubts about the Spanish commitment to religion in the New World, he wanted England to imitate their school of navigation in Seville and set up one in London.[120] Finally, Hakluyt mentioned what lay ahead in his book: John Cabot's letters patent, Sebastian's claim to Ramusio of his discovery of America, and the testimony of the English chronicler, Fabian, not to mention the voyages of Robert Thorne, Verrazzano, Cartier, Ribault, and others as well as Michael Lok's [Locke's] map.[121] In *Divers Voyages* Hakluyt had done much to contribute to this knowledge through translation and his own writing and collecting, but looked to the nobility for support to build an empire.

There is much to say about Hakluyt's long-unpublished state document, "A Discourse on Western Planting" (1584), but as I have discussed it extensively elsewhere, I wish to mention one aspect among many but one that relates to Philip II of Spain.[122] Unlike Richard Eden, who hoped for some benefits from the marriage of Philip II and Mary of England, Hakluyt showed little trust in the king of Spain. In Hakluyt's discourse, that king was the figure of the greatest threat to England, someone who must be faced with brave words: "So shall wee be able to crye quittaunce with the King of Spaine if he shoulde goe aboute to make any generall arreste of our navye, or rather terrifie him from any suche enterpryse, when he shall bethincke himselfe that his navye in newfounde lande is no lesse in our daunger then ours is in his domynions wheresoeuer."[123] The end of the fifth chapter of "Discourse" mixed plans to defy Spain, perhaps with Native support, with an implication that in this buildup to war each side blamed the other. Hakluyt wanted England to trade with Spain, but if it could not, he advised it to go fight the great power. It was as though Spain had rejected England and made life difficult for it. The desire for trade with Spain remained from 1555 to 1584, but tensions seemed to be heightening. How much rhetoric followed that increase in unease or contributed to it is not entirely certain. A mutual operation appears to have been at work.

VI

Even as France and England represented the model of Spain in the New World, they also influenced each other. The "American" group at the English court, which included Gilbert, Frobisher, Walsingham, Ralegh, and Hakluyt, from the 1560s until Elizabeth's death, provided money and arguments for their cause of expansion into the New World.[124] In England at this time there was no great public doubting voice like Michel de Montaigne's to question the right of the country to embark on empire, but there were many doubters, whose concerns and opposition the promotional literature often addressed.[125] John Florio did not translate Montaigne into English until 1603. Doubts obviously existed about the wisdom and effectiveness and profit of empire, but probably not about the right to expand, or the queen and court would have made a more concerted effort to colonize North America. Economic and political restraints, as we have seen, also constrained English monarchs from a systematic program of expansion. While in chapter 3 we shall discuss this opposition from within, the French, as well as the English, attempted to establish permanent colonies in North America despite skepticism at home. The very existence of apologies and polemics to promote empire suggest the fragility of the cause in both rivals to Spain: the French and English influenced each other as they both borrowed from Spain. The French Protestants, having suffered setbacks with Spain in the New World and in the civil war at home, looked to England to take up the cause of Protestant colonization in the Americas.

Martin Basanier's *Histoire notable de la Floride* . . . (1586), another example of a Huguenot history of French colonization, represented this intricate triangular relation and made Walter Ralegh a focus.[126] Protestant hopes for colonies in North America were shifting from France to England. The fleet that set sail for Ralegh's American colony on April 9, 1585 under the command of Sir Richard Grenville was established on Roanoke Island, under the governorship of Ralph Lane. Being without proper provisions, the colonists returned with Drake to England before a supply ship, which Ralegh had sent, arrived. Finding the colonists gone, Grenville, who, like Drake, had visited the colony, left fifteen colonists to retain possession of the territory for England. In 1587, the year after Basanier's book, Ralegh sent out a new group of settlers to Chesapeake Bay under the leadership of John White.[127] It was clear, then, that Ralegh was now the leading force in England concerning the colonization of America. The Armada and the subse-quent war with Spain slowed but did not stop Ralegh's push for permanent English settlements in the New World.

Ralegh's example as a colonizer was also known in France, especially among the Huguenots, whose leader Coligny was dead and who could find few leaders interested in colonization while a civil war raged in France. English Protestants were taking up in "Florida" where French Protestants left off. Part of the design was to thwart Catholic Spain and develop a Protestant colony in the area north of the Spanish colonies. Martin Basanier, a gentleman and mathematician, included a dedication to Ralegh in his *Histoire*, which collected three chapters on the French expeditions in Florida of 1562 and of 1564–65, the work of Captain Goulaine de Laudonnière, and another chapter concerning the revenge of Dominique de Gourges, a Gascon captain, against the Spanish in Florida, written by de Gourges. For French Protestants in the middle of the Wars of Religion, the events in Florida were still a controversy to keep alive.[128] Basanier celebrated the memory of Laudonnière in the service of Ralegh.[129]

In the body of Laudonnière's account of the events of 1564 in Florida, he addressed the temptations of avarice and ambition that led to sedition amongst the French. The mutineers wanted to go to Peru and the Indies to enrich themselves. Laudonnière made an observation that revealed that some amongst the French were no better than certain Spaniards in their desire for riches: "This talk of riches sounded so good in the ears of my soldiers."[130] In France, the queen recognized the precedence and right of the Spanish where they occupied colonies in the New World. On the basis of this passage in Laudonnière, the king of Spain was not imagining French incursions and piracy in Spanish America. Terrible events of revenge and counter-revenge between Spanish and French occurred in Florida. In this representation of the New World by the French and English, origins, crises, and golden ages were visited and revisited, so that the history of this discourse is like a helix, looping backward and forward in its attempt to make sense or justify its own policies and to imitate or vilify, sometimes simultaneously, the example of Spain. Certain traumatic events—such as Columbus's discovery of the New World, the papal donation of the new lands to Spain and Portugal, the first meetings of Natives and Europeans, the death of the Huguenots in Florida, the Revolt in the Netherlands, the Spanish Armada—recurred in the French and English writings about the New World. Sometimes within the same writers, there was support and opposition for colonization, and some writers were more skeptical about its benefits than others were.

Sir Walter Ralegh—courtier, explorer, landowner, and writer—was a central figure in the English settlement of America. The title page of Thomas Harriot's *Briefe and true report of the new found land of Virginia,* which was dedicated to Ralegh, described the author as "seruant to the abouenamed Sir WALTER, a member of the Colony, and there imploÿed in discouering": the quarto volume appeared in 1588 and Theodor de Bry's edition, which John White illustrated, appeared as a folio in Latin, English, French, and German.[131] In the Conclusion Harriot urged the English to follow in Virginia the example of Spain in its American possessions: "Why may wee not then looke for in good hope from the inner parts of more and greater plentie, as well of other things, as of those which wee haue alreadie discouered? Vnto the Spaniardes happened the like in discouering the maine of the West Indies."[132] It comes as no surprise that Richard Hakluyt translated John White's text from Latin, and that the title page and De Bry's prefatory address "To the gentle Reader" mentioned Ralegh as well as the French "discouerye" of Florida "longe befor the discouerye of Virginia" as a precedent and framed the work.[133] As a writer (historian and poet) Ralegh could also speak for himself. In *The Discouerie of the Large, Rich, and Bewtiful Empyre of Guiana* (1596) he tended toward the anti-Spanish and pro-Native position of the literature of the Black Legend, for he argued that the Spanish conquest was an illegal act that killed twenty millions, but his argument was also one of outconquesting the Spaniards and finding even more gold.[134] The English representation of Natives was at least partly mediated through the relation between England and Spain. In the body of *The Discoverie of Gviana* Ralegh developed the need to observe the Spanish model of colonization while using its own methods to subvert it. Although the text proper began with a description of the route from England to the New World, natural phenomena, and the situational friendship and trade of the English with the Spanish and Indians, it was clear that wherever he was, Ralegh had "*Guiana* (the *Magazin* of all rich mettels)" in mind.[135] Yet again in a French or English text about Spain's colonization of the New World, the Spanish were used as authorities to undermine their own imperial expansion. In exhorting the English to build an empire, Ralegh referred to Spanish discourses about the magnificent princes of Peru, and the words of Pedro de Cieza and Francisco Lopez seemed to have affected Ralegh's actions, or desire for action, as much as his writing.[136]

The French continued hopes for permanent settlements in the New World after the English were coming to terms with a new monarch, James I, and any shifts that might mean in relations with Spain and in the colonization of the New World. An important figure of the first two decades of the seventeenth century in French historiography of the New World is Marc Lescarbot, who, more than Samuel de Champlain, became the chronicler of Acadia and was more apt to comment on Spain. Lescarbot—lawyer, poet, humanist—was a Catholic but maintained friendships with Protestants and lived in the Port-Royal colony from July 1606 to the next summer when the expiry of Pierre Du Gua, Sieur de Mont's licence meant the return of the entire colony to France.[137] Lescarbot's *Histoire de la Nouvelle France* (1609, 1611–12, 1617–18), which concentrated on French discoveries in the New World, was popular in France and appeared in two English translations by Pierre Erondelle in 1609 and, subsequently, by Samuel Purchas.[138] In the prefatory matter of the first edition of 1609, Lescarbot presented a paean to France, expatiating on the greatness of his country, so that the Orient and south equate "Christian" with "French."[139] Still, Lescarbot was defensive about the relation of Spain to France: "The Spaniard shows himself more zealous than us, and has carried off the palm of navigation that was ours. But why envy him that which he has so well acquired? He has been cruel. This is what has soiled his glory, what otherwise would be worthy of immortality."[140] Cruelty and greed, elements of the Black Legend, appeared here. Moreover, France as a mother would produce "the Children of the West," who would settle New France: "Even if they do not find there the treasures of Atabalippa [Atahualpa] and others, which have lured them to the West Indies, they will, however, not be poor, for this province will be worthy to be called your daughter."[141] Like Richard Hakluyt the Younger, Lescarbot envisaged discontents and unemployed tradesmen going to the colonies rather than being lost to foreign lands, but, unlike his English predecessor, he emphasized the arts and, perhaps, following the model of Spain, spoke about "men of courage" settling in the New World.[142] Lescarbot differed from Hakluyt in his use of the language of Christian republicanism and of a French preoccupation—"la gloire"—which probably reached its greatest intensity under Louis XIV.[143] The French and English chroniclers of the New World in the late sixteenth century and late eighteenth century had similar goals to achieve permanent colonies beyond the areas of direct Spanish settlement. Spain was very much on their minds.

VII

The English were also on the minds of the Spanish. The Junta de Contaduría Mayor, or supreme board of accounts, wrote to Philip II that the "barbarous foreigner" looks for fertile lands to settle and that "It is greatly to be feared that so long as the Queen is alive they may extend still further the plundering of the Indies."[144] Roanoke, Virginia, and New England—in that order—were the places the English tried to settle. The Spanish were concerned that the English were seeking to settle Santa Maria Bay (Chesapeake Bay) in order to launch raids on the Spanish colonies in the West Indies and Florida.[145] I have mentioned a typology that existed between the Old World and the New, and the conflict in the eastern and western Atlantic had repercussions in Europe and the Americas. The war in the Netherlands in the 1580s and the friction in the West Indies and Florida helped to make the Spanish authorities build a case for an invasion of England by an armada. On August 7, 1586, Bernardino de Mendoza, Spanish ambassador to England until he was expelled in 1584 and then ambassador in France, wrote to Philip II, and maintained that Drake could not have taken 4,000 men in his raid in Florida because "any one who knows England will understand that so many men could not be sent out of the country, seeing the demands made for men in the Low Countries. The queen is making every effort to raise men for there, yet she cannot send all they ask for."[146] Francis Drake and Walter Ralegh [Rale to the Spanish]were both wreaking havoc with the Spanish colonies in the West Indies in the mid-1580s because while the one was raiding the Spaniards, the other was backing a colony. Philip II attended to this development: in a minute to the president of the Council of the Indies he referred to Drake, "the English viscount," and asserted: "It is to be feared that, if he has established a settlement on the Florida coast, the fact that he has changed its site is no indication of a decision to abandon it, but rather [of his intention] to improve its position."[147] The king and country had their own concerns over the challenge to Spanish power in the New World: they decided to find out where the colony was and to destroy it. When examining the example or model of Spain, from the point of view of the French and English, it is important, from time to time, despite the need for focus and the limits a study necessarily has, to point out the vantage of the Spanish. In 1588, Francisco de Valverde and Pedro de Santa Cruz, wrote to the Spanish embassy in Paris about the possible exchange of prisoners. Richard Grinfil [Grenville] is, for these authors, a "corsair" from Cornwall, who "brought to England twenty-two Spaniards whom he treats as slaves are treated in Algiers, making them carry on their backs all day stones and other materials for a certain building, and at night he chains them up."[148] The Spanish had their own dark views of the English.

The Spaniards had also destroyed the French settlement in Florida (which included the Carolinas) in the 1560s. For the French Protestants, the cruel villain of this episode was one Pedro Menéndez de Avilés: years later a certain Pedro Menéndez Marqués, his nephew, wrote to Philip II and warned him that if other nations master Florida and become allies with the Natives, it will "be most difficult to conquer and rule it, especially should the French and English settle it, as they are Lutheran peoples, and, because they and the

Indians are nearly of the one faith, as I have said, they will very easily make friends with one another."[149] Marqués was also involved in this operation to stop the English and French from establishing a foothold in North America. For a while this seemed like a phoney war. Thomas Harriot responded with something that made the war into a comic dance in a phrase Shakespeare would later use as the title of one of his comedies: "Much ado about nothing./Great warres & no blowes. Who is the fool now"?[150] Both sides were feeling the other out in a time when information was difficult to obtain, fragmentary, and often arrived late.

A Spanish relation of Pedro Diaz, someone "the English pirates imprisoned and took when he was going to Spain in the flag-ship of the Santa Domingo fleet," is signed and sealed by Pedro de Arana.[151] Richard Grenville, Diaz's captor, took goods from French ships en route to France and Flanders from San Lucár and Cadiz and later cargo from a Flemish fly-boat on the way to San Lucár.[152] On Porto Santo, northwest of Madeira, Grenville wanted to go ashore but the inhabitants offered him a tun of water for each of his Seven ships if the English would not land; this account stresses the bravery of those resisting the English, who are portrayed as bullies and pirates:

> The captain, angered by this, determined to disembark, intending to burn the island and destroy it with its inhabitants. To do this he armed his boats and placed men in them and sent them to land. The islanders, however, prevented them from coming ashore, and fought so bravely that the English returned to their ships. The next day the ships were brought close to the land in order to sweep the shore with artillery-fire, from which the inhabitants received no harm owing to the precautions they took. They defended themselves until noon, when the English ships withdrew and continued their journey to Florida where they had left settlers (which is latitude 36 $^{1/4}$ °).[153]

This colony at Roanoke Island, not to mention the English sea-captains, takes on a very different complexion when the point of view shifts to that of this Spanish captive. Diaz's relation also provided Grenville's motives: "The reason why the English have settled here is, he says, because on the mainland there is much gold and so that they may pass from the North to the South Sea, which they say and understand is nearby; thus making themselves strong through the discovery of great wealth."[154] Here is a motivation that is like that of the Spanish in the New World, where they had found great riches. Thirty-four of Grenville's crew died, and he later captured passengers on another ship, many of whom also died; Grenville returned to England and sailed once more; on that journey, near Madeira, a French ship overtook the ship that Diaz was on and although most on both sides were either wounded or killed, Diaz survived and, being a valuable asset because he was a pilot, the French took him and made him false promises until, through his wits, he was able to escape.[155] This relation, which did not make the English or the French look good, provided Diaz's view of the fate of the English colony at Roanoke: "The said Pero Diaz is of the opinion that the people who remained in the settlement should have, by this time, died of hunger, or have been exposed to great need and danger."[156] The Spanish tried to keep a close watch over the French and English in the Indies and in North America.

The possible permanent settlement of Virginia by the English was something that the Spaniards hoped to stop as they had the establishment of a colony in Florida by the French in the 1560s. Juan Menéndez Marqués commented on the attempts to locate the English settlements in Virginia, but part of that expedition was to see whether the land "contained any kinds of precious stones."[157] This possible campaign against the English in Virginia was subject to delays in communication and excuses. When Gonzálo Méndez de Canzo wrote to Philip III (February 18/28, 1600), he began "Your majesty's letter of November 9, 1598 I received on January 18, 1600" and then proceeded to recount how the French captured the ensign carrying the missive and he added another complicated set of circumstances.[158] One of the recommendations that this response to the king made was "If the settlement is really there, it seems fitting to me that your majesty should deal with the problem by supplying us with 1,000 men, not counting the sailors who man the ships carrying supplies and arms necessary for such an undertaking."[159] This document contained more detailed recommendations for preparations against the English. The Spanish themselves could record their own violence against the Natives in North America while showing an interest in keeping the English and French out of the Continent. For instance, Luis Jerónimo de Oré, who wrote about Francis Drake as a corsair who attacked Florida, also described the Spanish attack on the Indians, recording the orders of the king to rebuild the fort at Santa Elena to Pedro Menéndez Marqués, governor of Florida and its provinces and nephew to the adelantado, Pedro Menéndez de Avilés, and the subsequent actions there:

> When the general arrived he put in hand the restoration of the fort of Santa Elena. Taking 100 soldiers with him, they had many encounters with the Indians until the fort was built. From Santa Elena as a centre they went forth to burn the Indian villages and to inflict whatever damage they could. In one such attack they killed and captured 120 persons, while in the province of Guale they burned all the towns so that when the Indians saw themselves thus persecuted and their people dead or in captivity they submitted, made peace, and asked for clergy to instruct them in the things necessary for receiving baptism and embracing Christianity.[160]

This is the kind of force that Las Casas had complained about and that texts and images of the Black Legend had reproduced and multiplied in a kind of stereotyping of Spain and Spaniards. Here, there is a military–clerical complex that seems to have begotten cruel blessedness or a not-sparing salvation, something that Las Casas did not appear to desire. This text also marked where uncle and nephew had left their mark years apart.[161] The seizing of Natives is something that Columbus, Cabot, de Gonneville, and others from each European country seemed to have practiced.[162] The search for the English settlement and the rebuilding of Spanish power in Florida were also about the Natives: they became the actual, representational, and rhetorical mediators or go-betweens in the conflict between and among different European states in the New World and the Old.

The leadership of Spain in the New World, even as it was waning in the seventeenth century, was a persistent preoccupation in European representations of America in this period. Just when Spain seemed to drop from view, it was there again. Although this discussion has concentrated mainly on how the French and the English came after Spain, it has also, however briefly, attempted to include a Spanish point of view. In examining the opposition to and promotion of empire, I have selected writers of various backgrounds and their different ideas, which provide a more intricate view of European politics and expansion. Whereas some Europeans opposed expansion, others promoted it: within texts there are tensions between opposition and promotion. Chapter 3 discusses the opposition to expansion and empire and Chapter 4 turns to the work of the promotion of empire. Empire was contested early on within and between European states.

Chapter 3 ～

Opposition from Within

In the fifteenth century Portugal was cautious about expansion, looking after national self-interest and control. The Portuguese court had turned down Toscanelli's proposal for a westward voyage in 1474 and dismissed Columbus ten years later. During the fourteenth and fifteenth centuries, the French, Portuguese, and Spaniards attempted to make territorial claims and seek remedies through papal bulls, which were not permanent laws. For instance, in 1344, Don Luis de la Cerda, great grandson of Alfonso the Wise and admiral of France, obtained a bull from Clement VI to make Christian the Canary Islands, and, on January 8, 1455, King Alfonso of Portugal received exclusive rights in the African exploration and trade from the bull *Romanus pontifex* that Nicholas V issued. The Portuguese had their own plans for southern and eastern expansion but also reacted to Columbus's voyages, dividing the world unknown to Europeans with the Spanish by way of papal bulls.[1] Portuguese influence should not be forgotten, something quite possible when viewing the world too much in terms of Columbus and the New World, no matter how crucial the landfall of 1492 and its aftermath were to world history. The accomplishment of Columbus has two contexts involving the Portuguese that show the importance of a southern and eastern vantage: in 1488 Bartolomeo Dias rounded the southern tip of Africa, which the king is said have called the Cape of Good Hope and, in 1498–99, Vasco da Gama sailed to India and established a maritime link between Europe and Asia in the Carreira da India or the spice trade.[2] The papal bull *Ea quae* of 1506 addressed issues arising from da Gama's voyage. In interpreting the Treaty of Tordesillas of 1494 with Spain, which extended from 100 to 370 leagues west of the Cape Verde islands the line of demarcation set out in the bull *Romanus pontifex*, the Portuguese considered that the land that Cabot encountered might be in their sphere. Portugal and Spain gave each other rights of passage across each other's territory and, in the Treaty of Madrid in 1495, confirmed these terms and changes to the papal bull

Inter caetera. In the wake of John Cabot's or Giovanni Caboto's exploration of Newfoundland or Cape Breton for England in 1497, Portugal, as well as Spain and France (or regional fishermen like Bretons and Catalans whom we in later times came to label as French or Spanish), set out to take advantage of the cod fisheries in the Grand Banks. King Manuel of Portugal—on October 28, 1499—issued letters patent to João Fernandez for a voyage to Newfoundland and issued similar letters for the brothers, Gaspar and Miguel Corte Real in the years 1500 through 1503, but these men were lost, and Portugal seems to have had less interest thereafter in finding a northwest passage to Asia. In 1506 the Portuguese began to tax cod brought from Newfoundland to Portugal.[3] In 1500, at about the same time as the Corte Real brothers sought out Newfoundland, Pedro Alvares Cabral embarked for India from Lisbon with the largest fleet yet in this new trade, but in the region of the equator a storm forced him west and on Easter he sighted a land that Europeans came to call Brazil.[4] Portugal now had a foot in America as well as in Asia. After Columbus, each major Atlantic European maritime power sought some foothold in the New World. Cabot seems to have spurred additional activity in exploration. The Portuguese begot their own rivals: a Norman, Binot Paulmier de Gonneville, sailed to Brazil (1503–05) and at the opening of his account, he described how "Bastiam Moura" and "Diègue Cohinto," two Portuguese, helped defy the laws of Portugal at that time to help the Normans find the route to the lands in the western Atlantic.[5] The use of captains, navigators, and mariners of different nationalities occurred on the voyages of the various contending European nations in their quest for the New World no matter how restrictive their laws or their appeals to legal custom, treaties and bulls.

The Portuguese contribution to exploration has sometimes dwelt in the shadows of the Spanish achievement, particularly the legacy of Columbus. The quincentennial of Columbus's landfall in the New World was surrounded by the five hundredth anniversaries of Portuguese firsts from 1987 to 2000, however ambivalent some of these commemorations might be: the evangelization of the Congo, the passage around the Cape of Good Hope in Africa, the voyage by sea from Europe to India, and contact with the Tupinamba and Tupinikin in Brazil. Other important quincentennials of Portuguese firsts will happen in the next fifty years or so, as A. J. R. Russell-Wood notes: Jorge Álvares' achievement of the first European maritime trade mission to China; the passage around South America by Magellan (Fernão de Magalhães) in the service of Spain; the start of the Jesuit mission to Japan.[6] Although the example of Spain in the New World was primary, the example of Portugal in expansion generally was available to Spain and the other maritime powers of Western Europe.

The contexts for considering Columbus's proposals were complex even when they are limited to the forces for or against expansion beyond Europe and not also including the relation of this Columbian enterprise to what was happening within Europe. A royal council in Spain rejected Columbus's petition, so he sought an audience with Ferdinand and Isabella, whom he was connected to through his Portuguese wife. During their meetings in December 1486 and January 1487, the Columbus commission, composed of *letrados* (mainly university-educated lawyers at court) and *sabios* (men learned in cartography and astronomy), rejected Columbus's arguments and passed their findings along to the Spanish sovereigns.[7] This kind of opposition was not enough to stop Columbus's project, but it qualifies any notion of Spain, or Europe, embracing expansion and empire without reserve and caution.

Spain gave Columbus its support with reluctance, and even after the Columbian landfall, Columbus and the Crown of Spain were involved in a long battle over governance and ownership of, as well as profits from, the New World. Some important European clergy and intellectuals in particular opposed European expansion or the exploitation of the peoples of the New World. Columbus's exploration began a great legal debate between Portugal and Spain, which culminated in treaties between them in the 1490s and the papal bulls of the subsequent dozen years as well as setting up England's official challenge through John Cabot or Giovanni Caboto in 1497 and the unofficial French voyages under Gonneville in the first decade of the sixteenth century and the exploration of Verrazzano under the aegis of François Ier during the 1520s. It is sometimes easy to make Natives and Europeans into two groups with coherent and opposing interests, and to an extent there is some sense to this view, but conflicts amongst Europeans and amongst Natives, as well as, later on, trade blocs where different European and Native nations allied against similar but rival allies make this kind of opposition too bald.

Another kind of opposition from within occurs in the ambivalence in European representations of the lands and peoples of the New World. In these the Natives are fierce and paradisal. Columbus and Verrazzano (at least as we have his account in Italian) can display that ambivalent attitude in the same sentence. The idealization of the land and its peoples as comprising paradise, even as they are sometimes made into barbarians in rough places, is a promotional tactic that is meant to appeal to religious dreams of the Ten Lost Tribes of Israel and conjure the riches of Asia. Beyond this trope of God and gold, even in its implicit form, is the possibility for the ideal aspect of the representation of the Natives and the new lands to provide a standard against which to judge the corruption of Europeans. These early representations in Columbus and Verrazzano, as much as they might owe to classical myths and to Marco Polo, prepared the way for Las Casas, Montaigne, and others, who will turn the Natives into critics of Europe.

This second kind of opposition often combines with a third, that is the Christian critique of riches and power. Some church intellectuals used this tradition to call up the absurd and cruel aspects of European expansion into the New World. More immediate is the humanist critique, and, more particularly, that in Thomas More's *Utopia* (1516), written the year before Luther's Reformation, which gave the rivalry among European powers a religious dimension it did not have before. The opposition to expansion came within the church and court establishments themselves. Their opposing voices could be ambivalent, owing in part to their stake in political and religious institutions.

European expansion, then, was not as univocal and as triumphal as it might appear five centuries later. Nor was humanism, which has been subject to a critique in the Humanities in universities in the West over the past twenty years or so, the standard of the imperial theme. By humanists I mean those, even from different generations, who, trained in the classics, dwelt on the classical past, sometimes critically, sometimes not. This interpretation of the classical past affected their framing of scholarly and social problems in the present. The critics of humanists, like the humanists before them, often construe their intellectual movement as a matter of reform.[8] Those humanists I wish to discuss briefly here all had an interest in imperial expansion inside and outside Europe and came from various countries with connections to, or aspirations for, empire: Erasmus, More, Las Casas, and Montaigne.

As these figures have been discussed extensively elsewhere, I want to emphasize their views of expansion and Spain, the great colonial power in a century where France and England have no permanent colonies in the New World, expressed by their characters or in the essays. The reason Las Casas is not discussed at length here is because he was a principal focus of chapter 2, "After Spain," as other powers used his critique of his own country as evidence of Spanish cruelty in the Americas in what became known as the Black Legend of Spain. One of the strands of this book is that there is a typology between Europe and the New World in the writings of these European nations. This typological paradigm is evident implicitly and explicitly in the writings of intellectuals, such as Erasmus, More, and Montaigne. By placing these figures in the context of one another as well as in relation to Las Casas and other Spanish clerics in the "Indies," the following discussion should cast some new light on the opposition from within or alternative critique in regard to the expansion of the European powers. Satire, including the savage indignation of Juvenal, the irony of Horace, and the Menippean or Varronian mode of Lucian, were weapons these writers employed to explore the folly and greed of internecine wars in Europe and the extension of their violence in the New World. Wisdom and civility were left in the classical and biblical wilderness while Europe exploited itself and the Natives of the New World.

These writers contributed to the ambivalence and contradiction in the European representation of the imperial theme. In Latin literature there occurred the Virgilian motif of the founding of Rome as a prolepsis to the inception of Augustus's empire, but there was also the republican opposition to kingship and empire, from the story of the rape of Lucretia to Cicero's speeches against tyranny. The nature of eternal Rome, from the banishment of Tarquin, through the republic, the empire, the arrival of Christianity, the fall of Rome to the establishment of the papacy, contributed to the trope of the translation of the empire. Although *translatio imperii* inspired the states of early modern European, the opposition to the expansion westward was of a different nature in the early modern period. Later, republicanism or republican nostalgia became strong during the English Civil War and under Cromwell's rule and with the American War of Independence.[9]

Often, alternative or oppositional criticism of European violence and expansion derived from humanists like Erasmus, More and Montaigne. Skepticism was something that connected these three humanist figures in varying degrees. The rediscovery of classical learning meant that a skeptical strand of European tradition was kept alive. There is a line, as Peter Burke says, between Cicero's *Academica* (c. 45 B.C.) and Sextus Empericus's *Hypotyposes* through the work of William of Ockham (c. 1300–49) and Erasmus's *Praise of Folly* (1509), Gianfrancesco Pico della Mirandola's *Examination of the Vanity of the Doctrine of the Pagans* (1520), Agrippa of Nettesheim's *On the Uncertainty and Vanity of the Sciences* (1526), and Guy de Bruès' *Dialogues against the New Academics* (1558), to the œuvre of Montaigne.[10] To this group I would add More's *Utopia* (1516) and also include the critical and distancing irony of Socrates as a skeptical tool long before Cicero's and one that would have had a great effect through the influence of Plato inside and outside the Christian church. Montaigne had *Praise of Folly* in his library. Some humanists more readily advocated national interests and others criticized war and territorial longings: often, consciously or unconsciously, the humanists embodied contradictions of their own about violence, expansion, and imperialism. This chapter really addresses the contradictory positions in and among the learned, whether they considered themselves humanists or not, and I have done so as a means of destabilizing the term "humanist" and in calling attention to the intricacies of the situations of the clergy and other opponents to an expansion based on violence and commercial exploitation. Rather than begin with Erasmus and follow a strictly chronological analysis, I turn to an incident involving Columbus's son, Diego, and that comes down to us though that most important editor and filter, Bartolomé de Las Casas, who, was so crucial in the dissemination of Columbus's work.

I

Las Casas was not the first religious to attack Spanish excesses in their treatment of the Natives in the Caribbean. Although this section concentrates on Las Casas, who edited Columbus and who reported the good works of those who went before, it is important to say something about his predecessors. The Dominicans or Black Friars, an order founded during the thirteenth century in Spain, arrived in 1510 in Hispaniola, where they protested in private over the decline in the Native population of the island, focusing on the abuses of the Spanish domination of the indigenous peoples rather than their right to dominate. Ironies arose in their defense of the Natives, for the Dominicans were founded to travel the roads and preach against heresy and directed the Papal Inquisition in the Middle Ages and, later, the Royal Inquisition in Spain as well as being involved with the expansion of Portugal, Spain, and France.[11] Alternative critiques and opposition from within could not escape the cultural frameworks of European society of the period.

During December of 1511, one of the members of this order, Antón Montesino, preached two sermons that were critical of these abuses. In writing a history of the Indies, where Las Casas described the work of the Dominicans and tells of these advent sermons, he observed: "There were two kinds of Spaniards, one very cruel and pitiless, whose goal was to squeeze the last drop of Indian blood in order to get rich, and one less cruel, who must have felt sorry for the Indians; but in each case they placed their own interests above the health and salvation of those poor people."[12] All the Dominicans, according to Las Casas, signed the sermon to present a common front, and, as their representative, Montesino delivered it before Diego Columbus, the admiral, and other important people they had invited. Las Casas reports excerpts from the sermon given by Montesino on the theme: *Ego vox clamantis in deserto*, this voice that declared

> that you are living in deadly sin for the atrocities you tyrannically impose on these innocent people. Tell me, what right have you to enslave them? What authority did you use to make war against them who lived at peace on their territories, killing them cruelly with methods never before heard of? How can you oppress them and not care to feed or cure them, and work them to death to satisfy your greed? And why don't you look after their spiritual health, so that they should come to know God, that they should be baptized, and that they should hear Mass and keep the holy days? Aren't they human beings? Have they no rational soul? Aren't you obliged to love them as you love

yourselves? Don't you understand? How can you live in such a lethargical dream? You may rest assured that you are in no better state of salvation than the Moors or Turks who reject the Christian Faith.[13]

The sermon attacked the governor and the established settlers of the colony as infidels, so that it was not a case of apparent postmodern cultural relativism *avant la lettre*. This sermon did, however, hit home, for Las Casas said that the powerful in the congregation gathered at Diego Columbus's house where they decided to frighten and punish Montesino for questioning the king's authority in them: fortunately for the preacher, his superior, Pedro de Córdoba, would not heed the demand of the admiral and his royal officials that they see Montesino in person. The intimidation, including a demand for an apology and a threat to send the friars back to Spain, did not work. Rather than apologize the next Sunday, as Diego and his officials expected, Montesino amplified his condemnation of illegal Spanish tyranny and asked them to mend their ways, so the enraged Diego Columbus, appealed to the king directly, who ordered the Castilian provincial of the Dominican order to correct the situation.

This scene of Columbus's son using his power to try to control the religious in his colony because they did not share his view of the Indians and of conversion in the Indies contrasts with the dramatic situation that Lope de Vega created at the end of the sixteenth century in *El Nuevo Mundo descubierto por Cristóbal Colón* (c. 1598–1603) in which the Indian king, Dulcanquellín, says to Columbus's brother, Bartolomé, that a gentle and peaceful advocacy of Christianity will convert the Natives.[14] This later interpretation of the situation in the years after Columbus's landfall might sound similar to the position of the Dominicans and of Las Casas, but the Columbus family they encountered was not as supportive as Las Casas, the editor and keeper of Columbus's works and reputation, would project (perhaps Las Casas sometimes needed Columbus as a saint- at other times he could be critical of him) or that Lope de Vega would represent.

Las Casas himself seems to have been able to praise both Columbus and the religious, perhaps by separating Columbus from his immediate family, but doing so—Las Casas must have been adept—he also acted as Columbus's textual and ideological editor and so must have kept good relations with the Columbus family. Las Casas's father, who had sailed with Columbus on the second voyage, brought back a Native boy who became Bartolomé's servant. The ambivalence and contradictions here are instructive and suggest that it is ill-advised to assume clear lines in these ideological struggles over the relations with, and representations of, the Natives or in Spain's imperial policy and colonizing practice. From this incident surrounding Montesino, Las Casas drew a moral that reveals the free speech and the courage of the religious: "You see how easy it is to deceive a King, how ruinous to a kingdom it is to heed misinformation, and how oppression thrives where truth is not allowed a voice."[15] Las Casas, himself a landowner and later a Dominican, would become part of this crusade for the conversion and care of the Natives. This crusader, then, is part of the conversion narrative as surely as Saul and Paul were in the Christian imagination of the time.

A couple of examples from *A Short Account of the Destruction of the Indies* should suggest Las Casas's affinity with his Dominican predecessors. Speaking of himself as a witness and an eyewitness to the terrible events in the Indies, Las Casas wrote in the Synopsis:

> Some years later, he observed that not a few of the people involved in this story had become so anaesthetized to human suffering by their own greed and ambition that they had ceased to be men in any meaningful sense of the term and had become, by dint of their own wicked deeds, so totally degenerate and given over to a reprobate mind that they could not rest content with their past achievements in the realms of treachery and wickedness (when they honed to perfection the art of cruelty in order to wipe human beings from a large part of the globe), but were now pestering the Crown to grant them official authority and licence once again to commit their dreadful deeds, or even (if such a thing were conceivable) to devise yet worse atrocities.[16]

This recidivism is a main motivation that Las Casas claimed for writing his brief account of the Spanish colonies in the Indies. He brought up the atrocity we have come to call genocide and that, more specifically, became what Spanish historians in the early 1900s termed the Black Legend of Spain, a blackening of Spanish reputation by its rivals, especially, but not exclusively, by Protestants in France, England, and the Netherlands in the sixteenth and seventeenth centuries.[17] Like his Dominican predecessors, Las Casas suffered attacks: it is not surprising that other Spaniards attacked him for being heretical and disloyal to the Spanish crown. A famous instance of this friction occurred in the debate between Juan Ginés de Sepúlveda and Las Casas, who had been trained as a lawyer at Salamanca, over the treatment of the Amerindians represented two ways of incorporating America into European history.

Las Casas saw the contact as fulfilling Christian universal history in the conversion of the Indians, who were human and had souls to be saved. Sepúlveda argued for the growth of the Spanish monarchy and empire and denied the importance of the conversion of the Indians, whom he thought were not completely human.[18] In the history of Spanish colonization, Sepúlveda and Oviedo argued against the humanity of the American Indian, whereas Las Casas defended them. The Synopsis of *A Short Account of the Destruction of the Indies* (1542, pub. 1552) said he was speaking for Natives thus: "Prominent amid the aspects of this story which have caught the imagination are the massacres of innocent peoples, the atrocities committed against them and, among other horrific excesses, the ways in which towns, provinces, and the whole kingdoms have been entirely cleared of their native inhabitants."[19] Las Casas, whose family was of French origin and had settled in Seville, did not have enough of an effect on Spanish policy to save the Indians. While some intellectuals took up this oppositional stance, those who in France and England advocated colonization began to use Las Casas's passionate defense of the Natives as a means of creating distance between their own imperial ambitions and the expansion of Spain.

Las Casas himself, however, did not limit his critique to Spaniards in the New World. Much has been said about Las Casas's role in the Black Legend of Spain, and there is no doubt that "heretics" in rival countries used him in ways that he would have found unacceptable. A neglected passage in *A Short Account* shows that Las Casas was not willing to attribute cruelty to Spaniards alone, as if they were the only ones touched by original sin. Of the colonization of Venezuela, which he says the Spanish crown placed under the jurisdiction of German merchants (part of the Habsburg connection), Las Casas claims: "In my opinion, the Venezuela expedition was incomparably more barbaric than any we have so far described, and the men involved in it more inhumane and more vicious than savage tigers, more ferocious than lions or than ravening wolves."[20] Theodor De Bry, a German, and the English, French, and Dutch purveyors of the Black Legend of Spain, neglected this observation of the cruelty of northern Europeans. Even legends have their legends. Whatever their faults, the Spanish did debate the issue of the Natives and the New World, and some among them offered alternative and oppositional critiques. In the other nations, even if they were not always forgiving of the faults of the Spanish, a few among the clergy and intelligentsia offered a critique of the violence and injustice of war and expansion. Erasmus, a native of the Netherlands, where the French, English, and Spanish fought for influence, sought royal and papal favor but was also critical of aggression. His chief concern was with internecine wars in Europe.

II

This brief section on Erasmus should suggest that how aggression and war in Europe were viewed related to how violence in the New World was perceived. Whereas Erasmus often commented on European conflicts directly, Thomas More in *Utopia* created a distance, perhaps even a fictional space, in his critique, which was built in part on allusions to the Americas. Erasmus used satire, and his reputation as a leading scholar and intellectual to criticize violence in Christian Europe. Like his friend and fellow humanist,

More, Erasmus, a native of Rotterdam, represented the tension between nation and Christendom: Erasmus's life and work were concentrated at the end of Latin Europe and the beginnings of Reformation Europe. The European courts strove to glorify their respective nations by assembling scholars, artist, and scientists from throughout Europe. Henry VIII sent Erasmus an invitation; François Ier appealed to him to come to Paris; Charles of the Netherlands and Spain, later emperor, put him on a pension as imperial councilor, which, Margaret, the regent, cut off, to force Erasmus's return from Basel. These invitations came in spite of Erasmus's opposition to "nationalism" and European expansion.

When Erasmus had entered the University of Paris as a candidate for the doctorate of theology and as a poor scholar at the Collège de Montaigu in 1495, he had found a place given to scholasticism, still embodying the learning of one of its teachers a half century before: Pierre d'Ailly.[21] Two other humanists, Vives and Rabelais, satirized the scholasticism there, the Spaniard saying that to depart the University of Paris was to emerge from Stygian darkness while the Frenchman ridiculed the *théologastres*.[22] While in Paris Erasmus sought out people who were attempting to combine classical learning and Christianity in a new fashion. Humanism, which already had a long history in Italy, had been adumbrated at Paris in the middle of the fifteenth century in the work of Guillaume Fichet, who had tried in his teaching of theology and rhetoric to meld Italian humanist eloquence with scholastic theology. Erasmus met Fichet's successor, Robert Gauguin, a humanist who taught rhetoric at the Sorbonne, a churchman, a diplomat for the French Crown, a Gallican, a patriot who thought the French and the English could not get along. Gauguin had written a chauvinistic history of France, which did not fill out the quire, so he invited Erasmus to use the space. With characteristic irony, in that given space, Erasmus praised Gauguin and writing above France and expansion: eloquence is better than land grabs as a way for kings to find glory.[23]

In Rome, Erasmus heard a tedious Good Friday sermon in which Pope Julius was praised as Jupiter Optimus Maximus who was responsible for everything important in Europe and Africa. Enjoying the great libraries and scholars in Rome, Erasmus remained ambivalent about a papacy that could maintain this ambiance and invade Venice. Pope Julius asked Erasmus to write for and against his right to make war and used only the pro-war argument. Erasmus argued that the church, from priest to Pope, should not fight for territory.[24]

While visiting Thomas More in London, he wrote *Encomium Moriae* (1511), the praise of More or Folly as the pun would have it, a satire that combined Lucianic irony with the notion of the fool in Christ.[25] This satire excoriated misrepresentation of God and gold—theologians and grammarians who displayed their learning to avoid the world and worldly merchants who wore their wealth in gold. It was folly to praise wealth and war, the imperial theme, in which Italy was one of the battlegrounds. The Netherlands and the New World were other grounds on which Europeans fought their imperial wars.

Erasmus, like More, opposed expansion and was wary of Spanish designs and ambitions. In 1512, Pope Julius II, having taken Venice with French help, now turned on France with Venetian aid. Henry VIII, who joined this alliance with Venice and the pope, was ready to invade France. John Colet preached a Good Friday sermon against the war in Henry's presence, saying that a Christian prince would better imitate Christ than the Juliuses and Alexanders. In a letter from England to Cardinal Riario, Julius's nephew, in Rome, Erasmus wrote: "I came to England expecting the age of gold, literally mountains of gold, beyond the wealth of Midas, and now the trumpet of Julius has thrown the whole world into war."[26] This parody of Christian godliness, of Julius the Pope imitating Julius Caesar, would drive away the golden age, including the gold that even Erasmus must possess to have the freedom to live as he would. His patrons would leave eloquence for blood. When his friend, Andrea Ammonio, an Italian and secretary to Henry VIII, informed Erasmus of this league against France, Erasmus responded: "Suppose the French are expelled from Italy. Would you rather have the Spaniards as lords?"[27] Erasmus's question would become even more pressing, when Spain sacked Rome in 1527. The Black Legend is foreshadowed or has early origins in Italy and elsewhere.[28] Later, Las Casas, like Erasmus, questioned the abuse of religion in the quest for empire, but this time the Spanish in the New World were targets. Erasmus's friend, Thomas More, would also use the Spanish–Italian axis (this time Vespucci rather than a pope with Spanish connections) to expose the spoils of aggression.

III

Thomas More was a member of the establishment who did not seem to think that the establishment of empire was a mission as divine as Columbus might have thought. As a humanist, he embodied a European internationalism based on Latin and Rome as well as national service. *Utopia*, which the author sent to Erasmus on September 3, 1516, begins with More's letter to Peter Giles (c.1486–1533), whom he had visited in Antwerp in September 1515. Thomas More actually entrusted the publication of this text to Erasmus and Giles and both men seem to have contributed marginal glosses on the work.[29] More knew the account of Vespucci's voyages, which emphasized the Epicurean nature and communal property of the Amerindians, and was familiar with the interest that his brother-in-law, John Rastell, took in voyaging to North America (which he set out for in 1517).[30] The Italian captain in the service of Spain had, along with Plato, influenced More. On his return to England, More seems to have added to the parts of *Utopia* he had written in the Low Countries during his embassy.[31]

In the prefatory letter, More reported about his fictional character, Raphael Hythlodaeus, a Portuguese, as if he were a real friend. In a satire on travel accounts, which can display questionable geographical knowledge of the Americas and idle curiosity, More wrote to Giles:

> We forgot to ask, and he forgot to say, in what part of the new world Utopia lies. I am sorry that point was omitted, and I would be willing to pay a considerable sum to purchase that information, partly because I am rather ashamed to be ignorant in what sea lies the island of which I am saying so much, partly because there are several among us, and one in particular, a devout man and a theologican by profession, burning with an extraordinary desire to visit Utopia. He does so not from an idle and curious lust for sight-seeing in new places but for the purpose of fostering and promoting our religion, begun there so felicitously.[32]

The truth, of course, is More's object, so that he urges Giles to have Hythlodaeus check the narrative for verisimilitude and hopes that he has not preempted Raphael's own account of the "adventures" and commonwealth. Well in anticipation of Gulliver's letter to Captain Simpson in the second edition to *Gulliver's Travels*, More plays here on the conventions of true eyewitness reports in his fiction. More makes the oxymoronic Raphael Hythlodaeus (his personal name means healing of God and his family name learned in nonsense) Portuguese, perhaps owing to the long-standing importance of Portugal in exploration, of the voyages of de Gama and Cabral under Manuel I and John III.[33] Perhaps with an eye to Erasmus's Folly, who represents a fable of the fool in Christ, the central character in More's dialogue is a godly healer learned in nonsense who has sailed to a good place/no place and has reported the truth in a fiction. More plays with satire, irony, and comedy as Erasmus had.[34]

After the letter, the body of text begins with More, citizen and sheriff of London, reporting in order to make the fiction reflect his own diplomatic role in Europe in 1515. The opening sentences encapsulate a moment in the conflict in which Spain, England, and France were involved. They also seem to shower patriotic praise on More's king, although the irony of the book itself might modify this encomium: "The most invincible King of England, Henry, the eighth of that name, who is distinguished by all the accomplishments of a model monarch, had certain weighty matters recently in dispute with His Serene Highness, Charles, Prince of Castile. With a view to their discussion and settlement, he sent me as a commissioner to Flanders."[35]

Henry is invincible as he was victorious in the Battle of the Spurs and in occupying Tournai and Thérouanne.[36] The matter between England and Castile was the potential seizure of the English merchant fleet for back payment of tolls. Despite this conflict involving England, Spain, and France, More ignores this friction as it occurs in the New World.

More then provides his diplomatic mission as a context for the meeting of the three main characters. They meet at the end of Mass in Notre Dame church in Antwerp. The play between fiction and truth also occurs as Peter Giles, the character, as opposed to Giles, the man addressed in the prefatory letter, notes that Raphael is not an ordinary ship captain, not a Palinurus, but even more like Plato than the extraordinary Ulysses, for he is an itinerant philosopher of the high seas. More constructs a world of exploration that is clearly Portuguese and Spanish. He is silent about the English voyages, for the character Giles places the fictional Hythlodaeus, a humanist Greek scholar, in an actual Iberian context, although Vespucci, the pilot general of Spain, was Italian:

> He left his patrimony at home—he is Portuguese—to his brothers, and, being eager to see the world, joined Amerigo Vespucci and was his constant companion in the last three of those four voyages which are now universally read of, but on the final voyage he did not return with him. He importuned and even wrested from Amerigo permission to be one of the twenty-four who at the farthest point of the last voyage were left behind in the fort. And so he was left behind that he might have his way, being more anxious for travel than about the grave. These two sayings are constantly on his lips: "He who has no grave is covered by the sky," and "From all places it is the same distance to heaven." This attitude of his, but for the favor of God, would have cost him dear. However when after Vespucci's departure he had traveled through many countries with five companions from the fort, by strange chance he was carried to Ceylon, whence he reached Calicut. There he conveniently found some Portuguese ships, and at length arrived home again, beyond all expectation.[37]

More's Giles is drawing on Vespucci's accounts, such as *Cosmographiae Intoductio* (1507) from about ten years before. Raphael travels to Cape Frio in Brazil to Calicut and back home, a member of the Spanish expedition but saved by his own countrymen and perhaps his philosophy, which, if the sayings are a guide, derives as much from his reading of Lucian, Augustine, and Cicero as of Plato. The English More and the Flemish Giles are left to the defining example of a Spanish voyage in a new world divided between Portugal and Spain.

Part of the fiction of finding Utopia is that Raphael and his friends stayed behind at the fort in Brazil after Vespucci left. More, who plays with the slippage among the many Mores, the diplomat, author, and narrator, stresses how the generosity of a Native ruler allowed these Europeans to survive and what excellent institutions the aboriginal commonwealths had. More's ambivalence resides in the wonder that the compass caused among the Natives and the reliance of the Europeans on the Natives in the New World. Using the topos of inexpressibility, More says that on another occasion Raphael's story about the discourse of civilization and facts useful to the reader will be told, "but about stale travelers' wonders we were not curious. Scyllas and greedy Celaenos and folk-devouring Laestrygones and similar frightful monsters are common enough, but well and wisely trained citizens are not everywhere to be found."[38] As a good humanist, More ironically relates travelers' marvels to the monstrous fictions of Homeric and Virgilian epic. Then More shifts to the friction between the ethnological aspects the Utopians (a Ciceronian regard for customs and manners) that interests Raphael and the role of the adviser to European princes that preoccupies Peter Giles. More seconds Giles's belief that Raphael would make a good king's councilor, but Hytholdaeus speaks satirically against the monarchs' pursuit of war rather than peace and the flattery at court, which he has found in various places, including England.

Before Montaigne, More is satirizing Europe through the New World, except in Book I he includes direct satire that is not connected explicitly to life in the New World. For instance, Raphael opposes the view of an English lawyer that hanging is proper punishment for nonviolent theft by representing theft as an act of the economically desperate. Some thieves are veterans who were disabled in the battles in France in the late 1480s and early 1490s, such as Boulogne in 1492, and others in the Cornish rebellion in 1497. Implicitly, More has Raphael give a European context of poverty, violence, and injustice to the era of Columbus, Cabot, and Vespucci. Kings and nobles neglect their soldiers and loyal servants, and this abuse leads to social unrest, a homeless class of wandering thieves. Even in a dialogue, in which the dissident voice of Raphael, full of allusions to Plato, Cicero, Augustine, and others, is not equivalent to that of More, the author, his expression of this critique, and the high regard More builds for Raphael through the praise Giles and More, the character, have for him make Hythlodaeus both dialogic protagonist (the first among interlocutors) in Book I and narrator in Book II. Even though Raphael exalts Cardinal Morton (c. 1420–1500), in whose household More once served, More allows for a critique of England.

Nor does France escape criticism. *Utopia* places Europe in the context of a New World state of generosity and wisdom: Book I begins with mention of this trait in the New World and then proceeds to the corruption of Europe. Book II follows with an account of this good place/no place of the New World, partly as a corrective of the errors of Europe. Not all Europeans looked arrogantly West as if they were to bring civilization to the savages.

The oppositional or alternative critics, like More, who recalls Plato in the *Republic*, were raising embarrassing questions about the "discovery" of royal advisers and admirals. Perhaps More's patriotism allows him to have Raphael praise English draftee soldiers over French professionals, but Hythlodaeus, speaking to More, the character, cannot help criticizing England in the same breath: " 'France in particular is troubled with another more grievous plague. Even in peacetime (if you can call it peacetime) the whole country is crowded and beset with mercenaries hired because the French follow the train of thought you Englishmen take in judging it a good thing to keep idle retainers.' " [39] Raphael says that France has learned at its own cost, like Rome, Carthage, and Syria that such an idle army can turn on its own country. Raphael answers More, the character, who suggests that philosophers should counsel kings with the view that Plato means that kings will have to become philosophers first before they ask philosophers for their advice. To illustrate his view, Raphael supposes himself in the French king's privy council while the king's councilors advise how France can conquer Milan, Naples, Venice, the whole of Italy, then Flanders, Brabant, the whole of Burgundy, and other nations through various schemes: treachery in treaties, German mercenaries, bribes to the Swiss, and gold for the emperor, giving Navarre (someone else's kingdom) to the king of Aragon, a marriage alliance with the Prince of Castile, French pensions to Spanish nobles.

Raphael continues his satire on the French privy council by outlining its machinations concerning England. Then he sets up a situation where he would raise and refute their advice by a supposition that Italy should be left alone because France is almost too big itself to govern, so that the king should stay at home. He illustrates this principle by showing that the Achorians who live south-southeast of the isle of Utopia decided, after experiencing what France might, to offer their king the chance to rule only one of his two kingdoms. He chose his own. More, the character, admits that with such advice Raphael would not be a popular French councilor. But Raphael is not finished with his satire on the vanity of the French privy council. The advisers in Raphael's fictional scene call for corrupt uses of old laws to raise money through fines and related tricks and they agree with Crassus, "Nullam auri uim satis esse principi, cui sit alendus exercitus."[40] Raphael opposes this dishonest counsel by insisting that the people chooses a king for its own sake and not his, so his safety and honor depend on recognizing this political foundation and should, then, attend to the welfare of the people at home and make them prosperous rather than seek new lands. A nation is not a jail for paupers. Kings should not be indolent, arrogant, above the law, and greedy for private gold instead of public good. Raphael proceeds to tell another story of a people of the New World to correct France. The Macarians have learned their lesson about greedy kings and should serve as an example.

More, the character, counters with a rhetorical and dramatic position, saying that academic philosophy considers everything suitable to every place, whereas the practical philosophy of statesmen knows its stage, accommodating itself to the play at hand, performing his role with decorum. Why mix tragedy and comedy, Seneca with Plautus? Raphael should obey the decorum of genres and the harmony of proportion. More, the character, does not let Raphael satirize the king of France and his privy council without something of a fight between absolute academic philosophical truth and a more relational, rhetorical, and dramatic truth. Even still, the theme of gold also strikes at the heart of the French court, the most ambitious in Europe it seems, at least according to the representation in *Utopia*. France has the potential here to be the villain in a legend.

Columbus had written about the quest for God and gold in the New World but goes unmentioned here. If More had wanted to do so, he could have made Spain a monster, as he did Richard III in another work that Shakespeare seems to have employed later as a source for his play about that king. Instead, over sixty years later, the French then the English used Las Casas to create such a monster. Although not entirely spared in More's satire, Spain makes few explicit appearances in *Utopia*. The themes of God and gold, which occurred in Vespucci, who sailed under the Spanish flag, are central to More's fiction of the New World. Vespucci told of the baptism of many Natives, a topic More represents in the coming of Christianity to Utopia.[41] The Indians do not value gold or gems and almost despise them, Vespucci said, while educated Europeans would have read Peter Martyr's account of the Spanish lust for gold in *De orbe novo*.[42]

More's satire plays on this difference between the worldly greed for gold of Christians and the spiritual indifference to it of the Utopians. In Utopia there are gold and silver chamber pots, fetters for slaves, ornaments, and crowns for criminals. The children there play with gems as toys. The Anemolian ambassadors to Utopia cause disgrace and amusement by decking themselves out in precious metals and gems. Although probably alluding to Lysurgus's reforms in Sparta, where iron became legal tender in place of gold and silver, More's Lucianic allegory also amplifies the contrast between the Native indifference and contempt for gold and the Spanish greed for it.[43] One of the interpolated notes, which run through the text for emphasis on certain topics, reads: *Quanto plus sapiunt Vtopiani, quam Christianorum uulgus'*.[44] If the Spanish seemed ridiculous, the French and English, probably not to More's surprise, also showed this Christian gold-lust but were not as "fortunate" as the Spanish in finding precious metals.

This passage on gold, silver, and gems also raises the issues of communism and slavery, which both Vespucci and More represented. In a letter to

Lorenzo Pietro di Medici about the New World, Vespucci mentioned that the Indians hold goods in common and that they are their own masters without kings or government.[45] More's character, Raphael, emphasizes the egalitarian and communist values of the Utopians.[46] Vespucci discussed the Spanish plan to enslave the Natives, and More describes slavery in Utopia in the context of how fair and compassionate the Utopians were, representing a more ambivalent position than Vespucci's view from the New World.[47] Like the Indians Vespucci described, the Utopians do not fight war for glory.[48] The Utopians are noble, but do not live in a golden age without conflict.

More, the character, does not agree entirely with Raphael in Book I, where Hythlodaeus speaks most, but More, the author, has given most of *Utopia* over to Raphael's opinions and his representation of this place that does and does not exist in the New World. Spain appears and does not appear in More's book: besides a few references to its rulers, it presents itself in allegory, which is never precise and can constitute an interpretative El Dorado. That is why, as well as in keeping with the themes or argument of this study, no elaborate allegorical Castle of Castile appears here. The interest of More in the New World, and perhaps of other Christian humanists, depended on Spanish experience there, and seized on some of the ancient European themes that the Spaniards elaborate: gold, God, and strange peoples. Utopia and the New World, like Plato's republic, the Land of Cockaigne, and Mandeville's isle of Bragman, were possible worlds, different from Europe. The only catch is that the New World was actual as much as the Europeans wished to imagine it. The real and the imagined join in the actual. The opponents to imperialism and war, like More, found it difficult even in their dreams and fictions, to imagine a world, even a new world, without expansion and strife.

Even as the Spanish, English, and French were establishing empires, some from within those countries were questioning expansion or the way Europe was possessing the New World. For humanists, like Erasmus and More, the opposition derived in part from the sense that Christians should not war in Italy or in far-off lands. At the same time that opposition was an aspect of a critique of Europe, a kind of reform, whether religious, legal, or philosophical. Las Casas and Montaigne also become alternative thinkers about the relation between Europe and the New World. The example of Spain and the consequences of Columbus's encounter with this world unknown to the Europeans provided writers like Las Casas and Montaigne with new problems and a way of demanding justice as More had. These two critics of European exposed abuses in colonization in the sixteenth century, when Montaigne cast his skeptical eye on imperialism and when French and English translations of Las Casas appeared.

IV

Before preceding to the better-known example of Montaigne, I want to call attention to the critical aspects of Jean de Léry's views of European presence in the New World and how it relates to their mores in their own country, most particularly to the French in Brazil and in France. For the purposes of this discussion of Léry's *History of a Voyage to the Land of Brazil*, I concentrate on the edition of 1580, which is more readily available in French and English than that of 1578 and which did not accrue to itself the material concerning Spanish cruelty as taken from Las Casas that Léry's subsequent editions did. Léry, who wrote the first draft in 1563, himself did not oppose contact with the Tupinamba in Brazil or the establishment of French colonies, but he could, like his more famous compatriot, Montaigne, criticize the French above the Natives in a typological comparison of the Old World and the New. Brazil became something of a touchstone for Léry during the Wars of Religion that were tearing France apart. In addition to having been to Brazil in the 1550s and having nearly starved on the voyage back, Léry had witnessed the Saint Bartholomew's Massacre in La Charité-sur-Loire and lived through and wrote about the siege of Sancerre from January to August of 1573 in which many had little or nothing to eat.[49] These terrible experiences made him aware of the barbarity in Europe, so that he could be more critical of his compatriots than he could of the Natives in Brazil, even if he saw their shortcomings and his own as well.

It is important not to see Montaigne's satire on France in isolation. There is, as Peter Burke has noted, a danger in making Montaigne, or other forward-thinking writers of his time who considered culture, into social anthropologists, a professional designation that has its beginnings in the late nineteenth century, but ethnographer, in the sense of someone with an interest—whether neutral, hostile, or sympathetic—in different or exotic cultures, is more appropriate and could apply to Herodotus, Marco Polo, John de Mandeville, Francisco López de Gómara, Hernán Cortés, Girolamo Benzoni, André Thevet, Marc Lescarbot, John Smith, or Jean de Léry himself.[50] Here, I am focusing on those who were largely neutral or sympathetic to the Natives and less so to imperialism, hegemony, or warfare. Léry seems to have had begun this criticism before Montaigne and they share a use of ethnographical estrangement as a means of creating a comparison in which the French come out badly. This kind of chastisement occurs in the one example I wish to concentrate on and that is, in this history of Brazil, when Léry remembered the Saint Barthomew's Massacre, which occurred long after he had been in Brazil and after he had written the first draft but which came to play a prominent role in the published version of the *History*. What interests me about this incident, rather than in the 1585 edition when

Léry added other atrocities from the Old World and in the 1611 edition when he expanded the material about Spanish cruelty in the New World taken from Las Casas, is that in the 1580 edition he spoke about how cruel and barbarous both the Natives of Brazil and the people of France were.[51] After cataloguing "the cruelty of the savages," he reminded his readers that he wanted them to "think more carefully about the things that go on every day over here, among us."[52]

He chastised usurers and Christians in Italy who eat their enemies, livers and hearts, but it is for the French in the Wars of Religion (1562–98) that he saves his harshest words: "(I am French, and it grieves me to say it.)"[53] The cannibalism and hatred led Léry to conclude, along with someone whose verse he quoted, "that execrable butchery of the French people . . . surpassed all those that had ever been heard of."[54] In a passage that is akin to what Montaigne later wrote, Léry concluded his chapter on the Native ceremonies for killing and eating prisoners in Brazil, with a moral indignation, in which the ethnological lens is turned back on those who would use it on other peoples beyond Europe:

> So henceforth no longer abhor so very greatly the cruelty of the anthropophagous—that is, man-eating—savages. For since there are some in our midst even worse and more detestable than those who, as we have seen, attack only enemy nations, while the ones over here have plunged into the blood of their kinsmen, neighbors, and compatriots, one need not go beyond one's own country, not as far as America, to see such monstrous and prodigious things.[55]

In 1574 Léry had published his account of the siege of Sancerre, which he had experienced firsthand. Here was an eyewitness who had lived through hardship in the Old World and New. Looking back on Brazil, where he arrived in 1556 and where Nicolas Durand de Villegagnon led the French expedition, through the civil strife of France only a few years after his return in 1558, Léry provided a lament for his people. How could they feel superior to anyone?

Léry might have had some nostalgia for Brazil, but he was not idealizing that place or France in the double vision of his "typology." And I use this term from biblical interpretation advisedly. Léry combined biblical and classical allusions to tyrants in his quotation from a poem about the Wars of Religion in France:

> Laugh, Pharoah,
> Ahab and Nero,
> Herod too;
> Your barbarity
> By this deed
> Is buried from view.

Barbarism was an idea from classical Greece: French claims to the translation of empire were, owing to their barbarity, questionable. These French were more tyrannical than the worst the poet could muster. Léry's alternative critique to colonial attitudes was to uncover the pretensions of the French and their own heart of darkness. Between Las Casas and Montaigne, Léry was able to produce shards of an anatomy of cruelty. Like Montaigne, Léry concentrated on his own compatriots rather than, from 1585 onward, deflecting some of the horror in France to the borrowed descriptions of Spanish cruelty in Las Casas. I have chosen to mention only Léry's blame for Villegagnon for the failures in Brazil and his disagreement with André Thevet about this leader and about France's role in Brazil more generally because it was the indignation with the French and with what they had done to each other in France that called into question even more what they had said and done in the New World.

V

The critics of the abuses of colonization, like Las Casas and Montaigne, could not alter the kind of commercial development and treatment of Natives that their countrymen were bent on pursuing. Las Casas did not have enough of an effect on Spanish policy to save the "Indians." While some intellectuals took up this oppositional stance, those who in France and England advocated colonization began to use Las Casas's passionate defense of the Natives as a means of creating distance between their own imperial ambitions and the expansion of Spain. Michel de Montaigne, born to a Catholic father and a Jewish mother who had converted to Protestantism, also criticized European abuses against the peoples they were subjecting.

In his essay, "Des Cannibales" (1580), Montaigne uses a classical context, including the Greek habit of calling all foreign countries barbarous and Plato's representation of Solon's account of Atlantis, to criticize French and European expansion and commerce in the New World, so that the simple equation, now made too often from neglect or ignorance, of classicism with the ills of colonization is too simple an assessment.[56] Classicism bore an ambivalent relation to colonization, which was itself fraught with ambivalence. Montaigne framed his critique in terms of ancient Greece, but what is of more direct interest here is to recent events in French colonization, ones addressed by Jean de Léry, probably a source for Montaigne. In writing about Villegagnon and "Antarctic France," for one of Montaigne's employees had been on that expedition, Montaigne wondered whether so many "great personages" had been wrong about whether any other such "discovery" would be made in the future: "I am afraid that we have eyes bigger than the stomach, as it is said, ... I also fear that we have much more curiosity than we have capacity: we embrace all, but I fear that we grasp nothing but wind."[57] This criticism of French expansion, like Las Casas's critique of Spanish colonization, did not seek to blame another country and served as a balance to those in France who would criticize Spain in the New World. Montaigne represented the desire for colonization in an image worthy of Rabelais: clearly the French should be aware of their own limits. Unlike Las Casas, Montaigne did not advocate the expansion of Christendom and the conversion of the Indians as a justification for colonization. Montaigne's method was to compare and contrast the classical and the contemporary.[58] As this essay is much discussed, this section concentrates on a work of Montaigne's that is less familiar and more directly about Spain in the New World.[59]

Whereas in the essay on cannibals Montaigne had concentrated on the French and Europeans in relation to the New World, in "Des Coches" he focused on the Spanish.[60] He asked why the new lands could not have been conquered under the Greeks and Romans to bring the peoples virtue rather than teach them European avarice and "all sorts of inhumanity and cruelty, and by the example and pattern of our customs."[61] Instead, in search of pearls and pepper, the Europeans had exterminated nations and millions of people, so that Montaigne proclaimed "mechanical victories."[62] It is clear, however, that Montaigne meant to chastise the Spanish, the king of Castile and the pope, who appear in the usual Spanish ceremony of possession in which the Spaniards, searching for a mine, told the Natives that their king is "the greatest Prince in the inhabited earth, to whom the pope, representing God on earth, had given the principality of all the Indies" and that they want the Natives to be tributaries who yield up food, medicine, and gold, believe in one God, and the truth of the Spanish religion.[63] To this customary ritual, the Spanish added "a few threats."[64] The response that Montaigne gave the Natives is characteristic of the "savage indignation" he often attributed to their reaction to European folly: "concerning their King, as he begged, he must be indigent and needy, and he [the pope] who had made this distribution to a third party of something that was not his, was a man liking dissension to put it up for debate against its ancient possessors."[65] Montaigne reported that the Spaniards stayed only where they found the merchandise they sought, but when they did, they could be brutal, for instance, in ransoming and then killing the king of Peru, whose nobility Montaigne contrasted with the ignoble Spanish.[66] The noble king of Mexico was subjected to Spanish cruelty and torture, which diminished Spain and not the victim.[67]

These and other atrocities were a source of Spanish pride: "We have from themselves these narratives, for they not only confess but publish and extol them."[68] The Spaniards, according to Montaigne, exceeded the force necessary in conquest and have met with providential justice as they have fought one another in civil war and have had the seas swallow up some of their treasure.[69] Montaigne offered a king of apocalyptic judgment of the Spaniards who had not brought religion into the New World but death: their apparent use of God would bring the wrath of God and darkness.[70] While Montaigne's work, which was skeptical of empire, was making its impact felt in the 1580s, Richard Hakluyt was in Paris much of the time (1583–88), preparing and prompting England to pursue imperial expansion.[71]

VI

These critics from within, whether the erudite Erasmus or the rhetorical Las Casas, left their mark in European and "American" intellectual and cultural history. They contradicted themselves, but at least they contradicted others. No simple acceptance of violence, war, and colonial exploitation informed Montesino, More, Erasmus, Las Casas, Léry, and Montaigne in this crucial first century of European colonization of the western Atlantic. While they were disturbed with domination and greed, they used irony and satire to discipline their own cultures. These textual promptings were not always that effective in staying the material exploitation and the deaths of the indigenous peoples—the world is not a text only—but they are a disjunction to observe and build on. These dissident voices, sometimes as close to the king as possible, suggest the rupture within the bodies of Europe and America then and now.

The alternative or oppositional critiques of European violence and expansion often came from humanists who turned their classical knowledge of history, literature, and philosophy against the abuses of power in Europe both at home and in the New World. While in postcolonial theory it is easy to dismiss humanism as complicit in empire—and we have our own possible tendencies toward complicity—leading humanists, like Erasmus, More, and Montaigne, were often against a violent foreign policy.[72] Their chief weapon was satire—something they could use to excoriate their own courts and countries as well as those of their great, neighboring powers. Although Spain was becoming the "superpower" in sixteenth-century Europe, neither Erasmus nor More nor Montaigne focused exclusively on its abuses in Europe and the New World. They did, however, adumbrate the Black Legend of Spain, which became part of the way other European powers, and not simply those with large Protestant populations, depicted the Spanish Empire. Nonetheless, the massacres of the Huguenots by the Spanish in Florida in the 1560s and the Revolt in the Netherlands from 1580 to 1640 contributed to a blackening of the reputation of Spain. These countries translated the work of Las Casas, an opponent or alternative thinker from within Spain, and used those translations, as well as interpretations of his work, to criticize and excoriate Spain.

Las Casas is an aspect of the Spanish precedents that haunt the English- and French-speaking parts of the Western Hemisphere and the imperial centers that begot them. Las Casas was not the first or last Spaniard to raise questions about the right or morality of Spain in claiming lands and having dominion over the Natives. Francisco de Vitoria was a key figure in asking difficult questions of his country's involvement in the New World such as: by what right (*ius*) were the barbarians subjected to Spanish rule? What powers in temporal and civil matters did the Spanish monarchy have in regard to the "Indians"? In spiritual and religious matters what powers has either the monarchy or church in relation to the "Indians?"[73] This self-criticism, as well as the growth of the Spanish colonies, elicited notice and sometimes a grudging respect for Spain. The ghost of Spain, or what I have also called the example of Spain, depends on the ambivalence with which the French and English regarded Spanish power in the New World. Although this narrative of Spanish colonization in the Atlantic was involved with other countries, most notable with Italy, Portugal, the German states, and the Netherlands and although the balance in that ambivalence shifted over time, from the late fifteenth century and into the nineteenth century, the narrative found its greatest intensity and endurance in the rivalries between Spain and the other great powers, England and France.

In this war of propaganda, someone like Richard Hakluyt the Younger could use learning and the translation of modern European languages to help build an English empire, although he did not include Las Casas in his first edition as much as he did in later ones. While the English, French, and Dutch were ambivalent in their representations of Spain, for they wished to emulate Spanish wealth and commercial success in Asia and in the New World, they found, as their power grew, that they wished to displace Spain. It was not simply a matter of religion, as France came to purge itself of many of its Protestants by 1685, but coming after Spain had to do with legal, religious, economic, and political precedents that bore on the other European countries as they expanded into the Americas. As the Enlightenment approached, the Spanish were increasingly associated with feudalism and the medieval Church; but the propaganda and rhetoric could not mask that despite Spain's decline in Europe, it was still a formidable power in the New World.

In the Enlightenment, whose own means of incarceration and torture Michel Foucault has criticized, some writers sought rights for those who had been denied them.[74] Although this was an age when the Black Jacobins were not made beneficiaries of the French Revolution, it also should not be stripped of its advancements in human rights.[75] A figure of the

Enlightenment, the Abbé Guillaume Raynal, wrote, with Denis Diderot, *Philosophical and Political History of the Two Indies*, a scathing condemnation of European colonialism, and imagined a statue of Las Casas as an exemplum of benevolence in a ferocious age, a figure standing between an American and a European in order to defend the one from the other. Many such statues, as Anthony Pagden points out, can now be found throughout the Americas.[76]

What follows takes a step back to the sixteenth century, a time Las Casas was active, and focuses on three important writers—one Spanish, the other French, and still another English—Gonzalo Fernández de Oviedo, André Thevet, and Richard Hakluyt, the Younger respectively—who represent the New World. The discussion is structured deductively, proceeding from a more general influence of Spain on the promotion of empire by France and England through a specific comparison of three key promoters, Oviedo, Thevet, and Hakluyt to a discussion of Hakluyt and those indebted to him. These three steps, then, should provide a more up-close view of three key figures who have appeared in this chapter and in the book as a whole. A comparative European context allows for illumination of each national project of colonization. The promotion of empire had been and would continue to be a difficult and triangular if not angular endeavor, something that Spain, France, and England found from the beginning. In what follows, we shall look closely at the new angles that Oviedo, Thevet, and Hakluyt took to set the foundation for the imperial expansion of their respective countries.

Chapter 4 ∿

Promoting Empire

Within Europe, despite this opposition to exploration and settlement in distant lands, there were many key figures who promoted empire, so that a disjunction or tension existed within various Western European cultures over expansion. The contest over expansion was as internal as it was external and that tension varied from time to time, state to state, empire to empire. Often these promoters of "empire" had the ear of monarchs or counselors, and their writings were rhetorically pitched in persuading king, queen, and court of the wisdom as well as material and spiritual benefits of exploring and possessing overseas lands. While Spain had a head-start in creating settlements in the New World, the very knowledge it built up during its colonization became useful for other European countries in framing their desire to expand and in helping them to understand the practicalities of that expansion. The possession of knowledge of the New World helped the French and English, just as it had the Spanish, to the possession of the New World. Here, I concentrate on three major writers of the New World—Oviedo, royal historiographer in Spain; Thevet, royal cosmographer in France, and Hakluyt, editor, collector, and adviser to the English court—and their prefatory matter, which includes epistles dedicatory, Prefaces, addresses to readers, and patrons and commendatory verse. This matter, which is a genre and thus includes a code of expectations, is often promotional and involves the selling of an idea, if not of a book. When I speak of expectations here in regard to historiography, I am not focusing on the related expectations of Columbus, Cabot, and Cartier before they set out or when they saw land in the western Atlantic but of those who set out to collect and to reflect on these early voyages and the contact between Europeans and Amerindians and America.

The writers I have in mind are those historiographers who wished to retell or reconstitute the discovery, meaning, and development of the New World. More specifically, rather than discuss the whole range of historiography and historical collection, this chapter concentrates primarily on the prefatory matter of Gonzalo Fernández de Oviedo's *Natural History of the West Indies* (1526), André Thevet's *Les Singvlaritez de La France Antarctique, Avtrement nommée Amerique* (1558), and Richard Hakluyt's *The Principall Navigations of the English Nation* (1589). By limiting this selection, it is possible to focus on close reading and rhetorical analysis of the process of European possession of the New World. As this topic depends on the relation between rhetoric and history, it is important to show an inductive method, which complements the largely deductive framework of much of the work in the area. Evidence and argument should coexist as a mutual check. That these influential writers had to sell the idea of American colonies means that there was resistance at home and hardships overseas, so that the idea of a monological and monolithic European thirst for empire is not a complex enough view and the utopian descriptions of the Americas, which began with Columbus, were far enough from the actuality that it was often hard to get people to leave the various European nations for the New World.

These key promoters—who were not beyond self-promotion insofar as they wanted their ideas of colonization to prevail—had to set out carefully considered strategies of promotion to encourage colonization and the imperial destiny they saw for their respective nations and often did so through powerful and even royal patrons. While Oviedo, Thevet, and Hakluyt wrote at different times over a period of about seventy-five years, from 1526 to 1589, they all shared the framework of rhetoric, one of the foundations of the curriculum in the schools and universities of the time. The close reading in this chapter focuses on rhetoric, which is particularly appropriate in a study of promotion, as Aristotle called it the art of persuasion: to promote is to persuade others. In this case the writers sought to persuade the court of the importance of their views of expansion and their compatriots of the opportunities in settling and developing the New World. As the personal or ideological voice can surface more readily in prefatory matter, front material needs to be viewed seriously but not solemnly, carefully but not heavy with care. Some decades later, Cervantes would write in the prologue to the First Part of *Don Quixote*: "I would have wished to present it to you naked and unadorned, without the ornament of a prologue or the countless train of customary sonnets, epigrams and eulogies it is the fashion to place at the beginnings of books. For I can tell you that, much toil though it cost me to compose, I found none greater than the making of this Preface you are reading."[1] Prefatory or front matter is a central concern of this chapter. Cervantes's wry comment does address the nature of print and the making of books in the Renaissance or early modern period. Promoting empire could be about self-aggrandizement, a desire for profit, a cause of conversion, a search for markets, a turning from or solution to domestic problems.

Although the Spanish exploration and historical project set the tone for those of the English and French, by coming first, they also developed at an earlier time within a different context. Oviedo, Thevet, and Hakluyt all tried to define the national project of colonization and gave to it a collection or an attempted assimilation of an archive for public consumption. They took on the role of the scholar interpreting the mass of materials that made claims on their readers. They reflected on the New World, but Oviedo had been there, Thevet probably claimed to have been there more often and to more places than he had been, and Hakluyt, who traveled extensively in Europe, had not been to America at all. As Hakluyt came latest of the three, the role of experience in his project did not seem to be pressing, and in fact he appeared to have assimilated some of the work of Oviedo and Thevet. In the texts of all three writers there was a stress between the scholar who was coming to terms with new knowledge and representing the truth of that record and the eyewitness report of the experienced voyager who had been there and so knew more than theorists and scholars sitting in their studies. In Renaissance fashion, Oviedo, Thevet, and Hakluyt were men of "action" in the civic space and not monastic scholars living out a discipline in isolation. By examining their dedications and prefatory materials, I try here to ascertain what strategies and moves, tropes and schemes they used and to what ends.

I

Oviedo's *Natural History of the West Indies* (1526) appeared six years before Charles V appointed him official chronicler of the Indies.[2] In the Introduction, where Oviedo was addressing his "Sacred, Catholic, Imperial, Royal Majesty," he emphasized the importance of experience and eyewitness accounts and supported his view with an appeal to classical authority:

> The wonders of nature are best preserved and kept in the memory of man by histories and books in which they are written by intelligent persons who have traveled over the world and who have observed at first hand the things they describe and who describe what they have observed and understood of such things. This was the opinion of Pliny, the foremost of all natural historians, who wrote a history in thirty-seven books for the Emperor Domitian [*sic* Vespaciano].[3]

Oviedo advocated an observation of nature and a representation that depended on that rather than on other books, while he appealed to the authority of Pliny, whom, he said, included in his *Natural History* many things that were firsthand observations as well as accurate scholarly citations of the sources for the stories he read or heard.[4] Oviedo did not see a contradiction between history as representation based on other books or oral evidence and history as the account of observed results. Once again, he stressed that he was writing his book in "the manner of Pliny" when he proposed "to describe for your Majesty what I have seen in your Occidental Empire of the West Indies, Islands and Tierra Firme of the Ocean Sea."[5] Here was a new natural historian addressing a new emperor: Spain would take up where Rome left off. The trope of the translation of empire, of *translatio imperii*, was implicit.

Other ambitions informed Oviedo's rhetorical strategy. He wanted to set himself up as an authority, as if this natural history were a Preface to another larger project. This work, in turn, was already underway, so that the historian appealed to his copia. Although Oviedo was just one of many of the king's officials in the New World, he wanted to set himself apart. Even though he did not go to the New World until 1514, well after Columbus and others, he wished to connect his experience with these earlier feats:

> I have already written much more fully of these and many other things. These accounts are in the papers and chronicles I have been engaged in writing from the time I was old enough to become interested in such affairs. These writings are concerned with what has happened in Spain from 1490 up to now, as well as affairs in other lands and kingdoms where I have traveled.[6]

In one sentence, although Oviedo was not hidden when he first went to the New World, he yoked the time of Spain's exploration of the western Atlantic with his own travels. In search of patronage, it would seem, he said that his writings treated the lives of Ferdinand and Isabella, "of glorious memory," as well as events that had occurred in Charles's reign. Oviedo personalized Spanish history in the lives of the sovereigns.

But this was not all. Oviedo reminded Charles that he had another work based on his "observation" and "study" of the Indies, the two terms that gave Oviedo his authority. His papers were in the Indies with his family, as if to remind his sovereign that he lived in the New World as well as observing and studying it, so that he was writing to the king from memory. The book was meant for Charles's pleasure. But here is the crux:

> Even though these things may have been written about already and eyewitnesses may have described them, they probably are not so accurate as you will find them here. Those who have gone to the Indies on business or for other reasons may have spoken accurately about some or all of these things. Most men, however, would be inclined to forget the details since they have observed those wonders in a casual manner. I, on the other hand, by natural inclination have had keen desire to learn of these things and I have therefore observed them very carefully.[7]

Others may have studied and observed the New World, but Oviedo appealed to his own superior accuracy. He was, however, slippery. In his next breath, he was admitting that some of those who went on business or for other purposes, though not as a natural historian he implied, had been accurate about some things, or, as he then admitted, all things. Now Oviedo had to find a way of distinguishing himself and depreciating those who would compete with him through their representations for the attention of the sovereign. He had to say that most men did not have his memory—the historian who had left one of his histories in the Indies and had to remember it for Charles—and forget; they also were casual in their observations of wonders. Without mentioning it, it was also possible that Oviedo dwelt on memory in a kind of Ciceronian allusion, because, for Cicero, history was based on memory and witnessing: "to be the witness of time, the model of life, the life of memory, the light of truth, the messenger of antiquity."[8] Ultimately, history was Oviedo's "natural inclination" to curiosity and to careful observation. This was a kind of courtly waffling, a periphrastic giving and taking away, with the pleasure of the sovereign as the object and the assumed authority of this historian as the prize.

Using compression and a kind of synecdochic and metonymic strategy, Oviedo called the work he was introducing a *Summary*, as if it were standing in as a part of a great whole, for the much promised work that had stayed behind in the Indies. As if to reiterate and amplify his work, to show the fecundity of his pen and the extensiveness of his observations, Oviedo used a kind of topos of inexpressibility, a negatio, for he had already told the king the purpose of his historical project. The reminder was part of the purpose, a kind of unspoken supplement, because Oviedo would like the king's permission to send him "the longer and more complete history."[9] He dangled before Charles V the history that was "more complete" as if the king's pleasure, like Oviedo's, would be to desire to learn more.

Whether this longer history existed at this time is debatable, but as evidence, Oviedo reproduced or invented its beginning, which he reported from memory. The phantom great book was supposed to overshadow this prolegomena. Here he reported the beginning of a book that was absent. The opening phrase, "As everyone knows," built a consensus. Columbus's "discovery" of the New World was so famous that everyone knew about it. Next he reminded the reader, who was principally Charles, that this discovery occurred "in the time of the Catholic Sovereigns, Ferdinand and Isabella, your Majesty's grandparents."[10] He mentioned the Indian hostages Columbus took in the same breath as the "specimens of riches" and information about, not Cathay as Columbus would have thought it, but already Spain's "Occidental Empire." Columbus, for the next generations of Spaniards and their European neighbors and rivals, appeared to be inescapable as a moment of origin and precedent. Oviedo appealed to patriotism and nationalism, the nation building he hoped his history would be part of: anyone unaware of Columbus's feat was not a good Castilian or Spaniard. Each person was being called to glorify the empire. As Oviedo did not wish to repeat himself, he set out the outline of the book at hand. It was a strange and uncanny operation to introduce one book with another one.

He promised some of the thousands of things he could describe as if the New World was such a wonder that the king could not resist it. Instead, Oviedo summarized the contents of his so-called *Summary*, as something he had deferred to the end of his Introduction. The book would describe the voyage, people, animals, plants, and the land as well as "certain rites and ceremonies of those uncultivated people."[11] This last item in his list offered material that would now be considered topics appropriate to anthropology or comparative ethnology. It had, for Oviedo, a certain bias from the beginning as he thought of the people he was observing as uncultivated by Spanish standards.

Even in Oviedo's advertisement for this book, he could not resist closing the Introduction with a repetition of a misrepresentation of it as a summary of the larger study. He asked the king "to pardon any lack of order or arrangement that may be found in this book, for indeed it may be less orderly than the larger work I have written."[12] In admitting the artlessness of this work Oviedo emphasized the art of the book for which he was seeking patronage. His excuse for the lack of order was that he was preparing to return to the Indies to serve the king and so could not arrange the work as he would have liked. Nonetheless, he could not discount this shorter book that he was presenting to the king and so appealed to its novelty:

> But I should like you to observe the new things in it, for this has been my chief purpose. I write this accurately, as could many trustworthy witnesses who have been to the New World and who have now returned to Spain. There are also others in your Majesty's court, who ordinarily live in the New World, who could write about these things.[13]

This was a curious way to end as Oviedo had insisted on the uniqueness of his observation and study, on his accuracy. Although he waffled before, praising others in these areas, he held himself out as the only one who could do the job properly. Now, even while he appealed to the newness of his material, he threw his uniqueness away and admitted that others who have been to the New World could have written thus. Whether this was a rhetorical squint or a topos of modesty or false modesty to show himself part of the king's great enterprise in the Indies or whether this was an allegorical indirection that the king was supposed to see through, all of which was to lead to the triumph of Oviedo as the king's historian, is difficult to say. What is certain is that this brief Introduction was full of rhetorical moves that presented Oviedo's *Natural History* as a modest offering from a great natural historian to his king, as Pliny had written for his emperor, in preparation for a greater gift—the absent larger study that might have been completed and waiting in the Indies or might have been a fiction waiting to become historical representation—to the king if he would give him an incentive to work on it and a means of publication.

The classical past played a key role in the translation of study and the translation of empire. While Columbus had created a rupture in received authority and the medieval worldview and helped, wittingly or not, to usher in a modernity that displaced the classical world, his successors, like Oviedo, had both to seize the opportunity of this New World that would eclipse the past and to frame the imperial longings of the Spanish king and court in terms redolent of Rome. Oviedo's natural history would supplant Pliny's but was of it just as the king would eclipse the Roman emperor but was of that tradition. The eyewitness, Oviedo, like Acosta finding that his experience made him leave behind Aristotle's cosmology and geography, had to set aside his book learning but could not do so entirely as the rhetoric that underpinned his language and the way he set out to frame his knowledge and persuasion derived from the classical tradition. A tension between form and content, between observation and received learning, characterized the work of Oviedo and other key chroniclers of the New World in the sixteenth century.

II

This disjunction between observation and experience also affected historians and cosmographers in France, who sought to be authorities on parts of the world hitherto unknown to their compatriots. André Thevet, cosmographer to the king of France, also insisted on his unique ability to combine astute observations of the New World with strong scholarship. Thevet was a controversial figure: whereas Jean de Léry and François de Belleforest ridiculed his scholarship and character, Ronsard and Du Bellay esteemed his achievement.[14] In this century some scholars have tried to defend Thevet and to achieve a balanced view of his work: even still, some ambivalence remains. Frank Lestringant has said that this cosmographer was really a writer of fiction and not a savant, although he has praised Thevet's promotion of the colonization of Canada and his discussions on the political will as being sufficient for the birth of a nation.[15] In discussing Thevet's reputation, Roger Schlesinger and Arthur Stabler remain ambivalent. They have summarized his faults:

> Certainly Thevet cannot be taken at face value—as a fountain of learning on virtually all subjects, and especially on geography and ethnography. Besides, his tiresome criticisms of the authors who dared to infringe upon "his"

territory, his pretensions to infallibility, and his occasional "impudent lies" and clumsily concealed plagarisms, executed in the same breath as his repeated claims that he had "refused to publish anything other than that which I have seen with my own eyes or heard when I was in the countries about which I have often spoken to you," do him little honor.[16]

But Schlesinger and Stabler also list Thevet's good qualities, his insatiable curiosity and courage as a Renaissance tourist, and recommend that his works would be best treated as a kind of encyclopedic conflation or genre: travelogue, natural history, ethnography, anthropology, and romance. Without Thevet, we would lack some of the information we have about sixteenth-century America. Unlike Oviedo, Thevet did not live and serve long in the New World, but, like Oviedo, he claimed the authority of observation and the eyewitness.[17] Both historians sought the favor of their sovereigns and wished to be the sole authority on the New World for their respective countries. They wanted to chronicle the expansion and the desire for empire at court.

In this respect the preliminary matter to *Les Singularitez* provides Thevet's own rhetorical moves in his representation of the New World and his intellectual project. This book gained the privilege of the king: however formulaic the privilege is, it does place the king's authority behind Thevet. The Epistle, however, was to "the Most Reverand Cardinal de Sens, Guardian of the seals of France," and not the king himself.[18] Thevet hoped that the cardinal would recreate his spirit after reading, seeing, and tasting the history and would give him a delectable intermission from the most grave and serious negotiations. Thevet said that "the American Indie" or "the Antarctic France" could be called "the fourth part of the world."[19] Although Thevet placed the natural history and climate above the extension of French horizons, he did mention this growth in worldview. He implied that until his work cosmographers had not done the research necessary to extend beyond what the ancients had described. Even though Thevet said that the thing, presumably his book, seemed too small to Thevet to offer for the cardinal's perusal, "still the grandeur of your name will aggrandize the smallness of my work."[20] Here is a rhetoric that sought patronage, a comprobatio, that is, a seeking of favor by praising the audience. In this trope of modesty the cardinal's greatness would make great the smallness of Thevet's book, although the author had already implied that he was breaking new ground by supplementing the ancients and not simply by receiving their view of cosmography. As with Oviedo's rhetorical stance, Thevet's represented large claims for his work in regard to others placed beside declarations of modesty. Both hoped that the greatness of the person addressed would fulfill their books. Here Thevet repeated the trope that the aim of his book is to divert the spirit just as a doctor orders a change in diet: the cardinal will want with this pleasant diversion to relieve the burdens of the government of the republic. This comparison led Thevet to the ancient republics, where philosophers and others retired from public affairs. He cited the example of Cicero and compared the cardinal to him, for like that great orator among the Romans, among the French, "for your singular erudition, prudence, & eloquence, you are like the chief and principal administrator of the triumphant French Republic, and such for truth, which Plato describes in his Republic, it is to know great Lord, & man who is a lover ['amateur'] of science and virtue: also it is not beyond reason to imitate and follow it in this place."[21] From Plato's truth, Thevet moved to the singular virtue of the cardinal, his patron, whose grace, reception, and welcome Thevet had come to know. Thevet presented his little labor to this great patron, to whom he would dedicate it, if his Lord ("Seigneur") would accept it. The author also reiterated that he thought that if the cardinal read the book, it would recreate him. Moreover, Thevet said that he was much obliged to his Lord, to whose domain he would like to render very humble and obedient service and implore the Creator to give prosperity.[22] Like Oviedo's history, Thevet's was a historiography in search of official support even if it was not at this stage official history. By winning the favor of the king and his officers, of the deciding powers who determined factors (secular and ecclesiastical), each of these historians hoped to make his version the official version that would guide colonization and empire in his respective court.

Between Thevet's Epistle and his Preface to Readers there were three poems, two in French and one in Latin. These dedicatory poems were tributes to Thevet by illustrious people, so that they advertised the book as something large and important and not small and insignificant as Thevet had represented it to the cardinal at the end of the Epistle. Estienne Iodelle, Seigneur du Limodin, began with an ode. In it Iodelle praises the author—"*Thevet you would be assured/The harvests of your labour*"—but used the book as a pretext to contrast America with France to show France and its kings beset by triumphant enemies from within:

> *For who would like a little to blame*
> *The country that we should love,*
> *He would find Arctic France*
> *Has more monsters I believe*
> *And more barbarism in it*
> *Than does your France Antarctic.*
> *These barbarians walk all naked,*
> *And we walk unknown,*
> *Disguised, masked. This strange people*
> *Settle down to piety.*
> *We our own despise,*

Deceive, sell & disguise.
These barbarians to behave
Do not have as much reason as we do,
But who cannot see that plenty
Only serves to harm one another.[23]

This is the kind of opposition from within that we observed in chapter 3: it turns the ethnological and cultural glass back on France as a means of critique. Before Montaigne, whose famous chapter 31 in *Essais* (1580) compared cannibals favorably with the French, Iodelle, and indeed Thevet, Léry, and Ronsard (*Discours contre Fortune*), had represented material that would make the Amerindian nations seem ideal compared to France.[24] This Utopian satire could be found as early as More's *Utopia* (1516) and the righteous indignation of Iodelle may be found in Juvenal.

Belleforest's ode was written before its author became a critic of Thevet. It begins with the image of the harvest, proceeds to Thevet's achievement in representing the peoples of the Levant, to a multitude of peoples, to voyages whose dimensions outstrip those of Strabo beyond the horizons Ptolemy limited. Belleforest's Thevet, at least in 1557–58, discovers two Frances in the New World, expresses what has never been expressed before, creates a truth in which obscurity itself would be clear, a world of variety, which he knows how to color so well that he could cause idolatry or move people like Pan. Belleforest builds up the hyperbole to the point that it seems that God, France, and Europe all marvel at Thevet's work. The poem ends with the image of a tributary Europe, which will exalt Thevet, and a France that will not be able to remain quiet in its admiration, "*Reading these hidden marvels*" not yet touched and "*honouring you.*" Europe will honor Thevet for the marvels he has uncovered for his readers.

In keeping with the honor that Thevet has brought through his travels to the New World and descriptions of it and with the classical allusions that he and those who have written dedicatory poems have uses, Io. [Iohannes] Auratus, "literarum Gracarum Regius professor," records in Latin the feats of Thevet whose eye has seen the New World. Auratus concludes his brief poem with the appeal to the eye over the ear: "*Tantum aliis hic Cosmographis Cosmographus anteit, / Auditu quanto certior est oculus.*" ["This Cosmographer excels all other Cosmographers, / As much as sight is more sure than hearing."] Here Thevet is the greatest cosmographer who is the eyewitness and whose authority is, as Auratus implies, that of observation over orality or rumor.

Thevet's "Preface to Readers" set out a catalogue of the great philosophers, writers, and politicians of antiquity who traveled or understood travel. His premise thus began by considering "*how the long experience of things, &*

faithful observation of several countries & nations, together with their customs *['meurs'] & ways of life, brings perfection to man.*" Combining the experience of things and faithful observation of nations and their morals and ways of living was, for Thevet, the most praiseworthy exercise and a means of enriching his spirit with heroic virtue and solid science. Thevet also appealed to his voyages to the Levant, Greece, Turkey, Egypt, and Araby to make him an authority, for those travels gave him such wisdom and experience that under the grace of God, he sailed toward the south pole, not known to the ancients, as it appeared from the writings of Ptolemy, to places that were thought to be uninhabitable. Thevet distinguished himself from the ancients and made his voyage appear new and original, but when he says that he wanted to write down his experience, he did so in imitation of the greats of antiquity: "*That* *which I dared to undertake in imitation of several great personages, whose more* *than heroic acts [gestures], & high enterprises celebrated by histories, make them* *still live today in perpetual honour & immortal glory.*" History, like the epic, is a representation of the heroic—a memorial to fame and glory. Thevet used Homer as an example: he virtuously celebrated in his writings the long peregrination of Ulysses. He then turned to Virgil's representation of Aeneas, who is to be admired for his journey to Italy.

The Creator, Thevet said, made two types of men, the first elementary and corruptible and the second celestial, divine, and immortal. In this view God lets man execute his designs by land and sea, something that he can abuse. Thevet illustrated his point with the authority of Horace's *Epistles*, which argued in favor of the public good, a virtue practiced by Socrates, Plato, and Aristotle. Plato receives special mention because he voyaged in strange lands to learn philosophy and communicate with the public without recompense. Actually, before Thevet got to Aristotle, using an appropriate rhetorical question, he detoured through Cicero, who sent his son Mark to Athens partly so he could learn philosophy from Cratippus and partly because he could learn the customs ["meurs"] of the Athenian citizens. Lysander, Antiochus, Themistocles, and others are examples of virtuous men who show how virtuous the art of navigation is, while experience and Aristotle are witnesses to virtue. Appealing to the authority of Anacharsis, Thevet emphasized the dangers of the sea, and after an allusion to Alexander, Plato, Aristotle, and Diogenes, Thevet turned to himself, the object of the allegory of the combination of wisdom with physical courage all along.

After setting out this epic catalogue, Thevet seemed to want to be more useful than Diogenes among the Athenians: "I would like to put into writing several notable things, which I diligently observed during my navigation, between the Midi [south (of France)] and the Occident ['Penent,' Atlantic ocean]." He then listed what would follow, which included climate, geography, natural history, way of life of the inhabitants. Belleforest's ode says that

Thevet's pen sings to his audience of the customs ["meurs"] of the peoples of the Levant and makes them see the most diverse peoples, *"Men naked, & Savage, / Until now never discovered."* Vivid representation was also Thevet's aim: *"all of it represented vividly and without particular preparation by the most exquisite portrait that was possible for me."* After the epic simile of the wanderer as hero, which culminates in Thevet, he returned to the trope of his little book, an old trope that Geoffrey Chaucer used, saying that he would be happy if the reader would receive *"this my little labour."* But Thevet could not resist making explicit his epic comparison to the reader and said that it would be especially agreeable if he *"think about the great travail of so long & painful peregrination, which I wanted to undertake, for the eye to see, & then to make apparent [put into evidence] the most memorable things that I could note & collect, like those we shall see next."* The artistic and rhetorical ability to represent is a key purpose of Thevet's book. He used exempla, that is a rhetorical proofs by analogy employing the deeds of historical and fabulous men, to build his argument for this work, so that he could be the author/character as hero. He also appealed to testatio, his book as a confirmation of his experience for the reader. What Thevet, like Belleforest, is stressing about his work is how its representations use description to move the audience. What Thevet has implicitly promised is the following uses of description: demonstratio, a description of something that is so vivid that it seems to appear before the eyes of the audience; effictio, a representation of the body of any person; and locus, a description of any real place.

Thevet's critics would, however, add that he also used topothesia, or the description of an imaginary place. He conflated the fabula of Homer and Virgil with the lives of philosophers like Plato, so that from the beginning there is the possibility, if not the expectation, that the story and inquiry in history will yield a mixture of fiction and truth. What Thevet did not mention is that the Platonic Socrates impugned Homer for making such powerful fictions that they stand in for truth and have distorted Greek education. It may be in a post-modern context, as in an early modern one, that this mixture of rhetorical and "scientific" history did not trouble most of his readers, though we have seen that he was not without contemporary critics and has been criticized to this day for his claims of historical verisimilitude while having a penchant for fiction. Nor would Thevet be the only cosmographer whom Richard Hakluyt the Younger criticized in his attempt to collect essays and define what was necessary for the successful building of empire in North America.

III

Richard Hakluyt the Younger, as seen earlier, is a central figure in the historiography and literature of European, and not just English, expansion. Having discussed his lesser known works—one, the "Discourse," was published nearly three hundred years later—I now examine his best-known work: *The Principall Navigations of the English Nation* (1589), which helped Hakluyt, the collector, to carve out a place for himself and England in the making of empire and the knowledge necessary for imperial design. Although Hakluyt was also in the tradition of Oviedo and Thevet, he sometimes distanced himself from such company. Hakluyt needed his Continental predecessors, as England did, but in recognizing this need, he also had to erase it to some extent. To make its way in the future of the Americas, England had to suppress or displace its burden of the past or its anxiety of influence.[25]

Near the beginning of the Preface to *The Principall Navigations of the English Nation* (1589), Richard Hakluyt the Younger took a crack at unnamed universal cosmographers, apparently like Thevet and Belleforest, who published their cosmographies in 1575:[26]

> for I am not ignorant of Ptolemies assertion, that Peregrination is historia, and not those wearie volumes bearing the titles of universall Cosmographie which some men that I could name have published as their owne, beyng in deed most untruly and unprofitablie ramassed and hurled together, is that which must bring us to the certayne and full discoverie of the world.[27]

This trope of peregrination was one that Thevet borrowed from Ptolemy for his Preface, "Aux Lectures," in *Les Singularitez*, but he did not seem to have convinced readers like Hakluyt. In Hakluyt's view these cosmographies were a miscellany of other people's views rather than the observations of voyagers.

Before proceeding to Hakluyt's Preface to the First Edition, it is better to begin at the beginning of his Epistle Dedicatorie to Sir Francis Walsingham Knight, principal secretary to the queen and a member of the Privy Council, in order to compare his appeal to a patron with those of Oviedo and Thevet. Hakluyt began with a story about his own life in order to remind Walsingham of his connections to the Crown and to Walsingham himself. He evoked memory, of when he was "one of Her Majesties scholars at Westminster," and his visit to his cousin, Richard Hakluyt the Elder, "a Gentleman of the Middle Temple, well knowen unto you."[28] In the elder Hakluyt's chamber, young Richard found books of cosmography and a universal map. His older cousin proceeded to give him a lesson on ancient and modern geography. After speaking on the specific bodies of water and land, Hakluyt the Elder brought the Younger to the Bible and directed him to Psalm 107, verses 23 and 24, "that they which go downe to the sea in ships, and occupy by the great waters, they see the works of the Lord, and his woonders in the deepe, &c."[29] The words of the prophet and his cousin convinced Hakluyt the Younger to "prosecute that knowledge and kinde of literature" at the university. At Christ Church, Oxford, he did just that. Like Thevet, Hakluyt saw God in the great ocean, but he stressed the religious element even more as he began his dedication with a conversion experience. As with Oviedo's and Thevet's preliminary matter, Hakluyt's appealed to the authenticity of private experience and study.

Hakluyt explained that he read about discoveries in Greek, Latin, Italian, Spanish, Portuguese, French, and English. Like Oviedo and Thevet, Hakluyt also claimed a first. In his public lectures he "was the first, that produced and shewed both the olde imperfectly composed, and the new lately reformed Mappes, Globes, Spheares, and other instruments of this Art for demonstration in the common schooles, to the singular pleasure and generall contentment of my auditory."[30] Hakluyt's mode is narrative. His story now involved a movement from study to observation in travel in a case of cause and effect:

> and by reason principally of my insight in this study, I grew familiarly acquainted with the chiefest Captaines at sea, the greatest Merchants, and the best Mariners of our nation: by which meanes having gotten somewhat more then common knowledge, I passed at length the narrow seas into France with sir Edward Stafford, her majesties carefull and discreet Ligier.[31]

It was the uncommon knowledge of Hakluyt that allowed him to serve his nation through the learning garnered from his travels.

Five years Hakluyt spent with Stafford—when in Paris he would have known Huguenots like Duplessis-Mornay—"in his dangerous and chargeable residencie in her Highnes service."[32] Hakluyt appealed to what he heard in conversation and read in books, that is "other nations miraculously extolled for their discoveries and notable enterprises by sea," but not the English, who, despite their enjoyment of peace, were "either ignominiously reported, or exceedingly condemned."[33] The author hoped to arouse English patriotism through praeexposito, a comparison of what has been done with what should have been done. The English should have made more discoveries, but have thus far squandered the opportunity. Like the comparisons between the Old World and the New World in the first two dedicatory odes to Thevet's *Les Singularitez*, Hakluyt's comparison between other European nations and England was meant to show the shortcomings of his own country.

Hakluyt called on La Popelinière's *L'Admiral de France*, noting that it was "printed at Paris. Fol. 73. pag. 1, 2," and quoted him in French to shame the English.[34] La Popelinière was a prominent Huguenot: while in Paris during the early 1580s, Hakluyt seems to have had access to French Protestants, who had been prominent in the French expeditions to Brazil and Florida, and this intelligence, as we saw in chapter 2, had helped him with his *Discourse on Western Planting*, a private document that promoted the English settlement of North America and was meant for Queen Elizabeth I and her advisors only. In this passage, La Popelinière wondered why the Rhodians, an Island people, were so good at navigation, and why the English did not surpass them.[35] La Popelinière thought that that "les Anglois, qui ont d'esprit, de moyens, & valeur assez, pour s'aquerir un grand honneur parmi tous les Chrestians, ne se font plus valoir sur le' element qui leur est, & doit estre plus naturel qu'à autres peoples."[36] Hakluyt took these musings as an obloquy or detraction, as if the French were challenging the English.

In the dedication to a work devoted to translating accounts that were not in English and placing them beside those in English, Hakluyt chose to emphasize the foreignness of La Popelinière by quoting him in the original French. He did not domesticate the insult. He may also have wanted to show his learning. Like Thevet, who emphasized his own hard work, Hakluyt made his labors epic: he was the only one to take up La Popelinière's challenge. Hakluyt cut through the excuses of the others, except Lady Sheffield, who claimed ignorance, lack of leisure, or argument, "whereas (to speake truely) the huge toile, and the small profit to insue, were the chiefe causes of the refusal."[37] The author, forgetting Lady Sheffield, then concentrated on what he called his "burden" because "these voyages lay so dispersed, scattered, and hidden in severall hucksters hands."[38] As Pliny had complained about the malice of men in his time, so too did Hakluyt by quoting his predecessor in Latin. Thus, with an excitatio, an arousal of the audience by the invocation of La Popelinière's alleged critique of the English nation, Hakluyt rushed into intellectual battle. His new scholarship would triumph in its vindication of England.

Instead, Hakluyt represented an England with a long history of voyages. Here, the author emphasized Elizabeth I's unequaled expansion of these English contacts with foreign lands. In an epic catalogue to rival that in Chaucer's "The Knight's Tale" Hakluyt listed theses contacts in Persia, Constantinople, Tripoli, Aleppo, Balsara, Goa, the river Plate, Chile, Peru, Nova Hispania, and so on. He did so with a series of five rhetorical questions, the last of which is long, involved, and climactic. This incrementum celebrated the valor and seamanship of the English, which through the author's hyperbole or dementiens, outstripped all other nations. It is far from certain whether the English had such an advantage as Magellan and the enemies of England, to whom Hakluyt alluded, seem to have got to the places he chronicled first by being there in his very account of English glory.

China is a pivot in Hakluyt's narrative. English ships have returned laden with Chinese goods, and the Seres, whom he interpreted as the people of Cathay, sent ambassadors to ancient Rome, as Lucius Flores recorded, to seek friendship and to pay homage to the fame of Rome. Hakluyt then compared this tribute with the desires of the Kings of Java Major and the Moluccaes to have the favor of Elizabeth and the commerce of her people, although the comparison may have paled as Cathay or China was probably a much greater empire than the ones Hakluyt listed. The places he mentioned were, nonetheless, important locations for trade, especially of spices. By extension, the reader may wonder if the same diminishment does not occur in the comparison between Rome and Elizabethan England. Beyond the "wonderful miracle" of the Seres' visit to Rome, Hakluyt saw in the presence of Japanese and Philippinos speaking English and living in England "as a pledge of Gods further favour both unto us and them: to them especially, unto whose doores I doubt not in time shalbe by us caried the incomparable treasure of the trueth of Christianity, and of the Gospell, while we use and exercise common trade with their marchants."[39] Just as Hakluyt had read Lucius Florius on the Seres, he had read the *Origines*, a history by Joannes Goropius, which included a testimony by Elizabeth's father, Henry VIII, to seek glory in Asia. Once again, Hakluyt cinched his case in quoted Latin, making Henry "Regio sumptu me totam Asiam."[40] Like Alexander the Great, Henry would move east as a conqueror. Hakluyt made a virtue out of Henry's inability to carry out these plans, for just as Solomon built the temple that David promised, so too will Elizabeth, "our Solomon her gratious Majesty," complete Henry's work.[41] In Hakluyt's representation, she had the same heroic spirit and honorable disposition as her father.

At the end of the Epistle, Hakluyt turned to Francis Walsingham, to whom he was dedicating his book. Like Thevet, Hakluyt praised his audience, who was in the first instance his patron, to seek favor and thereby uses comprobatio. For Hakluyt, Walsingham had sought the honor of the queen, the good reputation of the country, and the advancement of navigation, so, the author implied, he too would answer the implicit criticism that La Popelinière had leveled at the country. If Walsingham helped to fulfill project, England would be the greatest seafaring nation in Europe. He had, as Hakluyt reported, encouraged the author's travels by letter and speech, so that Hakluyt saw himself "bound to make presentment of this worke to your selfe, as the fruits of your owne incouragements, & the manifestation both of my unfained service to my prince and country, and of my particular duty to your honour."[42] Hakluyt attempted to answer his patron's "expectation" partly by letting Doctor James look at the work and censure it "accordingly to your [Walsingham's] order."[43] Official approval had cleared *Principall Navigations*. The author ended his Epistle Dedicatorie with a benedictio or blessing for his patron, who was the principal hearer while the reader overheard. In the background it is Elizabeth I for whom this work is ultimately made.

The Preface also bore the title, "Richard Hakluyt to the favourable Reader."[44] Here was a direct address to the reader in which Hakluyt set out the method of his book and to acknowledge those who helped in his endeavor. He had sought out all testimonies relating to his topic and has recorded them word for word with the author or authority's name and the page number. If the work had not been translated, "I have first expressed it in the same termes wherein it is originally written, whether it were a Latine, Italian, Spanish or Portingall discourse, or whatever els, and thereunto in the next roome have annexed the signification and translation of the wordes in English."[45] It is clear that Hakluyt's project of building up England as a naval power and celebrating its glory through its great voyages and famous victories rested on a kind of collecting, translation, and observation of other Europeans, ancient and modern.

This "nationalism" had nothing to do with isolationism and everything to do with assimilating the experience of other nations into its own. There has been a long debate over the nature of nations and nationalism, which calls into question earlier forms of statehood as being a nation in the sense that developed from the later eighteenth century onward. Regionalism, religious division, and even language (in Cornwall and the borders with Wales) qualified the later definition of an English nation in Hakluyt's time. What we can see him doing, with some of his contempories, is making a nation or the idea of an English nation, which, of course, became more intricate once James I, a Scot, ascended the throne. Long before Walter Bagehot said of "nation-building" that "We know what it is when you do not ask us, but we cannot very quickly explain or define it," Hakluyt and others were helping to forge an English state that was an earlier form and laid the groundwork for a British state and empire.[46] Ernst Gellner, E. J. Hobsbawn, and others have discussed whether the national and political units should be congruent, but do so in the context of the period following the late Enlightenment.[47] Translation in forming national identity and the expansion of the nation beyond its territory into empire suggest interesting paradoxes. Hakluyt used texts and knowledge from other states with different languages to bolster the English nation, language, and writing (including travel literature). So by defining Englishness, he did so through the assimilation of difference. But expansion meant coming into contact with and perhaps assimilating new cultures, some vastly different from the European tongues and states. So just as England was consolidating a new identity—a Protestant one, Hakluyt and his circle would hope—it was expanding its influence in Ireland, America, and elsewhere and would soon press for an English-British then British (formalized after 1707) identity that would take on new forms while creating myths of continuity and race as well as progress. A decade after Hakluyt's first edition of *Principall Navigations*, Shakespeare had various characters use cognates of nation in *Henry V* (1599). Near the beginning of the play, Canterbury says: "Let vs be worried, and our Nation lose / The name of hardinesse and policie."[48] A little like Bagehot, Canterbury knows he lives in a nation, but might not give a ready definition if asked. Later, Exeter answers the king of France with Henry's claim to the French throne:

> He wills you in the Name of God Almightie,
> That you deuest your selfe, and lay apart
> The borrowed Glories, that by gift of Heauen,
> By Law of Nature, and of Nations, longs
> To him and to his Heires, namely, the Crowne.[49]

Exeter appeals to the law of nature and the law of nations, so that he assumes that the national exists as much as the natural. Before Hakluyt and Shakespeare, Vitoria had made a contribution to the law of nations, which Grotius would build on. Even at Agincourt, in the Middle Ages, and certainly in Shakespeare's representation of the battle, Scots, Welsh, and Irish join the English in fighting the French. Shakespeare's dramatization of these nations as a nation under Henry's command explores the nature of nation:

> *Welch.*
> Captaine *Mackmorrice*, I thinke, looke you,
> vnder your correction, there is not many of your Na-tion.
> *Irish.*
> Of my Nation? What ish my Nation? Ish a
> Villaine, and a Basterd, and a Knaue, and a Rascall. What
> ish my Nation? Who talkes of my Nation?
> *Welch.*
> Looke you, if you take the matter otherwise
> then is meant, Captaine *Mackmorrice*, peraduenture I
> shall thinke you doe not vse me with that affabilitie, as in
> discretion you ought to vse me, looke you, being as good
> a man as your selfe, both in the disciplines of Warre, and
> in the deriuation of my Birth, and in other particula-rities.
> *Irish*
> I doe not know you so good a man as my selfe.[50]

These soldiers speak their own form of English but contest what a nation is, so there is as much friction as unity in this army that is battling the French. The comedy underscores the divisions, the dramatic conflict between the nations as Henry makes a claim to sovereignty in France based on genealogy and precedent, a kingdom beyond the territory of England. Although the word "nation" is not widely used in *Henry V*, Shakespeare, like Hakluyt, raises questions and doubts about the English nation while representing its glory. There is an inspirational and motivational aspect to this promotion or commotion of England, which, in the 1580s and 1590s, felt under threat from Spain and was not as strong as the Continental powers.

Whatever Hakluyt meant by translation, be it literal or otherwise, he appealed to his project as a means of allowing "the paynefull and personall travelers" to "reape that good opinion and just commendation which they have deserved."[51] Furthermore, Hakluyt had "referred every voyage to his Author, which both in person hath performed, and in writing hath left the same" so "that every man might answere for himselfe, justifie his reports, and stand accountable for his owne doings."[52] Evidence and experience could be represented. Hakluyt allowed the voyagers to speak for themselves, so they could be tested in what they said and could gain any honor from what they had done and the events they had recorded. He would not ventriloquize for them or take their glory unto himself. He would not be a rhetorical or editorial magpie but let people speak for themselves. This is the context for Hakluyt's allusion to Ptolemy "that Peregrination is historia" and his caustic remark about universal cosmography. Hakluyt elided the question of editorial selection being more than just a collection on the topic, but on the other hand he did bring together a vast array of materials and was cosmopolitan in the way he did it.

Hakluyt's project was, however, ambivalent about these foreign sources. He wanted to concentrate on the navigations of the English nation but had found that "strangers" have cast more light on them than have English historians, except for Bale, Foxe, and Eden.[53] In setting out further his method of selection, Hakluyt used a form of occupation or telling something by pretending to leave it out. Although he was not going to talk about English voyages to any part of Europe where English ships usually sail, he did list briefly examples of English glory there. Using the anaphoric "Not upon," he arrived at "I omit," even though he had just listed the defeat of "that monstrous Spanish army," the Portuguese expedition, and two of Francis Drake's exploits. Despite his rhetorical and thematic shifts, Hakluyt did not concentrate on these victories closer to home but on the "discoverie of strange coasts."[54]

Hakluyt divided this work into three classes: voyages to the south and southeast, north and northeast, and the west. He established his nation in ancient times through its voyages to the south and southeast. The voyages by the ancient Britons and the English were to the Holy Land, mainly for the sake of devotion, although he had read in Joseph Bengorion that "20,000. Britains valiant souldiours" participated in "the siege and fearefull sacking of Jerusalem under the conduct of Vespasian and Titus the Romane Emperour."[55] Like other European nations, England must have had a classical past in the Roman Empire, as if the trope of *translatio imperii* were often implicit in the translation of classical texts into the vernacular. Hakluyt also recorded early voyages of the English to Africa and India.

The English voyages to the north and northeast were later than those to the south and southeast and earlier than those to America and thus were second in his classification. The journeys to the north and northeast began with Arthur and ended with Jenkinson's opening of sea of the "Empire of Russia" and the voyages of "the Companie of Moscovie Marchants."[56] This company earned Hakluyt's praise as having "performed more then any one, yea then all the nations of Europe besides."[57] To support his view, Hakluyt said that it "is also acknowledged by the most learned Cosmographers, and Historiographers of Christendome," so that he never abandoned the authority of books and scholars.[58] Presumably these cosmographers were not the universal cosmographers who had earned his earlier derision.

The western English navigations "came last of all to our knowledge and experience."[59] There followed the usual claim by European nations of being the first to look for or arrive in America. In this instance a son of a prince of North Wales sailed west more than four hundred years before. Hakluyt told of Columbus "that renowned Genouoys to the most sage Prince of noble memorie King Henrie the 7. with his prompt and cheerefull acceptation thereof, and the occasion whereupon it became fruitlesse, and at that time of no great effect to this kingdome."[60] The author had to thread his way between representing the lost opportunities of English navigation and praise for the queen's ancestors and predecessors. Henry VII at least gave Cabot his letters patent "to discover & conquer in his name, and under his Banners unknowen Regions," and Hakluyt made much of Cabot being the first Christian to see the land from the Arctic circle to Florida.[61] Henry VIII's contribution seems to have been glossed over, with three unnamed voyages and four intended for Asia. Even in talking about John Hawkins, it was difficult for Hakluyt to conceal that Mexico City in Nova Hispania and Hispaniola were marked in their very names as part of the Spanish Empire, in which the English, as in Portuguese Brazil, were trading partners at best and pirates and interlopers at worst. Hakluyt was especially proud of six discourses by Englishmen on New Spain, "wherein are disclosed the cheefest secretes of the west India, which may in time turne to our no smal advantage."[62] Eyewitness reports became spying.

Various English achievements merited celebration and served as *exempla* to promote the cause of colonization. Hakluyt celebrated the "enterprise" of Drake on Nombre de Dios, where he robbed the Spanish of their gold. The Northwest Passage, as sought by Frobisher and Davis, became a challenge to the English, and Hakluyt redoubled the challenge by calling it hopeful, probable, certain. He called attention to Humphrey Gilbert's reasons for believing in a passage, though, as in the case of John Oxnam, he admitted that the voyage was a failure. Then Hakluyt continued in this vein with Ralegh's two colonies in Virginia, which failed because of a lack of follow-up. He proceeded to "the two voyages made not long since to the Southwest, whereof I thinke the Spanyard hath had some knowledge, and felt some blowes"—that is, those of Edward Fenton and Robert Withrington.[63] For

Hakluyt, the account of Thomas Candish's voyage into the south seas and circumnavigation supplemented and was more exact than that of Drake. The Candish account substituted for Drake's, which "(contrary to my expectation)" would allow another man to collect Drake's writings, and provided an excuse for the omission of Drake's first voyage in this volume.[64]

In the last section of the Preface—the acknowledgments—the reader can observe the network in which Hakluyt works. As he relied on other eyewitnesses, the men who actually traveled to distant lands, he served as a compliler, editor, and synthesizer of their work, which he brought together with his own work as a reader and translator. After a general thanks to Edward Dier, there were more specific thanks: for the first part or class of the south and southeast, Richard Staper, merchant, for help with Turkey and the East; for the north and northeast, William Burrowgh and Anthonie Jenkinson; in the west, "besides myne owne extreeme travaile in the histories of the Spanyards," he thanked Hawkins, Ralegh, and his cousin and namesake. Hakluyt returned to study and observation as Oviedo and Thevet had: he listed the wonders of nature "and such other rare and strange curiosities, which wise men take great pleasure to reade of, but much more contentment to see."[65] What is curious is not the fascination with the strange but that Hakluyt had not seen most of the distant lands of which he collected accounts. Nonetheless, he could speak of his great pleasure in reading, translating, editing: "herein I my selfe to my singuler delight have bene as it were ravished in beholding all the premisses gathered together with no small cost" in the cabinets of Richard Garthe and William Cope. It is as if the metonymy and synecdoche of relics and manuscripts could allow for vision and observation to be viewing and reading, as if word and object became the world. These were officials of the government, the latter serving Lord Burleigh, the treasurer of England, whom Hakluyt called "the Seneca of our common wealth" in a Romanizing move worthy of Thevet turning the French monarchy into a republic. Another dimension of viewing is the map, and Hakluyt described the one "collected and reformed according to the newest, secretest, and latest discoveries, both Spanish, Portugall, and English."[66] In this advertisement, which promised knowledge that came from state secrets, Hakluyt even named the mapmaker and his patron.

What remains for the reader, Hakluyt said, is the profit and pleasure of the book, which represents Hakluyt's pains and labor "in bringing these rawe fruits unto this ripenesse, and in reducing these loose papers into this order."[67] He ended the Preface with the customary classical Latin closing, *vale*, but translated it into "Farewell."[68] As an editor, Hakluyt shaped the narrative, so that the reader should have reason to enjoy and learn from it. This ripening of the fruit was something that Hakluyt did not explain despite his brief comments on method in this Preface.

IV

Oviedo, Thevet, and Hakluyt hoped to spur their governments into more effective policies in navigation and colonization in the New World. By building up pride in the nation, each historian wanted to see a translation of empire from the Romans to his country, even if metaphorically as an inspiration to further exploration. To this imperial theme, they added the Christian dimension of the translation of faith. While being implicitly critical of his nation's lack in its policy in the New World, each historian sought a favor from monarch and court, so that each had also to flatter and to seek patronage. As this prefatory matter shows, Oviedo, Thevet, and Hakluyt all wanted (lacked, desired) official or quasi-official roles in molding and recording policy in America. They had great expectations for their respective countries in their navigation on the route to empire.

Here, I have tried to show the rhetorical means and motives that these texts yield in their intricate and ambivalent relation internally to their reader, whether it is the patron addressed or the general reader. Elsewhere I have discussed how other images of America or the New World, in words and pictures, created a rhetoric of seduction and exploitation in which the land was a woman or its strangeness caused sexual anxiety in European writers. This sexing of America, both as a woman to seduce or exploit and as an object of homoerotic interest, is another aspect of the imperial theme.[69] The promotion of empire was about perception and persuasion as well as about expanding markets, changing change routes and the balance of power in Europe and on other continents. Comparing these promoters of expansion, from different empires, suggests homologies in their common rhetorical heritage, which derived from classical Greece, as well as implying distinctions even as the English and French courts had to pay careful attention to Spain because it had forced the hand of every leading Western European country, including Portugal, as a result of Columbus's landfall. The papal bulls had long balanced Spanish and Portuguese interests in expansion and this continued in 1494 and beyond, whereas England and France, which had been left out of the division of this "unknown" world, began to perform a double action of imitating and challenging Spain. Historiographers, cosmographers, collectors, editors, translators, and writers, as we have seen, all tried to frame the debate on empire and expansion, its drawbacks and advantages, and in the process representing, inadvertently or not, its inconsistencies and amphibologies.

Even in Thomas More's *Utopia*, there was slavery, so that one of the great contests, contradictions, and gaps in inconsistent and ambivalent human behavior was the proclamation of liberty while enslaving others. The Utopians would go to war to obtain land for colonies and they enslaved prisoners in wars when they fought for themselves and did not employ mercenaries.[70] The gap between being free and allowing for slaves or the exploitation of slave or cheap labor was the case especially in the Netherlands, England/Britain, and the United States—lands of professed democracy and freedom—and can still be the case. Even if the United Nations has outlawed slavery, it is still practiced and there are forms of servitude and economic dependence that, while not as horrific and degrading as the slavery of the Atlantic slave trade from the fifteenth to late nineteenth century, include some oppressive conditions. One of the missed opportunities for abolishing the institution of slavery was the American Revolution or War of Independence. That is why in chapters 5 and 6 I have made it the watershed. To live free or die was not nearly as often a choice for Native or African Americans as it was for Anglo or Euro-Americans. The backgrounds and aftermath of the American Revolution and Civil War produced a legacy that in some forms, no matter how transmuted, is still with us.

Chapter 5 ~

Slavery to the American Revolution

The buying, selling, and holding of slaves is an ancient practice that is especially repugnant to a world that, while still having this institution in its midst, has, through the United Nations, affirmed its abolition in law. Slavery is illegal, but persists. This is a cultural and economic practice that robs people of their humanity, breaking up families, controlling bodies, minds, and spirits and profiting from unpaid labor. As lust is to prostitution, so is greed to slavery. Slavery is a dark side of human experience, not simply in empires but in other forms of political organization as well. The matter of slaves is a vast topic, so that any discussion of it is a selection and ordering from a welter of evidence. Amid the statistics and texts, human voices push through, and the pain and death of multitudes of slaves haunt the topic even when they are not recalled or asked to testify.

I

The fifteenth-century expansion of Portugal into Africa was a crucial event in the European involvement in the slave trade. The Moors in Portugal and Spain had pushed the Christians north, but by the end of this century the Iberian peninsula was under the control of Christian rulers. Thus, some European expansion was reactive to the once-expanding Muslim empire into Europe, but the pursuit of gold, spices, and slaves soon motivated some of the European policy and voyages to other continents. In the east of Europe, the Russians would begin a kind of counter-expansion against the very groups who had expanded into the traditional lands of the Rus, surrounding Kiev and later Moscow.

Cultural capital was also invested in European expansion and its use of slaves. There were many biblical and classical antecedents in the matter of slavery. For instance, Exodus describes the oppression of the Israelites in Egypt and the freedom from this suffering that Moses delivers. The Egyptians feared the multiplication of the Jews, even though they had built Pithom and Raamses for them. They attempted to curb and control the population of the Israelites: "And Pharaoh charged all his people, saying, Every son that is born ye shall cast into the river, and every daughter ye shall save alive."[1] Aaron and Moses find hope for the Jews before Pharaoh, "Thus saith the Lord God of Israel, Let my people go, that they may hold a feast to me in the wilderness."[2] This early liberation narrative calls on divine aid to allow the Israelites cultural and religious integrity and dignity and to take them out of servitude and tyranny. Later, the lyrics of spirituals by African slaves in the English American colonies and the United States echoed this call. The opening chapters of Matthew represent Herod's tyranny in trying to destroy the infant Jesus. This episode involves a reversal: an angel appeared to Joseph and said that he should "flee into Egypt."[3] Egypt, a place of bondage or of refuge, came to have different meanings in the typological world of the Bible. Over the course of empire, various uses of typology recur. Isaiah prophesies that Israel will be restored from the Babylonian captivity. An individual, tribe, or people can be sold into slavery or subject to its poison.

Classical Greek and Roman antecedents underlie the later use of and trade in slaves in Western Europe. An example from the beginnings of the Roman Republic is apt. The last king of Rome, an Etruscan, Tarquin the Proud, was expelled from Rome in about 509 B.C., an event that instituted an aristocratic republic. In a later political or military crisis the Senate could advise the consuls to appoint a dictator who had *summum imperium* or supreme powers. In 396 B.C., when Camillus, the dictator, finally took the great Etruscan city of Veii, he had the population massacred or sold into slavery, the city razed and looted, and the territory annexed. Slavery could be wholesale in war, and this practice persisted well into the era of medieval and early modern Europe.

During the Middle Ages, some of the practices would contribute to a later extension and intensification of slavery. In the late 1200s, the Catalans also appeared on the Atlantic coast of Morocco and the Genoese navigators seem to have reached islands—inhabited by Neolithic inhabitants—the Canaries. Here, in the mid-fourteenth century, the Genoese, Mallorcans, and Andalusians traded and slaved. By this time, European mariners had come across the Madeiras, which contained no inhabitants. Slavery, as Charles Verlinden has noted, was continuous from Rome into European society after the fall of the empire, so that this slavery found itself in an adaptable legal context: just as an evolved and adapted form of Roman law became accepted in the late Middle Ages, so too did early European colonies in America accept but change feudal law.[4] Law, exploration, and trade were intertwined with slavery. Continuity must not be forgotten in the transformation of Europe through expansion and the slave trade.

Others had been involved in the slave trade in Africa before the Portuguese became involved. As early as the *Catalan Atlas* of 1375, there was some idea of the markets and trade routes of the Niger basin. Portugal was on the main route between Flanders and Italy: the Italians had opened trade with the Portuguese in the early fourteenth century and English merchants had privileges there as well. Antwerp and Bruges became the principal markets for the Portuguese, and Flemish capital and shipping grew in significance. Portugal also became an important center in the slave trade—in the 1430s the first African slaves were brought to Lisbon.[5] Before the Portuguese voyages along the coast of Africa, an acquaintance with the Niger and the Gulf of Guinea is evident. This knowledge implied, as G. R. Crone has said, that these expeditions from Portugal were not "thrusts into the unknown" but an attempt to take control from others of different cultures of this lucrative trade.[6] At the capture of Ceuta in 1415, Prince Henry the Navigator might well have become interested in African trade. That trade involved the caravans of slaves, gold, ivory, and ebony from beyond the Sahara to the ports of Barbary. There, Christian galleys brought European goods to the Moorish merchants who controlled the trade.

Although a transformation in slavery occurred in the era of the expansion of Western Europe in the fifteenth century, there was, beyond this medieval context, an underpinning from the ancient world. Slaves from Africa transformed the European economy, but this change also had an intellectual dimension that reached beyond that time. Aristotle set out a theory of natural slavery in his *Politics*: he divided the world into masters and slaves. Natural law was another part of the debate over slavery. St. Augustine and St. Thomas Aquinas in the Middle Ages (and William Blackstone in the eighteenth century) wrote of natural law and were inheritors of Cicero and others who considered the connection between law and nature. Ideas traveled like goods. This theoretical framework of Aristotle's theory of slavery was in circulation about 1,800 years before the court chronicler, Gomes Eannes de Azuzara [Zuzara], a chronicler attached to Prince Henry of Portugal, represented a key event in the new slavery. Azuzara described how in August 1444, the Portuguese landed 235 African slaves near Lagos in southern Portugal, sobbing, lamenting, throwing themselves prostrate as they were divided family members, one from the other. This scene began the transformation of the ancient and lamentable practice of slavery. Controversies between Portugal and Castile were not uncommon, and one of them was over Africa. After the conquest of Ceuta in 1415 with military expeditions in Morocco and with voyages to Guinea, Portugal made its claim in Africa. In the 1440s and 1450s slaves and gold provided a lucrative trade there.

This trade affected Christian, Muslim, and pagan cultures in the Mediterranean and Atlantic worlds and beyond. Africa, which had seen Islamic powers involved in slavery, now had to face European involvement. The Iberian powers intervened. In pursuit of their delegated monopolies, the Portuguese and Spanish, enslaved Africans, who were considered pagans and savages, and sold them in Portugal, Spain, and the Atlantic islands. In the fifteenth century the black slaves were sometimes considered to be ill-formed and inferior. Whereas this racial attitude was not yet a developed systematic racism, as occurred in the nineteenth-century onward, it was there and insidious nonetheless.[7] A great change would affect the Iberian powers in the decades ahead.

Textual evidence provides an interweaving of themes at the moment of contact between Iberian and African cultures. A text that is particularly instructive in this early expansion of the Iberian powers is Alvise Cadamosto's narrative because of its descriptions of economics, culture, and slavery and because it has a rich and complex textual history. Works in one language would often find their way, sometimes without delay and other times after centuries, into other European languages. Thus, the texts that helped to build up the knowledge and myth of empire in one state would also become part of the identities of other countries and empires. Cadamosto's text, which is another instance of the importance of Italians to the expansion of many of the Western European empires, seems to have been begun in 1463 and completed by 1468. It first appeared in the collection, *Paesi*, in 1507 and was translated into Latin in Milan and into German in Nuremburg both in 1508 and into French in Paris in 1515. A circulation of texts about exotic places often occurred through translation in Europe.

Cadamosto's narrative showed Portugal expanding into Africa and becoming part of the nexus of slavery. Cadamosto represented Black Africa, a region that was so crucial in the slave trade for Islamic North Africa, for Europe, and for the Americas. Economics and religion were part of cultural exchange. In Cadamosto's account there is a kind of paradigmatic ethnographical description. Cadamosto said that the Portuguese settled Madeira, "which had never been inhabited," but saved many observations of cultural difference and conflict for his writing about the Canary Islands: "the inhabitants of the four Christian islands are wont to go by night with some of their galleys to assail these islands, and to seize these heathen Canarians, both men and women, whom they send to Spain to be sold as slaves."[8] Cadamosto then described what happened when these slaving raids went awry: "And it happens that at times some from these galleys are taken prisoners: the Canarians do not put them to death, but make them kill and skin goats, and prepare the meat, which they hold to be a most vile and despicable occupation, and they make them serve thus until they are ransomed by some means or other."[9] The Canarians (Guanche) showed leniency toward those who would enslave them.[10] Cadamosto described the role of the Portuguese in the African trade: "You should know that the said Lord Infante of Portugal has leased this island of Argin to Christians [for ten years], so that no one can enter the bay to trade with the Arabs save those who hold the licence."[11] For "slaves whom the Arabs bring from the land of the Blacks, and gold tiber" or dust, the Portuguese exchanged alchezeli (perhaps a rough cloth), corn, cotton, woolen cloths, silver, carpets, and cloaks.[12] For Berber horses, an item of trade that Arabs brought to Blacks, "Ten or fifteen slaves are given for one of these horses, according to their quality."[13] Moreover, the Arabs traded silver and Moorish silk from Granada and Tunis for gold and slaves, who were bound for Sicily, Tunis, and Portugal. Since 1448, when Gomes Eannes de Azurara had described the African slave trade, the Portuguese had expanded it fast, for Cadamosto said: "every year the Portuguese carry away from Argin a thousand slaves."[14] The organization of the slave trade, terrible in and of itself, replaced practices that were also insidious. The Portuguese used four or more caravels to raid the land at night: "Thus they took of these Arabs both men and women, and carried them to Portugal for sale: behaving in a like manner along all the rest of the coast, which stretches from Cauo Bianco to the Rio di Senega and even beyond."[15] The Portuguese were now part of the plunder and the trade in human beings and would be involved for about four centuries to come. Across the divide between Arab and Black Africa, the Portuguese were involved in raids not unlike those the Spanish practiced in the Canaries. The Iberian experience in Africa and the Atlantic islands provided precedents for the ways Spain and Portugal overcame and settled the New World. Violence and impressments into slavery were two invidious aspects of the economic and social practices of these empires and many of those that followed in their wake. A typology between Africa and America was in the making and the perspective that brought them into focus was from the Iberian peninsula.

Class and profit also drove slavery. Moreover, hierarchy and greed played a role on the many sides of the capture, sale, and exploitation of slaves—trade, too, was at the center of the exchange between Africans and Europeans. During the late Middle Ages, the shortage of gold in Europe helped to drive Europeans to find new sources and at this market sought "further strange sights" but also "to find out whether any came thither with gold for sale," although there was little to be found.[16] Later, Columbus would search for gold in the New World. From Barbary, the Arabs and Azanaghi brought horses and exchanged them for slaves: "A horse with its trappings is sold for from nine to fourteen negro slaves, according to the condition and breeding of the horse."[17] After having bought a horse, a chief would send for his horse-charmers. This animal had taken on a spiritual or supernatural role as well as being a product in trade: a horse was worth many human slaves. Possibly, the charms worn on horses contained texts from the Koran (Quran).[18] Moreover, in Cadamosto's account, the Barbazini (Barbacenes) and Sereri (Serer) question the connection between lordship and enslavement: "They will not recognize any lord among them, lest he should carry off their wives and children and sell them into slavery, as is done by the kings and lords of all the other lands of the negroes. They are exceedingly idolatrous, have no laws, and are the cruellest of men."[19] For Cadamosto, they seem to be without class, religion, law, restraint, and civility, but the tactics of these people might appear to be sensible today. A certain ambivalent and ironic situation occurred in the descriptions of the encounters between European and the people overseas.

Mediation and slavery were also connected. The Crown of Portugal seems to have recognized that interpreters, who could be slaves, were necessary to their success in trading in Africa: "These slaves had been made Christians in Portugal, and knew Spanish well: we had had them from their owners on the understanding that for the hire and pay of each we would give one slave to be chosen from all our captives. Each interpreter, also, who secured four slaves for his master was to be given his freedom."[20] Language and religion were part of the Black African's training—only enslaving others would free him. Spanish, as opposed to Portuguese, was the language taught to the slaves. Through an interpreter, Cadamosto traded with Lord Batimaussa, exchanging many articles for gold and slaves, but differences in values and valuation occurred in this relation between Portuguese and the Blacks of Gambra: "Gold is much prized among them, in my opinion, more than by us, for they regard it as very precious: nevertheless they traded it cheaply, taking in exchange articles of little value in our eyes."[21] These Africans spoke many tongues and traded varieties of colorful cloth, apes, baboons, civet, and wild dates and did not venture from their own country because they were "not safe from one district to the next from being taken by the Blacks and sold into slavery."[22] In addition to gold and slavery, Cadamosto also described the hunting of wild elephants. Cadamosto gave a sense of what was happening on the ground in Africa during Portuguese expansion in the fifteenth century, but there were also those from afar at court and in the Church who attempted to regulate and frame this change.

Legal and political differences marked the Iberian expansion. One way of addressing controversies between Spain and Portugal was canon law, a mixing of legal principles with religious politics as the name would suggest. For instance, on January 8, 1455, Nicholas V issued the bull *Romanus pontifex* that gave exclusive rights to King Alfonso of Portugal in this African exploration and trade. This ruling extended the bull *Dum diversas* (June 18, 1452), in which Nicholas had given Alfonso the right to conquer pagans, enslave them, and take their lands and goods. Thus, the issue of slavery arose early in the expansion of Spain and Portugal. As the bull *Romanus Pontifex* had given the Portuguese the right to reduce the infidels to slavery, the inhabitants of these new lands—"so unknown to us westerners that we had no certain knowledge of the peoples of those parts"—had no rights because they were not Christian.[23] This pattern was like the one the popes made in their donations concerning the New World, except as the Natives were deemed barbarous and not infidels, they were saved from slavery—at least theoretically—by their potential for conversion. After Columbus's landfall in the New World, the papacy continued to play a role in legitimizing exploration. Expansion and slavery owed something to the authority of the Church, whose regulations were meant to underpin the political and economic power of Catholic Europe. Slavery was to become a key factor in the Portuguese role in the colonization of the New World.

Slavery in the sugar trade spread from Europe and the Atlantic islands to the New World. A taste for sweetness fueled the bitterness of slavery. Europe would now use African slaves to feed its production of sugar. First in Europe and in the islands that Portugal and Spain possessed in the eastern Atlantic and then in the West Indies and the mainland of the Americas, slaves would underwrite the sugar economy: slavery would never be the same. Slave labor later maintained cotton and coffee as lucrative crops. African slaves were also heavily engaged in mining and domestic service. During the Middle Ages, Muslim merchants in Spain and Africa practiced *razzias*, or the seizure of slaves, rather than acquiring them through purchase. Christian merchants had similar practices. Using slaves on the sugar plantations that the Genoese had established in the Algarve, the Portuguese also sold slaves into Spain. By 1475, Spain appointed a magistrate, Juan de Valladoid, who was black, for the growing population within the country itself of *loros* (mulattos) and Africans. Governments were a part of the slaving enterprise. The Portuguese Crown began by requiring that its Casa da Guiné approve expeditions to coastal Africa and subjected them to taxation. The Spanish Crown required a license and imposed a tax on the slaves acquired from the Portuguese before they were shipped to the New World. France, England, and the Netherlands would all come to develop financial interests in the slave trade. In 1482, the Portuguese established the castle at São Jorge da Mina on the Gold Coast of West Africa (Ghana) and after that year it attracted hundreds of Europeans of various nationalities. A Florentine banker who was one of the wealthiest people in Lisbon and had agents in Seville, Bartolommeo Marchionni was involved in the African trade and also had connections with Christopher Columbus (Colón). The New World would make a difference to Africa, America, and Asia as well as in Europe.

Along with the Portuguese exploration of Africa, Columbus's landfall changed the face of slavery. Africa now became the predominant source of slaves, whereas Slavs, Turks, and Western Europeans had also been part of a slave economy based on war and piracy. The demand for slaves increased sharply when the sugar economy spread from the estates of southern Portugal and the Portuguese Atlantic islands to the large plantations of Brazil and the West Indies. Although the Muslim rulers of West Africa had increased the trade in slaves, the European demand for slaves after the coming of the Portuguese in the sixteenth century intensified the trade and its devastation. So many people were fed into American sugar plantations, a machine that helped to ruin families, tribes, and states in Africa. Columbus, as Hugh Thomas has observed, was a product of a new Atlantic economy in which sugar and the slavery played a great role. Columbus himself sent from Santo Domingo the first known shipment of slaves—Taino Indians—to his Florentine friend in Seville, Juanotto Berardi, an associate of the great merchants the Marchionni. The Crown was soon annulling such sales of Native slaves because of the uncertainty over the legality of this scheme. Reportedly, the queen was said to be cross with Columbus over his repeated attempts to sell or give her vassals away as slaves.[24] Slavery was a concern for Columbus during his first contacts with the inhabitants of the western Atlantic.

II

In less than twenty years after Columbus's landfall in the New World the nature of the relation between the Crown and its colonies changed. Even though Columbus and his king were content with Native slaves, a shift soon occurred. In 1510, owing to the decimation of the indigenous labor force, King Ferdinand ordered that 200 African slaves be sent to the New World. From the Philippines to Peru—in the Spanish colonies—the three chief institutions were the audiencia (judicial tribunal), the office of the viceroy (captain-general), and the Church, the first two representing the royal interests and the third attending to "the conversion of the infidels and the subsequent care of their souls."[25] Crown and Church were key aspects of Spanish colonization and had to come to terms, or even contend, with viceroys and settlers.

While the whole relation between the Crown and those who served it was multifold, when Columbus took certain risks and they seem to have paid off, the Crown changed its strategy. Once the wealth of the New World was proven and the population of settlers grew there, the Crown asserted its control over these dependent territories. Through law, Ferdinand and Isabella had exerted their authority in Castile. Courts and the Roman law they dispensed were instruments of that strategy. In Castile, the royal administration made much use of judicial bodies, which in the form of audiencias, became crucial in major colonial cities and whose powers extended beyond those at home. In 1511, the first audiencia or tribunal in the Americas appeared in Santo Domingo. As part of an extension of authority in the colonies, the Crown retracted the privileges granted to Columbus, and Charles I kept his eye on *encomenderos*. The problem for the Crown, as J. M. Ots y Capdequí has maintained, was to conquer the conquerors (*conquistadores*). The solution for the Crown was to extend the Castilian administration to the New World.[26] Politics, law, and economics were key issues—especially the matter of slavery—that were intertwined in the history of Iberian overseas history.

In the early sixteenth century, a critical tradition developed among European humanists, who wrote about the various new lands in Africa, America, and Asia. The Portuguese experience is important in this regard. Paolo Giovio (b. 1448) was apparently the first to mention that printing had originated in China. João III of Portugal (ruled 1521–57) had himself received a humanist education, invited humanists to his court, and appointed an official historian—João de Barros (1496–1570)—who wrote about the Portuguese in Asia (Persia, India, and China). The chroniclers— Gaspar Correia, Fernão de Castanheda, Diogo do Couto, and Barros himself— concentrated most on the deeds of the vassals of the Portuguese crown in Asia. Even Correia and Couto, although less sympathetic to matters of rank, did not leave us with a full view of the marginalized, more particularly of exiles and renegades, these go-betweens who moved from one culture to the other.[27] For China, Barros used Chinese sources and bought a Chinese slave to interpret them. Slaves, as in ancient Rome, could perform more than physical labor. Various perspectives were available to the Portuguese and the Spanish as they expanded their influence and territories.

During the sixteenth century, the presence of colonies in the New World affected the slave trade radically. Columbus and Diego Colón, his son, were interested in slave labor to drive their enterprise of the Indies. Diego became governor of the Spanish possessions in the Caribbean in 1509. He encouraged the kidnapping of Native slaves from adjacent islands and wrote to King Ferdinand, saying that the Natives were not able to bear the work and asking for African slaves. Despite Ferdinand's irritation with this kidnapping, he did, in January 1510, authorize the sending of 50 African slaves to go work in the gold mines of Hispaniola. Sugarcane was cultivated in the Caribbean very soon after Columbus's landfall in the western Atlantic. Ferdinand was the same king who had deported Jews and Moors from Spain and had enslaved many of his Moorish and some of his Jewish subjects. Sometimes slavery was as much about jurisdiction and power as it was about the practice itself.

The Iberian powers set the example for the other Western European powers, both in expansion and in slavery. From Portugal, Spain learned about how lucrative the slave trade could be. More slaves were shipped to Europe than to America until about 1550. In that year, one in ten people in Lisbon were slaves. João III, who extended his empire to and in Brazil, had a black slave as his jester. Not all slaves were African: the Portuguese sent back slaves from Malacca and China. By 1565, slaves made up about 7 percent of the population of Seville—among the African slaves the blacks outnumbered the Berbers or "white slaves." Africans worked in mining, textiles, and agriculture in the New World. In the sixteenth century, Bartolomé de Las Casas and Pope Leo X could argue contra Aristotle and his followers, like Ginés de Sepúlveda, that slavery was unnatural and inhumane in the case of the Indians in the New World, but they did not make the same argument for Africans. Las Casas saw the Natives as open to conversion and as being part of a great tide of Christian expansion. His outrage at genocide and his defense of the humanity of the Natives defied Sepúlveda's application of Aristotle's theory of natural slavery and drew on a radical New Testament distrust of class and race that institutional Christianity has sometimes perverted.

An ambivalence over empire and the treatment of the peoples encountered in new lands was there from Columbus's first letter and Las Casas and many clerics who went before and after him.[28] This division, although not perfectly symmetrical or oppositional, went back to the Spaniards in the New World. The Crown and the Church could extend, or try to extend, protection to the indigenous peoples. The Dominicans or Black Friars protested the treatment of the Natives in Hispaniola, a year after they arrived there. In particular, in a sermon of 1511, Father Antonio Montesinos (Antón Montesino) protested to the colonists in his congregation: "With what right . . . and with what justice do you keep these poor Indians in such a cruel and horrible servitude?. . . . Are you not obliged to love them as yourselves?"[29] Bartolomé de Las Casas, who was a colonist and later a Dominican, did not react immediately to this sermon but came to defend the Natives, having met with King Ferdinand of Spain just before Christmas 1515 to lecture him about the ills of the colonists against the Indians ("los Indios"). The Natives themselves in North America reacted to the ways they were treated by the European settlers (Spanish, then English, later British, and still later American) settlers. Juan Ponce de Leon came to Florida in 1539, had enslaved the Natives of south Florida, and sent some of the people he had captured to speak with Acuera, a leader of the Timucua, to meet him, but this Native leader was defiant. The Spanish Crown had tried to address these abuses, but sometimes its legalistic responses were grotesque, such as the Requirement ("Requerimiento"). This document ranged from Adam through the papal donation of the lands to the Spaniards and a demand for homage to a threat of destruction if they did not agree. It was to be read to Indians before battle. And it was, in a language and a part of a legal tradition, the Natives could not understand, and sometimes it was read afar or while villages slept. The Laws of Burgos constituted the first legislation of the Crown that forbade Spaniards from addressing Natives as "dogs" and tried to make the hard working conditions of the indigenous peoples better. Later, the Crown would pass the New Laws of 1542 and Las Casas would argue against Aristotle's theory of natural slavery to defend the humanity of the Indians against the position of Juan Ginés de Sepúlveda, Charles V's official chronicler and chaplain. From the first years of expansion, a tension existed between king and councilors, Crown and settlers. The experience in North America, although different, had some affinities with, if not roots in, this example of Spain.

An opposition from within—as discussed in chapter 3—extended to violence, war, and slavery. In addition to the well-known figures we discussed there, others raised their voice against the dark side of expansion and empire. There were others, like Domingo de Soto, Alonso de Montúfar, and Martín de Ledesma, Spanish Dominicans who spoke out against slavery and including that of Africans—and Fernão de Oliveira, a military writer and captain who also criticized the slave trade in Portugal and Africa for its illegitimacy and immorality. Diseases had destroyed the indigenous slaves, small pox in 1520 in the Caribbean and Mexico, and dysentery and influenza in Brazil in the 1560s. The destruction of the Native population in Pernambuco and Bahia led to the importation of blacks from Angola and the Congo to work the sugar plantations. These Africans, whether bought, kidnapped, or taken in war, were severed from their families and worked in the most brutal fashion. Brazil supplanted São Tomé, which had succeeded the Canaries, Madeira, and the Mediterranean islands, as the greatest supplier of sugar for Europe. The Italians produced sugar equipment, Madeira and the Canary Islands artisans, Lisbon the marketing representatives of the Fugger commercial interests in Augsburg. Moreover, the Dutch provided much of the capital and many of the ships for transporting the sugar to Europe. Multinational interests and trade were long part of basic global trade networks, which were intensifying. The paintings of the Dutch masters came to show the effect on the teeth of the subjects of the increasing consumption of sugar in Western Europe. Further, the teeth of Elizabeth I and more and more people in England showed the effect of a taste for sweets. Slaves suffered to feed a taste for sugar: their backs bent while the teeth of Europeans rotted.

While the slaves in the colonies did the backbreaking work, the peoples of Europe did the manufacturing. This situation was a kind of mercantilism in which resources from overseas fed European manufactures. In 1572, black African slaves were sold for almost three times what Native slaves were bought for in Brazil. By 1580, the Spanish officials in Mexico and Peru (where the vast silver mine at Potosí was located) decided to feed Spain's hunger for precious metals with a flow of black African workers. In that year, the merger of Spain and Portugal under one Crown meant that the Spanish acquired the Portuguese expertise in slaving and its trading posts in Africa. For the next 60 years, Spain tried to keep foreigners, especially the Dutch and English, from its overseas trade.

Slavery was long part of the Iberian trade that the French and English disrupted. In 1545, Pierre Crignon wrote a discourse about Jean Parmentier, a sea captain from Dieppe, and described Norumbega, which he said was discovered by Verrazzano 15 years before. In *La Cosmographie*, Jean Alfonse, Roberval's pilot, enhanced Crignon's description of Norumbega, but in his *Voyages avantureux* (1559), a work on navigation, Alfonse attributed the discovery of the river named after the Cap de Norombègue to the Portuguese. This attribution went contrary to expectations of chauvinism in these national rivalries in the New World, except that it seems that Alfonse came from Portugal.[30] In this text, Alfonse set out general observations about the New World. He made, as Jean-Paul Duviols has observed, a similar point to one Las Casas used in his defense of the Natives, for both thought that it was illegal to reduce the indigenes to slavery because they were delicate: "The men of this land of Peru are small, feeble and good. But the Spaniards mistreat them and make them their slaves."[31] In addition to the Spanish involvement with slavery, the Portuguese were involved in the black African slave trade in the fifteenth and sixteenth centuries and beyond. The Portuguese, according to André Thevet, altered their tactics when French corsairs and English privateers attacked a caravel, which had slaves as a crew.[32] This is the context for Nicolas Durand de Villegagnon's voyage to Brazil in 1555. Jean de Léry commented on the monopoly that Portugal and Spain held so dear, the Spanish and Portuguese claiming to be the lords of the countries whereas the French maintained and defended themselves valiantly.[33] If Portugal had rivals to its power, so too did Spain.

The Netherlands rebelled against Spain in 1568 and the rebellion occurred on and off for eighty years. In the final years of the sixteenth century the Dutch attacked Iberian colonies. When Spain and Portugal were united under Philip, the arrangement prohibited Spaniards from settling or trading in the Portuguese Empire and the Portuguese from doing the same in the Spanish Empire. This long colonial war against the Netherlands was for the sugar trade in Brazil, the slave trade in West Africa, and the spice trade in Asia. The Portuguese won the war in Brazil, drew in West Africa, and lost in Asia.[34] The Portuguese contested first with France and then with the Netherlands.

Various empires vied for the possession of key overseas territories. Each empire used various ceremonial means of possessing territories. The French and English still occupied and wanted to occupy the lands of the Natives, something that, with good reason, met with resistance, even as they differed from more horrific forms of Spanish possession. The one Las Casas focused on was the *Requerimento*, or Requirement, which traced the history of creation, gave the grounds for Spanish possession, and threatened the Natives in a language they could not understand with enslavement and loss of their lands if they resisted.[35] The Natives of the New World were attacked, displaced, and enslaved.

African chieftains and the sultan from Marrakesh were also involved in the nefarious slave trade. Slaves came from many different places. The King of Morocco had Western European slaves, who suffered horrific punishments. Slavery knew a savagery all its own. Black Africans, as Hugh Thomas has said, had the misfortune of having Christian and Muslim traditions against them. Ham was supposed to be—in this traditional view—the ancestor of those with black skin because Noah had cursed him after seeing him naked and drunk and had been turned black with sin.[36] The kidnapping and treating of African people as chattel or beasts for labor without regard for their very humanity drove national and imperial expansion. The economics of bondage underpinned commerce, trade, industry, art, education, and many of the institutions of the Western European empires and their colonies. Legal and illicit trade was interwoven in this period and this was also the case in slavery.

Piracy was an ancient practice: it was always a part of commerce on the Atlantic. Even in the fifteenth century, French pirates benefited from Portuguese shipments. Jean Ango of Dieppe built ships for his king but also plundered for him when the opportunities arose with Portuguese and Spanish ships from Africa and Asia. Even a Portuguese, João Affonso, known in France as Jean Alphonse, sailed under a French flag to take advantage of this triangular trade between Africa, America, and Europe. The English and French traded goods with Africa as the Portuguese did. John Hawkins was interested in slaving: however, Elizabeth I wanted slaves taken only of their free volition because otherwise divine vengeance would punish those who did otherwise. Even this contradiction and ambivalence, as in the case of the Dutch, did not prevent slaving from proceeding. The queen herself came to invest in Hawkins's ventures. The Dutch Revolt meant a challenge to Spain not just for independence but for commerce. As Portugal was joined with Spain through the Crown, the Netherlands attacked Iberian interests in Brazil as well as elsewhere. In the 1590s, Amsterdam and Middelburg refused to allow Dutch ships to trade in slaves in their ports. By 1600, the Dutch carried about half the goods from Brazil to Europe. In time the Dutch settlements in Brazil started to import slaves. The French, too, had early scruples about trading in slaves: during the 1570s, a court in Bordeaux forbade trading slaves there. But France also gave into the temptation of slavery.

Marseille had its own slave market. In the seventeenth century, slavery would become part of the economies and practices of colonization of the Northern European powers.

~

III

In the seventeenth century the slave trade in the English, Dutch, and French colonies had ambivalent beginnings, as people favored and opposed it. Early on, the Dutch had also been weary of or had opposed the slave trade with Africa. In 1596 the city fathers in Middelburg had freed a hundred slaves brought as cargo there and in 1608 Usselincx had opposed the use of black slaves in Dutch America. A Dutch ship brought 20 black slaves to Virginia in 1619, perhaps having captured them through piracy from a Portuguese slaving ship. Like sugar before it and cotton afterward, tobacco came to rely on slave labor. Ambivalence over slavery occurred among the English, Dutch, and French. The demand for slaves after the Dutch capture of Paraíba and Pernambuco in 1634 to 1636 changed the Dutch position. Johan Maurits chose to go the route of African slaves in the sugar-mills rather than use German labor. The conflict between an immediate economic fix and the longer ethical view divided people from themselves or from their neighbors. Despite the Netherlands benefiting from booty from the 547 Iberian ships taken between 1623 and 1636, the West India Company was bearing great financial burdens.[37] Even though the Dutch navy was powerful and its economic clout was substantial, a friction between the public sphere of politics and private realm of finance made it more difficult for the Netherlands to succeed in this struggle in the southern part of the New World.

The Dutch looked as though they would come to rule Brazil. Between 1637 and 1641 Johan Maurits, the Dutch governor-general in Brazil, proved successful in expanding Dutch holdings and influence in this region. The local Portuguese were subject to Roman–Dutch law and were guaranteed equal rights with the subjects of the United Provinces. Furthermore, Maurits permitted Jews and Roman Catholics freedom of conscience and worship and allowed some French Capuchin friars to enter the colony. Willem Piso was a physician to the governor of Dutch Brazil from 1638 to 1644: he edited a key book from this brief Dutch sojourn in this area of Portuguese influence.[38] Portugal traded with Brazil and Africa, where it found gold, ivory, and slaves. In the 1630s, the Dutch, who employed many Germans in the Dutch West India Company, attacked the Portuguese slaving stations on the Atlantic coast of Africa as well as their posts in Brazil. Michael Hemmersam was one such German employee: he was in Brazil from 1639 to 1644 and described the slave trade and the peoples of West Africa.[39] The multinational aspect of trade and empire recurred time and time again. Willem Usselincx advocated free rather than slave labor. This issue of slavery would be a crucial one in the Netherlands as profit and labor overcame early opposition to the trading and holding of slaves. The temptation toward slavery, despite an awareness of how questionable such a trade was morally, was too much.

Long after Columbus, the Spaniards had understood the importance of black slaves to their imperial wealth. For instance, in Lima in 1646, José de los Ríos complained that a shortage of black slaves would ruin Peru because the riches of the hacienda and kingdom were based on the labor of those Africans. The Netherlands also understood how important the links were among their various spheres of influence. In 1652 the Dutch East India Company (VOC) founded a refreshment station at Table Bay for crews fighting scurvy in their journeys between Europe and Asia and in 1657 they began to encourage permanent settlement. This would be the basis for the future of the southern tip of Africa.

Opposition to slavery was there from the beginning. The groundwork for a movement against slavery had been laid as early as the fifteenth century. In the seventeenth century more examples of antislavery voices arose. Pope Urban VIII had condemned slavery in a letter of 1639 and threatened excommunication to those who practised it; Richard Baxter insulted slaveholders by comparing them to conquistadores; in 1688 Aphra Behn published a novel, *Oroonoko*, which exposed the inhumanity of slavery.

This work of fiction—that might also be in part a memoir because the Dedication claimed it was a representation of Behn's experience in Surinam— was a defense of a noble African prince who was enslaved. The narrative is full of ambivalence. Shakespeare's *Othello* (1604) represented a noble Moor, whose military prowess had made him a general in Venice in its wars with the Turks. Like Othello, Oroonoko kills his wife, but, unlike the Moor, he is tricked into slavery. The treachery of white men ruin both men.

The narrator and the characters create an ambivalent narrative landscape concerning Europeans and Africans and the institution of slavery. Is the narrator a character or an expression of Aphra Behn in something approaching a memoir in the form of a novella, romance, or travel narrative? The various characters find themselves in shifting contexts. The eponymous Oroonoko is an African prince who becomes a slave: the English call him Caesar. His lover, Imoinda, also called Clemene, is enslaved as well. Oronooko conquers, Jamoan, a chief who becomes his vassal. More reversals occur besides a prince turns slave and a conqueror is conquered. Oroonoko serves the king of Coramantien and later betrays him and is in turn betrayed by him. The European characters include an English ship captain who runs slaves and various English colonists like the plantation overseer, Trefrey, the colony's deputy governor, William Byam, Colonel Martin, and an Irishman, Bannister. Oroonoko has come to know the narrator while he is a slave in Guiana and tells her his story. This tale is that Oroonoko was a warrior of some prowess who fell in love with Imoinda. Unfortunately, the king is also attracted to her. When the surreptitious love of Oroonoko and Imoinda is discovered, Imoinda is sold as a slave. Oroonoko is a slaveowner himself: he despairs over Imoinda's slavery and nearly loses a battle to Jamoan. Ironically, a captain of an English ship who had traded slaves with Oroonoko, tricks him and takes them as slaves to South America. In Guiana, Oroonoko and Imoinda reunite. Oronooko comes to lead a rebellion against his masters in the cause of freedom. The conclusion of the story involves the capture of Oronooko and the murder of his own wife as well as his own subsequent torture and execution at the hands of the English slaveowners. Ambivalence surrounds the noble prince turned slave, the slaveowner become slave, the man who would kill for honor and freedom and who is killed by those who enslaved him. The actions in the plot or the representation of events questions the notion of race and exposes the inhumanity of slavery.

The textual details—the language itself—complicates the text further. The title, *Oroonoko: Or, The Royal Slave. A True Story. By Mrs A. Behn*, announced that this person with an exotic name was the apparent oxymoron of a monarch enslaved, that the narrative was true and not fiction and that a woman wrote it.[40] In the Epistle Dedicatory, which is addressed to Lord Maitland, Aphra Behn speaks about the poet, in relation to the painter, and this reference qualifies the "True History" of the title. History can mean a story or a story about the past, fiction or history as we might say today, alive to the blurring of boundaries between them as Behn herself seems to have been. Of the "Picture-drawer" Behn says that he chooses the most agreeable of "many Lights" to give the face "the best Grace; and if there be a Scar, an ungrateful Mole, or any little Defect, they leave it out; and yet make the Picture extreamly like."[41] The artist lets light reflect in such a way as to achieve a more graceful likeness. This is a subtle assessment of the relation between world and representation. The analogy gathers more subtlety still: "A Poet is a Painter in his way; he draws to the Life, but in another kind; we draw the Nobler part, the Soul and Mind; the Pictures of the Pen shall outlast those of the Pencil, and even Worlds themselves."[42] The poet is and is not a painter, his monument outlasting that of lead and even what Behn refers to, in a suggestive way, in the plural "Worlds." That leads her to something that Philip Sidney, who modified Aristotle's hierarchy of philosopher, poet, and historian by reversing the first two, would have recognized, but she complicates this move by leading her allusion to the poet to a connection, even conflation, with the historian. The writer of history, like Sidney's poet, can move people to right action: there is an ethical aspect to this representation of universals. Behn continues: "'Tis a short Chronicle of those Lives that possibly wou'd be forgotten by other Historians, or lye neglected there, however deserving an immortal Fame; for Men of eminent Parts are as Exemplary as even Monarchs themselves; and Virtue is a noble Lesson to be learn'd, and 'tis by Comparison we can Judge and Chuse."[43] Innate nobility becomes the moral lesson here. The dedication creates an implied diptych between Lord Maitland and Oroonoko. Both are truly noble and do not rely on titles. In a book about a black royal slave part, of the message—no matter how mixed in the execution—is that neither race nor class nor gender can determine true nobility. Behn does not mince her words. Addressed to a noble, Behn contests conventional or titular nobility. Lord Howard is an exemplar of nobility: "'Tis by such illustrious Presidents, as your Lordship, the World can be Better'd and Refin'd; when a great part of the lazy Nobility shall, with Shame, behold the admirable Accomplishments of a man so Great, and so Young."[44] Age is not a factor of nobility. Lord Maitland is like St. Augustine, full of youthful gaiety while "Teaching the World divine Precepts, true Notions of Faith, and Excellent Morality" and being the pattern of a great man.[45] Behn also appeals to God for a blessing to Maitland's wife, "a Lady, to whom it had given all the Graces, Beauties, and Virtues of her Sex; all the Youth, Sweetness of Nature; of a most illustrious Family; and who is a most rare Example to all Wives of Quality for her eminent Piety, Easiness, and Condescension."[46] This is only a slice of the praise for Lord and Lady Maitland. The conventional appeal to beauty, virtue, and a good family is as much a social move as one that comes from comedy and romance. A small sample of the extended eulogy is the exalted claim: "Methinks your tranquil Lives are an Image of the new Made and Beautiful Pair in Paradise."[47] This paradise regained is a religious as well as a romantic image, a sexual innocence involving "Passion and Resignation" as well as "Tenderness."[48] This kind of romantic–religious love and innate nobility will create a complicity and typology between Lord and Lady Maitland on the one hand and Oroonoko and Imoinda on the other.

The connection is intricate because although this analogy might be implicitly drawn, part of the moral of Behn's story is the lack of power she had, as highly placed as she was in the colony, to protect Oroonoko and her wish that Maitland had been there to place this royal slave under his protection. Behn says she lays "such humble Fruits" at his "Lordships Feet," so that her prologue is no less begging than the epilogue that Shakespeare's Rosalind speaks in *As You Like It*. Behn herself was a dramatist with an eye for the dramatic. Behn's other analogies among painter, poet, and historian complicate the idea of history and representation further. She claims in this dedication: "This is a true Story, of a Man Gallant enough to merit your Protection; and, had he always been so Fortunate, he had not made so inglorious an end."[49] This unnamed slave who is called Oroonoko in the narrative itself is part of the problematics of a story that is true. This unfortunate man did not have the power himself or of those about him to save himself from a horrible end. Behn emphasizes her own impotence despite her high social standing: "The Royal Slave I had the Honour to know in my Travels to the other World; and though I had none above me in that Country, yet I wanted power to preserve this Great Man."[50] Class could not engender power enough in the face of the slave trade and the institution of slavery.

As a witness of these events, the author tells the dedicatee and, by extension, the reader, of what her motives are. Behn wants to assure Maitland that she speaks the truth and has not been given over to romance: "If there be any thing that seems Romantick, I beseech your Lordship to consider, these Countries do, in all things, so far differ from ours, that they produce unconceivable Wonders; at least they appear so to us, because New and Strange."[51] The marvelousness that Columbus saw in the New World, taking up the wonders that the ancients and the later writers of travel narratives described, was still a point of discussion in Behn's time. She insists on her truthfulness: "What I have mention'd I have taken care shou'd be Truth, let the Critical Reader judge as he pleases."[52] Having let the reader into the dedication, she brings back his lordship, says she wrote the book in hours and asks that he "Excuse some of its Faults of Connexion," so to stress the more the true object of the book—not the author but the protagonist: "'Tis purely the Merit of my Slave that must render it worthy of the Honour it begs."[53] This book is about "my Slave," an innocent enough description but also an expression of possession and a generic representation, perhaps to call attention to his state. It is only on the title page and in the story itself that he finds a name.

In this dedication one of the implications is that this royal slave can serve as an example to those who are called nobles and is worth the attention of a truly noble man like Maitland himself. As if in a satirical or ironic gap between the audience and the character, the nobles and the man, the readers themselves could behold their shortcomings and learn through admiration for this noble man. Maitland is a great example, a man worthy of a dedication. Oroonoko is a person worthy of a book to which that dedication is attached. Like Las Casas and Montaigne, Behn uses a figure from other cultures to show up some ill-advised Europeans who seek out power or abuse it. In case Lord Maitland might think he were numbered among "the lazy Nobility," she praises him as a reader who seeks knowledge and not novelty and uses it for the public good in service of religion and country. If Maitland could not be there to protect Oroonoko in life, he will do so in the story. If he is a patron to Behn, he can help her to achieve as an author what she could not as a member of the upper echelon of an English colony—preserve

Oroonoko. She is aware that it would have been better to save his life, but in her work she pays homage to a man much wronged and sacrificed by the very institution that he had been involved in—slavery.

In the body of the text, Behn emphasizes verisimilitude and history as opposed to the fiction of the poet both because the opening page echoes the title page with another rubric—"THE HISTORY OF THE ROYAL SLAVE"—and because the very first sentences of the narrative insist on the truth being told.[54] This plea is made at length:

> I Do not pretend, in giving you the History of this *Royal Slave*, to entertain my Reader with the Adventures of a feign'd *Hero*, whose Life and Fortunes Fancy may manage at the Poets Pleasure; not in relating the Truth, design to adorn it with any Accidents, but such as arriv'd in earnest to him: And it shall come simply into the World, recommended by its own proper Merits, and natural Intrigues; there being enough of Reality to support it, and to render it diverting, without the Addition of Invention.

Behn is claiming the status of nonfiction for her work. "Truth" and not "Invention" underpins her recounting of the life and death of this royal slave. Although insisting on the status of this book as a history and appealing to "Reality" and not to entertainment, Behn underscores her role of eyewitness:

> I was my self an Eye-Witness, to a great part, of what you will find here set down; and what I cou'd not be Witness of, I receiv'd from the mouth of the chief Actor in this History, the *Hero* himself, who gave us the whole Transactions of his Youth; and though I shall omit, for Brevity's sake, a thousand little Accidents of his Life, which, however pleasant to us, where History was scarce, and Adventures very rare; yet might prove tedious and heavy to my Reader, in a World where he finds Diversions for every Minute, new and strange.[55]

This text is then a curious history as it is really a mixture of autobiography, biography, reportage from an eyewitness, and editing by the author herself. Behn speaks about "us" and notes that "we, who were perfectly charm'd with the Character of this great Man, were curious to gather every Circumstance of his Life."[56] This is a gesture beyond the author into an anonymous group of admirers and to Oroonoko's life beyond the text. Besides this body who received his words, Behn, a little like Desdemona, listened to the stories of the royal slave, who presented himself from his point of view.

Behn's narrator unabashedly calls him the "*Hero*," so that there is a little of the life of saints here or history more as the life of a great man, something Thomas Carlisle picked up on in the nineteenth century. There is little criticism or distance between Behn and the person whose history she is telling. This is like one of Plutarch's *Lives* but with a difference. Before proceeding with her story, Behn enumerates rarities and exotic animals and objects, such as "a thousand other Birds and Beasts of wonderful and surprising Forms, Shapes, and Colours."[57] Behn describes the bodies of the exotic inhabitants of Guiana—men and women. She likens their dress to Adam and Eve and amplifies this identification with Eden: "And though they are all thus naked, if one lives for ever among 'em, there is not to be seen an indecent Action, or Glance; and being continually us'd to see one another so unadorn'd, so like our first Parents before the Fall, it seems as if they had no Wishes."[58] Behn's narrator identifies nature with innocence and elaborates her connection of these Natives with the first humans in the Scripture: "And these People represented to me and absolute *Idea* of the first State of Innocence, before Man knew how to sin."[59] This innocence will face European corruption.

Like Las Casas, Léry, Montaigne, and others before her, Behn turns the tables on Europeans. She tells the story of an English governor who did not keep his word, only to have the term *"Lyar,"* which he teaches them when they describe behavior similar to his, thrown back in his face: "Then one of 'em reply'd, *Governor, you are a Lyar, and guilty of that Infamy.*" The narrator (Behn wants this to be her in a history) expresses her own opposition from within, which shows the innocence and superiority of the Natives vis-à-vis Europeans long before Jean-Jacques Rousseau's "noble savage": "They have a Native Justice, which knows no Fraud; and they understand, no Vice, or Cunning, but when they are taught by the *White Men.*"[60] These Natives, as perceptive as they are about the faults of Europeans, have their own drawback, although the author does not present it as such: "and unless they take Slaves in War, they have no other Attendants."[61] The narrator says she and her peers get along well with the indigenous people with whom they exchange food for "Trifles."[62] This imbalance of power is something the narrator seems to reveal inadvertently as the reason they deal with the Natives with some fairness: "So that they being, on all Occasions, very useful to use, we find it absolutely necessary to caress 'em as Friends, and not to treat 'em as Slaves; nor dare we do other, their Numbers so far surpassing ours in that *Continent.*"[63] Friendship, rather than slavery, is the relation between the English and the aboriginal peoples here only because of the ratio in population, but this amity is based on the usefulness of the Natives.

As in Las Casas's *Short Account*, here the local peoples are able to avoid slavery whereas Africans cannot: "Those then whom we make use of to work in our Plantations of Sugar, are *Negro's, Black*-Slaves altogether."[64] The narrator then describes the buying and selling of slaves, especially in Coramantien, a war-like country, that acquired many captives, "for all they took in Battel, were sold as Slaves; at least, those common Men who cou'd not ransom themselves."[65] The king of Coramentien was over hundred years old and had only one successor left, his seventeen-year-old grandchild—Oroonoko, who the narrator praises as "one of the most expert Captains, and bravest Soldiers, that ever saw the Field of *Mars*: So that he was ador'd as the Wonder of all the World, and the Darling of the Soldiers."[66] Behn has emphasized the beauty of the Native men and women and, beyond this praise of Oroonoko's military prowess, also extends this concern with looks to this African prince: "Besides, he was adorn'd with a native Beauty so transcending all those of his gloomy Race, that he strook an Awe and Reverence, even in those that knew not his Quality; as he did in me, who beheld him with Surprize and Wonder, when afterwards he arriv'd in our World."[67] Long after Columbus, who professed wonder at the marvels of the New World, Behn expressed similar wonderment in her text.

The emphasis on "his gloomy Race" and "his Quality" suggest that racial and class differences are embedded in the cultural framework of Behn's language even if there is an attempt to get beyond them. Oroonoko was away from court from five to seventeen years but had a natural nobility: "where was it he got that real Greatness of Soul, those refin'd Notions of true Honour, that absolute Generosity, and that Softness that was capable of the highest Passions of Love and Gallantry" amid constant war?[68] One answer the narrator gives is the Royal Tutor, "a *French*-Man of Wit and Learning" who found Oroonoko "very ready, apt, and quick of Apprehension," and so taught "him Morals, Language and Science" and the other is that the African warrior-prince "lov'd, when he came from War, to see all the *English* Gentlemen that traded thither; and did not only learn their Language, but that of the *Spaniards* also, with whom he traded afterwards for Slaves." His magnanimity and learning come, it seems, in large part from European tutelage. The narrator bases her authority on the many times she saw "and convers'd with this great Man, and been a Witness to many of his mighty Actions," asserting that "the most illustrious Courts cou'd not have produc'd a braver Man, both for Greatness of Courage and Mind, a Judgment more solid, a Wit more quick, and a Conversation more sweet and diverting."[69] To this catalogue of virtues, the narrator adds civility, still anchoring the description in the culture of the reader. The narrator elaborates: "He had nothing of Barbarity in his Nature, but in all Points address'd himself, as if his Education had been in some *European* Court."[70] Hyperbole continues to be the language that describes Oroonoko for the reader. Behn's hero is framed in terms of Europe even in a tale that shows the failures of European values.

The narrator returns to physical appearance in her representation of Oroonoko: difference and similarity mark the description—he is "a perfect Ebony" but "His Nose was rising and *Roman*, instead of *African* and flat."[71] Oroonoko is and is not African: his Roman bearing leads the English to call him Caesar. When the general and foster-father who had guided Oronooko died, he left behind his daughter, "the beautiful *Black Venus*, to our young

Mars."[72] Through these descriptions, the narrator emphasizes physical attraction, and if the author's claim in the dedication and the beginning of the narrative itself is accepted, Behn herself is concerned with physical presence and beauty. This erotic, sexual, or romantic element, despite what Behn says in the dedication, plays an important role. The narrator makes it explicit: "I have seen an hundred *White* Men fighting after her, and making a thousand Vows at her Feet, all vain, and unsuccessful: And she was, indeed, too great for any, but a Prince of her own Nation to adore."[73] This textual sway, involving a rhetoric of seduction but also this shift from multifold White desire to singular Black adoration, contains its own surprises and its own reconfigurations of convention in race and romance. When Oroonoko meets Imoinda, he comes "to present her with those Slaves that had been taken in his last Battel, as the Trophies of her Father's Victories."[74] Slaves, then, are part of the landscape of these lovers before they are seized and sent separately and against their will from Africa to Guiana. They are prizes of their power, prestige, and honor and serve as a memorial to the dead father— the general. A beauty, Imoinda holds sway over Oroonoko: "and the Sweetness of her Words and Behaviour while he stay'd, gain'd a perfect Conquest over his fierce Heart, and made him feel, the Victor cou'd be subdu'd."[75] Behn appears to be using romance to underscore their love and to set up the violence done to them: what makes them most human is most violated. The language of conquest and slavery is part of the terms of love here and makes it more intricate and problematic. The passage that follows intensifies the curious mixing of love, war, and slavery—of Oroonoko, the narrator says:

> So that having made his first Complements, and presented her an hundred
> and fifty Slaves in Fetters, he told her with his Eyes, that he was not insensible
> of her Charms; while *Imoinda*, who wish'd for nothing more than so glorious
> a Conquest, was pleas'd to believe, she understood that silent Language of
> new-born Love; and from that Moment, put on all her Additions to Beauty.[76]

This love scene, a little like Cleopatra's conquest of Anthony as Enobarbus and others describe it in Shakespeare's play, reverses the usual gender roles. A woman conquers the conqueror. The soldier yields to love. Strangely, in this love and first sight is the spectacle of 150 slaves in chains, a gift that does little to enhance the romantic atmosphere. These two will-be lovers will be slaves. Retrospectively, the reader will come to experience the irony of the situation.

The old king, Oroonoko's grandfather, summoned Imoinda, to court to be one of his mistresses.[77] Oroonoko, the old king and Imoinda all have an intricate relation of obligations, love, and power: the king lacks military and sexual prowess but desires Imoinda; he sells her into slavery when he learns that she has been with Oroonoko, to whom she was betrothed, and Oroonoko forgives his grandfather, but is despondent at the news of what the king has done. Before being punished with slavery, Imoinda, to protect her life, lied that Oroonoko had forced her. Oronooko, so taken with European culture, finds himself tricked and kidnapped, taken into slavery, by an apparently cultured but unscrupulous English captain. Paradoxically, Oroonoko is seized by the very captain to whom he has "sold abundance of his slaves."[78] The narrator leaves no doubt when she describes the capture of Oroonoko as "treachery" and says that he and his fellows were "betrayed to slavery."[79] This is not the last dishonor of the English captain toward Oroonoko. The African prince would sell his slaves to save himself from slavery in Surinam, but this does not work out. Reunited with Imoinda in Surinam through Trefay, Oroonoko and his beloved are now slaves. Slavery and love come into conflict:

> They soon informed each other of their fortunes, and equally bewailed their fate, but, at the same time, they mutually protested that even fetters and slavery were soft and easy, and would be supported with joy and pleasure while they could be so happy to possess each other, and to be able to make good their vows. Caesar swore he disdained the empire of the world while he could behold his *Imoinda*, and she despised grandeur and pomp, those vanities of her sex, when she could gaze on Oroonoko.[80]

Unfortunately, for the reunited couple, love had a harder time than that conquering slavery. What begins as such a promising transcendence of love and the human spirit turns to a tragic sacrifice. Later, to Byam, who said that Caesar/Oroonoko "ought to have regard to his wife, whose condition required ease and not the fatigues of tedious travel," the royal slave, according to the narrator, rails against Europeans. Caesar would not heed Byam:

> But Caesar told him, there was no faith in the white men or the gods they adored, who instructed 'em; though no people professed so much, none performed so little; that he knew what he had to do when he dealt with men of honour, but with them a man ought to be eternally on his guard, and never to eat and drink with Christians without his weapon of defence in his hand, and for his own security never to credit one word they spoke.[81]

This indignation against the abuses of the Christians is something that Montaigne, Swift, and others were so good at representing. The voices of others are used to target European excesses and weaknesses. Thomas More also employed similar techniques to express dystopic or ironic elements of his fictional utopian community.

Nonetheless, the English are a mixed lot as are the Africans. There are English men and women, like Colonel Martin, Trefry, and the narrator, who are disgusted by the treachery of Bannister and the governor toward "Caesar." The violence of Oroonoko/Caesar in his gruesome murder of his wife Clemene/Imoinda and the torture and quartering of this royal slave suggests the horrors of slavery both for the English who practice it and the Africans who are caught in the trade and institution.

The narrator set out at length the state of mind and the motivations of Caesar in the killing of his wife. Caesar wanted to be revenged on the governor but knew he could not survive that vengeance, so he turned to "black designs": "He considered, if he should do this deed and die, either in the attempt or after it, he left his lovely Imoinda a prey or, at best, a slave to the enraged multitude. 'Perhaps', said he, 'she may be first ravished by every brute, exposed first to their nasty lusts, and then a shameful death.' No, he could not live a moment under that apprehension, too insupportable to be borne."[82] The narrator and her party responded to his story after the gruesome murder. First, she reported his frame of mind and then their reaction to it:

> These were his thoughts, and his silent arguments with his heart, as he told us afterwards, so that now resolving not only to kill Byam, but all those he thought had enraged him, pleasing his great heart with the fancied slaughter he should make over the whole face of the plantation, he first resolved on a deed that (however horrid it at first appeared to us all) when we had heard his reasons, we thought it brave and just.[83]

The narrator described the awful deed of Oroonoko murdering Imoinda, but, here beforehand, although the representation is based on what the royal slave said to them after the murder, the narrator and her party express ambivalence to his action—it is horrible, brave, and just. This slaveholder is held as a slave, this royal soldier is driven to a violence that might be noble at one level but is also repugnant and mean at another.

During the 1680s, when *Oronooko* had appeared, the French were codifying slavery in their Caribbean colonies. The first *Code Noir*, was promulgated under Louis XIV (r.1643–1715) under the influence of Jean-Baptiste Colbert (1616–83), and the second under Louis XV in 1724. This later version shed Articles 5, 7, 8, 18, and 25 of the version of the *Code Noir* of 1685. Both codes, while insisting on the humanity of slaves, codified slavery and linked blackness to slavery. For example, the code of 1685 opened with a declaration of a paternalistic and providential view of the king's role in the French Empire. The document stated that it is the king's duty to extend his care or protection to "all the peoples that Divine Providence has placed under our obeisance" and in response to memorandums "sent by our Officers of our Islands of America, by which having been informed of the need that they have of our authority & our justice, for maintaining there the discipline of the Catholic, Apostolic & Roman Church, & for regulated that which concerns the state & the quality of Slaves' there."[84] There were some important protections in this code, but it also allowed masters to treat their slaves with great severity in the face of violence, insubordination, or any strong challenge to their authority and the hierarchy that sustained it. A sample of the content of the various articles should suggest the coexistence of the protection and the exploitation of slaves, of their treatment as people, and as property and beasts of burden. For instance, Article 1 prohibited Jews unless they converted. Article 2 set out that slaves were to be baptized and instructed as Catholics. Moreover, Article 3 interdicted the practice of any religion except Catholicism. Article 13 regulated marriages so that, whether free or enslaved, black children would inherit the legal status of their mothers. Article 15 forbade that slaves be in possession of offensive arms. Further, Article 16 prohibited slaves belonging to different masters from assembling in groups (" 's'attrouper") and said that recidivists could be given lashes, branded with a fleur-de-lys or, in severe cases, put to death. In Article 27 the document showed a stark contrast to this severity by declaring that masters would nourish and maintain slaves who were infirm, old, or sick and, if they abandoned their slaves, would pay 6 sols a day for the hospital to care for them. Article 33 swung back to the other extreme by condemning to death any slave who hit his master, mistress, or children causing "contusion of blood" or in the face. Precise in its punishment and the way it marks and controls the body of the slave according to the nature and frequency of the offence, Article 38 stated that "The fugitive Slave will have been in flight for a month, counted from the day his Master will have denounced him in Justice, will have his ears cut, & will be marked with a fleur-de-lys on one shoulder; and if he repeats his offence ['récidive'] an other time, counted similarly from the day of the denunciation, he will have the hollow of the knee cut, & will be marked with a fleur-de-lys on the other shoulder, & the third time he will be punished with death."[85] The brutality and violence of such a code, despite glimpses of humane treatment of slaves, is something that has the power to shock more than three centuries later. The legacy of this regime is multifold. With the Enlightenment, more opposition to slavery would arise even if the institution was persistent.

Besides Aphra Behn, women in the seventeenth and eighteenth century, wrote about slaves and slavery in the New World. During King Philip's War in New England, the young Hety Shepard (1660–78?) mentioned slavery in a diary entry of October 6, 1676: "There is much talk about Philip's son, a boy of nine years, who was taken prisoner with his mother. They know not what to do with him. The ministers are bitter against him and would have him sold into slavery or even worse. How can so tender a child be held accountable? But perhaps it is a sin to feel this."[86] A sympathy for Natives, for cultural difference, and for children allowed Hety to question the position of her own religious leaders, although she felt guilty about this feeling.

Almost four decades later, Sarah Kemble Knight alluded to slaves in a journal from October 2, 1704 to March 3, 1705 during a trip to settle her cousin Caleb Trowbridge's estate that recounts the trip from Boston to New Haven, Connecticut. Knight spoke about the severity of the law and judges in Connecticut even if the people were governed by similar government to that in Boston. She provided a critique of the legal system generally:

> And much the same way of Church Government, and many of them good, Sociable people, and I hope Religious too: but a little too much Independant in their principalls, and, as I have been told, were formerly in their Zeal very Riggid in their Administrations towards such as their Lawes made Offenders, even to a harmless Kiss or Innocent merriment among Young people. Whipping being a frequent and counted an easy Punishment, about wch as other Crimes, the Judges were absolute in their Sentances.[87]

This legalistic rigidity and harsh corporal punishment provided a context for a comic tale that arose from an insidious institution—slavery. In Connecticut "They told mee a pleasant story about a pair of Justices in those parts, wch I may not omit the relation of. A negro Slave belonging to a man in ye Town, stole a hogs head from his master, and gave or sold it to an Indian, native of the place. The Indian sold it in the neighbourhood, and so the theft was found out."[88] This world at the turn of the eighteenth century was one made up of aboriginal peoples and black slaves as well as English settlers. The Indian, in this account, was caught: "Thereupon the Heathen was Seized, and carried to the Justices House to be Examined. But his worship (it seems) was gone into the feild, with a Brother in office, to gather in his Pompions. Whither the malefactor is hurried, And Complaint made, and satisfaction in the name of Justice demanded."[89] The pompion derives from Greek and Latin through the French: as the *Oxford English Dictionary* notes, "In Eng. *pompon* has undergone two anomalous transformations, first to *pompeon, pompion, pumpion*, and finally to *pumkin*" or, what we call, pumpkin.[90] So in a comic situation the judges found pumpkins for their bench: "Their Worships cann't proceed in form without a Bench: whereupon they Order one to be Imediately erected, which, for want of fitter materials, they made with pompions—which being finished, down setts their Worships, and the Malefactor call'd, and by the Senior Justice Interrogated after the following manner."[91] Knight sets out what she portrays as a comic scene in the examination:

> You Indian why did You steal from this man? You sho'dn't do so—it's a Grandy wicked thing to steal. Hol't Hol't cryes Justice Junr Brother, You speak negro to him. I'le ask him. You sirrah, why did You steal this man's Hoggshead? Hoggshead? (replys the Indian,) me no stomany. No? says his Worship; and pulling off his hatt, Patted his own head with his hand, sais, Tatapa—You, Tatapa—you; all one this. Hoggshead all one this. Hah! says Netop, now me stomany that. Whereupon the Company fell into a great fitt of Laughter, even to Roreing. Silence is comanded, but to no effect: for they continued perfectly Shouting. Nay, sais his worship, in an angry tone, if it be so, *take mee off the Bench.*[92]

The tables are turned on the administration of justice and the "Company" gathered laugh the judge off his make-shift bench, so that it appears that the black slave and the Indian do not suffer the harsh punishments that Knight had described in relation to youths who were mildly transgressive in the English American community. Through language, humor, misapprehension, and hurt dignity become themes of this encounter. The judge is judged and does not like it.

Other references to slaves and slavery in the eighteenth century suggest that women in the northern as well as the southern colonies observed their role in families and communities of the time. In New York, which included many different places of worship, Bilhah Abigail Levy Franks (1696–1756), a Jewish woman born in London and a member of a mercantile family, wrote letters in the 1730s and 1740s that referred to particular slaves in her life.[93] Patience Greene Brayton (1733–94), born in North Kingston, Rhode Island, worked as a Quaker minister for forty years. She and her husband, Preserved Brayton, became abolitionists and freed their slaves. In her diary for November 1771, she wrote: "On the 7th we went to Deer Creek meeting; afternoon being overtaken by a storm, as we rode in the rain, I thought if I brought no dishonour to God and his truth, there was no hardship but what I could endure in the rain and the darkness of the night; we at length reached a Friend's house; but oh! the black people, how does their slavery wound my spirit within me."[94] The Quakers were important to the abolitionist movement. For Brayton, trading and of holding slaves was a spiritual gash. Just before the American Revolution, in Antigua, Isabella Marshall Graham (1742–1814) wrote a letter to her husband, army surgeon, John Graham, on January 16, 1773, professing her love, expressing religious sentiments, and hoping for his preservation, but adding as a postscript: "I am told that you have taken a number of prisoners. I know not if you have any right to entail slavery on these poor creatures. If any fall to your share, do set them at liberty."[95] Amid these personal matters, Isabella Marshall Graham (1742–1814) worried about liberty and spoke out against slavery. Before Antigua, they had lived in Quebec, Montreal, Fort Niagara and she would later extend her social concern to the care of widows and poor children in New York. During the tensions between Britain and its American colonies, Abigail Smith Adams (1744–1818) wrote from Braintree, Massachusetts to John Adams on July 31, 1775: "Those who do not scruple to bring poverty, misery, slavery, and death upon thousands, will not hesitate at the most diabolical crimes; and this is Britain. Blush, O Americans, that ever you derived your origin from such a race."[96] She blames the British much and connects their penchant for crime with their bringing of slavery to America while trying to distance Americans from their origins in Britain. The trading and holding of slaves becomes part of the framework of the tensions between Britain and its colonies. The discussion about slavery intensified as the 1700s went on.

IV

During the eighteenth century, an ambivalent attitude to slavery became more widespread. The abolition of the slave trade, if not of slavery itself, occurred in some jurisdictions then. Africa, Asia, and the Americas became more closely connected to the European economy: slavery still helped to drive international trade. Africa was no longer the preserve of the Portuguese Empire among the European powers. There were many areas of the world in which empire was being contested.

Although the permanent population grew slowly in southern Africa, German, Dutch, and, to a lesser extent, French Huguenot settlers—some freeburgers and others not—helped the population grow. The Dutch stopped granting free passage in 1707. After that, natural increase was responsible for demographic growth. Among the people there were some former Asian and African slaves: some of them came to own land. Some of the white settlers married former slave women—their children were assimilated into the white community.[97] Relations between those who were settlers and who were not and between black and white populations in South Africa were complicated then. These connections became even more so over time. Slavery seems to have touched many places in this network of world trade, whether far from Europe or at its heart.

France and Britain took different approaches to the encouragement of trade and slavery. Whereas the French Crown taxed a port like La Rochelle— so important in the trade with the West Indies and West Africa—the British government encouraged Liverpool and Glasgow. The French government did not protect La Rochelle against the Royal Navy, which seized its merchant ships, disrupted its slave trade, and destroyed its markets in Louisiana and

Canada. France also allowed its colonists to trade with neutral shipping during wars. The British government picked up the Atlantic trade while its French counterpart neglected the importance of profit and the exchange of goods. The French monarchy, after the reign of Louis XIV, seemed to have trouble raising enough money to direct a full and sustained military effort.[98] Trade, shipping, and war all had an intricate relation.

In the eighteenth century, the British stressed commerce, although at times the French challenged them in this domain. A reason that Britain prospered was that it was well placed to take advantage of the shift from the Mediterranean to the Atlantic, from land routes to Asia to sea routes that connected Europe with East and South Asia, the West Indies, and the Americas. Sea power was necessary to national wealth and political clout: overseas trade bolstered metropolitan center and outlying territories. The navy supported trade and the colonies, but, as Paul Kennedy has noted, agriculture was still the basis of the British economy in the eighteenth century and British trade with the Baltic, Germany, and the Mediterranean was important even as the colonial trade in sugar, spices, and slaves was growing more rapidly.[99]

The City of London made money from slaves as did some of the prominent citizens of colonies like Salem and New York. Newport, Rhode Island, developed into a major port that traded in slaves (the greatest merchant of slavers, taxpayer and benefactor in Newport in 1775 was Aaron Lopez, of Portuguese Jewish origin). By 1710—succeeding the Portuguese, the French, and the Dutch as the great transporters of slaves—the British were transporting about ten thousand slaves a year to the Indies, including the Spanish colonies there. In 1713, they took over the *asiento*, or official monopoly for carrying slaves and a few other goods to the Spanish colonies. In the 1690s Liverpool entered the slave trade and later grew to be the greatest slave market. In the eighteenth century the African slaves passed from Nantes to Saint-Domingue, which Spain had ceded to France in 1697. Dutch merchants handled the sugar trade from the refineries in and about Nantes to various places in northern Europe, and cotton was also a part of the industry and commerce of this city. Britain intensified the slave trade and other northern European nations emulated it. Between 1740 and 1750 Britain carried about two hundred thousand slaves to the Americas and about two hundred and fifty thousand between 1761 and 1770. Spain and France had been rivals in North America for two centuries, but they would come to an agreement that, along with the British victory in the Seven Years' War, would see the end of the French Empire on the Continent (in a complicated series of events Napoleon would later sell Louisiana to the United States in 1803). The British capture of Havana on August 4, 1762 strengthened the war party in England while weakening the position of the British cabinet because the

British victory placed the French and Spanish colonies in the Caribbean and on the Gulf coast at the mercy of the British fleet and made the terms of peace more severe. France under Louis XV was willing to give up Louisiana to compensate Spain for the loss of Florida, which Charles III of Spain gave up for Cuba.[100] Still, the British transformed Cuba from 1762 onward, importing many more African slaves to fuel the boom in sugar. Britain had also driven the French from West Africa in 1758 and retained most of the French African colonies at the Treaty of Paris in 1763.[101] The French government had much to resent Britain for in the wake of this war. Between 1763 and 1778, when the French entered the American War of Independence, the Western European commercial nations as well as British North America prospered in the slave trade. France was beginning to overtake Britain as a sugar producer. The Portuguese continued sending slaves into Brazil.[102]

Governments backed trade and enabled the trading and holding of slaves. In the seventeenth century the Netherlands, Denmark, Sweden, France, England, and Brandenburg tried to establish permanent posts on the Gold Coast of West Africa, but by 1719 only the English, Danish, and Dutch remained. One of the arguments for slavery was that white men could not survive the tropics and so they had to rely on those—usually Africans—who could. By studying the mortality rates among the Europeans who worked for the Netherlands West India Company from 1719 to 1760, H. M. Feinburg determined that there was a much lower rate than published in earlier studies, so that Feinburg thought it might be prudent to revise downward these estimates of European morality there.[103] In mapping out the European movement into the interior of Africa in the eighteenth century, Robin Hallett did so from a worldwide perspective of European expansion from an earlier period: "For in the initial contact between peoples of different stages of technological development, power inevitably lay with the more highly organized, and imperialism whether predatory or paternalistic in form – came to assume the inevitability of a force of nature."[104] There were actual problems that nature caused after these first contacts, and ones that had devastating religious, social, political, and economic consequences. Nature and nurture, biology and culture were closely intertwined in the encounter between Europeans and local inhabitants. Disease and other biological factors relating to agriculture also contributed to European ecological imperialism in various parts of the world and often with devastating effects.[105] All the countries created companies given the rights and privileges to carry slaves from Africa to the Americas, and some merchants and ship captains in these countries became wealthy from trading at least in part in slaves. People of all religious persuasions were involved in human traffic. Some bishops and cardinals of the Catholic Church in Portugal and Spain partook in the fifteenth-century slave traffic; slave merchants in Bahia in Brazil had their own religious brotherhood; various Jewish merchants played some part in the slave trade in some Western European countries and the Americas; some of the Quakers in England and British America were engaged in the slave trade; Freemasons in Bordeaux had a connection to slaving at the end of the eighteenth century.

Politics and slaving were also connected: some members of legislatures or parliament in France, Britain, and British North America were slave merchants; some aristocrats and foreign merchants (first from Florence in Lisbon and Seville) were also involved. The cargoes altered over the centuries as the European suppliers responded to changing demand in Africa. In 1721, the Royal Africa Company (RAC) asked its agents in Africa about many details of the trade, including whether the slaves were taken in war or traded. Most were obtained by trade, some by war, and very few by kidnapping after 1448. For so many centuries, the causes of slavery were captivity from war; punishment; poverty; kidnapping. African monarchs later bought slaves to sell them again to Arabs, Africans, and Europeans. The RAC lost almost a quarter of their slaves shipped across the Atlantic between 1680 and 1688 but by the 1780s, at the apogee of the slave trade, the death rate had been reduced to under 6 percent. There was probably a violent insurrection every eight or ten European slaving voyages and these accounted for many deaths. By the end of the 1700s, about 80,000 black African slaves crossed the Atlantic annually.

Slavery, as we have seen, was a preoccupation and problem from the start in the exploration and exploitation of the New World. In the eighteenth century any objections and scruples some Europeans had to slavery intensified, so that during the American Revolution, both the British and Americans began to abolish the slave trade and ultimately the holding of slaves. In France, there was a notable condemnation—Montesquieu's *L'Esprit des lois* (1748) scorned the slave trade: "The state of slavery is in its own nature bad. It is neither useful to the master nor to the slave; not to the slave, because he can do nothing through a motive of virtue; nor to the master, because by having an unlimited authority over his slaves he insensibly accustoms himself to the want of all moral virtues, and thence becomes fierce, hasty, severe, choleric, voluptuous, and cruel."[106] Besides, this mutual disadvantage was the less than reassuring historical circumstances in which Europeans had established slavery in the New World: "The Europeans, having extirpated the Americans, were obliged to make slaves of the Africans, for clearing such vast tracts of land."[107] Montesquieu also questioned a philosophical argument for enslavement: "Aristotle endeavors to prove that there are natural slaves; but what he says is far from proving it."[108] The support for slavery is not something that history, philosophy, or law justify in Montesquieu's view.

The conditions of the crossing for the slaves were so crowded, painful, degrading, and pestilential that it is hard to bear even at the distance of time and textual description. One such representation based on experience was that expressed in the autobiography of Olaudah Equiano (Gustavus Vassa) in 1789. About half the slaves carried to the New World during this period were on British ships and, in the year that Britain recognized the independence of the United States, William Pitt estimated that the West India trade, which included a large slavery component, accounted for about 80 percent of Britain's income from overseas. Despite the declarations and writings against slavery—for some there had been a certain ambivalence in the religious communities and beyond, it was not until the end of the eighteenth century that abolitionists became an important political force.

In 1758 Frei Manuel Ribeiro da Rocha produced a call for the abolition of slavery and the use of free labor. Figures of the French Enlightenment, unlike their Renaissance counterparts, were against slavery: Marivaux, Montesquieu, Voltaire, Diderot, and Rousseau circulated ideas about the liberation of slaves and about freedom generally. Laws prohibited slavery in Portugal in 1750 and in 1779 the last black slave was sold in Britain: in British North America, from 1780 to 1800, following Pennsylvania, other British and former British colonies in North America abolished slavery (even though certain qualifications sometimes weakened the prohibition).

Thomas Jefferson also owned slaves, and although he was not a supporter of slavery as an institution, he did not go as far as Benjamin Franklin in working against the institution. In the Declaration of Independence Jefferson may well have omitted a condemnation of slavery because of pressure from some representatives from southern colonies whose commerce depended so heavily on slaves. The condemnation of George III in such a declaration, as important as it would have been, would also have been full of contradiction and might have smacked of hypocrisy. Jefferson was disturbed by slavery and at least did not want to encourage it as an institution. Franklin took this to heart on a personal level. He began a dialogue of 1770 on slavery among a Scot, an Englishman and an American by having the English interlocutor complain:. "You Americans. make a great Clamour upon every little imaginary Infringement of what you take to be your Liberties; and yet there are no People upon Earth such Enemies to Liberty, such absolute Tyrants, where you have the Opportunity, as you yourselves are."[109] The American emphasized that the British "began" the slave trade and profited from it, then retorting: "You bring the Slaves to us, and tempt us to purchase them. I do not justify our falling into the Temptation. To be sure, if you have stolen Men to sell to us, and we buy them, you may urge against us the old and true saying, that the Receiver is as bad as the Thief."

Violent confrontations with Natives were also a key part of the history of British America no matter how much the English, then the British and British North Americans, tried to distance themselves from the example of Spain and the cruelty to the Indians. The English colonists came to accuse the king of inciting rebellion among them and the Natives against them: "He has excited domestic insurrection among us, and has endeavored to bring on the inhabitants of our frontiers the merciless Indian savages, whose known rule of warfare is an undistinguished destruction of all ages, sexes, and conditions." The Natives were not included as equals in the birth of this new nation just as African slaves would not be.

On September 22, 1774, from Boston, Abigail Adams had written to her husband, John, about a petition by black slaves to the newly appointed governor of Massachusetts, Thomas Gage, that they would serve him in arms in exchange for their liberty: "There has been in town a conspiracy of the negroes. At present it is kept pretty private, and was discovered by one who endeavoured to dissuade them from it. He being threatened with his life, applied to Justice Quincy for protection. They conducted in this way, got an Irishman to draw up a petition to the Governor, telling him they would fight for him provided he would arm them, and engage to liberate them if he conquered."[110] She also mentioned her position on slavery: "I wiſh moſt ſincerely there was not a ſlave in the province—it allways appeard a moſt iniquitous ſcheme to me" and added that each day we are "plundering from thoſe who have as good a right to freedom as we have."[111] Abigail Adams saw the irony of fighting for freedom while depriving others of it.

Another woman in New England expressed her views as well, but she was an African slave and poet—Phillis Wheatley (ca. 1754–84), kidnapped from Senegal-Gambia when she was about seven years old. In Boston, she was purchased in 1761 by John Wheatley, a prominent tailor, to attend on his wife. On December 21, 1767, Phillis published her first poem in the *Mercury* in Newport, Rhode Island. As no one in Boston would publish her poems, Phillis, with the support of the Wheatleys, found a publisher in London, where, in 1773 *Poems on Various Subjects, Religious and Moral* appeared, containing elegies and poems on religious, classical, and related themes.[112] Perhaps Abigail Adams was not entirely right about the British and slavery as London seemed to be more hospitable for an English American of African descent than Boston was. Nonetheless, the shock of an African writing in English was such that the following attestation accompanied the poems and, owing to its very strangeness, deserves to be reproduced in full:

To the P U B L I C K.

A S it has been repeatedly suggested to the Publisher, by Persons, who have seen the Manuscript, that Numbers would be ready to suspect they were not really the Writings of PHILLIS, he has procured the following Attestation, from the most respectable Characters in *Boston*, that none might have the least Ground for disputing their *Original*.

W E whose Names are under-written, do assure the World, that the POEMS specified in the following Page,* were (as we verily believe) written by *Phillis*, a young Negro Girl, who was but a few Years since, brought an uncultivated Barbarian from *Africa*, and has ever since been, and now is, under the Disadvantage of serving as a Slave in a Family in this Town. She has been examined by some of the best Judges, and is thought qualified to write them.

*The Words "following Page," allude to the Contents of the Manuscript Copy, which are wrote at the Back of the above Attestation.

His Excellency THOMAS HUTCHINSON, *Governor.*

The Hon. ANDREW OLIVER, *Lieutenant-Governor.*

The Hon. Thomas Hubbard,	|*The Rev.* Charles Chauncey, *D.D.*
The Hon. John Erving,	|*The Rev.* Mather Byles, *D.D.*
The Hon James Pitts,	|*The Rev.* Ed. Pemberton, *D.D.*
The Hon. Harrison Gray,	|*The Rev.* Andrew Elliot, *D.D.*
The Hon. James Bowdoin,	|*The Rev.* Samuel Cooper, *D.D.*
John Hancock, *Esq*;	|*The Rev. Mr.* Saumel Mather,
Joseph Green, *Esq*;	|*The Rev. Mr.* John Moorhead,
Richard Carey, *Esq*;	|*Mr.* John Wheatley, *her Master.*

N. B. The original Attestation, signed by the above Gentlemen, may be seen by applying to *Archibald Bell*, Bookseller, No. 8, *Aldgate-Street.*

The soon-to-be reviled governor and John Hancock, who signed the Declaration of Independence, both signed to say that they could attest that this African woman had written these poems. Wheatley herself looked for examples of literary fame in Western literature:

> The happier *Terence** all the choir inspir'd,
> His soul replenish'd, and his bosom fir'd;
> But say, ye *Muses*, why this partial grace,
> To one alone of *Afric's* sable race;
> From age to age transmitting thus his name
> With the first glory in the rolls of fame?

*He was an *African* by birth.

Wheatley was writing in a framework had made her work a wonder and that had her look for precedents and for a transformation from barbarity to Christianity. While taking solace in Terence in "To M Æ C E N A S," she saw her being brought to America and her enslavement as a liberation through Christianity:

> On being brought from A F R I C A to
> A M E R I CA.
>
> 'TWAS mercy brought me from my *Pagan* land,
>   Taught my benighted soul to understand
>   That there's a God, that there's a *Saviour* too:
> Once I redemption neither sought nor knew,
> Some view our sable race with scornful eye,
> "Their colour is a diabolic die."
> Remember, *Christians*, *Negroes*, black as *Cain*,
> May be refin'd, and join th' angelic train.

There is, perhaps with some irony, a redemption of her blackness: William Blake's *Songs of Innocence and Experience* includes a satire against such discrimination. Whether Phillis Wheatley internalized the European symbolism of race or whether she is questioning it is hard to determine considering how hard it was for her to get published and to have her British and British American readers believe that she could write. This is similar to the doubts about Africans being capable of science as is the case surrounding the figure of Benjamin Banneker, an African American who had produced an almanac. In "To S. M. a young *African* Painter, on seeing his Works," Wheatley described the affect of an artist like her on her:

> TO show the lab'ring bosom's deep intent,
>   And thought in living characters to paint,
>   When first thy pencil did those beauties give,
> And breathing figures learnt from thee to live,
> How did those prospects give my soul delight,
> A new creation rushing on my sight?

Wheatley was not alone in breaking new ground in going against the grain of prejudice. She was freed before her mistress died and married a free black, John Peters, who abandoned her and the remaining child of their three children. Wheatley died in poverty and her last child died hours after she did. Amid the roar of revolution, this once celebrated poet, died unheard. In neglect and hardship, in a kind of freedom, Wheatley, far from the place of her birth, died young. Pursuing happiness for Africans in America was harder than it was for British and other European Americans.

The pursuit of happiness, then, long before its expression by Thomas Jefferson in the Declaration of Independence in 1776, was something Aristotle, who had contributed the Athenian Constitution, considered essential to individuals and states. Liberty and slavery were key elements in life and political life:

> For the same things are best both for individuals and for states, and these are the things which the legislator ought to implant in the minds of his citizens. Neither should men study war with a view to the enslavement of those who do not deserve to be enslaved; but first of all they should provide against their own enslavement, and in the second place obtain empire for the good of the governed, and not for the sake of exercising a general despotism, and in the third place they should seek to be masters only over those who deserve to be slaves. Facts, as well as arguments, prove that the legislator should direct all his military and other measures to the provision of leisure and the establishment of peace. For most of these military states are safe only while they are at war, but fall when they have acquired their empire; like unused iron they lose their edge in time of peace. And for this the legislator is to blame, he never having taught them how to lead the life of peace.[113]

Liberty and enslavement will be key subthemes of our exploration of the theme of empires and colonies. Here Aristotle developed a self-conscious assessment, a critical perspective or theory of empire as part of the notion of the good life and the good state. The good life and justice are the ends of politics, which is an art, unlike that of the physician or pilot, which some think is able to include domination: "Yet many appear to think that a despotic government is a true political form, and what men affirm to be unjust and inexpedient in their own case they are not ashamed of practising towards others; they demand justice for themselves, but where other men are concerned they care nothing about it."[114] The question for those who would modify justice and make the civil world of humans like the natural world of animals then becomes whether there are masters and subjects (even slaves) in nature. One of the complaints the Declaration of Independence had against the king was that "He has excited domestic insurrection among us, and has endeavored to bring on the inhabitants of our frontiers the merciless Indian savages, whose known rule of warfare is an undistinguished destruction of all ages, sexes, and conditions." Aristotle's theory of natural slavery framed the debate on whether the "savages" (wild men, *sauvages* in French) were human or whether they were barbarous or civilized. As Benjamin Franklin had noted in 1753, white men had imposed their way of life on the Natives, and a large number of White Indians, those of European descent who were captured by Natives, preferred this free-ranging life.[115]

Another aspect of the Declaration of Independence besides relations with the Natives or Indians was the way the document did not address slavery. This, along with the failure to abolish the slave trade in the Constitution of 1787, was an issue that would haunt the United States and would be a source of such conflict that it would be a preoccupation of the Civil War (1861–65) and beyond. One source for African American history cites the following omission from the Declaration of Independence as one of the accusations against George III:

> He has waged cruel war against human nature itself, violating its most sacred rights of life and liberty in the persons of a distant people who never offended him, captivating and carrying them into slavery in another hemisphere, or to incur miserable death in their transportation thither. This piratical warfare, the opprobrium of infidel powers, is the warfare of the Christian king of Great Britain. Determined to keep open a market where men should be bought and sold, he has prostituted his negative for suppressing every legislative attempt to prohibit or restrain this execrable commerce.[116]

A number of the founders of the United States had little fondness for slavery. In 1775, John Adams had proposed a Declaration of Independence and hoped to secure Virginia's allegiance to the revolutionary cause by suggesting that Congress appoint Thomas Jefferson to write a draft. Adams, who served as one of the editors, was a lifelong opponent of slavery. Nonetheless, Adams did not protest when Congress excised Jefferson's condemnation of slavery from the declaration because he, like Jefferson, believed the cause of independence was of paramount importance.[117] Aristotle's theory of natural slavery, which would play a significant role in the debate over the Spanish colonization of the western Atlantic, is more jarring in our world in which slavery is illegal but still practiced.

The legal underpinning of Iberian and Western European expansion is the papal bulls and their successors. Those laws engendered further interpretations, political documents, and reactions—such as the *Code Noir* in France (1688), the Declaration of Independence (1776), and the abolition of the slave trade in Britain and the United States (1808–08). In 1780, largely owing to the work of Quakers, Pennsylvania was the first of the British colonies (soon to be formally a state in the new United States). Between this time and 1800, most British or former British colonies on the mainland of North America had abolished slavery. The wealthy British Caribbean colonies did not. In 1773 alone, Jamaica exported five times the combined exports of the Thirteen Colonies. On February 4, 1794, the Convention of Paris declared the emancipation of slaves without outlawing the trade. Some of the other states who abolished the slave trade were Britain 1807; the United States 1808; Venezuela 1811; New Granada (Columbia—1812); Spain, Portugal, and the Netherlands, 1818.[118] In practice, slavery was harder to root out. The late eighteenth century and the nineteenth century were crucial to the debate on slavery and to the gradual abolition of the institution—the actual holding of slaves and not simply the first step—the slave trade itself. The rhetoric of rights that surrounded the Glorious Revolution of 1688, the American Revolution, and the French Revolution also affected debate on slavery, women, and reform. These rights go back much farther. In the early sixteenth century Las Casas fought against the enslavement of the indigenous peoples in the western Atlantic and later many would fight for rights based on gender, skin color, class, and other issues. The movement from subjection and slavery to liberty is not always linear.

Chapter 6 ∾

Slavery Since the American Revolution

The last quarter of the eighteenth century was crucial in the debate over slavery in the American colonies because when thirteen of the provinces in British America made their break with Britain, their inhabitants and leaders had a debate over what kind of country they would form. Although these colonies were not the only places with slaves or the only places that are discussed here, their role is prominent because of these critical circumstances. The American Revolution, like the French Revolution, declared liberty to be a principal theme. Freedom at this time, unlike that in the period of the English Revolution almost one hundred and fifty years before, was a product of the Enlightenment. The question of universal rights for human beings was being raised and even though questions of class, race, and gender took a long time to resolve in practice (and indeed continue to this day), at least the theory called into question the ascendancy of European males of substantial property. Slavery, then, was part of a wider movement to equal civil and human rights, a change that is still underway.

I

Women's writing about slaves and slavery in the dying years of the American Revolution and in its aftermath suggests some of the complex emotions for the white Americans and the "Negroes" they represent. Some of the letters and diaries tell tales of contesting and conflicting forces within and between these European Americans and in the minds, hearts, and communities of African Americans. The scar of the War of Independence was important in the representation of slaves and slavery. Both the British and the British colonists represented and made use of African slaves in their conflict.

A letter that sets this friction out is that of Eliza Yonge Wilkinson (1757–1813?), writing to a friend named Mary, in 1782 in which she describes a British attack on Charleston, South Carolina. That such discourse from the Revolutionary War remained popular can be seen as Wilkinson's letters were published in New York in 1839. This letter contains a narrative that is revealing in its excoriation of the British for being cruel to Americans and for the sense that justice and liberty, being attributes of heaven, will give the colonists success in the war if they fight in their service. Amid this danger, as the British had been routed, the two sisters had to walk home three miles escorted by two black men who worked in the service of their father and with the fear that some of the British lurked in the woods. African slaves were also drawn into this conflict:

> Two of Father's Negro men attended us, armed with great clubs; one walked on before, the other behind, placing us in the centre. It was not long before our guard had some use for their clubs; we were crossing a place they call the Sands, when one of the enemy's Negroes came out of the woods. He passed our advance guard with nothing but the loss of his smart Jocky cap, which was snatched from his head. He turned round, and muttering something, then proceeded on; when, attempting to pass our rear-guard, he was immediately levelled to the earth; he arose, and attempted to run off, when he received another blow, which again brought him down. I could not bear the sight of the poor wretch's blood, which washed his face and neck; it affected me sensibly.[1]

A violent clash between Africans also seems to be occurring while the British and their rebellious colonists are at war. On a personal level, Eliza Wilkinson could not bear to see the violence. The sight of blood bothered her. One African loyal to her family and the American cause had leveled another who served the British. This scene shows the greater conflict on a local and quotidian level:

> "Enough, Joe! enough," cried I; "don't use the creature ill, take him at once, I wont have him beaten so." "Let me alone, Mistress, I'll not lay hand on him till I have stunned him; how do I know but he has a knife, or some such thing under his clothes, and when I go up to him, he may stab me. No, no,—I know Negroes' ways too well." With that he fetched him another blow. I was out of all patience; I could not help shedding tears.[2]

The violence between Negroes reduces Eliza Wilkinson to tears. She and the Anglo-American culture in conflict and their use of the institution of slavery are partly responsible for this violent situation. This inhumanity is something in which they and she find themselves trapped:

> I called out again; "Inhuman wretch, take the Negro at once, he cannot hurt you now if he would; you shall not—I declare you shall not beat him so." With that he took him, tied his hands behind him, and gave him to the fellow

who went before; he himself stayed behind with us; but the poor wretch was sadly frightened. The fellow who had him in custody, walked on very fast, but he kept looking back on us.[3]

Eliza is able to help stop the violence, but its terror remains with the beaten black man. She has to mediate between those African Americans who are protecting her and this man whom she protects:

> At last he said to me, "Do, Mistress, let me walk by you." "Don't be afraid," said I, "they shan't hurt you again, I wont let them." But he looked on me so pitifully—his head continually turning round towards me, with such terror in his countenance, that I felt for the poor creature, and, to make him easy, walked, or rather ran, close behind him; for, to keep up with them I was obliged to go in a half run, the fellow who had hold of him walking at a great rate, for fear of being overtaken by the enemy.[4]

To protect this beaten man, Eliza had to run in the heat. He feared the men of his own background while Eliza and her party were afraid that the British would come upon them. This situation encapsulated some of the conflicts and contests of the war but at the level of personal experience:

> I was ready to faint; the exercise and extreme heat of the sun overcame me; but I would not quit the unhappy wretch as he claimed my protection, and my presence seemed some alleviation to his misery; so on I went, scarce able to support myself. I had got on a great way ahead of my sister and Miss Samuells, when I heard a confused noise, which, echoing in the woods, sounded like lamentations; my heart was at my mouth. "I'm afraid we are pursued," cried I; "I think I hear my sister and Miss Samuells crying!" The noise increased; I made a stop, and was ready to sink to the earth: the Negro, who had the prisoner in custody, heard what I said, and hearing the noise also, took it for granted that we were pursued, quitted his charge, and was making off.[5]

The pledge Eliza shows to a stranger, she white and he black, and the restraint she ensures to the black men who protect her, make for a complex situation well beyond any abstract stereotypes or ideology might lead people to expect. In some sense everyone is afraid of being pursued. The black prisoner, who was under Eliza's protection, seems to have feared this pursuit more than anyone else. Eliza expresses her concern, which takes her motives beyond the protection she provided to her survival and that of her family:

> I was then some distance behind, for not a step could I take after the stop I made; when looking, I saw the prisoner standing alone in the path, watching the road very sharply, as if expecting a speedy deliverance. I then found my tongue; for, thought I, if the enemy should find the Negro in such a bloody condition, they would use us very ill.[6]

In Eliza's concern we can see that the British would not tolerate violence against their black ally, so that the situation becomes more intricate still. Eliza does not want to see the black prisoner get loose:

> I called out as loud as I was able to the absconding fellow—"Stop, this moment, and take that Negro; make all the haste you can with him home, and keep him out of the way; remember, your life may be concerned in this matter, so take care." The mention of his life was enough; he grasped the prisoner's arm, and off he ran at such a rate, that they were both out of sight in a minute or two. In the mean time I stood trembling in the road, thinking it useless to attempt getting out of the way, for, so weak was I with the long walk (or rather run), that I could not have gone any distance in the wood if I had ever such an inclination so to do.[7]

The compassion, physical endurance, survival instinct, and political grasp coexist in this narrative in this letter of 1782. This document is obviously from one person's point of view and might have characterized herself and her actions in the best possible light, but the account shows the tensions between the British and the Americans and the violence that involved African Americans. This tension between the black men heightens:

> So, thought I, I may as well die here as anywhere else; but, upon my sister's coming up to me, I found the noise proceeded from the Negroes with the baggage, who were quarrelling about carrying it. When they heard, and indeed saw how I was frightened, (for they told me I looked as pale as death,) said Joe, "Do you think if it was so, I'd hab staid behind so long? Not I! Soon as ever I found how it was, I'd hab come out before, and that Negro should never hab told what *hurted* him. I'd have finished him, and got him out of the way; better for him to die, than all of us die for him."[8]

Eliza's fear comes out here, but the dramatic dialogue that the story of survival underpins is enlivened. The voice of Joe shows a loyalty to his own group and an unwillingness, despite what his mistress might partly have set up by feeling compassion for the prisoner, to let this other black man jeopardize their survival. Eliza has realized that the British should not find this bloodied man or they would have their revenge on her people, but Joe is willing to do the violence necessary to make sure this does not happen. In the people, even as they appear in some sense as characters, the drama of race and gender, of compassion and mistrust, of the verge of death and the turn of survival all come together. They all—it seems the prisoner, too—made it safely to Eliza's father's. Eliza mentions the words "fears" and "frightened" in describing the days that followed, but the only horsemen that made it to her father's house were "Major Moore, with three of his men" and "He staid and dined with us, spent a part of the afternoon, and returned to camp."[9] This is the same Major Moore, much earlier in this long letter, who is reported to have said the following: "For my part," continued he, "I would rather explore unknown regions, blessed with liberty, than remain in my native country if to be cursed with slavery."[10] Live free or die was a good stance for British Americans defending their homeland against what they saw as British tyranny and enslavement, but the lot of African American slaves is not something that he, or the letter at large, appears to consider.

Eliza Wilkinson herself had earlier responded in her letter to this captain's words on liberty. Her point of view concerned questions of gender:

> Pardon this digression, my dear Mary—my pen is inspired with sympathetic ardor, and has run away with my thoughts before I was aware. I do not love to meddle with political matters; the men say we have no business with them, it is not in our sphere! and Homer (did you ever read Homer, child?) gives us two or three broad hints to mind our domestic concerns, spinning, weaving, &c. and leave affairs of higher nature to the men; but I must beg his pardon—I won't have it thought, that because we are the weaker sex as to *bodily* strength, my dear, we are capable of nothing more than minding the dairy, visiting the poultry-house, and all such domestic concerns; our thoughts can soar aloft, we can form conceptions of things of higher nature; and have as just a sense of honor, glory, and great actions, as these "Lords of the Creation."[11]

That Wilkinson has read Homer and can criticize the notions of women in male authors before she gives an account of this violent three-mile walk and run provides a context that does not accept European men as those who define politics and the values in life generally. She is sarcastic about these lords who create stereotypes;

> What contemptible *earth worms* these authors make us! They won't even allow us the liberty of thought, and that is all I want. I would not wish that we should meddle in what is unbecoming female delicacy, but surely we may have sense enough to give our opinions to commend or discommend such actions as we may approve or disapprove; without being reminded of our spinning and household affairs as the only matters we are capable of thinking or speaking of with justness or propriety. I won't allow it, positively won't. Homer has a deal of morality in his works, which is worthy of imitation; his Odyssey abounds with it. But I will leave Homer to better judges, and proceed in my narration.[12]

The narrative Eliza will set out is one of female presence of mind, compassion, and courage in action. Her story is something that, while taking Homer into account, is one that is about female virtue beyond the domestic sphere and something that a woman has written and not spun delicately in a household. Her odyssey has its own sense of adventure in a dangerous world. Women can be fully human and are not earthworms. The humanity of slaves is implicit in the account that follows, but Eliza Wilkinson does not consider African slavery explicitly.

The terror had subsided at the end of the narrative but questions remain. Not once did the Africans on both sides of the British–American divide seem to consider in this incident that is described that they should join together to escape or to inflict violence on the white women or their family and friends. Nor does Eliza give a sense whether the British had freed this prisoner in return for his loyalty to their cause as this was a practice. Slavery and freedom play out in spoken and unspoken ways. After the revolution and after Eliza's death in about 1813, or even in 1839, when the book was printed in New York, the controversy over slavery continued. Independence was not enough for slaves.

At the end of the peace that capped off the American Revolution, on December 26, 1783, Abigail Adams wrote to her son, John Quincy Adams, counseling him in the ways of liberty and the lessons of the recent war with Britain. She did not address the enslavement of Africans but the notion of liberty:

> Let your observations and comparisons produce in your mind an abhorrence of domination and power, the parent of slavery, ignorance, and barbarism, which places man upon a level with his fellow tenants of the woods;
>
> "A day, an hour, of virtuous liberty
> Is worth a whole eternity of bondage."[13]

Slavery is a fellow of barbarism and ignorance, all of which power and domination engender. A moment of freedom is worth eternal enslavement, but if liberty is so precious, then, by implication, it would also be for African Americans, who are not mentioned here.

Until the end of the eighteenth century, American women mention slaves and slavery. For instance, in July, 1787, Patience Greene Brayton, a Quaker, was able to feel empathy for African slaves and to express it in her diary: "After seven or eight days contrary winds, and feeling poorly, the wind came fair, and we all began to grow better, but I felt low in spirit; Lord, make me contented, and sweeten every bitter cup, for what are my sufferings, accommodated as we are on ship board, compared with those of the poor Africans in their transportation to slavery."[14] A journey from the United States to England is not nearly as painful as what a slave would experience in - transport. In a diary entry of January 30, 1794, Elizabeth Sandwith Drinker (1735–1807), another Quaker, mentions "a memorial on the subject of the Slave-trade."[15] On Sunday May 29, 1796, Charlotte Sheldon (1780–ca. 1840) noted in her diary: "Attended meeting all day, heard two very indifferent sermons, read in the American Magazine found many good things in it & among the rest an extract from Mrs. Yearsley's poem on the slave trade, took a walk down to the brook it was too cool to be very agreeable walking finished my gown in the evening."[16] A published poem by a woman on the slave trade is at the center of Sheldon's description of the Sabbath. Slavery is still a subject in this newly liberated America. Still, that independence was a topic for women at this time. Isabella Marshall Graham writes a letter on the birthday of the independence of the United States (July 4, 1797) in which she describes the scene: "Waked this morning by the ringing of bells, beating of drums, firing of cannon, to usher in the anniversary of the glorious independence of America! The day in which she dared to be free, dared to say we will no longer be the tame, abject slave, of British tyranny. Liberty or death will be our motto."[17] Whereas some American women showed an awareness of the slavery of African Americans, others did not.

Elizabeth Drinker, in another entry (this one of July 22, 1799), wrestles a little with the selling of slaves, even if she denies that wrestling:

> Black Judy was here today. She is now about 52 or 53 years old. My sister and self sold her when 9 years old into the country. We did not think we were doing wrong, for we did not know what to do with her, as our parents were dead, and we were going to board out. We loved the child, and after a few weeks' consideration took a ride to her mistress's habitation, and offered her 40 pounds for ye child; they gave us 25, promising to use her very kindly. She said that she would not part with her for 100 pounds—she thought Providence had directed her to the child, and she meant to treat her with great kindness—we came away disappointed. She was afterwards sold again, but has been many years free, and her children are free when of age. We had formerly some uneasy hours on her account, tho' nothing to accuse ourselves of as a crime at that time, except parting with a little child that we loved, to be a slave, as we feared, for life.[18]

Once more, the role of kindness plays a part in the relation between white and black Americans. Providence is invoked, so that religious interpretations of slavery can differ over time. This entry also emphasizes the possibility of being a free black and Elizabeth and her sister being worried that a child will be caught in slavery for life. The issue of slaves was one of the strands in the letters and diaries of American women during the American Revolution and the years that followed. Quaker women contributed to the consideration and abolition of slavery in the American colonies and then the United States. In 1671 in England, the founder of the Society of Friends (Quakers), George Fox expressed opposition to slavery and, as early as 1696, Quakers in the American colonies began to work for abolition.[19]

II

The influence of the Quakers was one of the keys to the abolitionist movement in Britain and the American Colonies (later the United States). In 1780 Pennsylvania led the way with the abolition of the slave trade—if not the holding of slaves. An ambivalence over slavery or even a strong division among people over the institution occurred in British North America and especially in places where the Quakers were influential. As the first president of the Pennsylvania Society for Promoting the Abolition of Slavery, Benjamin Franklin was cautious—in 1789—about the abolition of slavery causing problems because of the debased nature of the institution: "Slavery is such an atrocious debasement of human nature, that its very extirpation, if not performed with solicitous care, may sometimes open a source of serious evils."[20] A certain caution prevailed even in the one of the greatest opponents of slavery among the founding fathers of the United States. Franklin and his fellow framers of the United States would have slavery before them and would not be able to abolish it from the new country.

Even at this time of revolution, the English then British Americans–turned Americans lived with the legacy of Spain in framing the expansion to and colonization of the New World. This inheritance also included slavery. As Jeremy Belknap declared in 1792, as part of the celebration of the three hundredth anniversary of Columbus's "discovery" of America, "It is not pretended that Columbus was the only person of his age who had acquired these ideas of the form, dimensions and balancing of the globe; but he was one of the few who had begun to think for themselves, and he had a genius of that kind, which makes use of speculation and reasoning only as excitements to action."[21] As was usual in the discourses in Dutch, French, and English about the New World, the author separated Columbus from Spain. For Belknap, that country did not measure up to Columbus, who inaugurated the settlement of America, to which the English Puritans had brought liberty from persecution and which their liberty-loving descendents had improved on with their revolutionary war against England. The Spanish were part of the Black Legend and "the first introduction of the negro slavery into America was occasioned by the previous destruction of the native inhabitants of the West-India islands, by the cruelty of their Spanish conquerors, in exacting of them more labour than they were able to perform"; contrary to the usual canonizing of Bartolomé de Las Casas in this Black Legend, Belknap's view blamed him in part for being responsible for one of the horrors of the European expansion into the New World: "The most remarkable and unaccountable circumstance attending the beginning of this traffic, is, that it was recommended by a Spanish Bishop, one of the most benevolent friends of the Indians, whom he could not bear to see so wantonly destroyed by his countrymen."[22] Belknap was making Columbus a precursor to English Puritans who were precursors to American patriots: this was New England radical Columbus. He was invoked to bolster the identity of America and its liberty in the wake of its War of Independence.

The tensions between regions and interests made matters more complicated in this new United States. While states in the union could abolish slavery, the federal state did not: the Constitution of the United States of 1787 delayed a discussion of the slave trade for the country for twenty years. In the arts as well as in politics, slavery was an issue—the tensions between justification and abolition expressing themselves in painting as well as in literature. In 1788, George Morland exhibited a painting at the Royal Academy in London. Now lost, it is still known from copies. This work represented slave traders on the coast of Africa—it was one instance of art contributing to the debate over, or representation of, slaves and slaving.[23] In a double movement, slavery and antislavery coexisted. Opposition had its eminent advocates: William Pitt and William Wilberforce were among important British leaders who opposed slavery. In 1791, the National Assembly of France condemned slavery, but more in principle than in practice. In 1792, Denmark abolished the slave trade. Still, at this time, the importation of slaves to places like Jamaica and Cuba was thriving. At the turn of, and in the early years of, the nineteenth century the British economy relied heavily on cotton and sugar that slaves produced. Portugal also depended much for prosperity on slavery in colonies like Brazil. This reliance was strong enough that C. R. Boxer began his study of the "golden age" of Brazil—1695–1750—by focusing on "the interdependence of Brazil and the slave markets of West Africa."[24] In religion, politics, the arts, and economics, slavery played a public role.

III

In the more personal realm of diaries and autobiography, as we have seen, the question of slavery is a recurrent topic as more of this kind of writing came to be practiced. A key autobiography was Olaudah Equiano's *The Life of Olaudah Equiano, or Gustavus Vassa, the African* (1789; rpt. 1814).[25] In the Dedication of 1792, Equiano (ca.1745–ca.97) addressed the House of Lords and the House of Commons: he described its "chief design" as "to excite in august assemblies a sense of compassion for the miseries which the Slave-Trade has entailed on my unfortunate countrymen. By the horrors of that trade was I first torn away from all the tender connections that were naturally dear to my heart."[26] Despite the misery of the institution of slavery and his own experience of enslavement and transport, Equiano also stressed how fortunate he was to be introduced "to the knowledge of the Christian religion, and of a nation which, by its liberal sentiments, its humanity, the glorious freedom of its government, and its proficiency in arts and sciences, has exalted the dignity of human nature."[27] He was presenting his book amidst the debate on abolition in the legislature. The Preface to the edition of 1814 mentioned that the subscription list included the heir to the British throne, his two brothers (princes), the duke of Marlborough, and other illustrious people in Britain and noted that Equiano would have been gratified "had he lived to peruse the Bill for the Abolition of the Slave-trade," which was passed in March 1807.[28] Equiano had been given various names— Olaudah by his parents—and in slavery, names like Jacob, Michael, and, Gustavus Vassa, which Michael Henry Pascal, one of his masters, insisted on calling him.[29] In a letter to the queen of Britain, he signed himself by that name, beneath which is the epithet, "The Oppressed Ethopian."[30] Amidst his courtly language, Vassa (Equiano) could be direct with the queen: "I supplicate your Majesty's compassion for millions of my African countrymen, who groan under the lash of tyranny in the West-Indies."[31] Vassa added that "The oppression and cruelty exercised to the unhappy negroes there, have at length reached the British legislature," which is deliberating on redress, and noted that even some slaveowners in the West Indies were asking for the abolition of slavery because it was inhumane. Vassa's plea to the queen on behalf of Africans in the Caribbean is not unlike that Las Casas addressed to the Spanish monarchy in defense of Natives in the West Indies more than two centuries before. Vassa spoke of the "wretched Africans" and appealed to the queen's benevolence, bounty, and compassion to put a time limit on the misery of slavery, so that the Africans "may be raised from the condition of brutes, to which they are at present degraded, to the rights and situation of freemen, and admitted to partake of the blessings of your Majesty's happy government."[32] This act would contribute to "the happiness of millions" and "the grateful prayers of themselves and their posterity": Vassa also prayed for the queen and her family that "the All-bountiful Creator" give them the blessings of this world and the joy of the next.[33]

The body of the narrative, which Equiano/Vassa—the title page gives both names—seems to have worked on in new editions, represented a variety of experiences from the customs of Equiano's homeland in Africa (he was an Igbo prince from what is now eastern Nigeria) through kidnapping and slavery under various masters in Africa, England, and the West Indies to manumission and freedom, all the while involving journeys overland and, even more, by sea. Although there are some parallels with Aphra Behn's narrative about Oroonoko, Equiano's account, though representing some grim actions, shows much more hope than Behn's. A technique similar to Montaigne, Léry, Swift, and others that Equiano uses is typology. Equiano's irony and satire can range from the gentle Horatian mode to the savage

Juvenalian turn, but he is usually generous to others and understates even his denunciation of European cruelty. He does not belabor the point or dwell on detail. For instance, very near the beginning, he is modest about whether the memoirs of an obscure stranger who was neither saint nor hero nor tyrant would be worthy of the kind of public attention that the publication of his memoirs might warrant but, in taking this stance, creates his own interesting turn that unsettles the relation between Africa and Europe, author and reader: "I believe that there are a few events in my life which have not happened to many. It is true the incidents of it are numerous; and did I consider myself an European, I might say my sufferings were great: but when I compare my lot with that of most of my countrymen, I regard myself as a *particular favourite of Heaven*, and acknowledge the mercies of Providence in every occurrence of my life."[34] These statements can be taken at face value as his life was much harder than most Western Europeans who would never be slaves and much harder than many slaves, who would never know freedom. At another level, he turned this fact on the reader who would see how unusual his case had been and should see the plight of the slaves for whom he was advocating because of the even larger gap between their lives and his. Moreover, the brethren of those European readers would be the ones most often responsible for cruel actions and practices. Like Las Casas, Equiano exposed the cruelty of Europeans, the one mainly of Spaniards and the other principally of the British.

The word "cruelty" and its cognates run throughout the book. Equiano's memoir or autobiography is imbued with slavery even before he is taken from his home and sold as a slave: "My father, besides many slaves, had a numerous family, of which seven lived to grow up, including myself and a sister, who was the only daughter."[35] Equiano and his sister, whose father had slaves, are twice separated once they are taken into slavery and never see each other again.[36] The inhumanity of this kidnapping and of how slavery unnaturally cut the bonds within families generally and between siblings in particular is something that the narrative stressed. If Equiano had given any thought to the situation of the slaves his family kept, he did not say. Only after his own kidnapping did he begin to empathize with the other slaves about him as well as feel for the situation that he and his sister found themselves in. According to Equiano, the problems of being a slave in Africa paled by comparison to being one shipped across the Atlantic. Equiano used words like "terror" and "horror" to describe his being handed over to Europeans.[37] Black people handed him over to these people who he thought were going to eat him—something he repeated—and he saw a multitude of Africans in chains. Equiano asked the black people about him whether "we were not to be eaten by those white men with horrible looks, red faces, and long hair."[38] Despite how horrific these white people looked, black people had kidnapped him and had turned him over to the Europeans: "Soon after this the blacks who brought me on board went off, and left me abandoned to despair."[39] His circumstances seemed even worse than those before: "I even wished for my former slavery, in preference to my present situation, which was filled with horrors of every kind, still heightened by my ignorance of what I was to undergo."[40] This slave trade—which used chains and brutality—was more cruel than any Equiano had experienced.

The theme of cruelty persisted in Equiano's narrative. He gave one of the reasons for his despair that was based in a meanness that included but also exceeded the matter of race: "But still I feared I should be put to death, the white people looked and acted, as I thought, in so savage a manner; for I had never seen among any people such instances of brutal cruelty: and this is not only shewn towards us blacks, but also to some of the whites themselves."[41] Equiano then proceeded to supply an example to illustrate this point: "One white man in particular I saw, when we were permitted to be on deck, flogged so unmercifully with a large rope near the foremast, that he died in consequence of it; and they tossed him over the side as they would have done a brute."[42] After exposing the terrible conditions on the ship, Equiano did not fail to amplify his theme of white cruelty: "Every circumstance I met with served only to render my state more painful, and heighten my apprehensions and my opinion of the cruelty of the whites."[43] Another example contributed to the cumulative effect of this horrific drama of cruelty, which, although less hyperbolic and more rooted in personal experience than that of Las Casas, contributed to the critique of European abuses. Two slaves in chains decided to jump overboard to commit suicide in their own version of live free or die. Another attempted suicide but did not die. The crew sent out a boat to try to rescue the three because they did not want this action to serve as a precedent and to urge a mass suicide: "two of the wretches were drowned; but they got the other, and afterward flogged him unmercifully, for thus attempting to prefer death to slavery."[44] The poor soul could not achieve what the other two had done, so he was punished for his attempt.

Balance also characterizes Equiano's narrative. In spite of these abuses by whites, he did not advocate revenge or stereotype Europeans. For instance, Equiano told of his friendship to Richard Baker, an amiable and well-educated American about the same age who became good friends with the young African and who was a "companion and instructor" to him over two years: "Although this dear youth had many slaves of his own, yet he and I have gone through many sufferings together on shipboard; and have many nights lain in each other's bosoms, when in great distress."[45] The death of Baker is noted in two places in Equiano's account.[46]

Equiano, although obscure in his modesty, said he met General James Wolfe on board a ship sailing to help in the attack on Louisbourg in Cape

Breton.[47] The question of nationality and religion came up: Equiano described himself as "almost an Englishman" and talked about his baptism.[48] Sometimes Equiano does sound like Gulliver describing the Europeans, and especially the English, as vermin: "I have often reflected with surprise that I never felt half the alarm, at any of the numerous dangers in which I have been, that I was filled with at the first sight of the Europeans, and at every act of theirs, even the most trifling, when I first came among them, and for some time afterwards."[49] This last phrase might, to some extent, apply long afterward as some Englishmen, including a former master, continue to brush him off or treat him badly. Even at the conclusion of his narrative Equiano continued to press for the end of the cruel practice of slavery in which the British were still engaged. Even as Equiano quoted Homer and spoke of "dreams of freedom," he could not control his fate: his life depended on the whims or judgment of his masters.[50] At one point, Equiano's master, Mr. King, was criticized for feeding his slaves well (at least in comparison to others) and he gave his slave scope, so Equiano was able to observe much: "When I was thus employed by my master, I was often a witness to cruelties of every kind, which were exercised on my unhappy fellow slaves."[51] One such instance shows the unequal treatment of whites and blacks: the injustice over sexual relations. Equiano was unable to offer protection when he was sailing with "cargoes of new Negroes in his care for sale" to prevent the clerks and other whites from committing "violent depredations on the chastity of the female slaves," some of whom were not yet ten years old.[52] Although one captain discharged a mate and others for this kind of brutal offence, other white authorities were less enlightened:

> in Monserrat I have seen a Negro-man staked to the ground, and cut most shockingly, and then his ears cut off, bit by bit, because he had been connected with a white woman, who was a common prostitute! As if it were no crime in the whites to rob an innocent African girl of her virtue; but most heinous in a black man only to gratify a passion of nature, where the temptation was offered by one of a different color, though the most abandoned woman of her species.[53]

Equiano set out many other instances of cruelty and abuse: he asked one man who had sold 41,000 black slaves how he as a Christian could cut off a man's leg for running away from slavery and reminded him that Christian doctrine instructed "'to do unto others as we would that others should do unto us.' "[54] The overseers, according to Equiano, were often tyrants and a problem caused by humane gentlemen acting as absentee landlords and he then named some humane masters in the West Indies. None the less, Equiano did not shrink from lamenting the brutal system that works and abuses slaves to death, so much so that tens of thousands are needed annually in places like Barbadoes to replace them.[55] Slavery was a matter of torture and sadism.

Equiano used the topos of inexpressibility and showed restraint when describing the instruments: "The iron muzzle, thumb-screws, & c. are so well known as not to need a description, and were sometimes applied for the slightest faults."[56] This tyranny, exercised by white men who espoused principles of liberty, was something that clearly offended Equiano.

He had a gift for dramatizing or seeing the drama in the scenes from life that he witnessed: "I have seen a negro beaten till some of his bones were broken, for only letting a pot boil over. It is not uncommon, after a flogging, to make slaves go on their knees and thank their owners, and pray, or rather say, 'God bless you.' "[57] This irrational rage and this indignity suggest that something more was simmering beneath the surface for these white tyrants. Equiano also criticized the West India code, which allowed a French planter to work his mulatto children in the field as slaves, which prompted the author to ask: "Pray, reader, are these sons and daughters of the French planter less his children by being begotten on black women?"[58] Appealing to poetry once more, Equiano quotes and adapts Beelzebub's defiant speech in hell in Book 2 of John Milton's *Paradise Lost*, altering the first line quoted a little from "for what peace will be giv'n" to "No peace is given" then keeping as is "To us enslav'd, but custody severe, / And stripes, and arbitrary punishment/ Inflicted?"— except that he places a dash where there was a question mark.[59] Either way, the main thrust is the situation of enslaved beings, perhaps both suffering hell, and seeking a way out. Closer and more precise comparisons might well complicate the analogy between slaves and fallen angels.

The moral Equiano pointed was to the reader and the British and Europeans more generally: "by changing your conduct, and treating your slaves as men, every cause of fear would be banished."[60] As with Las Casas, with Equiano repetition and repeating expressions that repeat by denying they are doing so play a part in the building up of a case against cruelty: "IN THE preceding chapter I have set before the reader a few of those many instances of oppression, extortion, and cruelty, to which I have been a witness in the West-Indies; but were I to enumerate them all, the catalogue would be tedious and disgusting."[61] He also describes a marriage between a white man and a black woman that has to take place on the water to circumvent the local laws and how a free black man was wrenched from his family illegally by those who would enslave him.[62] The danger of teaching Equiano navigation and the possibility of manumission (as the result of his master being a fair man), the physical cruelty inflicted on the author by Doctor Perkins of Georgia, and the achievement of freedom were other topics raised in this narrative.[63]

Equiano was forgiving to those who had not treated him well: buying his freedom, he wanted to "see Old England once more, and surprise my old master, Captain Pascal, who was hourly in my mind; for I still loved him, notwithstanding his usage of me."[64] After his friend, another captain, died,

Equiano was able to make 300 percent on trading some turkeys.[65] Equiano also emphasized once more "that throughout the West Indies no black man's testimony is admitted, on any occasion, against any white person whatever."[66] When Equiano did get back to London, from whence Pascal had sold him, he found just how disappointing and unfair his former master was.[67]

The sea was the way Equiano best earned his living, so he traveled to many places and this allowed him to make cultural comparisons. In Smyrna in Turkey, for example, "The natives are good-looking and strong made, and always treated me with great civility. In general, I believe, they are fond of black people; and several of them gave me pressing invitations to stay amongst them, although they keep the Franks, or Christians, separate, and do not suffer them to dwell immediately amongst them."[68] There were levels of exclusion—here religion and elsewhere race. The Turks would exclude Equiano and his British friends, although he suggested that they were well deposed to Africans, but he also had to deal with the Inquisition. Galley-slaves were one of the casualties of the conflicts in the Mediterranean world. At Spring Bath in Kingston, Jamaica, "each different nation of Africa meets and dances after the manner of their own country."[69]

Another strand of Equiano's story is his commitment to Christianity, so that part of his account from youth is a conversion narrative.[70] Father Vincent, a Catholic priest, promised him a free university education, so that "if I got myself a priest, I might in time become even Pope; and that Pope Benedict was a black man."[71] Soon Equiano, a convert who was involved in the work of conversion, was reading Foxe's *Martyrology* with a Musquito or Indian prince, who asked about its depiction of "Papal cruelties."[72] In this journey to the Caribbean, Equiano was much involved with the Natives but he did not forget the African slaves there: "All my poor countrymen, the slaves, when they heard of my leaving them, they were very sorry, as I had always treated them with care and affection, and did everything I could to comfort the poor creatures, and render their condition easy."[73] Because he was black, Equiano himself had a hard time collecting his wages in Jamaica even with the help of Dr. Irving.[74]

Back in England, Equiano noted three mulatto boys with fair hair, practiced Anglicanism, and became involved with mission work.[75] So often traveling the seas, Equiano commented on the Quakers during a trip to Philadelphia: "my pleasure was much increased in seeing the worthy Quakers, freeing and easing the burthens of many of my oppressed African brethren. It rejoiced my heart when one of these friendly people took me to see a free-school they had erected for every denomination of black people, whose minds are cultivated here, and forwarded to virtue; and thus they are made useful members of the community."[76] This was one of the Christian examples that impressed Equiano.

When he returned to London, he was involved with an ill-fated mission to transport poor blacks to Africa. He was philosophical about its failure to live up to expectations: "Thus ended my part of the long-talked-of expedition to Sierra Leona; an expedition, which, however unfortunate in the event, was humane and politic in its design; nor was its failure owing to government; every thing was done on their part; but there was evidently sufficient misman-agement, attending the conduct and execution of it, to defeat its success."[77] In concluding the body of his narrative, Equiano presented a petition on behalf of Africans to the queen on March 21, 1788; he also declared: "May Heaven make the British senators the dispersers of light, liberty, and science, to the uttermost parts of the earth!"[78] In referring to "British Senators," Equiano implied a translation of empire. He also set up a comparison between the trans-formation of the British economy from its aboriginal state to the present with the future change to Africa, which could be a market for British manufactures. He saw a "beautiful contrast" between trade in "articles of export" as opposed to "the cargo of a slave ship."[79] Except manufacturers of the means that people use to torture and punish slaves, everyone else would benefit: "The manufac-turing interest and the general interests are synonymous. The abolition of slav-ery would be in reality an universal good."[80] Through repetition, Equiano made his point more forcefully: "Tortures, murder, and every other imaginable barbarity and iniquity, are practiced upon the poor slaves with impunity. I hope the slave trade will be abolished."[81] If anything, Africa is even vaster than Europe, so will provide an even greater economic prospect.

The end of the narrative expressed indignation over the slave trade, recorded that Equiano listened to the debate on slavery in the House of Commons on April 2 and 3 and then went to Soham in Cambridgeshire, where on April 7, he married Miss Cullen, daughter of James and Ann of Ely. There is an element of romance to this long, hard journey of Equiano from a child kidnapped into slavery in Africa through a slave transported to the New World on a terrible slave ship to a free man married north of London. Equiano made a distinction between those who were show Christians and those who embodied its teachings, so he did not seem to oppose his new religion to the abolition of slavery or his African roots. In leaving off with the reader, the author asked: "what makes any event important, unless by its observation we become better and wiser, and to learn to do justly, to love mercy, and to walk humbly before God?"[82] Moral instruction as well as the travels and journey of the hero combined to give this narrative power and interest.

IV

The nineteenth century until the end of the American Civil War represented the denouement of legality of the institution of slavery in many parts of the world. A certain interconnectedness of economies and of the wealth that slavery generated connected various regions. As Britain sought new markets in Latin America, the West Indies, Africa, and Asia, its trade more than doubled between 1794 and 1816. As it had supported sugar, slavery under-pinned cotton, which was now Britain's largest industry. Sugar and cotton helped to tie the United States and the West Indian colonies to the British economic sphere.[83] Slavery was, then, an underpinning of this imperial and colonial regime.

France, the United States, and Britain were not always in step on the insti-tution of slavery. Napoleon revived slavery. Thomas Jefferson signed a bill in favor of the abolition of slavery on March 2, 1807. The House of Commons and House of Lords also abolished slavery in 1807. A modest illegal slave trade occurred in the United States over the next 50 years or so. The British sometimes supplied, invested in, or sailed in ships of nations that had not abolished slavery. In 1811, Parliament made slaving a felony with a penalty of fourteen years in an Australian penal colony, and the Royal Navy began to police the waters off western Africa.

Law, ideology, and naval power were important aspects of the context of slavery. William Blackstone's commentaries on natural law, an ancient subject in legal study and practice, were important in the period. Even though natural law was never adopted explicitly, it did qualify the civil law and law of nations, for instance, in making legal rules more humane as in the evolution of the juridical standing of slavery.[84] The question of slaves also entered into the debate of the French philosophers and other figures of the Enlightenment. An interesting figure in this regard is Antoine Destutt de Tracy (1754–1836), a pioneer in discussions of ideology, because he connects the French thinker Montesquieu with Thomas Jefferson and because he partly does so through a discussion of slavery. De Tracy wrote a commentary on Montesquieu, and Thomas Jefferson published his translation of de Tracy's work in Philadelphia in 1811. Jefferson wrote de Tracy from Monticello on January 26, 1811, discussing his translation. Here, Jefferson praised Montesquieu but de Tracy the more for his commentary because the author whom he was commenting on needed correction because Montesquieu's work was "so much of paradox, of false principle, & misap-plied fact, as to render it's value equivocal on the whole."[85] So even in the case of a book that mocked slavery, de Tracy and Jefferson could find some fault. About nine years later, M. de Bovis expatiated on the spirit of the laws in the French colonies in the Caribbean and appealed to the *Code Noir* of 1685 to argue that slavery did not exist there "as it existed or exists in other countries, in an arbitrary law, or of life and of death, over the individuals who are in this slavery."[86] In terms of ideology—as at an economic, political, and legal level—slavery engendered debate and controversy.

The debates over liberty, democracy, and slavery continued after the American and French Revolutions and into the Napoleonic wars. For instance, in March 1812, the Cortes of Cadiz promulgated a constitution. It was based on universal suffrage for men, a responsible executive and a representative legislature. After the defeat of the French, who had occupied much of Spain at this time of promulgation, Ferdinand VII returned in March 1814. By declaring null and void all the acts of the Cortes and abolishing the Constitution, he restored absolutism. After revolts, on March 6, 1820 the king agreed to call the Cortes. The next day he restored the Constitution. In this period, Jeremy Bentham wrote "Rid Yourselves of Ultramaria, "which appealed to Spaniards to rid itself of its empire and grant independence to the colonies because they were a threat to the progressive government now in effect in Spain itself.[87] Moreover, Bentham called on Spaniards to be an example to Britain and the world: "More than forty years have elapsed since the men of the Anglo-American United States shook off the yoke of our Kings: the yoke—the fouler yoke of—our lawyers, is even hugged by them, and remains still upon their necks. Ridding yourselves of this Nightmare, what a lesson will you thus read to England!"[88] By divesting itself of its empire, Spain would be the greatest and highest example in the world as regards to slavery. It would be above what Bentham liked to call "the Anglo-American United States," a country he clearly admired as a leader in liberty: "In the endeavour to stop the traffic, they were, it is true, the first. Yet still has the poison maintained possession of their veins."[89] For Bentham, the shedding of empire would bring economic, political, and moral benefits as much for Britain or any other European empire as for Spain. Britain was on the threshold of being the dominant world power for a hundred years despite not having rid itself and its colonies entirely of the scourge of slavery. Nevertheless, slaves had impact in the world economy.

The practice of the slave trade persisted among the French, Spanish, and Portuguese merchants. In Africa itself blacks and Arabs continued in this commerce. Without the British, slavery continued in Africa. The Americans and African slave-traders, Europeans, Muslims, and others, plied their trade. In 1824, when the king of Ashanti died, about a thousand of his slaves were sacrificed. By 1810, the only places in the Spanish Empire to use black African slaves in great numbers were the territories that are today Cuba and Venezuela. They did so to maintain their sugar and cocoa plantations respectively. Cuba and Brazil had large populations of free blacks owing to a lenient view of manumission. Although part of the Spanish Empire, many Latin American colonies had become part of the informal British Empire. To encourage trade with Britain and to have its protection, many of these colonies relied less and less on slavery. Simon Bolívar, who freed his own slaves, considered the abolition of slavery to be a key to the independence of

Spain's colonies in America. Tensions over the commerce and administration of the colonies existed between the *criollos* (Spaniards born in America) and the *peninsulares*, some of whom were in the slave trade. The British government and abolitionists, like William Wilberforce, began to pressure Spain, Portugal, France, and Russia to abolish slavery in their empires. Moreover, the British foreign minister, Castlereagh prevailed upon the governments of Russia, Austria, Prussia, Sweden, Portugal, Spain, France, and Britain to sign a declaration that the African slave trade was "repugnant to the principles of humanity and universal morality" and those powers with colonies promised to abolish this trade as soon as possible.[90] Not since the early days of the Atlantic slave trade had Europeans been so divided over slavery. Early on, the Dutch and the French had qualms about trading in slaves as did Elizabeth I of England, but they had all given in to it.

Britain had broken ranks and led the way against slavery. The British continued to police the waters of Africa in search of Portuguese and Spanish slavers on the slightest pretext. In 1815, during the "hundred days" of Napoleon's return to France, he reversed his revival of slavery in 1802 by abolishing it uncategorically. The British navy had its problems enforcing antislavery laws. In a short period, Lord Liverpool, who had been honored by the great slaving city whose name he bore, and his foreign secretary, Lord Castlereagh, set out to abolish slavery. They also wanted to have a group of great powers preserve peace and ethical action in the world. This charter at Vienna, as Hugh Thomas has pointed out, formed the basis of the Covenant of the League of Nations and the Charter of the United Nations.[91] The opposition to slavery was moral as well as economic.

Religion became a vehicle for those who opposed the trading and holding of slaves. Britain was taken up with an almost religious fervor in the abolition of the African slave trade. As this human commerce continued, the Royal Navy was supposed to use the right of search, something done in war since the fourteenth century, in times of peace. The British found resistance to their zeal, especially from Chateaubriand in France, so they tried a new tactic. Having replaced Castlereagh, George Canning proposed a boycott of countries engaged in the slave trade and had the backing of the duke of Wellington, who thought that traffic to be scandalous. This policy took hold haltingly. Canning followed Castlereagh's approach of setting up treaties with individual countries. Although the illegal trade in slaves was nefarious, Britain also had its own inconsistencies or even hypocrisy. For example, it had long taken half then almost all of the cotton from the slaveholding southern United States. British naval and economic power played a key role. As much as ideas of morality and humanity, military power and finance impressed on others like Spain, Portugal, the Netherlands, and the countries of Latin America the importance of the abolition of slavery. Owing to the legacy of the War of Independence and the War of 1812, relations with the United States were sometimes strained. This situation made it more difficult to reach an agreement between the two countries over searching slaving ships and enforcing the antislavery laws. France also continued to resist British pressure. However, it also had its own strong antislavery movement that included Madame de Staël and the marquis de Lafayette, long an opponent of slavery. Many key products relied on slavery—coffee in Brazil, sugar in Cuba, cotton in the United States, and sugar in the British and French West Indies. Literature and art portrayed slavery. For instance, Auguste-François Biard's oil painting, "The Slave Trade," was shown at a salon in Paris in 1835 and then at the Royal Academy in London in 1840. It helped increase opposition to the trade and is now housed at Wilberforce House in the Kingston upon Hull Museum and Art Galleries.[92] In 1838 Lord Palmerston, the British foreign secretary, threatened Portugal over the slaving to Brazil. Slavers soon shifted to the American flag as a way of avoiding British enforcement or harassment. As the House of Representatives was full of slaveowners, the U.S. government did not do much to curtail the slave trade. President Martin Van Buren did try to curb this practice in late 1839 by sending cruisers to patrol the western coast of Africa. As the British searched ships that disguised themselves as American vessels, some friction remained. The U.S. government seemed glad that France did not ratify the Quintuple Treaty signed in London by France, Britain, Austria, Prussia, and Russia. Unfortunately, this treaty prevented the right of search from becoming a common practice in Europe. The slavers came to face patrols off Africa by British, French, Spanish, Portuguese, and American ships in the 1840s. Even though it took some time, the weight of Western governments came down increasingly against the slave trade.

The story was not, however, straightforward and progressive. The contradictions of imperialism were also apparent. Even though the French became involved in combating the slave trade in Africa, France had invaded Algeria in 1830. Over the next two decades, French, Maltese, and Italian colonists settled there and often took control of the lands of the native inhabitants. In the wake of the rebellions in Canada during 1837, Britain granted more self-determination there, but it also annexed New Zealand in 1840 (as it had Singapore in 1819), extended its control of India through the British East India Company, and used the same private group of merchants to establish a trade in opium in China against the wishes of the government. In addition to banning the import of opium, the Chinese government forbade Western merchants from going beyond Guangzhou in Canton and prohibited the export of precious metals. Nor was British policy in China about reform. When the Chinese government expelled British merchants from the south of China, Britain bombarded the cities on the Chinese coast from Hong Kong to Shanghai. In this First Opium War of 1839 to 1842, Britain had China open up four more ports to Europeans, assumed sovereignty over Hong Kong, received indemnity, and continued with the opium trade. The Portuguese had brought opium from China to Europe in the sixteenth century. Now it was something the British government came to condemn and regulate at home while forcing its use on China. The revolutions of 1848 in Europe showed a crisis at home while questions of trade, slavery, and empire persisted. When concerns over slavery were still pressing in the British government, a second war over opium in China was fought between 1856 and 1858. A tension occurred between celebrating empire and curbing its excesses and criticizing its moral shortcomings. In 1851, for example, Reverend George Clayton gave a speech at the opening of the Exhibition of the Works of Industry of All Nations in London in which he praised Britain and its strength through its colonies. Approaching the high tide of imperialism, Britain had abolished the institution of slavery a generation before and the slave trade two generations ago.

Centers of slavery moved to the New World. By the middle of the nineteenth century, the slave ports had shifted from Nantes, Amsterdam, Bristol, and Liverpool to Pernambuco, Bahia, Rio, Havana, New Orleans, and New York. This was a phase that constituted an illegal slave trade. Partly to avoid detection, the dealers, or "ebony merchants" as the French called them, shipped slaves in even worse conditions than before, sometimes packing the human cargo into smaller and more horrific spaces. Thus, vile conditions occurred after the British and North American abolition of slavery in 1808. Witnesses before a House of Commons Committee in 1848 testified to that effect. The illegal trade was not always lucrative. Many of the largest merchants transporting slaves to Cuba and Brazil went bankrupt unless they also invested in sugar or coffee plantations. To deal with slaving under the flag of the United States, the American government tried to curb the slave trade off the coast of Africa and, to a lesser extent, off the coast of Brazil. Like their counterparts in the southern United States, slaveholding Brazilians considered the long-time institution of slavery as being natural. Friction occurred within the two largest settler countries in the Western hemisphere— Brazil and the United States.

The American experience suggests that gender and race were related in matters of social change. The situation of African Americans and of women were closely connected in this struggle for human rights. The five women organizers of the First Women's Rights Convention thought of themselves as abolitionists as they were married to prominent abolitionist leaders, worked as leaders of female antislavery societies, or were friends of the national leaders and thinkers of the abolition movement. The U.S. Park Service emphasizes the link between these two important movements in the achievement of human rights: "When Abby Kelley Foster came to Seneca Falls in 1843 to give an abolitionist lecture, she started a chain of events that founded a congregation and a host for the First Women's Rights Convention five years later. Her career started in 1838, when she gave her first address to an audience of men and women in Philadelphia at Pennsylvania Hall two days before it was set ablaze." The Park Service also stresses Frederick Douglass, who wrote to Foster, "'in token of my respect and gratitude to you, for having stood forth so nobly in defense of Woman and the Slave . . . Our hearts have been cheered and animated and strengthened by your presence.' The experience confirmed her deep commitment to sexual and racial equality."[93] Debates over the abolition of slavery and the rights of women were controversies in the United States, whose economy was closely connected with that of the British Empire.

Friction also occurred at the heart of the world's foremost empire. Some of the British, like William Cobden, who came from Manchester, the center of cotton manufacturing, thought that Britain was being hypocritical. While appealing to morality, Britain was the greatest seller of textiles to Brazil that were made from cotton that slaves grew and then refused to receive sugar that was slave grown. Planters in the West Indies were also puzzled why Britain would condemn slavery and then buy Cuban sugar that slaves had grown and harvested. Slavery aroused intense feelings in the House of Commons. While trade in ivory, gold, and palm oil grew, the British navy increased its presence and scared off many slavers. None the less, from 1831 to 1855, about half a million slaves were imported into Brazil. In 1851, about six million slaves lived in Brazil, roughly twice as many as in 1793. The curtailing of slavery also encouraged European emigration to the Americas. This changed the demography of a number of colonies.

Black leaders in the United States attempted to work against the hard conditions in which their people found themselves. Discrimination based on color was entrenched. In the United States and elsewhere, for peoples who were not of European background, a double standard existed. In May 1854, Frederick Douglass's speech before the American and Foreign Anti-Slavery Society underscored how Americans of African descent were excluded from the rights and freedoms set out by the founders of the United States: "Aliens are we in our native land. The fundamental principles of the republic, to which the humblest white man, whether born here or elsewhere, may appeal with confidence, in the hope of awakening a favorable response, are held to be inapplicable to us." Douglass recalled the American Revolution and how the principles of liberty had been twisted against African Americans: "The glorious doctrines of your revolutionary fathers, and the more glorious teachings of the Son of God, are construed and applied against us. We are literally scourged beyond the beneficent range of both authorities, human and divine." Besides the misapplication of the revolution, black Americans suffered because of a misconstrual of Christianity by white Americans: "American humanity hates us, scorns us, disowns and denies, in a thousand ways, our very personality. The outspread wing of American Christianity, apparently broad enough to give shelter to a perishing world, refuses to cover us." If this were not bad enough, a parodic piety uses violence against Douglass and his community: "To us, its bones are brass, and its features iron. In running thither for shelter and succor, we have only fled from the hungry blood-hound to the devouring wolf—from a corrupt and selfish world, to a hollow and hypocritical church."[94] Irony informs the words "American humanity," as if it were white only, and Douglass makes it parallel to "American Christianity." The structure of his analogies make the fugitive slave flee the blood-hound tracking the fugitive slave for the ravenous wolf of an empty and hypocritical church. State and church in matters temporal and divine scourge those who are strangers not in a strange land but in the country of their birth. Douglass uses the displacement of the biblical echo here of the Jews' exile and exodus to stress the point. The principles of the republic have been given over to a corruption and selfishness that allow for racial discrimination. The United States was hardly representative. Exclusion, exploitation, and injustice troubled a sizable portion of the white population of the country as well.

The relation between European and African inhabitants in the United States was something that abolitionists and a lawyer and politician who would lead his country during a civil war—Abraham Lincoln—recognized in social, historical, and religious terms. Lincoln would not turn from the possibility that God was punishing the British and Continental European settlers for getting rich from slavery. In his notes, he begins with the supposition: "If we shall suppose that American slavery is one of those offenses which, in the providence of God, must needs come, but which, having continued through His appointed time, He now wills to remove, and that He gives to both North and South this terrible war as the woe due to those by whom the offense came." He also sees the possible consequence of divine vengeance for the sin of slavery: "if God wills that it continue until all the wealth piled by the bondsman's two hundred and fifty years of unrequited toil shall be sunk, and until every drop of blood drawn with the lash shall be paid by another drawn with the sword, as was said three thousand years ago, so still it must be said "the judgments of the Lord are true and righteous altogether." As "American slavery" created wealth built on cruelty and unpaid work, then so be it if God were to wipe those riches away. Although Lincoln expressed that the righteous indignation of God would be a just punishment, he ended his address with a prayer for charity without malice, for healing the country, for caring for soldiers and their widows and orphans and for doing "all which may achieve and cherish a just and lasting peace among ourselves and with all nations."[95]

Years before becoming president, slavery was a topic on Lincoln's mind. In 1855, Lincoln had made notes on the history of the slave trade and, while not a member, had attended and addressed the meetings of the Springfield Colonization Society (he did so on January 4, 1855). Lincoln began these notes with the year 1434—"A portaguse captain, on the coast of Guinea, seizes a few Affrican lads, and sells them in the South of Spain." He then moved through Spanish, English, and American events and laws and ended in 1816 with the "Colonization Society is organized—it's direct object—history— and present prospects of success—Its colateral objects—Suppression of Slave trade—Commerce—Civilization and religion."[96] The idea of rights in the United States are inextricably related to slavery. As Lincoln set out in his notes, early in the eighteenth century, some Quakers had agitated for its abolition and, even before, he included a much earlier instance in Spain of an antislavery stance: "Soto, the catholic confessor of Charles 5. opposed Slavery and the Slave trade from the beginning; and, in 1543, procured from the King some amelioration of its rigors." The Board of Directors of the American Colonization Society adopted a constitution for the Commonwealth of Liberia in Africa as early as January 5, 1839. This document set out more rights for black citizens than Africans in the United States and some of those of European descent there. For instance, Article 20 declared that "There shall be no slavery in the Commonwealth"; Article 21 stated that "There shall be no dealing in slaves by any citizen of the Commonwealth, either within or beyond the limits of the same"; Article 25 said that "Every male citizen of the age of twenty-one years shall have the right of suffrage."[97] Lincoln was not a member of this antislavery society, but he showed sympathy to the unfairness of the situation in which African Americans found themselves. In a letter to James N. Brown in 1858, Lincoln had also demonstrated his opposition to slavery and his support for Americans of African descent: "I have made it equally plain that I believe the negro is included in the word 'men' used in the Declaration of Independence—I believe the declaration that 'all men are created equal' is the great fundamental principle upon which our free institutions rest—That negro slavery is violative of that principle; but that, by our frame of government, that principle has not been made one of legal obligation."[98] Lincoln had seen slavery as something that was there in the American colonies. For him, freedom and equality applied to all men and was the basis of government. A storm was gathering in the United States because of the unresolved issue of slavery.

V

Servitude and slavery, although so focused on the Atlantic slave trade built on the backs and lives of Africans, extended to Central and Eastern

Europeans as well. In Russia war with powers such as Britain and France helped to bring internal reform that outlawed human bondage. During the 1850s, the Crimean War checked Russia because with the Peace of Paris it lost the right to base its navy in the Black Sea and the Straits of Dardenelles. This defeat helped to bring reform to Russia. Serfdom had been debated in Russia. In Prussia serfs had been emancipated in 1810 and in Austria in 1848. In 1852, Turgenev's representation of their lot in *A Hunter's Sketches* and a translation of Harriet Beecher Stowe's novel about slavery, *Uncle Tom's Cabin*, appeared. In 1861 Alexander II (r.1855–81) emancipated 22,000,000 privately owned serfs and, a few years later, freed 25,000,000 publicly owned serfs. Despite the problems, such as the landowners getting the best land, this emancipation, coupled with judicial reform, set out principles of the equality of people before the law.[99] At about the same time, slavery would be part of the crisis of the period before and during the American Civil War (1861–65).

The tensions over slavery for the United States had a foreign as well as a domestic dimension. To fight the slave trade, President James Buchanan sent additional ships to Africa and others off Cuba in 1859. On February 21, 1862, the hanging of Nathaniel Gordon, the only North American to be executed for being engaged in the slave trade, became one of many events that showed that the tide was turning against slavery in the United States. As Abraham Lincoln needed his ships in the Civil War, he recalled the Cuban and African squadrons that had been operating against slavers. Perhaps hoping that Britain would side with the north, Lincoln and his secretary of state, William Seward, asked the British to send a force into Cuban waters. Consequently, both Britain and the United States came to allow warships from one nation to search the merchant vessels of the other country for slaves. Further, the British and Americans agreed to a mixed court from both countries at New York, Sierra Leone, and Cape Town for those accused of trading slaves the Americas and in Africa. In Seward's view, if Britain and the United States had made such a treaty in 1808 there would have been no civil war. Abraham Lincoln's government introduced the thirteenth amendment to the Constitution that abolished slavery in the United States. As some members of the government of Spain recognized, the Spanish colony of Cuba's wealth was based on slaves. In 1863 almost 25,000 slaves entered Cuba. The Africa to Cuba slave route, which had endured 350 years, was coming to an end by the close of the American Civil War in 1865. From 1492 to 1820 five times as many Africans went to the New World as white Europeans. Even from 1820 to 1870 the numbers of Europeans and Africans were equal. Black slaves had been servants throughout the Americas. They had also been crucial to cotton in the Guianas and then North America, rice and indigo in Virginia and South Carolina, gold in Brazil, and silver in

Mexico, and sugar in Brazil and then in the Caribbean. Black Africans had helped to build the New World and often without receiving credit. In the realm of social myth and official or school history the contribution of Africans was often displaced or repressed.[100]

Even those European Americans who came to oppose slavery and to fight for its abolition were not always consistent or did not always come to combat that institution in a linear or progressive fashion. For example, President Abraham Lincoln's road to the emancipation of the slaves was not a direct one. His public words did not indicate that he was going to take such a step. In his inaugural speech of March 4, 1861, for instance, he attempted to reassure the South: "Apprehension seems to exist among the people of the Southern States that by the accession of a Republican Administration their property and their peace and personal security are to be endangered. There has never been any reasonable cause for such apprehension."[101] On the contrary, he attempted to allay such fears: "I have no purpose, directly or indirectly, to interfere with the institution of slavery in the States where it exists. I believe I have no lawful right to do so, and I have no inclination to do so." Appealing to the balance of powers in the Constitution of 1787, Lincoln was attempting to balance the rights of states with the authority of the federal government. At this point, he was not willing to sacrifice peace and unity for the slaves. With the coming of war between North and South, that would change. On September 22, 1862, Lincoln proclaimed the emancipation of slaves to take effect on January 1, 1863: "That on the first day of January, in the year of our Lord one thousand eight hundred and sixty-three, all persons held as slaves within any State or designated part of a State, the people whereof shall then be in rebellion against the United States, shall be then, thenceforward, and forever free; and the Executive Government of the United States, including the military and naval authority thereof, will recognize and maintain the freedom of such persons, and will do no act or acts to repress such persons, or any of them, in any efforts they may make for their actual freedom." On behalf of the liberty of slaves throughout the United States, the whole power of the executive and armed forces was to be marshaled. In case there was any doubt, this was a point that Lincoln amplified, even in a brief proclamation: "And by virtue of the power, and for the purpose aforesaid, I do order and declare that all persons held as slaves within said designated States, and parts of States, are, and henceforward shall be free; and that the Executive government of the United States, including the military and naval authorities thereof, will recognize and maintain the freedom of said persons."[102] The southern states had tried to leave the United States peacefully and legally and a war erupted when the federal government would not let that happen, but this strategy had backfired. The American Civil War produced many casualties. One of the moments to remember that sacrifice was in Pennsylvania.

When dedicating a cemetery for fallen soldiers at Gettysburg, Pennsylvannia on November 19, 1863, Lincoln insisted that this civil war was being fought for liberty and implied that this nation reborn would give a wider scope to the words "people" and "equality": "that we here highly resolve that these dead shall not have died in vain, that this nation under God shall have a new birth of freedom, and that government of the people, by the people, for the people shall not perish from the earth."[103] Lincoln's public transformation was not over.

Entering into his second term, Lincoln interpreted the Civil War in wider terms. He gave of his own admission, by the second inaugural speech on March 4, 1865, a much briefer speech than the one he delivered the first time he took office. A gloss on the first address, this second speech also showed, retrospectively, an awareness of the terrible nature of the war: "On the occasion corresponding to this four years ago all thoughts were anxiously directed to an impending civil war. All dreaded it, all sought to avert it."[104] According to Lincoln, "insurgent agents" were in Washington at that time trying to dissolve the union by negotiation. Looking back, Lincoln explained why this peaceful solution was not satisfactory: "One-eighth of the whole population were colored slaves, not distributed generally over the Union, but localized in the southern part of it. These slaves constituted a peculiar and powerful interest." To emphasize his point so as to contradict those who skated the issue on the surface of things by saying that states rights and not slavery was the cause of the war, Lincoln continued: "All knew that this interest was somehow the cause of the war. To strengthen, perpetuate, and extend this interest was the object for which the insurgents would rend the Union even by war, while the Government claimed no right to do more than to restrict the territorial enlargement of it." In order to capture the tragic dimensions of the conflict, Lincoln added: "Neither party expected for the war the magnitude or the duration which it has already attained."[105] The intentions of people can seldom control events, especially those in war. Slavery and African Americans became the focus of an inaugural speech spoken by a president, perhaps more eloquent a speaker than any to hold his office. Slavery was a great unresolved issue at the founding of the great republic. The Civil War transformed the United States. Slavery was abolished after all that time. The country militarized, losing about 620,000 in the Civil War, about two-thirds to disease and one-third in battle. This was the first industrialized war that employed a vast array of new machines, guns, and bombs. Besides the Union navy, the great economic, financial, and manufacturing base of the populous North turned the tide of the war against the South. Britain would not intervene on the side of the South, despite the importance of its cotton for the "mother country."[106] The lives of the English-speaking peoples were still entwined in yet another civil war.

Although this chapter has often concentrated on the experience in North America, it is important to remember tensions over slavery in other parts of the world. In Africa, for example, the situation was difficult. The loss of lands by the peoples of Africa was also closely intertwined with the devastation of slavery. Muslim slave traders and Christians used new types of guns (the machine gun developed after the early 1860s) to subdue and subject the Natives. For instance, the Zulu, Xhosa, and neighboring peoples fought the Boers, descendents of the Dutch colonists who had settled the area in the seventeenth century, and British immigrants. Gold and diamonds were some of the riches at stake. Racial rationalizations for subjugating peoples were now a part of imperialism. The Europeans dispossessed the Africans culturally, politically, and economically. None the less, William Gladstone (1809–98) would become prime minister of Britain and would seek reforms. After an election campaign in 1879 in which he appealed to a wider franchise of voters—as more workers and middle-class men could vote after the most recent reforms of 1872—he called for more self-determination in Africa and India much to the dismay of Queen Victoria.[107] Antislavery and independence for colonies continued to be debated in Britain even at the height of its empire and while it was under pressure to compete with other European powers in the Scramble for Africa.

In the United States and British North America (Canada) related tensions occurred to those in Africa. Exclusion from liberty was not something that was exclusive to African Americans, even if they suffered so much from slavery. Native Americans struggled to survive and to preserve their language, culture, lands, and way of life. As the focus is on slavery here, one example will suggest the nature of this loss of life and liberty. Sitting Bull (Tatanka Yotanka), a chief of the Hunkpapa Sioux, related his views to a journalist, James Creelman, when held a prisoner of war between 1881 and 1883 at Fort Randall, "We were free to come and go, and to live in our own way. But white men, who belong to another land, have come upon us, and are forcing us to live according to their ideas. That is an injustice; we have never dreamed of making white men live as we live." The idea of force and cultural imposition are themes here. Reversing notions of American liberty, Sitting Bull declared: "The life of white men is slavery. They are prisoners in towns or farms. The life my people want is a life of freedom. I have seen nothing that a white man has, houses or railways or clothing or food, that is as good as the right to move in open country, and live in our own fashion."[108] Slavery and liberty, according to Sitting Bull, are not the same as European Americans proclaimed. Their lives were not as free as those of the Natives. The concern in British North American colonies over White Indians— Europeans who after kidnapping or other circumstances had ended up in Native communities seems to testify that enough Europeans living as Indians shared Sitting Bull's assessment. Many did not want to return to the farms and towns.

Even in the twentieth century in North America, the attraction of Native life for white people can be seen in the life and work of Grey Owl (Archie Belaney), an Englishman from Hastings who took on the identity of an Ojibwa, and in a film like *Dances with Wolves*, which won the Oscar for best picture in 1990. Just as there was guilt among some European Americans over slavery, there has been a sense of remorse in influential segments of white or settler society over the mistreatment of Native North Americans and the strangling of their way of life. As with the abolition of slavery, there has been—only much more slowly—a revisiting of the question of land claims and other injustices the Natives suffered. British North America (after the American Revolution) abolished the institution of slavery earlier than the United States, and its successor, Canada, has reopened land claims and questions of sovereignty. For all its flaws and injustices, Canada has been a leader in this field and countries like Australia (the Mabo case) have followed suit. The Mabo case in the early 1990s extinguished in Australia the legal fiction of *terra nullius*—no occupation of the lands in a European sense by indigenous peoples or others and therefore Europeans could settle them— something the Portuguese had used in Africa from the fifteenth century and variants of which François Ier of France and Elizabeth I had applied to lands in the Americas that neither Portugal nor Spain had occupied. Self-government is a key part of the ongoing negotiations between Natives and newcomers in territories like Canada. The question of aboriginal land claims and rights is one that is crucial throughout the world and a legacy of European expansion. Colonies and empire have left many legacies: slavery and Native loss of lands are just two related ones. Columbus brought these issues to the New World and Las Casas, after himself taking Native lands, tried to defend the indigenous peoples from slavery. They would be vassals but not slaves. In this last sentence lodge some of the complexities between being caught in the web of fealty and serfdom and being lost in the related realm of the kind of slavery the Atlantic slave trade imposed on Africans. This sad legacy is still with us.

VI

The writing of women, black and white, in the nineteenth and twentieth centuries, often in the form of diaries, oral narratives, letters, and autobiographies, contributed in important ways to the debate over slavery in North America. Some leading black male writers, like W. E. B. Du Bois, further helped to expose this institution and to complicate notions of slave-trading and slaveholding. Often these writings could uncover the abuses of slavery and the reach of its legacy, but they also gave hope. That the human spirit, regardless of skin color of the writer, rose up against and defied slavery is something that this section in particular emphasizes.

Some European American women were appalled by slavery because of religious qualms. This opposition to slavery gathered momentum in the nineteenth century. For instance, Mary Morton Dexter (1785–1822) wrote a letter to her sister, Mrs. N. N., on September 8, 1811:

> Though the New England States have not been deeply stained with the guilt of the slave trade, yet we are not wholly free. And as we are confederated with the Southern States, where slavery abounds, we, as a part of the nation, must feel ourselves very guilty on that account. Have we any right to expect national blessings unless national sins are repented of? And is it not the duty of every individual, however private may be the station in which he or she is called to act, to mourn and bewail over national sins, and to do all in his power towards their amendment? The awful prevalence, the indescribable cruelty of the slave trade is in my view a powerful argument in favor of the African Mission. Past sins cannot it is true be atoned for in this way.—We must look to him who alone hath power to forgive sins for the pardon of this as well as all other crimes.[109]

Dexter used the words "guilt" and "guilty" and the repeated phrase, "national sins," to stress the burden of slavery on European Americans. She emphasized that men and women are called privately to lament and to amend these national offences. The people of New England, although not given as much to slavery as those in the South, have to bear responsibility by association for being in a nation that allows slavery. Its prevalence, for Dexter, was awful and its cruelty was beyond description. She shared with Equiano this view as well as that in which real Christians could not tolerate the taking and keeping of slaves. The slave trade justified, for her, the idea of creating free settlements in Africa. Dexter further reiterated the term, "sins" and raised the only possibility for atonement—Christ's forgiveness. That is the only pardon for past sins. Speaking about the "unspeakable miseries of slavery," Dexter, who distinguished between those who hide behind religion and those who are religious, continued to emphasize hypocrisy and cruelty as attributes of those involved with slavery: "The name of Christian, in the minds of poor Africans, and indeed of many other nations, is associated with the basest crimes and the most detestable cruelty. May those who are real Christians be enabled by grace to make such benevolent exertions for the spreading of the gospel and the salvation of the poor heathen, as shall convince them of the excellence, the purity, and benevolence of real Christianity."[110] This exposure of cruel behavior is as much a concern for Dexter as it had been for Equiano.

The use of goods produced by slaves was also an issue at the time, not entirely unlike the debate today about goods produced in the global marketplace by slaves or cheap labor. In 1819, Anne Mott (1768?–1852) wrote a letter to James Mott in which she outlined one such case: "I have thought, frequently, how James got along with what he was once convinced was not consistent with justice, the use of West India produce" and added a wish: "May my dear child therefore not shrink from the trial, should he believe it right to set an example by endeavoring to supply his family with such articles as can be procured untinged with slavery."[111] The taint of the slave trade was something that affected the daily lives of families. Commerce and trade had and have ethical dimensions.

Another aspect of slavery for European Americans is that it could split families. One southerner who moved North and became an abolitionist had differences with her slaveowning mother. On October 4, 1829, Angelina Emily Grimké Weld (1805–79)—she later married another abolitionist, Theodore Weld, in 1838—recorded in her diary an incident that encapsulated part of that friction: "Last night E. T. took tea here. As soon as she began to extol the North and speak against slavery, mother left the room. She cannot bear these two subjects. My mind continues distressingly exercised and anxious that mother's eyes should be open to all the iniquities of the system she upholds."[112] Angelina's biography will provide some background to this instance of family tension over slavery. An abolitionist and women's rights activist and the youngest of fourteen children, Angelina was born on February 20, 1805 to John Faucheraud and Mary Smith Grimké, in Charleston, South Carolina. Her father served in the South Carolina judiciary in a post similar to that of chief justice. Angelina's well-off parents owned a rice plantation that depended upon slave labor. In 1829, Weld moved to Philadelphia to join her sister Sarah, who had settled eight years before. Both women, who opposed the institution of slavery, left the Anglican communion to become Quakers. Angelina joined the Philadelphia Female Anti-Slavery Society: in 1835, she served as a committeewoman and William Lloyd Garrison (1805–79) published one of her letters in the *Liberator*. The sisters broke with the group over the issue of immediate abolition and moved to New York, where they worked with its Anti-Slavery Society. Angelina published *An Appeal to the Christian Women of the South* in 1836 and *Appeal to the Women of the Nominally Free States* in 1837. Angelina also fought for the rights of women. In letters to the *Liberator*, later published as a pamphlet, Angelina argued that women should take part in the legislative process and, on February 21, 1838, she was the first woman to address the Massachusetts legislature. On this occasion, she gave lawmakers an antislavery petition.[113] The rights of women and slaves, as we have seen, were an important and sometimes inseparable pair in the nineteenth century.

A wider commitment to human rights was often an aspect of marriages in which husband and wife were both committed to the cause of freedom.

An example of this is the marriage of David and Lydia Maria Child (1802–80): both brought a commitment to rights before they married. A letter from Lydia Maria Francis Child to E. Carpenter on September 4, 1836 from South Natick set out the central issue in a trial about slavery: "In consequence of the amount of evidence ready to be proved by three witnesses, the pro-slavery lawyers did not pretend to deny that the intent was to carry the child back into slavery; but they took the new and extraordinary ground that Southern masters had a legal right to hold human beings as slaves while they were visiting here in New England."[114] Lydia Maria Child gave a sense of the tact taken by the lawyers on the side of slavery as well as the ensuing judgment: "The opposite counsel were full of sophistry and eloquence. One of them really wiped his own eyes at the thought that the poor little slave might be separated from its slave mother by mistaken benevolence. His pathos was a little marred by my friend E. G. Loring, who arose and stated that it was distinctly understood that little Med was to be sold on her way back to New Orleans, to pay the expenses of her mistress's journey to the North. The judges decided unanimously in favor of Med and liberty!"[115] Commerce and family ties, even if translated by courtroom drama and sophistry, were often at odds in the institution of slavery. Child remarked on bald motivation when she saw it in this case: "The Commercial Gazette" of the next day says: "This decision, though unquestionably according to law, is much to be regretted; for such cases cannot but injure the custom of our hotels, now so liberally patronized by gentlemen from the South." Verily, Sir Editor, thou art an honest devil; and I thank thee for not being at the pains to conceal thy cloven foot."[116] This is a brutal honesty based on profit rather than the hypocrisy of the lawyers trying to send the child back into slavery in the South.

The Childs were committed to unpopular causes for human rights. David Lee Child, a lawyer and editor, and Maria, who had become a member of intellectual high society in Boston, married on October 19, 1828. David's support for the Cherokees fight against President Andrew Jackson seems to have inspired Maria to write *The First Settlers of New England* about the Native Americans in her area. When David became an abolitionist, Maria also became involved with the antislavery movement. Her *An Appeal in Favor of That Class of Americans Called Africans* (1833) angered members of Boston society, and the Athenaeum spurned her. Undeterred, Francis then edited *The Oasis* (1834), an antislavery gift book, and two pamphlets, *Authentic Anecdotes of American Slavery* (1835) and *Anti-Slavery Catechism* (1836). Moreover, Maria funded biographies written by slaves, including Harriet Jacobs's *Incidents in the Life of a Slave Girl* (1861). Maria also edited the *National Anti-Slavery Standard* for the American Anti-Slavery Society. Her interests in rights also included those of women as well as of Natives and

Africans. Maria (Francis) wrote *History of the Condition of Women in Various Ages and Nations* (1835) and, in 1837, became the delegate from Massachusetts to a convention for women's rights in New York. Her home was a station on the Underground Railroad. After John Brown's raid on Harper's Ferry in 1859, her writing was widespread in the North.[117] The commitment to rights was not necessarily one-dimensional but could apply in a number of areas of American life.

Other writings showed the tensions between nations and the sexes when it came to slavery. A letter of May 8, 1837, by Sarah Pugh (1800–84), is instructive. Pugh was a teacher, abolitionist, and supporter of women's suffrage. Born in Alexandria, Virginia on October 6, 1800 to a Quaker couple, Jesse and Catharine Pugh, Sarah's father died when she was three, and the family moved to the home of her grandfather Isaac Jackson, an abolitionist, in Pennsylvania. George Thompson, a former member of the British Parliament, helped to inspire her to activism in the cause against slavery. Thompson gave a speech in Philadelphia in 1835: soon after, Pugh joined the Female Anti-Slavery Society, of which she was a member for thirty six years. Besides becoming a member of the American Anti-Slavery Society, Pugh attended the meeting of the American Women's Anti-Slavery Convention in 1837 as well as the British and Foreign Anti-Slavery Society's general conference in London in June of 1840. For instance, in this letter Pugh described that at a meeting in 1837, "The reading of the remonstrance against slavery from Scotland to the American people, containing more than four thousand signatures, made quite a sensation."[118] Some of the British public were pressing Americans to abolish slavery. Even in the movement against slavery, there were other forms of discrimination: "Women were not admitted as members. The first antislavery convention of women assembled in a church in the northern part of the city of New York in 1837."[119] To speak of a unified and fair white society from within would be to create too ideal a picture. Following the Civil War, Sarah worked to free slaves and to better the status of women. Pugh went to women's rights conferences Lucretia Mott, whose mobility was limited with age. Once more, here is a woman interested in the rights of her sex and the abolition of slavery: an extension of rights was a motivation for women like Sarah Pugh. Nor were women or other members of a church necessarily to bow down before the clergy. Another Grimké sister wrote something to this effect to someone she addressed as "sister." On October 20, 1837, a letter from Sarah Moore Grimké (1792–1873) to Mary S. Parker, said: "Let us keep in mind, that no abolitionism is of any value, which is not accompanied with deep, heartfelt repentance; and that, whenever a minister sincerely repents of having, either by his apathy or his efforts, countenanced the fearful sin of slavery, he will need no inducement to come into our ranks; so far from it, he will abhor himself in dust and ashes, for his past blindness and indifference to the cause of God's poor and oppressed: and he will regard it as a privilege to be enabled to do something in the cause of human rights."[120] These rights were, above all, an important part of the struggle and should not be sacrificed to those who would curtail them no matter who they were: "I know the ministry exercise vast power; but I rejoice in the belief, that the spell is broken which encircled them, and rendered it all but blasphemy to expose their errors and their sins. We are beginning to understand that they are but men, and that their station should not shield them from merited reproof."[121] Authority can be reproved if it opposes a just cause. The rights of slaves and women called into question laws and practices that did not allow these people their freedom.

The divisions between Britons and Americans, northerners and southerners, whites and blacks were also played out in the institution of and debate over slavery. Frances Anne Kemble (1809–93) brought a point of view from England in her observations on Georgia:

> On our drive we passed occasionally a tattered man or woman, whose yellow mud complexion, straight features, and singularly sinister countenance bespoke an entirely different race from the negro population in the midst of which they lived. These are the so-called pine-landers of Georgia, I suppose the most degraded race of human beings claiming an Anglo-Saxon origin that can be found on the face of the earth,—filthy, lazy, ignorant, brutal, proud, penniless savages, without one of the nobler attributes which have been found occasionally allied to the vices of savage nature. They own no slaves, for they are almost without exception abjectly poor; they will not work, for that, as they conceive, would reduce them to an equality with the abhorred negroes; they squat, and steal, and starve, on the outskirts of this lowest of all civilised societies, and their countenances bear witness to the squalor of their condition and the utter degradation of their natures. To the crime of slavery, though they have no profitable part or lot in it, they are fiercely accessory, because it is the barrier that divides the black and white races, at the foot of which they lie wallowing in unspeakable degradation, but immensely proud of the base freedom which still separates them from the lash-driven tillers of the soil.[122]

The misery of the indigent whites and their aspiration to own slaves helped to maintain slavery and the bondage of blacks, with whom they shared a degraded condition. Desperation and a politics of race are part of the equation. The poor whites wanted to lord it over the blacks and would envy them their freedom if they were not kept in their place and they also could dream that they could join their "Anglo-Saxon" brethren as great landowners and have slaves themselves. Fanny (Frances) Kemble arrived in Georgia through a circuitous route. An actress and writer, Fanny was born 1809 in London to Charles and Maria Theresa de Camp Kemble, the former a manager and coowner of the Covent Garden Theatre, the latter an actress. For financial reasons, the family moved to New York. In Philadelphia, she married a well-off plantation owner, Pierce Butler in 1834, but he was unhappy when she published *Journal of a Residence in America* (1835), in which she was critical of life in the United States. The family moved to Butler's plantation in Georgia: Kemble found the institution of slavery to be abhorrent. Husband and wife held very different views on slaveholding. In 1849, Fanny and Pierce Butler were divorced. This is quite a different story from the abolitionist couples, some of whom we have discussed. In 1863, while she was living in England, she published her antislavery memoir *Journal of a Residence on a Georgian Plantation*. Kemble moved back and forth between Europe and the United States.[123]

Education was also played a significant role in the antislavery movement. In May of 1849, Lucretia Coffin Mott (1793–1880), an abolitionist, minister, and women's rights activist, born in 1793 in Nantucket, Massachusetts, where many Quakers lived, wrote in a letter: "That large package, containing a variety of books and pamphlets, we made the most of; sending some to Ohio, and others to Canada, among the anti-slavery colored people there, where indeed not a few of our papers find their way."[124] Canada was a land of freedom for blacks who had escaped slavery and there is an educational bond across the border. Once more, the fight for rights went beyond the battle against slavery. In advocating women's rights Lucretia worked with suffragists like Elizabeth Cady Stanton. The role of women in opposition to slavery recurred over the decades leading up to its abolition. Another instance is Ella Gertrude Clanton Thomas (1834–1907), who made an observation about women in the heartland of slavery: "Southern women are I believe all at heart abolitionists but there I expect I have made a very broad assertion but I *will stand* to the opinion that the institution of slavery degrades the white man more than the Negro and oh exerts a most deleterious effect upon our children—But this is the dark side of the picture, written with a Mrs Stowe's feeling—but when I look upon so many young creatures growing up belonging to Pa's estate as well as others—I wonder upon whom shall the accountability of their future state depend."[125] Harriet Beecher Stowe affected through her writing, most notably *Uncle Tom's Cabin*, other people's perceptions of and writing about slavery. In Michigan on February 8, 1860, Elizabeth Leslie Rous Wright Comstock (1815–91)—who was born in England, lived in Canada and then the United States, and became a Quaker minister—wrote about a Southerner unimpressed with this book:

> he is bringing with him visitor No. 7, a somewhat singular looking man with the costume of the South, strong built, dark complexion, fierce-looking. . . . A slave-driver! Well, we have all sorts. All classes are at home here, all claim

fellowship with us, and I suppose all should have our sympathy. Poor man, he has lost his right arm. That arm that has often swung the cat-o'-nine-tails, and wielded the whip around the shrinking form of the poor slave, is gone for ever— it shall torture suffering humanity no more. It was torn off by the machinery of a "cotton-gin," as he was driving the poor slaves. On the whole, he seems a pleasant man in conversation. He does not think slavery *wrong*, he believes a slave is just as much the property of his master, as his horse or sheep is. He has read "Uncle Tom's Cabin," and does not like it. Thinks the slaves are a sort of middle class between men and beasts, and that they are generally well treated, that a man usually takes as much care of his negroes as of his cattle, and that, if set free, they could not provide for themselves, &c., &c. He has left the plantations, and is going home to his relatives in the north of this state.[126]

The sad irony for this man is that the machinery of cotton-picking tore off his arm. His view of slavery went against the grain of the author's. On the verge of the Civil War, the nature of slaves and slavery was contested. Their humanity was being debated more than three centuries after Las Casas and others disputed the status of the Indians in relation to Aristotle's theory of natural slavery. This division could also been seen in the writing of other women. For instance, Catherine Maria Sedgwick (1789–1867), a writer born in Massachusetts, averred: "It may be that he will permit the Southern suicidal madness to rage and *prevail* to the great end of blotting slavery from the land it poisons. Massachusetts is condemned as the hot-bed of abolition fanaticism—I hear nothing but ultra concession and conservatism."[127] The land was poisoned with civil war.

Emancipation was also a central topic in this contest over slavery. Lydia Maria Child alluded to how long this issue had been burning. On May 5, 1861, she wrote a letter in which she said:

> Twenty years ago, John Quincy Adams maintained on the floor of Congress the constitutional right of the United States to proclaim emancipation to all the slaves in time of war, either foreign or civil. He maintained that it was in strict conformity to the law of nations and the laws of war, and he challenged any man to prove to the contrary. No one attempted to do it. Let us hope and trust that a great good is coming out of this seeming evil. Meanwhile, I wait to see how the United States will deport itself. When it treats the colored people with justice and humanity, I will mount its flag in my great elm-tree, and I will thank you to present me with a flag for a breast-pin; but, until then, I would as soon wear the rattlesnake upon my bosom as the eagle.[128]

And that emancipation, amid great blood-letting, came in 1863. The wounds of slavery persisted long after the Civil War, something that black leaders like Martin Luther King called attention to a century later, and something that is still with us. Although much more could be said about the writing of European American abolitionists, it is important to pick up the tradition that Equiano helped to start—the slave narrative or the story of emancipation.[129] Writing about and by slaves affected the sense and the reputation of the United States.

After 1800, the example of Equiano before them, slaves published narratives of their own experiences. African women are a significant part of the writing about slavery.[130] In 1831, Mary Prince's book, the first published slave narrative by a woman, appeared in two editions in London and transformed the genre because she spoke for herself and claimed authority to speak for other slaves and helped to gain a voice for black women.[131] Prince, who was born in Bermuda, told of how her master, Mr. Williams was harsh and that his wife was kind but, by the time Mary was twelve, could not afford to keep so many slaves, so Mary was hired out to Mrs. Pruden, who treated her "unkindly."[132] When Mrs. Williams died, Mary and sisters were sold to pay for Mr. Williams wedding, so that the family was torn apart. The new master was cruel and beat "a French black called Hetty" and his wife "was a fearful woman, and a savage mistress to her slaves."[133] The sadism of this new mistress took on particular forms. For instance, "To strip me naked—to hang me up by the wrists and lay my flesh open with the cow-skin, was an ordinary punishment for even a slight offence."[134] The master beat a pregnant Hetty until she was bleeding and delivered a dead child: as a result, soon after, Hetty died. For five years, Mary did not escape further beatings as well. The master then sent Mary away to the Turks Islands without saying goodbye to her family, which led her to conclude about whites: "Oh the Buckra people who keep slaves think that black people are like cattle, without natural affection."[135] Mary's new master had her work in grueling conditions in salt ponds: he was calm in his cruelty to his slaves while Mary's previous master foamed with passion as he abused them. She concluded: "Oh that Turk Island was a horrible place! The people of England, I am sure, have never found out what is carried on here. Cruel, horrible place!"[136] This theme of cruelty, which was prominent in the narratives of Las Casas and Equiano, played a significant role in Prince's story. Mary Prince's plea is against this cruel institution and to the English to abolish it:

> Oh the horrors of slavery!—How the thought of it pains my heart! But the truth ought to be told of it; and what my eyes have seen I think it is my duty to relate; for few people in England know what slavery is. I have been a slave— I have felt what a slave feels and I know what a slave knows; and I would have all the good people in England to know it too, that they may break our chains and set us free.[137]

The voice of this African woman, born in "the still-vext *Bermoothes*," and called out against the institution that allowed for enslavement and the abuses of slaves and for freedom itself.[138] After giving more gruesome examples, of the cruelty of this master in Turk Island, Mary described her view of his son: "I must say something more about this cruel son of a cruel father.—He had no heart—no fear of God; he had been brought up by a bad father in a bad path, and he delighted to follow in the same steps."[139] Reading the Bible and religion played an important role for Mary.[140] Still a slave, Mary found that an impediment to her happiness after she married Daniel James, a free black.[141] Her tribulations continued.

There is a typological relation between the West Indies and England. Her masters took her to their mother country. When in England the Woods, her masters, drove Mary out of their house on a number of occasions, so she was taken in by Mash, the shoe-black, and his wife, who treated her well, and Prince met other English people who were good to her.[142] She contradicted the view that West Indian slaveowners propagated in England that "slaves do not want to be free" by recalling the abuses they have suffered and she observed: "Since I have been here I have often wondered how English people can go out to the West Indies and act in such a beastly manner. But when they go to the West Indies, they forget God and all feeling of shame."[143] Miss S—— recorded the narrative for Mary, but the antislavery stance comes through. While Mary saw many good things in England, she can be critical of it as well: "The man that says slaves be quite happy in slavery—that they don't want to be free—that man is either ignorant or a lying person."[144] She upbraids those who say they cannot do with slaves, because people in England do without them and masters can let servants go and servants can leave bad masters. There is, then, a distinction between being a servant and slave. English servants "have their liberty. That's just what *we* want."[145] Black people would then be able to keep the Sabbath and be treated fairly not like beasts. Mary ended her narrative with this admonition: "This is slavery. I tell it, to let English people know the truth; and I hope they will never leave off to pray God, and call loud to the great King of England, till all the poor blacks be given free, and slavery done up for evermore."[146] The voices against slavery came from men and women, black and white. How slaves saw slavery became a significant part of the movement afoot to abolish this institution.

In 1845, *The Narrative of the Life of Frederick Douglass* appeared with a Preface by the great abolitionist William Lloyd Garrison, who met Douglass at an abolitionist meeting at Nantucket in August 1841 not long after Douglass had escaped from slavery in the South. In a rhetorical flourish, Garrison repeated the word "fortunate" in relation to others for benefiting from Douglass's work against slavery, "fortunate for the cause of Negro emancipation and of universal liberty!—fortunate for the land of his birth."[147] Garrison, who was well aware of his outsized rhetoric in opposition to slavery, did place Douglass's contribution quite rightly into the context of rights and freedoms and the history of the United States as well as the history of African slavery. The power of Douglass's speech at that convention was something that Garrison emphasized, especially the effect on him and on the audience: "I think I never hated slavery so intensely as at that moment; certainly, my perception of the enormous outrage which is inflicted by it, on the godlike nature of its victims, was rendered far more clear than ever."[148] Garrison spoke about the greatness of Douglass, who was closer to being an angel than to being property, and the abolitionist framed his response to the fugitive slave's speech in terms of the rhetoric of freedom and the American Revolution: "As soon as he had taken his seat, filled with hope and admiration, I rose, and declared that PATRICK HENRY, of revolutionary fame, never made a speech more eloquent in the cause of liberty, than the one we had just listened to from the lips of that hunted fugitive."[149] Garrison also realized that Douglass would contribute to the cause in the North and South, something that can be elided: "It was at once deeply impressed upon my mind, that, if Mr. DOUGLASS could be persuaded to consecrate his time and talents to the promotion of the anti-slavery enterprise, a powerful impetus would be given to it, and a stunning blow at the same time inflicted on northern prejudice against a colored complexion."[150] The "northern prejudice" could have been of northern Europeans generally but also people living in the North in the United States. One person's promotion was another person's opposition.

The opposition to slavery were the promoters of emancipation. This group included a strong black presence that Garrison outlined in his Preface:

> It is certainly a very remarkable fact, that one of the most efficient advocates of the slave population, now before the public, is a fugitive slave, in the person of FREDERICK DOUGLASS; and that the free colored population of the United States are as ably represented by one of their own number, in the person of CHARLES LENOX REMOND, whose eloquent appeals have extorted the highest applause of multitudes on both sides of the Atlantic. Let the calumniators of the colored race despise themselves for their baseness and illiberality of spirit, and henceforth cease to talk of the natural inferiority of those who require nothing but time and opportunity to attain the highest point of human excellence.[151]

After this praise of Douglass and Remond and this dispraise of white illiberals, Garrison discounted racial theories as calumny and proceeded to say that no other people has endured so much "the privations, sufferings and horrors of slavery" as "slaves of African descent" and that white men who enslaved were also reduced to a state that brutalized their faculties.[152] Garrison thought it wise that Douglass presented his story without someone else's editing: "Mr. DOUGLASS has very properly chosen to write his own

Narrative, in his own style, and according to the best of his ability, rather than to employ some one else."[153] For Garrison, Douglass became a representative slave despite his talent: he was one example of a slave suffering in a terrible institution. Garrison's reading of Douglass was an advance interpretation for the prospective reader and he was not afraid to appeal to emotion—the tears shed over the inhumanity of slavery. Douglass's narrative "comes short of the reality, rather than overstates a single fact in regard to SLAVERY AS IT IS."[154] More specifically, Garrison pointed to a particularly poignant moment in Douglass's narrative when on the banks of Chesapeake Bay he considered, in a soliloquy and in an apostrophe to the white-winged sails, whether one day he would be free: "Who can read that passage, and be insensible to its pathos and sublimity? Compressed into it is a whole Alexandrian library of thought, feeling, and sentiment—all that can, all that need be, urged, in the form of expostulation, entreaty, rebuke, against that crime of crimes,—making man the property of his fellow-man!"[155] Garrison also expatiates on the abuses of slavery and its annihilation of human rights. The two unpunished murders of slaves as Douglass related them were also instances of the barbarity of slavery that Garrison called forth. So, too, is the "religious profession" of southern masters, a Christianity that Douglass called into question.[156] Garrison did not mince words and addressed the audience directly: "Reader! Are you with the man-stealers in sympathy and purpose, or on the side of their down-trodden victims?"[157] If with the masters, then the reader is "the foe of God and man" but if with the slaves, then he or she must be prepared to do something on their behalf: in concluding his Preface, Garrison exhorts the reader to take up "as your religious and political motto— 'NO COMPROMISE WITH SLAVERY! NO UNION WITH SLAVE-HOLDERS!' "[158] This was a prelude as much to civil war as to Douglass's account. The lines were being drawn, and they could only stretch so far—a little like conscience.

White abolitionists, then, as committed and as necessary as they were to the cause of emancipation, could also act as organizational, editorial, and interpretive filters for their black colleagues. In a letter from Boston on April 22, 1845, Wendell Phillips wrote to Frederick Douglass, in what became part of the front matter of Douglass's book. Before Karl Marx, Phillips used the fable of the man and the lion, "where the lion complained that he should not be so misrepresented 'when the lions wrote history.' "[159] Phillips rooted the parable in project at hand: "I am glad the time has come when the 'lions write history.' We have been left long enough to gather the character of slavery from the involuntary evidence of the masters."[160] The motivation for moving against slavery needed more than economics and a recognition of its harshness: "A man must be disposed to judge of emancipation by other tests than whether it has increased the produce of sugar,—and to hate slavery for other reasons than because it starves men and whips women,—before he is ready to lay the first stone of his anti-slavery life."[161] Amid the themes of the cruelty and abuses of slavery, Phillips called attention to the comparisons Douglass could bring to bear on North and South: "You have been with us, too, some years, and can fairly compare the twilight of rights, which your race enjoy at the North, and that 'noon of night' under which they labor south of Mason and Dixon's line."[162] Those who stood up to slavery had to break the law, so that fear and defiance mixed in Phillips's letter. Before he ended his letter with an appeal for "consecrating anew the soil of the Pilgrims as an asylum for the oppressed," Phillips likened Douglass to the founding fathers of the United States: "They say the fathers, in 1776, signed the Declaration of Independence with the halter about their necks. You, too, publish your declaration of freedom with danger compassing you around."[163] Freedom from religious persecution for the Pilgrims and freedom from British oppression for the founders of the United States become precedents or typological points of identity with Douglass and those who were fighting for freedom from slavery.

Douglass began his narrative with his birth but turned to the way slavery treated people like animals. He generalized from his own situation: "By far the larger part of the slaves know as little of their ages as horses know of theirs, and it is the wish of most masters within my knowledge to keep their slaves thus ignorant."[164] This lack of knowledge of his age made Douglass unhappy as a child: nor did he know his father, who was said to be white and might have been his master. He also noted the practice of separating mother and child at about a year old. The hard working conditions and long workday meant that Douglass did not see his mother during the day: she did not live long, dying when he was seven. In a couple of sentences Douglass summed up the inhumanity of the institution: "I was not allowed to be present during her illness, at her death, or her burial. She was gone long before I knew any thing about it."[165] The circumstances of Douglass's birth, parents, and the death of his mother made him consider one specific abuse in slavery:

> the fact remains, in all its glaring odiousness, that slave-holders have ordained, and by law established, that the children of slave women shall in all cases follow the condition of their mothers, and this is done too obviously to administer to their own lusts, and make a gratification of their wicked desires profitable as well as pleasurable; for by this cunning arrangement, the slaveholder, in cases not a few, sustains to his slaves the double relation of master and father.[166]

Profit and pleasure, but a breaking with the bonds of blood and affection, attended to slavery. In so many ways slaveholding was inhumane and cruel.

This cruelty took on different forms. Douglass described an overseer: "Mr. Severe was rightly named: he was a cruel man. I have seen him whip a woman, causing the blood to run half an hour at a time; and this, too, in the midst of her crying children, pleading for their mother's release. He seemed to take pleasure manifesting his fiendish barbarity."[167] This mistreatment caused woe as was expressed in the songs of slaves, which some people mistook as signs of contentment: "To those songs I trace my first glimmering conception of the dehumanizing character of slavery."[168] Not being forthright, especially about their condition and masters, was a means of self-preservation and protection for slaves: "They suppress the truth rather than take the consequences of telling it, and in so doing prove themselves a part of the human family."[169] Masters and overseers could be hard. Another overseer was inhumane: "Mr. Gore was proud, ambitious, and persevering. He was artful, cruel, and obdurate."[170] Douglass did not represent all white society as harsh: for instance, he described one of the slaveholders positively, his new mistress was "a woman of the kindest heart and finest feelings," for she had been a weaver and "had been in a good degree preserved from the blighting and dehumanizing effects of slavery."[171] Other intricacies in this institution appeared in Douglass' account—the distinguished between types of bondage: "A city slave is almost a freeman, compared with a slave on the plantation."[172] Education was contentious, so that Douglass had to employ stratagems in order to learn to read and write and build his skills, including learning from white boys. He read about masters and slaves and about Catholic emancipation but all the while wishing he were dead. As is often the case in slave narratives, the death of a master created a crisis in the slave's family or community and they were sold as property. In Douglass, the various deaths led to a selling off of the slaves: "We were all ranked together at the valuation. Men and women, old and young, married and single, were ranked with horses, sheep, and swine."[173] This is a point that Douglass amplified, thinking of the situation of his lonely grandmother and the loss of her children and their offspring in terms of the words of Whittier, "the slave's poet:" "Gone, gone, sold and gone / To the rice swamp dank and lone."[174] One misery piled up on another, Douglass's master Thomas was so bad that "I do not know of one single noble act ever performed by him."[175] Working for Mr. Covey the first six months he was whipped almost every week and Douglass felt he had become a brute. Douglass provided a poetic description of the sailboats on Chesapeake Bay: "Those beautiful vessels, robed in purest white, so delightful to the eye of freemen, were to me so many shrouded ghosts, to terrify and torment me with thoughts of my wretched condition."[176] None the less, Douglass was able to fight back and he used violence to quell the abuse that Covey had given him, something he saw as "a turning-point in my career as a slave" that allowed him to feel confident and determined to seek freedom.[177] Douglass also observed the strategy used "to disgust the slave with freedom," that is the abuses of holidays and forcing him to eat too much when he has displeased the master.[178] More violence occurred—the fight with the four white apprentices, for instance, in which Douglass's left eye was almost knocked out.[179] The cruelty accumulated and the pressure for freedom built up.

Douglass left slavery and recorded how he felt in achieving freedom: "It was the moment of the highest excitement I ever experienced."[180] He reviewed his options with David Ruggles in New York and together they made the following decision: "I thought of going to Canada; but he decided against it, and in favor of my going to New Bedford, thinking I should be able to get work there at my trade."[181] In New Bedford, Douglass was impressed with people "more able, stronger, healthier, and happier, than those of Maryland" and who experienced wealth without the extremes of poverty; above all, Douglass was impressed with "the condition of the colored people," many of whom had escaped "the hunters of men."[182] Their situation was such that Douglass "found many, who had not been seven years out of their chains, living in finer houses, and evidently enjoying more of the comforts of life, than the average of slaveholders in Maryland."[183] And in the time since, Douglass has felt a measure of freedom speaking in the cause of freedom and against slavery, including to white audience.[184]

In the Appendix, Douglass addressed the question of religion, which he was not against unless it was that of slaveholding. His stance is clear and forceful as he contrasts the slaving Christianity of the United States with the true form of that religion: "I love the pure, peaceable, and impartial Christianity of Christ: I therefore hate the corrupt, slave-holding, women-whipping, cradle-plundering, partial and hypocritical Christianity of this land."[185] These scribes and Pharisees and their religion were the forces against which Douglass was testifying. And he also began a poem entitled, "A Parody," with the satiric representation of that religious posture: "Come, saints and sinners, hear me tell / How pious priests whip Jack and Nell."[186] Douglass hoped that his book would cast light on slavery in the United States and hasten the day of deliverance of his people from slavery. He relied on "the power of truth, love, and justice" for success.[187] This was an author not afraid to speak directly about white cruelty and hypocrisy in the Appendix, even after the body of his narrative had represented the cruel aspects of slavery but had also ended with his feeling of freedom and confidence in addressing a white audience in Massachusetts. Douglass expressed himself with eloquence and directness and was an accomplished author independent of the endorsement that Garrison, a white abolitionist, gave him. The relation between the end of the body of the narrative and the Appendix complicates the text and makes it more ironic and satirical than it would have been otherwise.

A white woman, Olive Gilbert, helped Sojourner Truth (Isabella Baumfree), who could not read or write, to record her life, from slavery to freedom, from obscurity to renown. This narrative was published in 1850. An inhabitant of New York state, Isabella found refuge and freedom with a Quaker family, the Van Wagenens, in 1826. She was shunned by the women's movement because of the color of her skin but won white women over at a women's rights convention in 1851. Harriet Beecher Stowe wrote a tribute to her in the *Atlantic Monthly* in 1863 and Lincoln invited her to the White House in October 1864.[188] Sojourner remembered the cellar her master put his slaves into with a cruelty inherent in the institution of slavery and the effects on them: the inhumanity to other people.[189] Like Mary Prince, Isabella (Sojourner) was sold and later married. The inhumane institution did not respect either love or family: "Isabella was married to a fellow-slave, named Thomas, who had previously had two wives, one of whom, if not both, had been torn from him and sold far away."[190] The illegal sale of her son was another instance of this violation of human relations. The insensitive words of her mistress illustrate this inhumanity: "*Ugh!* a *fine* fuss to make about a little *nigger!* Why, haven't you as many of 'em left as you can see to take care of? A pity 'tis, the niggers are not all in Guinea!!"[191] There is also something heroic in Isabella's overcoming of the cruelty and the woes of slavery: after obtaining the freedom of her child, she found her brother and sister.[192] Isabella became more and more interested in religion and, more particularly, in the scriptures.[193] Olive Gilbert praised Isabella's power of mind and pure character, "untrammeled by education and conventional customs," and her principle and enthusiasm, "which, under different circumstances, might easily have produced another Joan of Arc."[194] Although Gilbert provided a service to the cause against slavery and to Isabella herself by translating her life for readers, Gilbert's editorializing also qualified the achievement of Isabella by noting the potential and the hard situation of Sojourner's life.

Harriet Jacobs's *Incidents in the Life of a Slave Girl* (1861), which was published under the name Linda Brent and which L. Maria Child edited, also uncovered the ills, bad-faith, hypocrisy, and predatoriness of slavery. As with narratives of the New World, or travel narratives generally, the figure, testimony, and authority of the eyewitness represent an important strand in slave narratives. Jacobs began her Preface with this appeal: "READER, BE assured this narrative is no fiction. I am aware that some of my adventures may seem incredible; but they are, nevertheless, strictly true. I have not exaggerated the wrongs inflicted by Slavery; on the contrary, my descriptions fall far short of the facts."[195] Understatement or litotes also accompanied the insistence on truth and the disavowal of the fictive.

Another aspect of the story of slaves is, owing to the prevailing biases, that some figure, a white editor, printer, or member of the abolitionist movement, had to testify to the good character or even the ability of the slave or former slave to tell or write the story. We saw that with science and how Thomas Jefferson was placed in a position of supporting a black scientist and some of the ambivalence that attended that situation. Child, who is the Lydia we have discussed but used L. Maria here, began her brief Introduction with "THE AUTHOR of the following autobiography is personally known to me, and her conversation and manners inspire me with confidence."[196] To her credit, Child, who revised the manuscript at Jacobs's request, explained her editorial principles and was put in a position where she felt it necessary to say why a former slave had so much talent as a writer:

> It will naturally excite surprise that a woman reared in Slavery should be able to write so well. But circumstances will explain this. In the first place, nature endowed her with quick perceptions. Secondly, the mistress, with whom she lived till she was twelve years old, was a kind, considerate friend, who taught her to read and spell. Thirdly, she was placed in favorable circumstances after she came to the North; having frequent intercourse with intelligent persons, who felt a friendly interest in her welfare, and were disposed to give her opportunities for self-improvement.[197]

Although this "surprise" seems patronizing, Child was apparently worried that readers would think that she wrote this book, so she went out of her way to set out her editorial practice and the three reasons for Jacobs's accomplishment. Another kind of uneasiness is in the "intelligent persons" she got to meet in the North as this phrase elided education with intelligence and may even have implied that these people were white. Another contradiction or complexity in the crusade against the cruelty of slavery was the kind and friendly white people—even in the slaveholding South or Caribbean—that were good to slaves. If slavery were so bad, then would not racial equality be its end, so that an intelligent slave or ex-slave would not be an oxymoron. Then, as now, human beings dwelt in their own internal contradictions as well as those that surrounded them.

Child also admitted that she might be going against decorum by publishing this work because of the indelicate nature of some of the subjects, but that she ought to lift the veil so the public could know about this "peculiar phase of Slavery . . . with its monstrous features."[198] Child, who explicitly takes responsibility for this public unveiling of slavery, herself has a talent for writing. Hers is the art of persuasion:

> I do this for the sake of my sisters in bondage, who are suffering wrongs so foul, that our ears are too delicate to listen to them. I do it with the hope of arousing conscientious and reflecting women at the North to a sense of their duty in the exertion of moral influence on the question of Slavery, on all possible occasions. I do it with the hope that every man who reads this narrative

will swear solemnly before God that, so far as he has power to prevent it, no fugitive from Slavery shall ever be sent back to suffer in that loathsome den of corruption and cruelty.[199]

This is a rousing end to a brief Introduction that used rhetoric to bolster the cause. More specifically, Child employed anaphora or initial repetition to swear her commitment in the cause against sending fugitive slaves back to the South to endure the slavery they had fled. The last word of her Introduction is "cruelty," a word that echoed down from Las Casas in setting out his account of the abuse and enslavement of Indians in the Americas. How cruel Europeans and their descendents could be was a matter of religion and morality and not simply an aspect of economics and politics. This was as true in 1861 as it had been in 1542.

Jacobs began her tale with the striking sentence: "I WAS BORN a slave; but I never knew it till six years of happy childhood had passed away."[200] She mentions how skilled and intelligent her father, a carpenter, was and mentioned how their family was considered mulattoes. Throughout Jacobs's book an amplification occurs of the friction between happiness and slavery in the first sentence. This elaboration can happen in small or at large, so that another sentence about her family and her parents draws out this frictional theme: "They lived together in a comfortable home; and, though we were all slaves, I was so fondly shielded that I never dreamed I was a piece of merchandise, trusted to them for safe keeping, and liable to be demanded of them at any moment."[201] Here, Jacobs represented the insidious role of property as a means of undermining the happiness and family life of slaves. The violence against families could also be seen when her maternal grandmother, a granddaughter of a planter, despite being left free and given money with her two siblings and mother in his will, were captured on their way to St. Augustine during the Revolutionary War and sold to different buyers. Jacobs described different members of her family as intelligent and she mentioned the Anglo-Saxon part of her heritage in describing how white one of her relations looked and also revealed how under Southern law a slave could not own property because he or she was property. The white foster sister of Jacobs's mother, who died when Jacobs was six, was also kind to the young girl until she died when the child was twelve.[202]

There are many suggestive parts to Jacobs's narrative, but I touch on a few only. The cruelty and violence against family ties was also a theme of Jacobs's account. Jacobs once heard her mistress abuse a young slave girl who wanted to marry a black man: " 'Do you suppose that I will have you tending *my* children with the children of that nigger?' "[203] Jacobs's interpretation of this exchange followed with this observation: "The girl to whom she said this had a mulatto child, of course not acknowledged by its father. The poor black man who loved her would have been proud to acknowledge his helpless offspring."[204] Matters became even worse when Jacobs's master struck her for wanting to marry a free black and when he said: "Many masters would have killed you on the spot."[205] Such an incident for this slave girl spoke loudly about tyranny. In chapter 15, entitled "Continued Persecutions," Jacobs summed up this master: "Dr. Flint loved money, but he loved power more."[206] Like Douglass, Jacobs, wondered about those clergy who would justify slavery in the South: "Are doctors of divinity blind or are they hypocrites? I suppose some are the one, and some the other; but I think if they felt the interest in the poor and the lowly, that they ought to feel, they would not be so *easily* blinded."[207] Northern clergymen came south and allowed themselves to be hoodwinked by the luxury and conversation with the master and a few favored household slaves who deny any desire to be free, so that the clergyman in question returned home and complained about "the exaggerations of abolitions. He assures people that he has been to the south, and seen slavery for himself; that it is a beautiful 'patriarchal institution'; that the slaves don't want their freedom; that they have hallelujah meetings, and other religious privileges."[208] The narrative that Jacobs wrote is a testimony that slavery was harsh and that slaves dream about gaining their freedom. Mr. Sands, who was elected to Congress, was the father of Jacobs's children and she had him promise that he would free the children.[209] Jacobs's cunning and dishonest master continued to make her life miserable and substituted his forged letter for hers to her grandmother, so that Jacobs could not be free, but she had set up a trick for him in the service of freeing her family.[210] Jacobs worried that her own children might be sold as she contemplated their new destination—their father's: "I had no trust in thee, O Slavery! Never should I know peace till my children were emancipated with all due formalities of law."[211] The children were caught between their old master, Dr. Flint, and their new one, Mr. Sands (their father), who disputed authority over them. The hypocrisy of congressmen, as representatives of a hypocritical white society, was another theme on which Jacobs expatiated:

> If the secret memoirs of many members of Congress should be published, curious details would be unfolded. I once saw a letter from a member of Congress to a slave, who was the mother of six of his children. He wrote to request that she would send her children away from the great house before his return, as he expected to be accompanied by friends. The woman could not read, and was obliged to employ another to read the letter. The existence of the colored children did not trouble this gentleman, it was only the fear that friends might recognize in their features a resemblance to him.[212]

The double-standard dwelt in the everyday and in the hearth. Jacobs had a less comfortable home, despite the exalted station of the father of her children, for she lived in a hole for almost seven years within earshot of her children.[213] Slavery literally had a darker side for her, and she did anything she could to avoid and escape it.

Some other forms of uncovering and recognition remained in this account. Some discoveries were hard and others liberating. Arriving from Canada became a pretext for Jacobs to be allowed to see her daughter in Brooklyn, New York, but she found that her daughter was being treated as property by one of Mr. Sands's relations despite the relationship she and her mother shared with him.[214] Jacobs got a job as a nurse with an employer who pleased her: "She told me she was an English woman, and that was a pleasant circumstance to me, because I had heard they had less prejudice against color than Americans entertained."[215] Mrs. Bruce, who was understanding when Jacobs limbs swelled and had a hard time doing her work, had a doctor attend to her. Although the Bruces also tried to shield Jacobs from prejudice in the North, they could not.[216] When finally Jacobs told Mrs. Bruce that she was a fugitive slave, "She listened with true womanly sympathy, and told me she would do all she could to protect me."[217] Mrs. Bruce did help and they went from New York toward Boston, which Jacobs described in terms of happiness: "The day after my arrival was one of the happiest of my life. I felt as if I were beyond the reach of the bloodhounds; and, for the first time during many years, I had both my children together with me."[218] The death of Mrs. Bruce came that spring, and Mr. Bruce asked Jacobs to accompany his daughter to England to see relatives, so she left her son, Benny, in a trade, and her daughter, Ellen, with a friend to go to school. Jacobs's visit to England was a revelation: "For the first time in my life I was in a place where I was treated according to my deportment without reference to my complexion. I felt as if a great millstone had been lifted from my breast."[219] She saw London and Steventon in Berkshire, where many poor laborers lived: "I had heard much about the oppression of the poor in Europe. The people I saw around me were, many of them, among the poorest poor. But when I visited them in their little thatched cottages, I felt that the condition of even the meanest and most ignorant among them was vastly superior to the condition of the most favored slaves in America."[220] Jacobs was not playing down the hard conditions of impoverished Europeans, but she was able to count the ways in which they were protected as compared to slaves. For instance, "Their homes were very humble; but they were protected by law."[221] Jacobs set up a typology between England and America. Grace entered her heart in England, where she saw religion and the Episcopal church as being positive and not the contemptuous institution that allowed members like Dr. Flint and whose ministers bought and sold slaves. Like Douglass, Jacobs distinguished between false and true religion. During ten months in England, "I never saw the slightest symptom of prejudice against color. Indeed, I entirely forgot it, till the time came for us to return to America." About her return to the United States, Jacobs concluded: "It is a sad feeling to be afraid of one's native country."[222] Ellen was well but Benny had suffered prejudice from Americans, some of Irish background, for being "colored," so even the North was alive with bias. Benny had gone out on a whaling voyage. All this was before the Fugitive Slave Law, before which the judges of Massachusetts began to stoop.[223] That law forced many prosperous fugitive slaves in New York to go to Canada, and Jacobs feared for her own safety and freedom as the nurse to the infant of Mr. Bruce and his new wife, who was also against slavery and helped Jacobs in evading Dr. Flint and his relatives after his death. The Bruces purchased the freedom of Jacobs and her children.[224] The title of the last chapter of Jacobs's book, "Free At Last," seems to have been echoed by Martin Luther King about a hundred years later in one of his most poignant public moments. Jacobs had a sense of the story she told as well as its genre: "Reader, my story ends with freedom; not in the usual way, with marriage. I and my children are now free."[225] With a sense of poetry, Jacobs ended her narrative, the sweet and bitter mingling: "Yet the retrospection is not altogether without solace; for with those gloomy recollections come tender memories of my good old grandmother, like light, fleecy clouds floating over a dark and troubled sea."[226] After such an image the testimonials of two people, Amy Post, a Quaker, and George W. Lowther, whom the editor, Child, called "a highly respected colored citizen of Boston," were given to attest to and to witness the truth of Jacobs's narrative.[227] This life of a slave girl needed mediators into a wider world, but its eloquence and perceptiveness also speak for themselves.

Since the American Civil War, black writers have considered carefully slavery and its legacy. In 1896, Harvard University Press brought out W. E. B. Du Bois's *The Suppression of the African Slave-Trade to the United States of America, 1638–1870*. Du Bois concluded his study with a meditation on the American Revolution and Civil War: "No persons would have seen the Civil War with more surprise and horror than the Revolutionists of 1776; yet from the small and apparently dying institution of their day arose the walled and castled Slave-Power. From this we may conclude that it behooves nations as well as men to do things at the very moment when they ought to be done."[228] Liberty can have no accommodation that does not threaten itself: either all people are free or none is. The question of race would not go away even after emancipation. In "The Forethought" to *The Souls of Black Folk* (1903), Du Bois spoke prophetically: "Herein lie buried many things which if read with patience may show the strange meaning of being black here in the dawning of the Twentieth Century. The meaning is not without interest to you, Gentle Reader; for the problem of the Twentieth Century is the problem of the color-line."[229] Race was not simply a cause of strife in the twentieth century but its construction was part of high imperialism and was at the root of the Second World War. In "The Souls of White Folk," Du Bois provided a provocative, informed, and compressed critical history of race:

> The discovery of personal whiteness among the world's peoples is a very modern thing,—a nineteenth and twentieth century matter, indeed. The ancient world would have laughed at such a distinction. The Middle Ages regarded skin color with mild curiosity; and even up to the eighteenth century we were hammering our national manikins into one, great, Universal Man, with fine frenzy which ignored color and race even more than birth. Today we have changed all that, and the world in a sudden, emotional conversion has discovered that it is white and by that token, wonderful![230]

There is a sensible satire to Du Bois's uncovering of whiteness and the recent conversion to it. And what is this new hue? According to Du Bois, "I am given to understand that whiteness is the ownership of the earth forever and ever, Amen!"[231] He left off this piece on the souls of white folk with these ghosts and with the modern Prometheus tethered to a fable of the past proclaiming his whiteness. But the speaker in Du Bois's essay answers this divine thief with a question "Why, then, devour your own vitals if I can answer even as proudly, 'I am black!' "[232]

Other voices questioned race and asserted the freedom of black people. In 1912 an anonymous work, *The Autobiography of an Ex-Colored Man* masqueraded successfully as a memoir until its author, James Weldon Johnson (1871–1938), a poet and diplomat, acknowledged it as his own in 1927. The text turned out to be a novel that followed important conventions that arose from the slave narratives. The protagonist, who has gone white, lamented his choices at the end of this work. Of the "colored men who are publically fighting the cause of their race," the first-person narrator said: "Even those who oppose them know that these men have the eternal principles of right on their side, and they will be victors even though they should go down in defeat. Beside them I feel small and selfish. I am an ordinarily successful white man who has made a little money. They are men who are making history and a race. I, too, might have taken part in a work so glorious."[233] This text, which was fiction in the form of truth, has its narrator, who was a character playing a person, conclude by amplifying this point: "I have sold my birthright for a mess of pottage."[234] We have encountered White Indians and now blacks who would be white in a world of the new whiteness Du Bois described. The matter of race divided a rising great nation that would displace the great Western European empires. Race and whiteness haunted the twentieth century, beyond the atrocities of the Nazis and Klu Klux Klan. Nations and empires contested within themselves, and race was part of that contestation and agony.

Not all people and all parts of government supported this prejudice and division. During the Great Depression of the 1930s, the U.S. government, attempted to provide unemployed writers with work. Through the Works Progress Administration (WPA), it funded the Federal Writers' Project. One of its legacies was the Slave Narrative Collection, which consisted in providing transcripts of interviews with over 2,000 former slaves. The memory of slavery, which is still with us, was living in the 1930s. The nature of slavery was sometimes ambiguous. Mary Anderson (b. 1851) noted that although the slaves were allowed to go the white people's church near Franklinton in Wake County, North Carolina, they did not have access to education: the whites "would not teach any of us to read and write. Books and papers were forbidden."[235] The arrival of the Union Army created a great moment: "The footmen stacked their shining guns and began to build fires and cook. They called the slaves, saying, 'You are free.'" Anderson continued her dramatic representation of this momentous and festive occasion: "Slaves were whooping and laughing and acting like they were crazy. Yankee soldiers were shaking hands with the Negroes and calling them Sam, Dinah, Sarah, and asking them questions." This soon led to a celebration: "The Negroes and Yankees were cooking and eating together. The Yankees told them to come on and join them, they were free." All the while, "Marster and Missus sat on the porch and they were so humble no Yankee bothered anything in the Great House."[236] After the slaves were freed and had wandered for a year, the master and his wife asked any they could find to come home and some did and were happy because they had been hungry: "Most all spoke of them as 'Missus' and 'Marster' as they did before the surrender, and getting back home was the greatest pleasure of all."[237] Here was a return that complicated the notions of slavery and freedom, white and black, and this is described by a former slave. The liberation was not always even, as Boston Blackwell explained:

> I reckon they was right smart old masters what didn't want to let they slaves go after freedom. They hated to turn them loose. Just let them work on. Heap of them didn't know freedom come. I used to hear tell how the government had to send soldiers away down in the far back country to make them turn the slaves loose. I can't tell you how them free niggers was living; I was too busy looking out for myself. Heaps of them went to farming. They was sharecroppers.[238]

Blackwell also talked about something beyond vestiges of slavery and the resistance to change among the masters. He had been a member of the Union Army and saw a great deal and witnessed other developments: "Them Ku Kluxers was terrible—what they done to people. Oh, God, they was bad. They come sneaking up and runned you outen your house and take everything you had. They was rough on the women and children. People all wanted to stay close by where the soldiers was. I sure knowed they was my friend."[239] Another aspect of the postwar period was how whites and black voted and how there were "colored" legislators and clerks everywhere until "The Jim Crow law, it put us out."[240] As he was an employed man with the army and not a soldier, he did not receive his pension from the army after he got sick from working on water closets.[241]

Other former slaves testified to the hardship of slavery. In an interview with Watt McKinney, Tines Kendricks, born in Crawford County, Georgia, also showed the variousness of slavery: "My old master, Arch Kendricks, I will say this, he certainly was a good fair man. Old Miss and de young master, Sa, dey was strictly tough, and, Boss, I is telling you de truth, dey was cruel."[242] Kendricks also remembered Reverend Dickey who advocated freedom for slaves.[243] He could also recall how hard the institution was: "Slavery time was tough, Boss. You don't know how tough it was. I can't explain to you just how bad all the niggers want to get dey freedom."[244] The free blacks were treated almost worse than slaves because they were often forced to work off their "taxes" and because "De slaveowners, dey just despised dem 'free niggers' and make it just as hard on dem as dey can."[245] Another aspect of slavery was part of Kendricks's recollection—the arbitrary and unpredictable breaking up of families because slaves were property. Many white people resisted after the war to make the formal agreements with blacks that the government insisted on: "De white folks at first didn't want to make de contracts and say dey wasn't going to. So de government filled the jail with dem, and after dat everyone make de contract."[246] The violence did not end with emancipation: "When my race first got dere freedom and begin to leave dere masters, a heap of de masters got raging mad and just tore up truck. Dey say dey going to kill every nigger dey find. Some of dem did do dat very thing. Boss, sure enough. I'm telling you de truth. Dey shot niggers down by de hundreds. Dey just wasn't going to let dem enjoy dey freedom. Dat is de truth, Boss."[247] Fannie Moore, born in Moore, South Carolina, also spoke about education and about violence. She observed: "None of the niggers have any learnin', weren't never allowed to as much as pick up a piece of paper"; the reason, she provided: "De white folks afraid to let de chillen learn anythin'. They afraid dey get too smart and be harder to manage."[248] Terror also awaited blacks: "After de War de Ku Klux broke out. Oh. Dey was mean! . . . Dey never go round much in de day. Just night. Dey take de poor niggers away in de woods and beat 'em and hang 'em."[249] This kind of legacy has poisoned the freedom of blacks and affected the consciences of many whites since. One last testimonial interview should round out this representation of slavery, that by Bill Simms, born in Osceola, Missouri, who spoke to Leta Grey. Even though Simms said that "Most masters were good to their slaves," he also pointed out implicitly or not when they were misguided.[250]

In one passage Simms brought together a number of strands: "Slaves were never allowed to talk to white people other than their masters or someone their masters knew, as they were afraid the white man might have the slave run away. The masters aimed to keep their slaves in ignorance and the ignorant slaves were all in favor of the Rebel army. Only the more intelligent were in favor of the Union army."[251] Simms himself was sent to work for the Confederate Army and then ran away to join the Union Army. Still, after the war, he returned to his master, who was kind to his former slaves. Unspecified people, perhaps those around the master's nephew and heir, wanted my master's land and were "afraid he would give it all away to us slaves, so they killed him, and would have killed us if we had stayed at home."[252] Any white, regardless of class, was in danger if he helped blacks even if they were his former slaves. Simms's two daughters received good educations and became teachers, "the oldest one being the first colored girl to ever graduate" from Ottawa University.[253] Education, despite the violence and neglect, was the key to freedom, for slaves and free blacks before and after the Civil War, something that Ishmael Reed suggests in his fictional slave narrative, *Flight to Canada* (1976).[254] Freedom and the "deslaving" of blacks and the weaning of whites from a politics of racism and "colonial" authority were widespread. In the United States some of these events were intense and well documented, but in the age of "decolonization" and the rise of universal human rights in practice and not simply in theory, many peoples of color in many nations pushed for their freedom and dignity. The voices of abolitionists and especially of slaves are reminders on the ground of the narrative of domination and slavery in peoples, bones, hearts, and minds and not simply in the hover of statistics and the distant perspective of time.

VII

The twentieth century has involved decolonization and problems with human and civil rights despite the legal abolition of slavery. The crises connected with the two world wars and the tensions between empires and their colonies affected discourses and practices of freedom. The Nazis enslaved and exterminated people in a fashion that might have part of its genealogy in the way the Spaniards treated the Natives in the New World. Other European empires and their successor states (former colonies) also mistreated aboriginal peoples and while some of them were fighting the Nazis, they, too, embodied their own forms of racial discrimination, which, although not as virulent or systematically violent or deadly, were bad enough. The legacies of these empires were ambivalent and contradictory. Paradoxically, the opposition from within Europe or its self-critical tradition became available as a weapon for others to use against European and even

American nationalism and imperialism. Sometimes, figures within the powers themselves—as Lincoln had done in the United States and Harold Macmillan would do in the disbanding of the British Empire—would call for an end to the abuses and advocate for a sense of equality and freedom for all. Gandhi, Martin Luther King, and Nelson Mandela were all able to use part of the education they took from the European tradition and employ peaceful means to curtail or end the violence of racism. The passive resistance of the suffragettes in their battles in Britain and the United States against discrimination against women was something, like the teachings of Christ, that affected leaders, such as these three well-known proponents of human rights and freedom and others, like Ralph Bunche, whose reputations are becoming more widespread, in their fight for justice.

In the twentieth century slavery persisted but came to be outlawed through the United Nations. The sheer numbers of slaves traded is so vast that this universal abolition was in reaction, in part, to the legacy of the Atlantic slave trade, perhaps the most nefarious commerce, a terrible dealing in human beings. Portugal became the principal slaving country: its part in the slave trade endured the longest. Up to the abolition of slavery, Portugal, including Brazil, would come to transport about 4,650,000 slaves in about 30,000 voyages. After Portugal, Britain was the leading trader in slaves: it transported about 56 percent of the number of slaves Portugal would in about 40 percent of the voyages. Spain (including Cuba) and France (including the West Indies) became major slave-trading empires. Although considerably smaller traders, the Netherlands, British North America (United States), and Denmark also had considerable involvement in this trade. The major destinations for slaves were as follows: Brazil about 4,000, 000 slaves, the Spanish Empire 2,500,000; British West Indies 2,000,000; the French West Indies (including Cayenne) 1,600,000; British North America and the United States 500,000; the Dutch West Indies (including Surinam) 500, 000; Danish West Indies 28,000; Europe 200,000. Portugal and Spain set the example for those who followed and became the largest slaveholders. Sugar plantations employed more slaves—6,000,000 of the over 11,000,000 transported—than all the rest of employments.[255] The beginnings of the Portuguese expansion—its economy and its use of slaves—were more modest than in its later empire. Madeira and the Azores in the fifteenth century produced wine and sugar, providing exports for Lisbon and a valuable example for those who would later colonize Brazil.[256] What the Portuguese began in the middle 1400s, Brazil ended in the later 1800s. Born of this historical slavery was an important aspect of human rights. The British had been leaders in the abolition of slavery. Africa was a place where historical changes had occurred in the institution of slavery. In Africa, a shift occurred from the traditional exchange directly or indirectly of slaves for manufactured goods.

The raw materials of Africa—such as cocoa, cotton, rubber, palm oil, and diamonds—attracted Europeans.[257] As the world's foremost naval and industrial power, Britain wanted to control the eastern and southern coasts of Africa, while controlling the Suez Canal, to maintain its empire in India and beyond. European direct political control was coming to Africa. Portugal, which began the expansion into Africa, was still there. France, Belgium, Germany, and Italy were all involved in the Scramble for Africa. But the British attempted to chase slavery from Africa, even, as it had absorbed African territory before the First World War.

These empires and powers had their own critics from within. In some ways, these critiques were based on a notion that the empires or the nation had not lived up to its ideals of freedom and rights. Henry David Thoreau's "On the Duty of Civil Disobedience" influenced Gandhi and Martin Luther King both, and, in *Stride Toward Freedom* (1958), King had also paid tribute to his debt to Gandhi, especially in articulating the power of love.[258] King would inspire others, like Nelson Mandela. Gandhi, who was educated in England, began his political life in South Africa and returned to India, where he made such a difference to independence. He presented an opposition to empire and an advocacy of one nation—India—on the subcontinent. His work, *Hind Swaraj* (1909), was self-expression, a work he also translated into English. It is a definition of home rule, a response to terrorism, a critique of modernity as being a worse threat than colonialism, an attempt to reconcile Indians and the British, a revision of dharma or practical philosophy in terms of civic humanism.[259] Reminiscent of the works of Plato, this dialogue has the Editor respond to the Reader: "the whole of India is not touched. Those alone who have been affected by western civilization have become enslaved." The work continued with a psychological insight into the internalization of slavery: "We measure the universe by our own miserable foot-rule. When we are slaves, we think that the whole universe is enslaved. Because we are in an abject condition, we think that the whole of India is in that condition." Freedom is a matter of imputation and insight: "As a matter of fact, it is not so, but it is as well to impute our slavery to the whole of India. But if we bear in mind the above fact, we can see that, if we become free, India is free."[260] In this context Western civilization is not the Christian, religious, or spiritual dimension but something that undermines its own spirituality. The swaraj, for Indians, is learning to rule themselves. Gandhi exposed the dynamics of the imperialist and the slave. Just before and after the First World War, opposition to imperialism intensified.

From that war a decline occurred in the European empires. Even though Germany was bombing Britain, it took years, although not as long as in the First World War, for the United States to come to the support of this democracy and its empire, which it had left at the end of the eighteenth century. For instance, in August 1941, Winston Churchill and Franklin Roosevelt met and established the Atlantic Charter with many principles. The first principle spoke of self-government and liberty—which had a long connection in the English-speaking world but most notably in the United States and Canada. In the second principle the Charter expressed opposition against the Nazis, who were a force of death, dominance, and slavery in the world. The third principle affirmed that Britain and the United States "respect the right of all peoples to choose the form of government under which they will live; and they wish to see sovereign rights and self government restored to those who have been forcibly deprived of them."[261] In December 1941, President Franklin Delano Roosevelt, who had been providing some support for Britain without committing to the conflict, brought his country into the Second World War. After the United States declared war on Japan for the bombing of Pearl Harbor, Germany went to war with the Americans. Roosevelt expressed his view to Congress—"the Imperial Government of Japan has committed unprovoked acts of war" and reported to it that "On the morning of December 11 the Government of Germany, pursuing its course of world conquest, declared war against the United States."[262] Despite the fine words of Hitler and his government, the German action came as no surprise to the president: "The long known and the long expected has thus taken place. The forces endeavoring to enslave the entire world now are moving toward this hemisphere. Never before has there been a greater challenge to life, liberty, and civilization." Freedom continued to be a theme in the wars of nations.

Frictions between the great powers, successors to the European empires—the United States America and Union of Soviet Socialist Republics—also marked the period from 1917 to 1989, mostly after the Second World War, when the ideological Cold War began. Churchill spoke of an iron curtain between east and west in March 1946 and the Soviets began to speak about being encircled and against Anglo-American world domination. The commander of the Allied forces in Europe, Dwight Eisenhower later saw this struggle in the postwar era as one of freedom against slavery. Both the United States and the Soviet Union spent vast amounts on their militaries and on their buildup of nuclear arms. This arms race in the Cold War characterized much of the period from 1945 into the early 1990s, despite various treaties to limit nuclear weapons between the United States of America and Union of Soviet Socialist Republics.[263] The notions of freedom and slavery are older than the Greeks, but has resonated in modern Western history over the past 500 years or so. As much as empires contested, they shifted allegiances and alliances.

An interest in human rights across the globe occurred in the wake of the Second World War. The United Nations played a central role in the attempt to widen rights. In 1948 Universal Declaration of Human Rights reinforced this emphasis on freedom, respect, and human dignity: "**WHEREAS** recognition of the inherent dignity and of the equal and inalienable rights of all members of the human family is the foundation of freedom, justice and peace in the world." This document also addressed the abuses of rights as they had just occurred in the Second World War: "**WHEREAS** disregard and contempt for human rights have resulted in barbarous acts which have outraged the conscience of mankind, and the advent of a world in which human beings shall enjoy freedom of speech and belief and freedom from fear and want has been proclaimed as the highest aspiration of the common people." Rights were not to be a privilege of elites. People should have freedom to speak and believe in security and plenty. The Declaration also provided a legal dimension to rights: "**WHEREAS** it is essential, if man is not to be compelled to have recourse, as a last resort, to rebellion against tyranny and oppression, that human rights should be protected by the rule of law." [264] There is an echo of the long-standing debate in political philosophy whether it is just to rid the state of a tyrant. For instance, Plato included discussions over tyranny; the expulsion of Tarquin, the last king of Rome, was well known even in the Renaissance in the various representations of the rapes of Lucretia (Lucrece); and the Declaration of Independence justified the taking up of arms against a tyrant. This declaration of 1948 also contained other related clauses that the General Assembly proclaimed. The ideal was that human rights were to be part of a rule of law that would not be tyrannous. These rights were to be universal and not the province of one group or people.

The Nazis had exterminated millions of Jews in the Second World War. The problems in Palestine intensified in the shadow of the Holocaust. One of the principal people who attempted to diffuse this crisis was Ralph Bunche, a pioneering Black American (1904–71), whose grandmother was born into slavery. He negotiated for eleven months to put into place agreements for armistice between the Arab States and Israel. Bunche told *Reader's Digest* that "his grandmother appeared white 'on the outside' but was 'all black fervor inside.' "[265] In 1950, the Nobel Prize was awarded to Bunche. His Nobel Lecture of December 11, 1950 raised the problem of lofty words as ideals, obfuscation, and aggression: "The words used by statesmen in our day no longer have a common meaning. Perhaps they never had. Freedom, democracy, human rights, international morality, peace itself, mean different things to different men. Words, in a constant flow of propaganda—itself an instrument of war—are employed to confuse, mislead, and debase the common man."[266] As in the UN Declaration of 1948, Bunche appealed to the situation of ordinary people. He also talked about the cultural relativism of these terms. Bunche quoted Voltaire on war as aggression and the tendency of the aggressor to rationalize his actions with the "pretext of justice." Moreover, Bunche called attention to the valuable but precarious contribution of the United Nations, which "seeks only unity, not uniformity, out of the world's diversity." The ideal of peace and the practice of peacekeeping were part of the mission of the United Nations.

The Second World War shattered the Western European empires. Nationalism, which had spread from Western to Eastern Europe, now encompassed the globe. Not something natural, but a passing phase, the so-called white man's burden or the Social Darwinist imperialism of the late nineteenth century and early twentieth culminated in the war with the Nazis and the second major phase in the self-immolation of Europe. Empire had altered the settler colonies through slavery and immigration. The decline of Europe and the slow and eventual rise of multicultural states like the United States, Brazil, Canada, and Australia altered the balance of power in the world. The massive movements of immigrants were a central characteristic of this period. Since 1945 a vast scale of global migration has taken place: as part of that movement, refugees have been moving decade after decade. It is possible that about one hundred million people have been victims of war, political persecution, and uneven economic development while tens of millions have fled in search of economic opportunity and safety. The United States, Canada, Australia, France, Britain, Sweden, Germany, Saudi Arabia, Nigeria, Singapore, Iran, and South Africa are among their destinations. In the United States, illegal immigration from places like Mexico and China became a matter of debate. Sweatshops in Western capitals have made for hard working conditions. Among other abuses have been modern slavery in the charcoal industry in Brazil and in the carpet business in India. No matter how prohibited by law, these invidious practices have continued. Children and women suffered much from these abuses and from migration.[267]

Not all the critics of racial discrimination and economic servitude were from peoples whom the imperial powers had enslaved or disadvantaged. Harold Macmillan, prime minister of Britain, advocated rights for Africans in South Africa just as later Presidents John Kennedy and Lyndon Johnson would seek to protect and extend civil rights for black Americans. Like Churchill, Macmillan had an American mother. As a result of the Suez Crisis, he became prime minister on January 10, 1957 and continued to preside over the decolonization of the British Empire. Macmillan met with President Dwight Eisenhower on March 20, 1957 in Bermuda and consulted with Eisenhower over the efforts to wind down empire. The end of one top secret telegram from Macmillan to Eisenhower in the late 1950s said that "all this 'liquidation of colonialism' is going so well that I would be sorry if there was any hitch, especially one in the Caribbean."[268] Macmillan was also concerned with Africa. He was the first British prime minister to speak before the Houses of Parliament in Cape Town, South Africa: his "Winds of Change" speech there on February 3, 1960 set out, diplomatically but directly, a vision of a world of equal nations where people of different backgrounds could come together in their countries and in the world as a community. Macmillan praised the economic development of South Africa and Britain's role in investment despite its exhaustion after two world wars.[269] He appealed to his own experience as a soldier in the First World War and a member of Churchill's cabinet in the Second and said "I know personally the value of the contribution which your forces made to victory in the cause of freedom."[270] Here, Macmillan came to the differences between Britain and South Africa. He thought that South Africa could be a leader in Africa owing to its wealth and knowledge as an industrialized country, but that it needed to embrace "the new Africa of to-day." Appealing to history, Macmillan justified African aspirations and the legitimacy of nationalism: "Ever since the break up of the Roman Empire one of the constant facts of the political life in Europe has been the emergence of independent nations. They have come into existence over the centuries in different forms with different kinds of government. But all have been inspired by a deep, keen feeling of nationalism, which has grown as the nations have grown." This use of history underpinned the decolonization over which Macmillan was presiding. His typology between past and present, Roman Empire and contemporary empires (including the British Empire) set out a sympathetic movement from empire to nation. Moving into the present, Macmillan was explicit that European nationalism would come to apply in other areas of the world: "In the twentieth century, and especially since the end of the war, the processes which gave birth to the nation states of Europe have been repeated all over the world. We have seen the awakening of national consciousness in peoples who have for centuries lived in dependence on some other power." This is an argument for the evolution of nations that arises from the growth and decline of empire. This devolution of power is what Macmillan was observing and advocating. From past to present, from the general to the specific, Macmillan moved, focusing on the most recent events that had caused anxiety for the white government of South Africa: "Fifteen years ago this movement spread through Asia. Many countries there, of different races and civilizations, pressed their claim to an independent national life. To-day the same thing is happening in Africa."[271] Macmillan attempted to soften the point, but he asserted that national policies must accept "this growth of national consciousness" as a fact and take it into account. In this view, South Africa—which "sprung from Europe, the home of nationalism" and which created "the first of the national Africanisms"— must face this actuality. This national consciousness was worldwide, but "The wind of change is blowing through this Continent." In speaking to the members of the white government of South Africa, Macmillan brought out a key paradox: "this tide of national consciousness which is now rising in Africa is a fact for which you and we and the other nations of the Western world are ultimately responsible." Nationalism, he continued, is part of the great advancements that "Western civilisation" has made in science, agriculture, communication, and, above all, education.[272] In many ways in the Cold War this nationalism has to be accepted and made part of the West. Not embracing this fact of the growth of national consciousness would imperil the precarious balance between East and West, between "the free world" and the Communists. There is then a political as well as a humane motive to the self-determination of nations beyond Europe and in Africa specifically. Macmillan asked whether non-aligned countries will become Communist or "will the great experiments in self-government that are being made in Asia and Africa, especially within the Commonwealth, prove so successful, and by their example so compelling, that the balance will come down in favour of freedom and justice?"[273] In this view, the struggle between Communism and freedom was one for minds. Each nation must make its own choice. Even though Macmillan makes a strong case, he implies that the imperial center in its last acts of devolution would not dictate to its last or former colonies: "It is a basic principle of the Commonwealth that we respect each other's sovereignty in matters of internal policy." Winding down empire and giving birth to nations constituted concerns and responsibilities for Britain: "If I may be frank, I will venture now to say this. What Governments and Parliaments in the United Kingdom have done since the last war in according independence to India, Pakistan, Ceylon, Malaya and Ghana, and what they *will* do for Nigeria and other countries now nearing independence—all this, though we must and do take full and sole responsibility for it, we do in the belief that it is the only way to establish the future of the Commonwealth and of the free world on sound foundations."[274] Further, Macmillan admitted that Britain had tried to learn and apply lessons from the past management of those affairs, basing its judgment of justice and right and wrong on Christianity and the rule of law. The extension of rights and sovereignty came to remake the world after the Second World War.

Macmillan continued to make his case with firm but gentle persuasion. In these territories that were achieving or were able to achieve independence, Britain had the aim "to raise the material standards of life" in "a society that respects the rights of individuals" and in which people share political responsibility and power and in which merit alone was the criterion for economic and political advancement.[275] Furthermore, minorities of all kinds in the various new and emerging nations needed "to live together in harmony." This was a vision not unlike that Nelson Mandela put into place in South Africa in the 1990s. Macmillan then quoted a speech of his foreign minister,

Selwyn Lloyd, to the General Assembly if the United Nations on September 17, 1959, in which he advocated all people of different backgrounds in territories had the right to security, freedom, and well-being: " 'we (that is the British) reject the idea of any inherent superiority of one race over another. Our policy, therefore, is non-racial; it offers a future in which Africans, Europeans, Asians, the Peoples of the Pacific and others with whom we are concerned, will all play their full part as citizens in the countries where they live, and in which feelings of race will be submerged in loyalty to new nations.' " Nation was more important than race and any theory that would be based on racial superiority. In doing their duty the British might, according to Macmillan, "sometimes make difficulties" for his South African hosts, while understanding that Africa is a longtime home for the Europeans who settled on its southernmost tip.[276] Macmillan, having been familiar with the attempt for equal rights in Africa and in the United States, saw the creation of many new countries in Africa and elsewhere, but did not live to see the release of Nelson Mandela and the birth of a renewed South Africa based on extended suffrage and equality.

   Martin Luther King, an internationally known figure in the fight for civil rights, had one eye on the lack of adequate human rights for African Americans in the United States and another on similar situations beyond its borders. On April 16, 1963, King had written his "Letter from Birmingham Jail," in which he had addressed to eight members of the clergy from Alabama, and had connected civil rights in the United States with independence from colonialism overseas: "The nations of Asia and Africa are moving with jetlike speed toward gaining political independence, but we stiff creep at horse-and-buggy pace toward gaining a cup of coffee at a lunch counter."[277] When arrested and jailed in Birmingham, King gained attention across the country. On August 28, 1963, King led a march on Washington, where, on the steps of the Lincoln Memorial, he began with a celebration of freedom and then appealed to the figure of Lincoln in his "I Have a Dream" speech: "I am happy to join with you today in what will go down in history as the greatest demonstration for freedom in the history of our nation. Five score years ago, a great American, in whose symbolic shadow we stand today, signed the Emancipation Proclamation. This momentous decree came as a great beacon light of hope to millions of Negro slaves who had been seared in the flames of withering injustice. It came as a joyous daybreak to end the long night of their captivity." This invocation of Lincoln emphasized the importance of a European American president committed to the cause of Africans but also the fact that the practice in the nation had fallen far short of the Proclamation: "But one hundred years later, the Negro still is not free."[278] King echoed Lincoln and appealed to his memory as a beacon. By appealing to American political, legal, and constitutional history, King focused directly on the problems for African Americans and for the country as a whole: "When the architects of our republic wrote the magnificent words of the Constitution and the Declaration of Independence, they were signing a promissory note to which every American was to fall heir. This note was a promise that all men, yes, black men as well as white men, would be guaranteed the unalienable rights of life, liberty, and the pursuit of happiness." King uses pacing and pauses to lead up to his declaration of what has happened to that promise: "It is obvious today that America has defaulted on this promissory note insofar as her citizens of color are concerned." King's people and the entire nation could put Lincoln's words into practice. That dream King had was of healing and community, not of violence and separation: "I have a dream that one day on the red hills of Georgia the sons of former slaves and the sons of former slave owners will be able to sit down together at the table of brotherhood." King meets the issue of slavery head-on. His speech culminates in a cry for liberty: "And when this happens, When we allow freedom to ring, when we let it ring from every village and every hamlet, from every state and every city, we will be able to speed up that day when all of God's children, black men and white men, Jews and Gentiles, Protestants and Catholics, will be able to join hands and sing in the words of the old Negro spiritual, 'Free at last! free at last! thank God Almighty, we are free at last!' " There was a religious dimension to this speech, so that heaven becomes a measure of how far short this earth has fallen short of justice but also represented a way of leading people of all faiths on to a just society here and now. A practical utopia—an actual activism built on a dream—was a key part of King's inclusive vision. This speech and the event it marked in Washington were a great success. They helped strengthen the movement to desegregation and contributed to the passing of the Civil Rights Act in 1964. King's search for freedom and equal rights were part of a larger rights movement and of devolution of colonies. His work in the United States might be called a decolonization from within.

More successes followed. For instance, King won the Nobel Prize. He began his speech on December 10, 1964 in Oslo in Norway with "I accept the Nobel Prize for Peace at a moment when twenty-two million Negroes of the United States of America are engaged in a creative battle to end the long night of racial injustice."[279] That long night had been going on before the Portuguese entered the slave trade in Africa. It was moonless after that. King, like Gandhi, appealed in this speech to spirituality. He spoke of the way nations and people ought to be not as they are. For him, Christianity was not about bullets or nuclear annihilation. Here, King brought up India and Africa, quietly but not directly alluding to the work of Gandhi and those who marched for Indian independence, but making a specific reference to the urgency in South Africa: "Civilization and violence are antithetical concepts. Negroes of the United States, following the people of India, have demonstrated that nonviolence is not sterile passivity, but a powerful moral force which makes for social transformation. Sooner or later all the people of the world will have to discover a way to live together in peace, and thereby transform this pending cosmic elegy into a creative psalm of brotherhood." Peaceful kinds of protest were the means and peace was the end. Like Harold Macmillan, King also focused on the need for justice in South Africa. Infused with the Bible, King also alluded to English Romantic poets, echoing William Wordsworth when calling attention to the injustice in South Africa: "Your honor, once again, Chief (Albert) Luthuli of South Africa, whose struggles with and for his people, are still met with the most brutal expression of man's inhumanity to man." Moreover, King ended his speech with an allusion to John Keats's "Ode to a Grecian Urn," in an aesthetic and spiritual moment : "I think Alfred Nobel would know what I mean when I say that I accept this award in the spirit of a curator of some precious heirloom which he holds in trust for its true owners—all those to whom beauty is truth and truth beauty—and in whose eyes the beauty of genuine brotherhood and peace is more precious than diamonds or silver or gold." Here is a moment where people find themselves amid the true and the beautiful regardless of their color. King gave a speech ("I've Been to the Mountaintop"),—the day before he was assassinated—in Memphis, Tennessee, enumerating different places in the stations of history where he would not stop: "I would go on, even to the great heyday of the Roman Empire. And I would see developments around there, through various emperors and leaders." Calling his own nation sick, King said it was in trouble. He witnessed a movement toward freedom in many parts of the world where black people wanted liberty: "The masses of people are rising up. And wherever they are assembled today, whether they are in Johannesburg, South Africa; Nairobi, Kenya; Accra, Ghana; New York City; Atlanta, Georgia; Jackson, Mississippi; or Memphis, Tennessee—the cry is always the same—'We want to be free.' " Here is an epic catalogue of suffering from the effects of slavery and subjugation and the desire to throw that legacy off for freedom. By comparing the situation of the United States with that in other countries, King placed this fight for liberty in context: "If I lived in China or even Russia, or any totalitarian country, maybe I could understand the denial of certain basic First Amendment privileges, because they hadn't committed themselves to that over there." King was clearly not in favor of totalitarianism, including Communism. In addition to the denial of free speech in the United States, which prides itself in freedom, he wanted to stress the strength and wealth of black Americans: "the Negro collectively is richer than most nations of the world. We have an annual income of more than thirty billion dollars a year, which is more than all of the exports of the United States, and more than the national budget of

Canada. Did you know that? That's power right there, if we know how to pool it." This speech complicated the boundaries between white and black people: King told of a "demented black woman" who nearly killed him when she stabbed him and a letter from a young white girl who heard that King might have died if he had sneezed after the stabbing, but she said: "I'm so happy you didn't sneeze." Then King could keep going toward the mountaintop and could take the entire nation back to the well the founding fathers dug so deep in the Declaration of Independence and the Constitution. With the Bible and Negro spirituals in mind, King's last words in his last public speech would be prophetic, his vision, like that of Gandhi, too great for his assassin: "We've got some difficult days ahead. But it doesn't matter with me now. Because I've been to the mountaintop. And I don't mind. Like anybody, I would like to live a long life. Longevity has its place. But I'm not concerned about that now." King continued in his religious as well as political commitment, which he hardly separated: "I just want to do God's will. And He's allowed me to go up to the mountain. And I've looked over. And I've seen the promised land. I may not get there with you. But I want you to know tonight, that we, as a people, will get to the promised land. And I'm happy, tonight. I'm not worried about anything. I'm not fearing any man. Mine eyes have seen the glory of the coming of the Lord."[280] Martin Luther King was shot on the balcony the next day by a white man, who could not let his people go there. Nearly thirty years later, on January 24, 1998, a statue of Mahatma Gandhi was unveiled in Atlanta at the Martin Luther King Jr. Historical Site as a way of marking the fiftieth anniversary of the independence of India and just a week shy of the fiftieth anniversary of Gandhi's assassination. During the 1990s, Nelson Mandela put his prison years behind him with magnanimous forgiveness and led South Africa into a peaceful and multilingual and multicultural democracy.

Like Martin Luther King, Mandela, too, won the Nobel Prize for his work on behalf of black people and civil rights. Just as King mentioned Gandhi in his Nobel speech, so too did Mandela refer to King in his: "It will not be presumptuous of us if we also add, among our predecessors, the name of another outstanding Nobel Peace Prize winner, the late Rev Martin Luther King Jr."[281] Among other webs of allusion, this one connected Gandhi, King, and Mandela. It also linked them to those in Britain and North America who advocated liberty, fought slavery, and favored civil disobedience. Moreover, others among the black population, like Bishop Tutu, and the white population, like F. W. de Klerk, who also fought apartheid, moved South Africa along from its apartheid past to its inclusive future. De Klerk, the cowinner of the Nobel Peace Prize for 1994, dedicated his prize to UNICEF and thereby the education of children as the hope for peace. He stressed the connection between economic development and democracy: "And hand in hand with economic development goes democracy. Wherever economic growth occurs it promotes the establishment of representative and democratic institutions-institutions which invariably develop a framework for peace. It is highly significant that there has never been a war between genuine and universal democracies. There have been countless wars between totalitarian and authoritarian states."[282] In South Africa, views on apartheid in the European population were always split. Now the peoples of African, European, Indian, and mixed ancestry would have to work together to make a democracy with universal rights work in that country. The legacy of empires and the act of decolonization can go on long after formal or legal independence.

Despite the great strides taken to end one of the great scourges of the nineteenth and twentieth centuries—racism—slavery persisted in some quarters. Despite its illegality, as set out in the declarations of the United Nations, the practice of slavery endures. The conditions still exist. In each country there is a danger that some form of slavery is being practiced, condoned, or supported both at home and abroad. Here, let us concentrate on one example almost twenty-five years ago. For instance, in 1980, Arab masters in Mauritania, where the Portuguese first carried away slaves in 1441, were said to have 90,000 black African slaves. This, to use William Blake's phrase, is a fearful symmetry.

Into the twenty-first century throughout the world, slavery persists. Whether among children working on rugs in India or charcoal operations in Brazil or among diplomats living with immunity in world capitals, slavery endures. The exploitation of work contains a shadowland between those who live on starvation-wages in poor conditions and those who are kidnapped, coerced, and terrorized as slaves for sex or cheap labor. This legacy goes on: so many saw exploitation from the eighteenth century into the early twentieth century from Adam Smith through Karl Marx to V. I. Lenin. It has not left us. William Wordsworth's "man's inhumanity to man" is as much a disease of the spirit as of law and economics. Black Africans suffered: Africa and other places now experience adverse effects. In another new era of globalization this suffering is a matter of lived experience. This pain and death are not merely a bird's eye view from high and far. These problems happen daily and on the ground. Statistics and economic analysis can hide this fact.

In the contest of empires paradoxes, contradictions, and ambivalences affected peoples' lives. Britain helped to put an end to the slave trade even as it benefited from it. Slavery ended at the apogee of British power and left scars in the United States. Despite how European empires rose and fell, slavery and its legacy remained. There were those who promoted and opposed empire, but even when the age of Western European empires had seemed to have passed, the ghost of the slave haunted the world. The United States would wrestle with the legacy of slavery even in its rise to the status of world power. This inheritance of slavery has been a part of world trade. Thus the trading and holding of slaves affected many people and their businesses and governments even in places that did not have slaves, or at least slaves from Africa.[283] The aftermath is never free of the planting and the harvest. The sins of the fathers are visited on the sons. Mothers and daughters play their part, too. The contest beneath contesting empires was a contestation within empires and nations, even within the consciences of people, of those who were slave masters or benefited from slavery. Then and now, the slave bore empire on his or her back. The agony of slavery was as much an agon from within as between and without. The long slow night of slavery is still lifting and the sun has not quite set on the empires even if ghosts wander the earth between dusk and dawn. Coming after or being post is something of a wish that takes a great deal of work as well as dreaming. Perhaps that is the true contest.

Chapter 7 ～

Conclusion

When Portugal entered the slave trade in the fifteenth century in Africa, a new phase of colonialism and imperialism was beginning, perhaps unbeknownst to those involved at court and on the ground. Almost 450 years of hardship and thralldom overcame Africans sent into Europe and West in the Atlantic to labor for sugar, cotton, and coffee. Columbus was interested in the Native Americans as slaves. Soon Africans were brought into the Americas to fill the gap that the dying Natives left under the yoke of slavery, abuse, and cruelty. The contest over empire was so often about making as much money as possible. Expansion could cause conflicts within empires: for instance, the Crown, landowners, and church in the Spanish colonies in the New World could find themselves at odds. The opposition to war, expansion, and empire coexisted, sometimes in the same people, with their promotion. Promoting and opposing empire were in Europe before and after Columbus and persisted from first expansion to decolonization in the twentieth century. The British Empire and the United States, together the two greatest political powers since the defeat of Napoleon, were as implicated in the trading and holding of slaves as were Portugal, Spain, the Netherlands, and other European powers. Some ambiguity remained in slavery, which is one of the key points where empires and nations contested, because as the British took American cotton for their mills, the British government and navy worked hard to close the institution down. The United States was also involved in contradictions because it had been founded on freedom, but that liberty did not extend to Native Americans and African Americans. The legacy of the United States as a settler nation torn by slavery from within has affected this great nation and informal empire from its very beginning to its rise to world power. Conscience haunts it and the European capitals of the former empires: slavery and cheap labor are topics still. The agon or agony of empire is still in the bones, hearts, and minds of the masters and slaves Hegel and Martin Luther King spoke about.

The early decades of expansion into the western Atlantic were about cooperation as well as contest. Antonio Pigafetta, who provided a narrative account of the Magellan expedition's circumnavigation of the globe, embodied conflict and Europeanness. Magellan was a Portuguese in the service of Spain, and Pigafetta was a nobleman from Vicenza who arrived in Spain and joined the expedition as a supernumerary in 1519. The voyage occurred from 1519 to 1522 and was of great moment in the expansion of Western Europe, both literally and in terms of knowledge. Apparently, as R. A. Skelton has maintained, Pigafetta was a military knight who took part in the guerilla war that the Christian pirates of Rhodes were waging against the Turks at sea in the Mediterranean.[1] His text has been translated from French into English, so the question of transmission has been difficult and provides, as with many medieval and early modern works, like those of Marco Polo and Columbus, a challenge of its own. Knowledge was part of this contest, but was also cooperative and involved translation. Pigafetta ended his narrative with such an emphasis: he gave the Emperor Charles V a book giving the daily events of the voyage, then traveled to see John III of Portugal and told him about what he had seen and then, before heading back to Rhodes, he left gifts from far-off lands with Louise of Savoy, mother of François Ier of France.[2] Although these states were in some ways rivals, they were also closely connected. The Spanish massacre of the French Protestants in Florida in 1565 and the French retaliation also showed that religion as well as national self-interest qualified any sense of an uncontested pan-European colonial or imperial project.

The contest was also one that involved the exploitation of Native and African labor. Some sentences at the beginning of the first chapter of Pedro de Castañeda's account of Coronado's expedition to Cíbola in 1540 suggest many contesting forces in the search beyond known territory. The president of New Spain, Nuño de Guzman, "had in his possession an Indian, a native of the valley or valleys of Oxitipar, who was called Tejo by the Spaniards."[3] The Indian was some kind of property and had been given a Spanish name even if the valley kept its Native name. Tejo (his Native name is not given) reported that his father had brought back a large amount of gold and silver from the back country, something that would have interested the likes of Columbus and Roberval as much as it did Guzman. This father had seen seven cities and Tejo himself had gone with him once or twice and had seen places comparable to Mexico City. There were streets of silver workers in these settlements. This information led Guzman to get "together nearly 400 Spaniards and 20,000 friendly Indians of New Spain."[4] The sheer number of Natives suggests how much the Spaniards relied on them and beyond this ratio was the description of the Indians as "friendly" and of "New Spain," so that, by implication, there were unfriendly Natives beyond the boundaries. The desire for riches drove the Spanish into the unknown based on stories told by Indians. These were the accounts Europeans sought out in the New World from Columbus onward. These narratives affected the social, economic, and political connections between Native and settler and were sometimes complicated by relations of dominance and servitude or slavery. The expedition of Coronado, as the one in which Magellan died, took a terrible toll. The road to riches and heaven were paved with good intentions.

Voices of women, Natives, and Africans qualified those dominant voices of male Europeans in the contest for empire. On January 6, 1836, William Apes (ca. 1798–1836), a Pequot, delivered a eulogy on King Philip and published his book in Boston in that year. King Philip was the name given to the Wampanoag chief who fought against the Pilgrims in the seventeenth century: Apes, who became a Methodist preacher, claimed to be his great-great grandson. He gave this speech, not about Alexander the Great or George Washington, but about this great Native leader, remembered by Indians as Washington lives in the hearts of whites, a reminder to "those few remaining descendents who now remain as the monument of the cruelty of those who came to improve our race and correct our errors."[5] Las Casas had spoken about European cruelty almost 300 years before. The figure of King Philip allowed Apes to meditate on liberty and the loss of rights for Natives and others of color: "I do not hesitate to say, that through the prayers, preaching, and the examples of those pretended pious has been the foundation of all the slavery and degradation in the American Colonies towards colored people. Experience has taught me that this has been a most sorry and wretched doctrine to us poor ignorant Indians."[6] A prejudice against Natives and Africans was, for Apes, a foundation of the British colonies that became the United States. Like Columbus and Guzman, the leader of the United States also pressed for riches but disguised that in terms of religion and civilization: "even the President of the United States tells the Indians they cannot live among civilized people, and we want your lands, and must have them, and will have them. As if he had said to them, we want your lands for our use to speculate upon, it aids us in paying off our national debt and supporting us in Congress, to drive you off."[7] In unmasking this charade, Apes returned to the question of rights and color: "We want trumpets that sound like thunder, and men to act as though they were going at war with those corrupt and degrading principles that robs one of all rights, merely because he is ignorant, and of a little different color. Let us have principles that will give every one his due; and then shall wars cease, and the weary find rest. Give the Indian his rights, and you may be assured war will cease."[8] The question of rights haunted a white society that proclaimed British then American liberty, particularly in the Declaration of Independence and the

Constitution. For Apes, King Philip was the greatest American "to the everlasting disgrace of the pilgrims' fathers."[9] The Natives had fed the Pilgrims and kept them alive and they had turned on the Indians.[10] Such was their shame. About a hundred years after Apes delivered his speech on King Philip at the Odeon Theater in Boston, Mary Reynolds, who was over hundred herself and might well have been alive at the time of Apes's speech, was interviewed in Dallas, Texas, and, in detail, testified to the color line that Du Bois talked about: "Master sold me cheap, 'cause he didn't want Miss Sara to play with no nigger young'un."[11] The ghost of myths and theories of color and civilization had practical and painful consequences for Native and African Americans. Friction and social strife were some of the consequences of these widespread and long-standing daily practices. Even in 1564, John Hawkins had come upon an African settlement, after being advised by Portuguese; was involved in a gruesome battle in which Africans and English were killed; carried African slaves to New Spain; witnessed with his men how Caribs deceived, lured, and killed Spaniards; met with the French in Florida who had conflicts with the Natives and some of who had cheated them for gold; traveled to Newfoundland and caught fish before returning to Cornwall.[12] Departing Sierra Leone for the West Indies, Hawkins's ships were becalmed for eighteen days, so that the water supply would be under pressure, "for so great a company of Negroes, and ourselves, which pinched us all, and that which was worst, put us in such fear that many never thought to have reached to the Indies, without great death of Negroes and of themselves: but the Almighty God, who never suffereth his elect to perish, sent us the sixteenth of February the ordinary breeze."[13] They did reach Dominica, an island inhabited by cannibals. The religious interpretation in this early English narrative was the kind of "Calvinist" certainty, a providential certitude that troubled some of the former slaves in their narratives and Du Bois in his writing on slavery and black culture. The "elect" considered themselves spared even as they were intent to take other people and sell them.

Nor was the taking of African slaves confined to the Atlantic slave trade. The Cape Colony in South Africa began with freeburghers having a farm economy founded on slave labor under the Dutch East India Company (VOC) to the British takeover in 1795 and beyond. Slaves on the Cape were from a greater variety of peoples from Africa and Asia than those in the New World, but, according to N. A. Worden, institutional racism in South Africa did not come about until after contact with peoples in the interior and after industrialization, but even still, by the early nineteenth century, in the hinterland of Cape Town, settlement was divided by race and was enforced after emancipation in a way based on the slave system of the eighteenth century.[14] The slave trade in the Indian Ocean was active along the coast of

Africa, except among the Somalis and the people of mixed ancestry in Mozambique who were protected by the Portuguese. Paradoxically, the Royal Navy tried to shut down the trade among Asians, Arabs, and other Europeans while Britain expanded from the Napoleonic wars to 1850. Until the 1840s, the Royal Navy had only six war ships to patrol the immense Indian Ocean. The British were accused of benefiting from the slave trade, for being hypocritically humanitarian while beating the competition by making goods in places like Birmingham from commodities slaves produced. However, according to G. Graham, this view is hard to justify and there is "a good deal to point the other way."[15] The British, then, were willing to experience some friction with other states and empires in order to end the slave trade. The French and the Americans were still involved in the trade in Africa, and not until 1845 did France reach an agreement with Britain. One French official wrote as far back as October 1685, that if the Company of Senegal sends to the coast (of St. Domingue) "more than 150 negroes each year," then it will diminish the colony and might lead to a neglect that involved not bringing the French to the area and thereby creating a demographic imbalance—"and the Colony will become feeble and exposed to the insults of Spaniards and other nations."[16] Opposition to or doubts over slavery occurred early, even in the West Indies. Ambivalence and contradiction—the tension between promotion and opposition—shifted emphasis over time but never entirely went away. There were other positive efforts, opposition to the promotion of slavery, such as the establishment of the British colony of Sierra Leone in 1787, mainly as a refuge or home for recaptives or slaves that the Royal Navy brought to Freetown and freed. In 1807 the Crown took over the colony, where the Royal Navy brought as many as 3,000–4,000 slaves annually to free from all over West Africa. While the majority were Yorubas and the second largest group were Ibos, a mix of people with different religions and languages was transported to this colony in the nineteenth century. Many remarkable people were involved with Sierra Leone and the relations between blacks and whites were quite contrary to the experience in the southern states of the United States because education was something encouraged by the British government. Sir Charles Macarthy, governor from 1814 to 1824, wanted to develop European culture and religion in Sierra Leone through missions and missionaries, like Hannah Kilham, a Quaker gifted in languages, who knew and taught in Joloff, Yoruba and Mende. The first Sierra Leonean called to the Bar—in 1850—was John Thorpe, and in 1876, Christien Cole, of Ibo descent, followed suit and also came to graduate from Oxford, where he read Greats (a course involving Greek and Latin). James Africanus Horton, of Ibo background, and William Davies, of Yoruba parentage, trained in London in 1858 and later in Scotland to be army doctors.

Bishop Adjai Crowther, an African, published a Yoruba grammar in 1852, so he wrote about his language for the benefit of Europeans as well as his own people. Not all was ideal in Sierra Leone. Perhaps, as C. H. Fyfe suggests, because Horton wrote political books, the British government did not train other doctors from that colony in Britain.[17] Not all the people the Royal Navy brought were recaptives. One group was the Maroons, runaway slaves who in the late 1600s took refuge in the mountains of Jamaica and who, in the 1790s, opposed the Jamaican government: 800 were sent, by way of Nova Scotia, where some black Nova Scotians joined them, to Sierra Leone.[18] Political issues in Jamaica and Africa also affected the lives of these free blacks: the British government seems to have balanced among peace, profit, and ideals.

The contest of empires, within and without, knew many qualifications and contradictions. For instance, in the 1582, Richard Hakluyt dedicated his *Divers voyages touching the discouerie of America* to Sir Philip Sidney, who later died fighting the Spaniards in the Netherlands during the Dutch Revolt, and Sidney and Sir Francis Walsingham, prominent Protestants, were involved in a Catholic colony in Florida that Sir Humphrey Gilbert was undertaking for prospective Catholic colonists like Sir George Peckham and Sir Thomas Gerrard. The question, then, was in the contest with Spain and Portugal in the New World did a person put his state or his religion first.[19] The Huguenots had faced the same quandary in the establishment and destruction of their colony in Florida in the 1560s. Notions of state, religion, and empire were in such flux, within decades let alone over centuries, that the nature of the contest was constantly in question. Competition and cooperation were elements that gave and took in this change.

The contest between Britain and its American colonies is central to this notion of internal and external contesting. Richard Price (1723–91), for example, was torn himself over the ways of reconciling liberty to a unified British Empire. In 1778, he wrote in his conclusion to his *Two Tracts*: "Having said so much of the war with America, and particularly of the danger with which it threatens us, it may be expected that I should propose some method of escaping from this danger, and of restoring this once happy Empire to a state of peace and security."[20] Price was conflicted in his discussion of liberty. The war with America over liberty threatened the very liberty of all in the British Empire—in Britain and overseas. A certain vigilance was necessary to preserve freedom:

> These are reflexions which should be constantly present to every mind in this country. As moral liberty is the prime blessing of man in his private capacity, so is civil liberty in his public capacity. There is nothing that requires more to be watched than power. There is nothing that ought to be opposed with a

more determined resolution than its encroachments. Sleep in a state, as Montesquieu says, is always followed by slavery.[21]

Liberty became one of the great themes in England, then Britain and the British Empire, and in the American colonies that became the United States. Living free or dying and not giving up to the sleep of slavery were themes in the eighteenth century. In 1831, William Lloyd Garrison linked the liberty proclaimed in 1776 with opposition to slavery: "Assenting to 'the self-evident truth' maintained in the American Declaration of Independence 'that all men are created equal, and endowed by their Creator with certain inalienable rights—among which are life, liberty, and the pursuit of happiness,' I shall strenuously contend for the immediate enfranchisement of our slave population."[22] Before the slaveholding author of the Declaration of Independence, Thomas Jefferson, Aristotle, also lived in a state that allowed slavery, also recommended happiness as a pursuit. *Contesting Empires* has discussed the ways rivals came after Spain in the New World; how, in a comparative context, More, Erasmus, Léry, Montaigne, and others opposed or complicated notions of war, expansion, politics, and empire; and how others, like Oviedo, Thevet, and Richard Hakluyt the Younger promoted empire, but the book then set out a consideration of liberty and slavery and how human rights, however painfully and haltingly, were extended and are still being contested. Men and women of different colors—and I have tried to stress the voices of women in the chapters on slavery—wrestled within themselves and beyond with moral and political power and the fragile rights that must stand up to power and cruelty, which Machiavelli, who wrote about acquiring and maintaining power, recommended for discipline in an army and held up as an example Hannibal's "transcendent cruelty" that was "joined with numberless great qualities."[23] Cruelty was also what Las Casas wrote against with such passion and what former slaves and abolitionists exposed. It was also something that could be found in later genocides like the one the Nazis perpetrated on Jews and gypsies. This struggle within people, states, empires—formal and informal—and other international bodies is something still with us. The agony of contests sadly remains in the first years of the twenty-first century. The clash of cultures, states, religions, and the division within nations persists. In 1912 Rabindranath Tagore (1861–1941) published *Gitanjali* (*Song Offerings*), and the fifth poem expresses an aspect of that agon for liberty and human rights that, as Richard Price said, is private and public:

> Where the mind is without fear and the head is held high;
>   Where knowledge is free;
>   Where the world has not been broken up into fragments by narrow domestic walls;

Where words come out from the depth of truth;
Where tireless striving stretches its arms towards perfection;
Where the clear stream of reason has not lost its way into the
dreary desert sand of dead habit;
Where the mind is led forward by thee into ever-widening thought
and action—
Into that heaven of freedom, my Father, let my country awake.[24]

Notes ⌒

Chapter 1

1. On earlier travel and on wonder, see Mary Baine Campbell, *The Witness and the Other World: Exotic European Travel Writing, 400–1600* (Ithaca, NY: Cornell University Press, 1988) and her *Wonder and Science: Imagining Worlds in Early Modern Europe* (Ithaca, NY: Cornell University Press, 1999).
2. J. H. Elliott, *First Images of America*, ed. Fredi Chiapelli (Berkeley: University of California Press, 1976), II:880, see I:12–21.
3. *The Spanish Origin of International Law: Francisco De Vitoria and His Law of Nations*, trans. J. S. Brown (Carnegie Endowment Classics of international Law, 1934), ix–xl.
4. For an excellent discussion on this background, see Anthony Pagden, *The Fall of Natural Man: The American Indian and the Origins of Comparative Ethnology* (Cambridge: Cambridge University Press, 1982, rev. 1986); on lordship, see a full analysis in Pagden's, *Lords of All the World: Ideologies of Empire in Spain, Britain and France c.1500–c.1800* (New Haven: Yale University Press, 1995).
5. See, e.g., Robin Law, *The Slave Coast of West Africa, 1550–1750: The Impact of the Slave Trade on an African Society* (Oxford: Clarendon Press, 1991).
6. Hugh Thomas, *The Slave Trade: The Story of the Slave Trade: 1440–1870* (New York: Simon & Schuster, 1997), 790. For a specialized study of this problem, see Urs Peter Ruf, *Ending Slavery: Hierarchy, Dependency, and Gender in Central Mauritania* (Bielefeld : Transcript Verlag, 1999).
7. Pierre Bourdieu, "Participant Objectivation," *The Journal of the Royal Anthropological Institute* 9 (2) (2003), 281–94.
8. Bourdieu is distinguishing his idea of the observer from that in Marcus and Fisher (1986), Geertz (1988), or Rosaldo (1989): See G. Marcus and M. Fischer, *Anthropology as Cultural Critique* (Chicago: University of Chicago Press, 1986); C. Geertz, *Works and Lives: The Anthropologist as Author* (Stanford: Stanford University Press, 1988); R. Rosaldo, *Culture and Truth: The Remaking of Social Analysis* (Boston: Beacon Press, 1989).
9. Bourdieu has in mind Clifford and Marcus (1986) and the "interpretive skepticism" that Woolgar (1988) refers to (Gupta & Ferguson, 1997). See J. Clifford and G. Marcus, eds., *Writing Culture: The Poetics and Politics of Ethnography* (Berkeley: University of California Press, 1986); S. Woolgar, "Reflexivity is the Ethnographer of the Text," *Knowledge and Reflexivity: New*

Frontiers in the Sociology of Knowledge, ed., S. Woolgar (London: Sage, 1988), 14–34; A. Gupta and J. Ferguson, eds., *Anthropological Locations: Boundaries and Grounds of a Field Science* (Berkeley: University of California Press, 1997). See Mary Louise Pratt, *Imperial Eyes: Travel Writing and Transculturation* (London: Routledge, 1992), 2; see, 6, 10.

10. Bourdieu, "Participant Objectivation," 281–94; see P. Bourdieu, *Science de la science et réflexivité* (*Cours et travaux*) (Paris: Raisons d'agir Editions, 2001).

11. For instance, see Jonathan Hart, *Representing the New World* (New York and London: Palgrave Macmillan, 2001) and with the same publisher, *Columbus, Shakespeare and the Interpretation of the New World* (2003), and *Comparing Empires* (2003).

Chapter 2

1. Richard Hakluyt, *The Principall Navigations . . .* (London: George Bishop, 1589), no pagination; the actual Latin inscription is "AMERICA SIVE IN DIA NOVA Ao 1492 a Christophoro Colombo nomine regis Castelle primum detecta." Noua Francia appears to the east.

2. Ibid., 2.

3. P. Fauchille, *Traité de Droit International Public*, vol. 1, part 2 (Paris: Rousseau & cie, 1925), 687, cited in L. C. Green and Olive P. Dickason, *The Law of Nations and the New World* (Edmonton: University of Alberta Press, 1989), 7. For similar references to François Ier on Adam's will, see Lyle N. McAlister, *Spain and Portugal in the New World 1492–1700* (Minneapolis: University of Minnesota Press, 1984), 199 and Anthony Pagden, *Lords of All the World: Ideologies of Empire in Spain, Britain and France c. 1500–c.1800* (New Haven: Yale University Press, 1995), 47.

4. Raymonde Litalien, *Les explorateurs de l'Amérique du Nord 1492–1795* (Sillery: Septentrion, 1993), 53.

5. Foreign merchants sometimes lived and traded under the protection of the government where they lived: the merchants of the Hanseatic League in the Steelyard in London, the English wool merchants in Bruges, the English in Andalusia, and the Florentine community in Lyon, one of whose syndicates financed Verrazzano. See Lawrence C. Wroth, *The Voyages of Giovanni da Verrazano 1524–1528* (New Haven: Yale University Press, 1970), 58–9.

6. Unfortunately, we do not have Verrazzano's original report in French for the king, but four Italian versions have been preserved, Ramusio's version of 1555 [1556?] being the only one known for years. An English translation of the Italian text in Ramusio appears in Hakluyt's *Divers Voyages* (1582) and *The Principall Nauigations* (1589). René Herval's French translation, *Giovanni da Verrazzano et les Dieppois à la Recherche du Cathay (1524–1528)* (Rouen and Caen, 1933), was based on Alessandro Bacchiani's Italian text (1909 edition) and was republished in *Les Français en Amérique pendant la première moitié du XVIᵉ siècle*, ed. Charles-André Julien, René Herval, Théodore Beauchesne (Paris: Presses universitaires de France, 1946). There are four versions of

Verrazzano's narrative of the voyage, three of which are full accounts in the form of a letter from the leader of the expedition, Verrazzano, to François Ier, who authorized the voyage. For a detailed account of the versions of the text, see Wroth, *The Voyages*, 93–5.

7. John Parker, *Books to Build an Empire: A Bibliographical History of English Overseas Interests to 1620* (Amsterdam: N. Israel, 1965), 21–3. See *Of the new landes . . . , see Edward Arber*, ed. *The first Three English books on America [?1511]–1555 A.D. . . .* (Westminster, 1895), xxiii–xxxvi.

8. W. P. D. Wightman, *Science in a Renaissance Society* (London: Hutchinson University Library, 1972), 101–2. On the knowledge of theoretical science and of practical navigation of Columbus, Vespucci, and others, see Wightman, *Science in a Renaissance Society*, 65–75. Concerning science in England and France, see E. G. R. Taylor, *Tudor Geography 1485–1583* (London: Methuen, 1930); D. Stone, Jr., *France in the Sixteenth Century: A Medieval Society Transformed* (Englewood Cliffs, NJ: Prentice-Hall, 1969).

9. John Rastell, *A new interlude . . . of the iiii elements* (n.p.n.d.), fol. Ci verso, quoted in Parker, 24–5. See also Parker's discussion on those pages. See M. E. Borish, "Source and Intention of *The Four Elements*," *Studies in Philology* 35 (1938), 149–63.

10. Richard Eden, *A treatyse of the newe India, with other new founde landes and Ilandes, as well eastwarde as westwarde, as they are knowen and found in these our dayes, after the descripcion of Sebastian Munster in his boke of universall Cosmographie: wherein the diligent reader my see the good successe and rewarde of noble and honeste enterpryses, by the which not only worldly ryches are obtayned, but also God is glorified, and the Christian fayth enlarged. Translated out of Latin into Englishe. By Rycharde Eden* (London, 1553), 7.

11. Ibid., a,i, verso-a,ii, recto.

12. Ibid., 171 recto, 172 verso-173 recto. I have quoted from Eden's translation of the bull into English, which appears to be the first extant, because this would have been the first time that the English reading public would have been able to read this donation in their mother tongue.

13. Ibid., c,i, recto.

14. Ibid., c,iii, recto.

15. A detail concerning Bermuda will illustrate the triangular relation amongst Spain, England, and France. One history of Bermuda claims that Menendez's massacre of Huguenots in Florida started as a request to look for his son whom he thought shipwrecked in Bermuda. The king agreed that Menendez go to Florida to establish a colony, but there he massacred the Huguenots as Lutherans. This version probably underestimates the deliberate nature of Philip's foreign policy, but, regardless of the intricacy of the intention, one detail is telling here: Menendez had gone with the king—Philip II—to England in 1554. Bermuda was a meeting place of various European ships and nations. Henry C. Wilkinson, *The Adventures of Bermuda: A History of the Island from Its Discovery until the Dissolution of the Somers Island Company in 1684* (1933; London: Oxford University Press, 1958), 20–1; see 1–53. On Spain's influence in Bermuda, see Henry C. Wilkinson, *Bermuda in the*

Old Empire: A History of the Island from the Dissolution of the Somers Island Company until the end of the American Revolutionary War: 1684–1784 (London: Oxford University Press, 1950), II, 117–57. See also Wesley Frank Craven, *An Introduction to the History of Bermuda* (1938; Bermuda: 1990). An important source for information on Spain is J. H. Lefroy, *Memorials of the Discovery and early Settlement of the Bermudas or Somers Islands 1515–1685* (Toronto, 1981). The Bermuda Historical Society and Bermuda National Trust, 1981 offered this reprint—volume 1, 1511–1652 and volume 2, 1650–87. This is a selection from ten volumes in the archives of Bermuda. The chronology in Lefroy is good. It includes the Spanish influence in Bermuda maps as well as discussion of Bermudez, Oviedo, Camelo as well as the inscription on Spanish rock. While in Bermuda, I examined a number of maps and books that showed the influence of Spain. For instance, I looked at two versions of the so-called Somers's maps—MAP OF BERMUDA, 1609–1617, [PA 337 (Bermuda National Trust)]. Paget donated the original to the British Museum. One map has writing. In the upper left hand corner there a note that situates the island in relation to Cape Cod, Virginia, England Madeira and Puerto Rico. On this map there is a Flemish wrack in the Northeast of Bermuda. In the bottom right hand corner this description is found:

> The Island of Bermuda was so named by Juan Bermudes a Spaniard, the first Discoverer thereof: It is seated in the Latitude of 33 Degress, distant from the Coast of Spayne 1000 Leagues/And from St. Juan de Porto Rico 200. Charles th'Emperor (considering that the fleetes homeward bounde from the Weste Indies muste passe by yt Island) thoughte it conveynient (it being then desarte) to have it habited. (And to that end In Anno 1527, he Covenanted wth Hernando Camelo a Portugues granting him the whole benifitte of the Island Custome free for 20 yeares to himself & his sonne wth the title of Govnor thereof duringtheyre lives uppon condition that he shoulde inhabite the same wthin 4 yeares next ensuing. Notwthstanding theesegreat Priviledges it does not appeare that ever the said Hernando Camelo did/people the Islands. Historia General de Las Indias Decad. 4 Pag. 39: written by Alfonso de Herrera.

In the early seventeenth century the English seem to have been well aware of the origins and precedents of Spain regarding the lands the English now wanted to occupy.

16. French privatering intensified and led to the burning of Havana in 1555. The Peace of Cateau-Cambrésis in 1559 ended the Habsburg-Valois wars, but, as Ian K. Steele notes, it failed to bring peace to American waters even if Philip II had reasons to claim exclusive rights to America in the formal treaty; see Steele, *Warpaths: Invasions of North America* (New York: Oxford University Press, 1994), 11–2.

17. The phrase is James Froude's; see his 'England's Forgotten Worthies' (1852) in *Short Studies on Great Subjects* (1867; London, 1888), I, 446. For a brief discussion of Froude's views of Hakluyt, see Jeffrey Knapp, *An Empire*

Nowhere: England. America, and Literature from Utopia to The Tempest (Berkeley: University of California Press, 1992) 1, 3 and Mary C. Fuller, *Voyages in Print: English Travel to America, 1576–1624* (Cambridge: Cambridge University Press, 1995), 14, 159–62.

18. On the abdication of Charles V and the transition to Philip II in the Netherlands and for the English intervention, see Charles Wilson, *Queen Elizabeth and the Revolt in the Netherlands* (London: Macmillan, 1970), ix–xiv, 1–20 respectively. Wilson also discusses the French hatred of the English (16) and the possible alliance of France with the rebels in the Netherlands (32).

19. I am not sure, however, that the papal bulls had been superceded as much as W. J. Eccles claims. See his *France in America* (Vancouver: Fitshenry and Whiteside, 1972, rpt. 1973), 7 8 for below. Like Marcel Trudel's scholarship, Eccles work in the field of French America is seminal. See also W. J. Eccles, *Canada Under Louis IV, 1663–1701* (Toronto: McClelland and Stewart, 1964).

20. Eccles, *France*, 8.

21. Ibid.

22. The Spanish failure to conquer Florida seems to have created a vacuum for the French. See Steele, *Warpaths*, 7–20. On the French failure in Florida, including dissension amongst the French, and their piracy, as well as a balanced account of the conflict between Spain and France in this region, see ibid., 25–8. Apparently, the Spanish expedition to Florida, 1565–68, would cost the king one-fifth of the military budget for his empire; ibid., 27. For other discussions of this conflict, which, along with the war in the Netherlands, fed the Black Legend, see Eugene Lyon, *The Enterprise of Florida: Pedro Menéndez de Avilés and the Spanish Conquest of 1565–1568* (Gainsville, FL: University Presses of Florida, 1976) and Paul E. Hoffman, *The Spanish Crown and the Defense of the Caribbean, 1565–1585: Precedent, Patrimonialism, and Royal Parsimony* (Baton Rouge: Louisiana State University Press, 1980), 218–28.

23. On the pretensions of claims amongst the European powers, including those made by Spain and France in Florida, see Steele, *Warpaths*, 22–3.

24. On Geneva and America, see Frank Lestringant, *Le Huguenot et le sauvage: L'Amérique et la controverse coloniale, en France, au temps des Guerres de Réligion (1555–1589)* (Paris: Aux Amateurs de livres [Klincksieck], 1990), ch. 3, 83–132.

25. In *Les Singvlaritez* Thevet gave his account of his voyage to Brazil with Villegagnon in 1555, including his preference for the religion of the Natives, who recognized the eternal God, and the Protestants. For a discussion of Thevet regarding this voyage, see Myron P. Gilmore, "The New World in French and English Historians of the Sixteenth Century," *First Images of America: The Impact of the New World on the Old*, ed. Fredi Chiapelli et al., 2 vols. (Berkeley: University of California Press, 1976), II, 520–1 and Lestringant, *Le Huguenot*, 13–4.

26. Roger Schlesinger and Arthur P. Stabler, eds., *André Thevet's North America: A Sixteenth-Century View* (Kingston and Montreal: McGill-Queen's University

Press, 1986), xxxiii, xxxix; see Jean Céard, *La Nature et les prodiges: L'insolite au XVIe siècle, en France* (Geneva: Droz, 1977), 283. In this century some scholars have tried to defend Thevet and to achieve a balanced view of his work. Even then, some ambivalence remains. Frank Lestringant, a specialist on Thevet, says that this cosmographer is really a writer of fiction and not a savant, although he praises Thevet's promotion of the colonization of Canada and his discussions on the political will as being sufficient for the birth of a nation. Frank Lestringant, "L'Avenir des terres nouvelles," *La Renaissance et le Nouveau Monde*, ed. Alain Parent et al. (Québec: Musée du Québec, 1984), 50–1. See also his *L'Atelier du Cosmographe ou l'image du monde à la Renaissance* (Paris: A. Michel, 1991) and Schlesinger and Stabler, *André Thevet's North American*, xxxix–xl. In discussing Thevet's reputation, Schlesinger and Stabler remain ambivalent. They summarize his faults—plagiarism, conceit, territorialism, pretensions as an eyewitness—but also his good qualities: his insatiable curiosity and courage as a Renaissance tourist, and recommend that his works are best treated as a kind of encyclopedic conflation or genre: travelogue, natural history, ethnography, anthropology, and romance. Without Thevet, we would lack some of the information we have about sixteenth-century America. Unlike Oviedo, Thevet did not live and serve long in the New World, but, like Oviedo, he claimed the authority of observation and the eyewitness; see Lestringant, *L'Atelier du Cosmographe ou l'image du monde à la Renaissance*, 29. Both historians sought the favor of their sovereigns and wanted to be the sole authority on the New World for their respective countries. They wanted to chronicle the expansion and the desire for empire at court.

27. For a discussion of the French in Florida, see Olive P. Dickason, *The Myth of the Savage and the Beginnings of French Colonialism in the Americas* (Edmonton: University of Alberta Press, 1984), 193–202.

28. Parker, *Books*, 58–9.

29. Ibid.

30. Nicolas Le Challeux, *Discours de l'histoire de la Floride, contenant la trahison des Espagnols, contre les subiets du Roy, en l'an mil cinq cens soixante cinq.* (Dieppe: Pour leffé le Sellier, 1566), 51. Vallemande is, apparently, Pedro Menéndez. All translations of Le Challeux are mine.

31. Nicolas Le Challeux, "The Epistle," *A true and perfect description*, A .iv. verso. I am using the British Library copy of Hacket's translation and have consulted original French versions in the Houghton at Harvard as well as Gravier's edition of 1872 and the one in Julien, *Les Français*, II, 201–38. Gravier and Julien both include the verse epistle and the "Reqveste."

32. The Spanish themselves took into account the piracy or challenge of Huguenot then English corsairs and, from their point of view, this encroachment demanded retaliation or containment. The role of the Flemish is also considered in a letter whose writer and recipient are now lost, who, in June 1569, is considering the economics of the trade between the West Indies and Spain; see *Documents Concerning English Voyages to the Spanish Main 1569–1580*, ed. I. A. Wright (1932; Nendeln/Liechtenstein: Krause reprint, 1967), 5–6.

33. See note 12 above.

34. In the "Epistle" he addresses the "tres-illvstre, et tres-vertvevse Dame Madame Clavde de Tvraine Dame de Tournon, & Contesse de Roussillon" with great praise for her bravery and exemplary behavior. François de Belle-forest Comingeois's *L'Histoire Vniverselle dv Monde* . . . (Paris: G. Mallot, 1570), ij. Hereafter referred to as Belleforest.

35. Ibid.

36. On Belleforest and Thevet, see Olive P. Dickason, "Thevet and Belleforest: Two Sixteenth-Century Frenchmen and New World Colonialism," *Proceedings of the Annual Meeting of the French Colonial Society* 16 (1992): 1–11.

37. Thevet uses the phrase "cruels jusques au bout;" André Thevet, *La Cosmographie Vniverselle D'André Thevet Cosmographe dv Roy . . . Tome Second* (Paris: Chez P. L'Huilier, 1575), in *Les Français en Amérique pendant la deuxième moitié du XVIᵉ Siècle: Le Brésil et les Brésiliens*, ed. Charles-André Julien, and notes by Suzanne Lussagnet (2 vols., Paris: Presses Universitaires de France, 1953), II, 29.

38. Thevet, *La Cosmographie* 82. Thevet also discussed American diseases the Spanish may have brought back from the New World; see ibid., 142.

39. Ibid., 221.

40. Ibid., 251. Portuguese slaves and rivalry with the Spanish appeared in Thevet's account; see ibid., 263. He also discussed the Cannibals, figures Columbus originally represented; see ibid., 271.

41. "Sonet," in Chauveton *Histoire Novvelle* (Geneva: Par Evstace Vignon, 1579), no pagination; my translation here and in the main text.

42. Villegagnon supplemented Coligny's support for the Brazilian enterprise with that of the Cardinal de Lorraine, a member of the Guise family and the leader of the Catholic clergy in France. See Janet Whatley, "Introduction," Jean de Léry, *History of a Voyage to the Land of Brazil*, trans. Janet Whatley (Berkeley: University of California Press, 1990), xx.

43. Jean de Léry, *Histoire d'vn voyage faict en la terre dv Bresil, avtrement dite Amerique* (Geneva: A. Chuppin, 1580), Aij.

44. Ibid., Aij verso.

45. Lancelot Voisin, sieur de La Popelinière, "Av Roy," *L'Histoire de France* . . . (n.p. [La Rochelle]: Abraham H[autin], 1581), I, CC iij verso and CC recto; see I, 55 recto (Spanish pride); I, 74 verso (Spanish cruelty); I, book 14, 52 recto and verso (Spanish dishonor); The pagination began at 1 after the tenth book. The descriptions were brief "statements of fact" woven into detailed accounts of war but were not long and sensational as in Las Casas, Benzoni and others.

46. Ibid., I, book 14, 52 recto. On La Popelinière, see Lestringant, *Le Huguenot*, 156–8, 226–34, 258–61.

47. Ibid., I, 101 verso.

48. Francisco López de Gómara, *Histoire Generalle des Indes Occidentales et Terres Nevves, qui iusques à present ont estre descouuertes. Traduite en françois par M. Fumee Sieur de Marly le Chatel.* (Paris: Chez Michel Sonnius, 1578), āiv verso; my translation.

49. Thomas Nicholas, "The Epistle Dedicatory," *The Pleasant Historie of the Conquest of the VVeast India, now called new Spayne, Atchieued by the vvorthy Prince Hernando Cortes Marques of the valley of Huaxacac, most delectable to Reade, Translated out of the Spanish tongue*, by T. N. (London: Henry Bynneman, 1578), aij recto-aij verso.

50. On the English history plays, see, for instance, E. M. W. Tillyard, *Shakespeare's History Plays* (London: Chatto & Windus, 1944) and Irving Ribner, *The English History Play in the Age of Shakespeare* (1957, New York, 1965); for the English and European history play, see Herbert Lindenberger, *Historical Drama: The Relation of Literature to Drama* (Chicago: University of Chicago Press, 1975), Walter Cohen, *Drama of a Nation: Public Theater in Renaissance England and Spain* (Ithaca, NY: Cornell University Press, 1985) and Jonathan Hart, *Theater and World: The Problematics of Shakespeare's History* (Boston: Northeastern University Press, 1992), 203–16, 231–50.

51. Nicholas, "The Epistle Dedicatory," aij verso.

52. Ibid., aiv recto.

53. Ibid., aiv verso.

54. A Latin poem by Stephen Gossan, the author of a number of anti-theatrical tracts, preceded the main text of Nicholas's translation. For his anti-representational stance, see Stephen Gossan, "Schoole of Abuse," in *Early Treatises on the Stage: Viz. Northbrooke's Treatise Against Dicing, Dancing, Plays, and Interludes; Gossan's School of Abuse; and Heywood's Defence of Stage Plays* (London, 1843), 7–34 . For a discussion of Gossan's anti-mimetic and anti-theatrical works, see Jonas Barish, *The Antitheatrical Prejudice* (Berkeley: University of California Press, 1981), 1–37, 80–191. The connection with Gossan, who later turned his back on the theater with which he had been associated, might suggest an instability in the views of "imitation" in this circle.

55. The Quinns seem certain that Hakluyt knew this work; see David B. Quinn and Alison M. Quinn, "Introduction," Richard Hakluyt, *Discourse of Western Planting* (London: Hakluyt Society, 1993), xvii.

56. "Discours au Henri III. Sur les moyens de diminuer l'Espaignol," cited in Quinn and Quinn, xx- xxi.

57. "Discours au Henri III. Sur les moyens de diminuer l'Espaignol," *Mémoires et Correspondence de Duplessis-Mornay* . . . Tome Second (Paris: Treuttel et Würtz, 1824), 580. The title page of this work, just over 200 years after the death of Duplessis-Mornay in 1623, proclaimed that these memoirs and correspondence were published from original manuscripts and preceded the memoirs of Madame de Mornay on the life of her husband, written by herself for the instruction of her son. This work did not have a straightforward textual history. My translation here and below. I use "grandeur" to indicate the double meaning in French, which suggests splendor and largeness. I have chosen Christendom as opposed to Christianity.

58. Ibid., 581.

59. Ibid.

60. Ibid.

61. Ibid.
62. Ibid.
63. Ibid., 281–82.
64. Ibid., 582.
65. Ibid.
66. Ibid.
67. Ibid.
68. Ibid., 583.
69. Ibid.
70. Ibid., 583–4.
71. Ibid., 584.
72. Ibid.
73. Ibid.
74. Ibid., 585
75. Ibid.
76. Ibid.
77. Ibid., 585–6.
78. Ibid., 586.
79. Ibid.
80. Ibid., 586–7.
81. Ibid., 587–8.
82. Ibid., 588.
83. Ibid.
84. Ibid., 588.
85. Ibid., 588–9.
86. Ibid., 589.
87. Ibid.
88. Ibid.
89. Ibid.
90. Ibid., 590.
91. Ibid.
92. Ibid. What is interesting here is that "stout Cortez" appears in "On First Looking into Chapman's Homer," a kind of conflation of the translation of study with the translation of empire. At the end of this sonnet, Keats's Cortez, with "eagle eyes," "star'd at the Pacific—and all his men/Look'd at each other with a wild surmise—/Silent, upon a peak in Darien." See John Keats, *The Poetical Works of John Keats*, ed. Francis T. Palgrave (London: Macmillan, 1884).
93. Duplessis-Mornay, 590.
94. Ibid., 590–1.
95. Ibid., 591.
96. Ibid.
97. Ibid., 592.
98. Ibid.
99. Ibid.
100. Ibid., 593.

101. For a mention of the friendship, see Christopher Hill, *A Tinker and a Poor Man: John Bunyan and His Church, 1628–1688* (1988; New York: Alfred A. Knopf, 1989), 32.
102. Ibid., see W. Hunt, *The Puritan Moment: The Coming of Revolution in an English County* (Cambridge, MA: Harvard University Press, 1983), 61.
103. Hill, *A Tinker*, 163.
104. John Bunyan, *Miscellaneous Works* (Oxford: Clarendon Press, gen. ed. Roger Sharrock 1976–), vol. 2, 43–4. See Hill, *A Tinker*, 328–9.
105. Yelverton MS. XIV British Library Additional MS. 48014 [555 b], 131 recto.
106. Ibid., 203 recto.
107. Ibid., 206 recto.
108. Ibid., 208 recto.
109. Ibid., 228 recto-verso.
110. White Kennett, "To the Worthy Society Established *For the Propagation of the* Gospel in Foreign Parts," [Dedication], *Bibliothecæ Americanæ Primordia: An Attempt Towards laying the Foundation of an American Library, In several Books, Papers, and Writings, Humbly given to the Society For the Propagation of the Gospel in Foreign Parts, . . . By a Member of the said Society* (London: J. Churchill, 1713), ii. My thanks to Stephen Ferguson, Curator of Rare Books at Princeton, for pointing this passage out to me. This Society was founded in 1701.
111. Anon., "A Discovery of Lands Beyond the Equinoctial" [*Landsdowne MS., C.*, fol. 142–6], in Martin Frobisher, *Three Voyages*, Richard Collinson ed. (London, 1867), 4. Whereas Hakluyt would look to North America, this adviser and promoter of colonization is apparently thinking about the southern end of South America.
112. "A Discovery," 7.
113. Urbain Chauveton, "Sommaire," *Histoire Novvelle dv Novveav Monde, Contenant en somme ce que les Hespagnols ont fait iusqu'à present aux Indes Occidentales, & le rude traitement qu'ils ont fait à ces poures peuples-la* (Geneva: Par Evstace Vignon, 1579), no pagination [1st page recto]. *Brief Discours* and *Requeste au roy* are numbered together and continuously after Benzoni's work, which was first published in Italian in 1565. For a discussion of Chauveton, see Benjamin Keen, "The Vision of America in the Writings of Urbain Chauveton," in *First Images of America: The Impact of the New World on the Old*, ed. Fredi Chiapelli et al., 2 vols., (Berkeley: University of California Press, 1976), I, 107–20.
114. Chauveton, "Sommaire," no pagination [1st page verso]. My translation of Chauveton here and below.
115. Ibid., no pagination [1st page verso-2nd page recto].
116. Richard Hakluyt, *Divers Voyages Touching the Discoverie of America, and the Islands Adjacent unto the Same . . .* (London: for Thomas Woodcocke, 1582), ¶ recto.
117. Ibid., ¶ recto-¶ 2 verso.
118. Ibid., ¶ 2 verso.
119. Ibid.

120. Ibid., ¶ 3 recto.
121. Ibid., ¶ 3 verso-¶ 4 recto For John Cabot's letters patent in Latin and English, see ibid., A recto-A 2 verso and the note by Sebastian Cabot (including the taking of 'three sauage men' back to England), see A 3 recto-A 3 verso and Ramusio's discussion of Sebastian Cabot in his Preface, see A 3 verso-A 4 recto.
122. See my *Representing the New World*, chapter 4 and the portrait (Fitzwilliam Museum M. 64 Philip of Spain) on the dust jacket of my *Columbus, Shakespeare and the Intrepretation of the New World*.
123. Richard Hakluyt, *Discourse of Western Planting*, ed. David B. Quinn and Alison M. Quinn (London: Hakluyt Society, 1993), 36.
124. Samuel Eliot Morison, *The European Discovery of America: The Northern Voyages A.D. 500–1600* (New York: Oxford University Press, 1971), 567–71; see *Voyages and Colonising Enterprises of Sir Humphrey Gilbert*, Hakluyt Society, 2nd. ser. vols. 83, 84 (London: Hakluyt Society, 1940).
125. As Nicholas Canny points out, individual cases, like Thomas Stukely's fraud for an Anglo-French settlement in Florida in 1563, could put off potential backers and colonists for Ireland and America, but other more practical objections occurred amongst the English, for instance that, in Ireland, only financing from the Crown could lead to successful colonies and that private profit had been placed before social and religious reform; Nicholas Canny, *Kingdom and Colony: Ireland in the Atlantic World 1560–1800* (Baltimore: Johns Hopkins University Press, 1988), 1–6.
126. For a discussion of the relation amongst Basanier, the Hakluyts, and Ralegh, see Lestringant, *Le Huguenot*, 163, 170–1.
127. Parker, *Books*, 121.
128. The passage reads: "My Lord, history being like a mirror, the means by which we form our actions to fit the virtues of those that we represent there, and reading the feats of men, is nothing other than to frequent and associate with them to profit in their company and continual conversation, so that historians are marvellously well received and welcome amongst those who make a profession of virtue." M. Basanier, "Epistre," *Histoire notable de la Floride située ès Indes Occidentales,* . . . (Paris: N. Roffet, 1586), ã ij recto. My translation here and below. For a modern edition, see Charles-André Julien, ed., *Les Français en Amérique pendant la deuxième moitié du XVIᵉ Siècle: Les Français en Floride*, vol. 2, (Paris: Centre de documentation universitaire et Société d'édition d'enseignement supérieur réunis, 1958), 27–251.
129. Basanier, "Epistre," ã ij verso-iii recto.
130. Laudonnière in Basanier, ed., *Histoire notable*, 64 recto. For another account of this mutiny and other events on this expedition to Florida, see Jacques Le Moyne, *Brevis narratio eorum quae in Florida Americae provincia Gallis acciderunt, secunda in illam Navigatione, duce Renato de Laudonniere classis Praefecto*, ed. Théodore de Bry (Frankfurt-am-Main, 1591), 10–13.
131. Thomas Harriot [Hariot], *Briefe and true report of the new found land of Virginia* (London, 1590) reprinted New York, 1972. In his Introduction to

the Dover reprint (Rosenwald Collection Reprint Series), Paul Hutton discusses briefly the textual history of this work (vii).

132. Harriot, *Briefe and true report* (London, 1590), 31.

133. John White, *The Trve Pictvres and Fashions of the People in That Parte of America Novv Cal-led Virginia* . . . in Harriot, *Briefe and true report* (1590), [41].

134. Walter, Ralegh, *The Discouerie of the Large, Rich, and Bewtiful Empyre of Guiana, with a Relation of the Great and Golden Citie of Manoa (which the Spanyards call El Dorado* . . . . (London: Robert Robinson, 1596), q 2, 76–9.

135. Ibid., 3.

136. According to Ralegh, Guiana had more gold than Peru. His evidence was the word of the Spaniards he had spoken to, they who called Manoa, the imperial city of Guiana, El Dorado. These same Spaniards attested to the riches of this city: "it farre exceedeth any of the world, at least of so much of the world as is known to the Spanish nation." Ibid., 10. While undermining the Spanish, Ralegh relied on them. He quoted at length in Spanish from chapter 120 of Lopez's history of the Indies, which described the magnificent court of Guaynacapa, the emperor of Peru, whose descendant was, in Ralegh's account, emperor of Guiana. His family had escaped the Spaniards. Ralegh was implicitly building a coalition against Spain. So that no one missed the description of gold and more gold in all shapes and sizes, Ralegh translated the passage. He also furnished a translation from chapter 117 from Lopez that amplified the quantity of gold.

137. All of the editions of Lescarbot's *Histoire de la Nouvelle France* (1609, 1611–12, 1617–18) included an appendix consisting of a short collection of poems, *Les Muses de la Nouvelle France*. The last two editions involved a reshaping and a completion of the account of New France until the date of composition. Although there was a strong tendency for anti-Spanish sentiment to be Protestant, there were Catholic examples of the Black Legend. One of the functions of my discussion of Lescarbot is to provide an illustration of this modification of the stereotype of what constitutes the Black Legend. Anthony Pagden has made a similar point: "Most of what was said about Spain during the Eighty-Years War was inevitably, harnessed to the war effort. Spanish atrocities in general, and the sack of Antwerp in 1576 in particular, led to the creation, at Flemish and English hands, of the so-called Black Legend. The Spanish image in Protestant Europe (and it must be said, in many areas of Catholic Europe as well) as proud, cruel, and overbearing was in large part based on Dutch, and later English, propaganda"; see Pagden, *Spanish Imperialism and the Political Imagination, Studies in European and Spanish-American Social and Political Theory 1513–1830* (New Haven: Yale University Press, 1990), 4.

138. It is a shame that no copy of the contemporary biography of Lescarbot by the poet, Guillaume Colletet, has been found. See René Baudry, "Lescarbot, Marc," in *Dictionary of Canadian Biography*, gen. ed., George W. Brown, vol. 1, 1,000–1,700 (Toronto and Québec, 1966), 469–71. W. L. Grant, the translator of Lescarbot, writes of him: "Lescarbot, like Herodotus, whom he so much resembles, should be read in the original;" see Grant, "Translator's

Preface," in Marc Lescarbot, *The History of New France*, trans. W. L. Grant and introduction by H. P. Biggar (3 vols., Toronto, 1907) I, vii. Grant notes "How lightly his Catholicism sat upon Lescarbot may be judged from the fact that his frequent quotations from the Bible are from the Geneva version of Olivetan, revised by Calvin" (I, xx). On Lescarbot, see Biggar, "Introduction: Marc Lescarbot" in *History of New France*, ix–xv.

139. Marc Lescarbot, *Histoire de la Nouvelle France* . . . . (Paris: Iean Milot, 1609), b ij verso. France is the mother in this address. Lescarbot emphasized the Roman connection with France, first with Julius Caesar civilizing Gaul and second with the French saving the Popes from persecution; ibid. b ij verso-bij recto.

140. Ibid., b iij recto-b iij verso.

141. Ibid., b iiij recto.

142. Ibid. H. P. Biggar called Lescarbot, "the French Hakluyt," although Lescarbot is probably more elegant and puts more of himself in the text as he was an eyewitness in New France and Hakluyt never voyaged to America; see H. P. Biggar, "The French Hakluyt: Marc Lescarbot of Vervins," *American Historical Review* 6 (1901), 671–92. Frank Lestringant thinks that Lescarbot imitates La Popelinière and puts him in the legal and historical contexts of Chauveton, Hakluyt, and Jean Bodin. Like Lestringant, I think that Lescarbot's history goes farther than Hakluyt's in establishing a new form, what Lestringant calls "the digressive narrative of the failures of France in the New World"; Lestringant, *Le Huguenot et le Sauvage* (Paris, 1990), 267; my translation. He also points out Lescarbot's debt, in the third book, to Acosta and Lafitau, and whereas Lescarbot mostly borrowed from Léry (ten chapters), he did defend Thevet's imaginative Brazil as a means of inciting others to support and transform the colony (which drew so much sarcasm in Belleforest); ibid., 266–70. Lescarbot, like a number of the French chroniclers of the New World I am discussing, is relatively unknown outside a small group of specialists. He deserves to be much better known. In a recent history of Canada, e.g., he is barely mentioned, except as the first playwright in the country; see Christopher Moore, "Colonization and Conflict: New France and Its Rivals (1600–1760)," in *The Illustrated History of Canada*, ed. Craig Brown (1987; Toronto: Lester Pub., 1991), 158, 169.

143. Lescarbot, *Histoire* (1609), b iv verso. In his address to Pierre Jeannin in the 1612 edition, Lescarbot used this language of republicanism; see Marc Lescarbot, *Histoire de la Novvelle-France* . . . (Paris, 1612), jx.

144. August 24/September 3 1586; trans. from transcript in Brit. Mus., Additional MS 36315, fo. 92 (from A.G.I. 140.7.35), quoted in *The Roanoke Voyages 1584–1590*, ed. David Beers Quinn (1955; New York: Dover, 1991), II, 717.

145. See ibid., II: 722.

146. Simancas, Estado K. 1564, no. 100–168; deciphered and trans.; ibid., II: 759–60

147. May 16/26 1587, Brit. Mus., Additional MS 28363, fo. 86; trans; in ibid., II: 769.

148. February 27/March 9 1588; extract, Simancas, Estado K. 1564, no. 100–168,; trans., ibid., II: 770.
149. A. G. I., Patronado I. I. 1/19, in E. Ruidíaz y Caravia, *Florida*, II, 324, quoted in ibid., II: 772.
150. Thomas Harriot [Hariot], on a slip attached to Brit. Mus., Additional MS 6785, fo. 436, in ibid. Here, as I have done elsewhere, I would like to acknowledge the work done by the Hakluyt Society, and here and in other places particularly by David Beers Quinn. Such work makes research in the field much easier.
151. Seville, A. G. I. 54. I. 34, Santa Domingo 118, in Quinn, *Roanoke Voyages*, II: 786.
152. Ibid., II: 787–8.
153. Ibid., II: 789.
154. Ibid., II: 791.
155. Ibid., II: 792–4.
156. Ibid., II: 795.
157. "Relation," June 7 1606, Seville, A. G. I., Patronado I. I. I/19, in Eugenio Ruidíaz y Caravia, *La Florida su conquista y colonización por Pedro Menéndez de Avilés*, II (Madrid: J. A. García, 1893); trans, in ibid., II: 818.
158. Seville, A. G. I. 54.5.9 (Santo Domingo 224); trans, Quinn, II: 826.
159. Ibid., II:829–30.
160. Ibid., II:802–3.
161. Ibid., II: 809.
162. Ibid., II: 810, 815–6.

Chapter 3

1. See Max Savelle, *The Origins of American Diplomacy: The International History of Anglo-America 1492–1763* (New York: Macmillan, 1967), 3–16; Felipe Fernández-Armesto, *Before Columbus: Exploration and Colonisation from the Mediterranean to the Atlantic 1229–1402* (Philadelphia: University of Pennsylvania Press, 1987), esp. 151f.; Jonathan Hart, *Representing the New World* (New York and London: Palgrave, 2001), 16–21.
2. Dagmar Schäffer, *Portuguese Exploration to the West and the Formation of Brazil.* (Providence, RI: John Carter Brown Library, 1988), 3.
3. Henry Harrisse, *Jean et Sébastien Cabot* (Paris: Leroux, 1882) and *Les Cort-Real et leurs voyages au nouveau -monde . . .* (Paris: Leroux, 1883). H. P. Biggar, *Voyages of the Cabots and of the Corte-Reals* (Paris: Leroux, 1903); James A. Williamson, *The Voyages of the Cabots and the Discovery of North America under Henry VII and Henry VIII* (London: Argonaut Press, 1929), 200–3; Hart, *Representing*, 18–28.
4. Schäffer, *Portuguese Exploration*, 3. For a wider context for the western expansion of European powers, see Edward Burman, *The World Before Columbus 1100–1492* (London: W. H. Allen, 1989), 189–99.
5. Binot Paulmier de Gonneville, *Relation authentique . . .* in *Les Français en Amérique dans la première moitié du XVIᵉ siècle*, ed. Charles-André Julien (Paris: Presses Universitaires de France, 1946), 10.

6. A. J. R. Russell-Wood, *The Portuguese Empire, 1415–1808: A World on the Move* (1992; Baltimore: Johns Hopkins University Press, 1998), 3–4. For earlier key studies of the Portuguese empire, see Hernani Cidade, *A literatura portuguesa e a expansão ultramarina*, 2nd. ed., 2 vols. (Coimbra: Armenio Amado, 1963–64) and Charles R. Boxer, *The Portuguese Seaborne Empire, 1415–1825* (London: Hutchinson, 1969). On the Portuguese in Africa, see Burman, *The World Before*, 171–88.

7. William D. Phillips, Jr. and Carla Rahn Phillips, *The Worlds of Christopher Columbus* (Cambridge: Cambridge University Press, 1992), 110–24. At his death Cecil Jane left an unfinished introduction, which he worked on until two days before he died and in which he covered 7 of 21 topics for the proposed Introduction and printed in that form because the Hakluyt Society thought "no other person could complete it in a manner which would do justice to its author," as Edward Lynum describes in his brief "Prefatory Note" to the second volume of Jane's edition of Columbus's *Voyages*. Nonetheless, Jane left a detailed, balanced, and useful examination of contemporary Spanish representations of these negotiations, including a discussion of the views of Peter Martyr and Bartolomé de Las Casas; see Cecil Jane, "Introduction: The Negotiations of Columbus with Ferdinand and Isabella," *The Four Voyages of Columbus*, ed. Cecil Jane (1929 and 1932; New York: Dover, 1988), vol. 2, xiii–lxxv. This second volume was originally of the third and fourth volume and was later bound into one volume to include all four volumes. Jane wrote the Introduction, and there are two indices, to both original volumes that came to be combined (which leaves the separate pagination of the original volumes from the Hakluyt Society). For another helpful account, see John Cummins, "Planning and Persuasion," *The Voyage of Christopher Columbus: Columbus' Own Journal of Discovery Newly Restored and Translated by John Cummins* (London: Weidenfeld and Nicolson, 1992), 31–45 and see also "Appendix I," the procurator's questions to Columbus, 195–203, in the same volume for subsequent questioning.

8. This is a vast field of postmodern, postcolonial, and other recent theories, so that I have refrained from creating a vast list. There is, e.g., a debate over the status of narrative in fictions and history, something I have discussed in relation to the dramatic in a number of places, including *Theater and World* (Boston: Northeastern University Press, 1992) and in relation to theory in *Northrop Frye: The Theoretical Imagination* (London and New York: Routledge, 1994), so that I have avoided repeating myself here. For a recent discussion of narrative and history in the possession of the New World, see Howard Marchitello, *Narrative and Meaning in Early Modern England: Browne's Skull and Other Histories* (Cambridge: Cambridge University Press, 1997), 92–123. For a view of contemporary Latin America in terms of the relation between fiction and history, see Lois Parkinson Zamora, *The Usable Past: The Imagination of History in Recent Fiction of the Americas* (Cambridge: Cambridge University Press, 1997), esp. 1–39, 196–210. On the relation between truth and lying, Montaigne had much to say, particularly in "Du démentir." In a chapter appropriately called "The Storyteller," Natalie Zemon

Davis raises an interesting relation between the culture of truth and fiction as opposed to ideas of their relation: "Where does self-fashioning stop and lying begin?" Long before Montaigne posed that question to his readers in a self-accusatory essay, Pansette's inventiveness posed it to his judges;" see *The Return of Martin Guerre* (Cambridge MA: Harvard University Press, 1983), 103.

9. On the relation between politics in the British Empire on both sides of the Atlantic, see Eliga H. Gould, *The Persistence of Empire: British Political Culture in the Age of Revolution* (Chapel Hill: University of North Carolina Press, 2000).

10. Peter Burke, *Montaigne* (Oxford: Oxford University Press, 1981), 141–17. On Montaigne's library, see ibid., 15.

11. Marvin Lunenfeld ed., *1492: Discovery, Invasion, Encounter Sources and Interpretations* (Lexington MA: DC Heath, 1991), 201.

12. Bartolomé de Las Casas, *History of the Indies*, trans. and ed. André Collard (New York: Harper & Row, 1971), Book III, 181–7.

13. Ibid.

14. See Lope de Vega Carpio, *El Nuevo Mundo descubierto por Cristóbel Colón* in *Obras de Lope de Vega* (Madrid: La Real Academia Española, 1900) and, in translation, *The Discovery of the New World by Christopher Columbus*, trans. Frieda Fligelman (Berkeley: Gillick, 1940).

15. Ibid.

16. Bartolomé Las Casas, *A Short Account of the Destruction of the Indies*, trans. Nigel Griffin. (Harmondsworth: Penguin, 1992), 3–4. For Las Casas' life, see "Bartolomé de las Casas," *Catholic Encyclopedia*, Online edition, K. Knight, 2003; see www.newadvent.org/cathen/03397a.htm

17. On the Black Legend see, e.g., Julián Juderías, *La Leyenda Negra* (Madrid [s.n.] (Tip de la "Rev. de arch bibl: y museós"), 1914); Rómulo D. Carbia, *Historia de la Leyenda Negra Hispano-Americana* (Buenos Aires: [Orientacíon Española] 1943); Manuel Cardenal, "La Leyenda Negra," in *Diccionario de Historia de España*, 2 vols. (Madrid: Revista de Occidente, 1952), II, 231; Pierre Chaunu, "La Légende Noire Antihispanique," *Revue de Psychologie des Peuples* (Caen, 1964), 188–223; Benjamin Keen, "The Black Legend Revisited: Assumptions and Realities," *Hispanic American Historical Review* 49 (1969), 703–19; William S. Maltby, *The Black Legend in England* (Durham, NC: Duke University Press, 1971); Miguel Molina Martinez, *La leyenda negra* (Madrid: NEREA, 1991); Inga Clendinnen, "'Fierce and Unnatural Cruelty:' Cortés and the Conquest of Mexico," *Representations* 33 (1991), 65–100; Anthony Pagden, "Introduction," in de Las Casas, *Short Account*, xiii–xli. Jonathan Hart, "The Black Legend: English and French Representations of Spanish Cruelty in the New World," *Comparative Literature Now: Theories and Practice/ La Littérature comparée à L'Heure Actuelle. Théories et réalisations*, ed. S. Tötösy and M. V. Dimić with Irene Sywenky (Paris: Honoré Champion, 1999), 376–87.

18. On Las Casas, history, and conversion more generally, see, e.g., André Saint-Lu, *Las Casas Indigeniste: études sur la vie et l'œuvre du défenseur des Indiens*

(Paris: L' Harmattan 1982); Santa Arias, "Empowerment Through the Writing of History: Bartolomé de Las Casas's Representation of the Other(s)," in *Early Images of the Americas: Transfer and Invention*, ed. Jerry M. Williams and Robert E. Lewis (Tuscon: University of Arizona Press, 1993), 163–79; Luca Codignola, "The Holy See and the Conversion of the Indians," in *America in European Consciousness, 1493–1750*, ed. Karen Ordahl Kupperman (Chapel Hill: University of North Carolina Press, 1995), 195–243.

19. Las Casas, *Short Account*, 3.

20. Ibid., 96.

21. Roland Bainton, *Erasmus of Christendom* (New York: Scribner, 1969), 3, 32–6. My discussion is indebted to Bainton, whose account remains a fine and useful general view of the life and work of Erasmus.

22. L. Vives, *Opera*, 2 vols. (Basel, 1555), I, 390–2, cited in Bainton, *Erasmus* 36. See also Louis Dulieu, "Les 'Théologastres' de l'Université de Paris au Temps d'Erasme et de Rabelais," *Bibliothèque d'Humanisme et Renaissance* 27 (1965), 248–71. On the relation of Erasmus and Vives and their reception in their different home territories, see *Erasmus in Hispania Vives in Belgio*, ediderunt J IJsewijn et A. Losada (Lovanii: In Aedibus Peeters, 1986). This axis between Spain and the Netherlands is crucial in the period, something I have examined specifically in relation to the example of Spain for France and England in *Representing*.

23. *Erasmus Epistolae*, ed. P. S. and H. M. Allen (Oxford, 1906–58), vol. 1, 25, cited in Bainton, *Erasmus*, 40; see also 39.

24. *Lugduni Batavorum*, the Leiden ed. of Erasmus, ed. Leclerc, 1703, rpt. 1963, vol. 1, 993, quoted in Bainton, *Erasmus* 87–88; vol. 5, 898–9, cited in Bainton, *Erasmus*, 89.

25. In their Introduction to More's *Utopia*, Logan and Adams briefly compare the complexity of the satire in this work and Erasmus's *The Praise of Folly*; see Thomas More, *Utopia*, ed. George M. Logan and Robert M. Adams (Cambridge: Cambridge University Press, 1989, rpt. 1999), xxi; see, e.g., 6n12, 67n53.

26. *Erasmus Epistolae*, vol. 2, 333, 70, quoted in Bainton, *Erasmus*, 104. See Latin original.

27. Ibid., vol. 1, 245, 492, quoted in Bainton, *Erasmus*, 104.

28. Sverker Arnoldsson has done detailed work on anti-Spanish sentiments in sixteenth-century Italy and Germany; see his *La Leyenda Negra: Estudios Sobra sus Orígenes* (Göteborg: Almqvist & Wiksell, 1960).

29. More, *Utopia* (Cambridge: Cambridge University Press, 1989, rpt. 1999 ed.), xxx, 125n26.

30. On Vespucci and More, see Martin Waldseemüller, *The Cosmographiae Introductio*, ed. C. G. Herbermann (1907), 97–8 and More, *Utopia* (1989, rpt. 1999), 10, 63n44; on Rastell, see R. W. Chambers, *Thomas More* (London, 1935), 141–3 and J. H. Hexter, "Introduction, Part I," *The Complete Works of St. Thomas More*, vol. 4, ed. Edward Surtz and J. H. Hexter (New Haven: Yale University Press, 1965), xxxi.

31. On the composition of *Utopia* and on Vespucci, see Hexter, "Introduction Part I," xxi–xxiii, xxxi; see Logan's and Adams's Introduction to *Utopia*, xvi.

32. Thomas More, *Utopia*, ed. Edward Surtz (New Haven: Yale University Press, 1964), 6. George Logan's and Robert Adam's Introduction to the recent edition of More's *Utopia* with Cambridge is an important work and discusses the Lucianic tradition and complex irony in Erasmus's *In Praise of Folly* (1509) and Thomas More's *Utopia*, [ed. G. M. Logan and R. M. Adams (Cambridge: Cambridge University Press, 1989, rpt. 1995), xx–xxi]. For an earlier but suggestive discussion of More, see Stephen Greenblatt, *Renaissance Self-Fashioning From More to Shakespeare* (Chicago: University of Chicago Press, 1980), where he discusses More's self-fashioning and self-cancelation, e.g., in a letter in 1516 where he wrote in jest to Erasmus that he dreamt he had been made king of the Utopians, with a crown of wheat, but that he had asked Erasmus to find recommendations for his book by statesmen as well as scholars in order to get word out in the right places; see Greenblatt, *Renaissance*. 55 but also 32–58 on *Utopia*. For the More's letter to Erasmus, see *St. Thomas More: Selected Letters*, ed. Elizabeth F. Rogers (New Haven: Yale University Press, 1961), 85.

33. Surtz, Introduction and notes, *Utopia*, xi, 12n19.

34. I have argued that Erasmus and More satirize war and hegemony. Erasmus, More, and Montaigne all provide critiques of cruelty. As David Quint notes, in contrast to the twelfth chapter of Xenophon's *Cynegeticus*, which justifies the aristocratic nature of hunting, Erasmus's *In Praise of Folly* satirizes the connections among hunting, war, and nobility and More takes up this satire on hunting in *Utopia*, (see Surtz, *Utopia*, ed. 4) while Montaigne later attacks hunting as not being worthy of the aristocracy in "De la cruauté"; see Quint, 61–63. On some of these links between these writers between cruelty and hunting, see Robert M. Adams, *The Better Part of Valor: Erasmus, Colet, and Vives on Humanism* (Seattle: University of Washington Press, 1962), 43–54; on Montagne and hunting, see Timothy Hampton, *Writing from History: The Rhetoric of Exemplarity in Renaissance Literature* (Ithaca: Cornell University Press, 1990), 170 and on cruelty and hunting, see Giordano Bruno, *Spaccio de la bestia trionfante* (Parigi: [s.n.], [London: John Charleswood], 1584).

35 More, *Utopia*, (Yale, 1965 ed.) 9.

36. Ibid., 9n3–4.

37. Ibid., 12–13. Original Latin in text.

38. Ibid., 15.

39. Ibid., 23

40. More, Book I, 92; the translation reads: "no amount of gold is enough for the ruler who has to keep an army" (93).

41. More, "Book II," 218–9; Amerigo Vespucci, *Quatuor Americi Vespucij nauigatones* (St. Dié, 1507), vol. 1, sig.c8, rpt. *The Cosmographiae Introductio of Martin Waldseemüller in Facsimile, Followed by the Four Voyages of Amerigo Vespucci, with Their Translation into English*, ed. C. G. Herbermann and trans. Mario E. Cosenza (New York: The United States Catholic Historical Society, 1907).

42. Vespucci, vol. 1, sig. c1v; Peter Martyr (Petrus Martyr Anglerius), *De orbe nouo decades* (Alcalá de Henares, 1516), Decades 1, 3; in French, see

Peter Martyr (Petrus Martyr Anglerius), *Extraict ov recveil des ilses nouuelleme[n]t touuees en la grande mer Oceane ou temps du roy Despaigne Ferna[n]d & Elizabeth sa femme, faict premierement en latin par Pierre Martyr de Millan, & depuis* (Paris, 1532); in English, see Richard Eden, *The Decades of the newe worlde of west India,* . . . . (London: G. Powell, 1555).

43. More, Book II, 150–9, 428.
44. More, Book II, 156; the translation reads: "*How much wiser the Utopians Are than the Common Run of Christians!*" (157).
45. Amerigo Vespucci, *Mundus novus: Letter to Lorenzo Pietro di Medici*, trans. G. T. Northrup (Princeton: Princeton University Press, 1916), 6, cited in *The Complete Works of St. Thomas More*, vol. 4 , ed. Edward Surtz and J. H. Hexter (New Haven: Yale University Press, 1965), 378.
46. More, Book I, 102–3.
47. Vespucci, *Quatuor Americi*, vol. 1, sig. d2v-3, quoted in *The Complete Works of St. Thomas More*, vol. 4., 475; More, 184–87.
48. Vespucci, *Quatuor Americi*, vol. 1, sig. b7v, quoted in *The Complete Works of St. Thomas More*, vol. 4., 497; More, Book II, 200–1.
49. Janet Whatley, "Introduction," Jean de Léry, *History of a Voyage to the Land of Brazil*, trans. Janet Whatley (Berkeley: University of California Press, 1990), xvii.
50. Peter Burke, *Montaigne*, 44–7. On the relation between history and anthropology, see Anthony Pagden, "History and Anthropology, and the History of Anthropology: Considerations on a Methodological Practice," *Imagining Culture; Essays in Early Modern History and Culture*, ed. Jonathan Hart (New York and London: Garland, 1996), 27–40. See also Charles Taylor, "Interpretation and the Sciences of Man," *Philosophical Papers* 2 (Cambridge: Cambridge University Press, 1985), 15–57.
51. Janet Whatley, "Editions and Reception of Léry," Jean de Léry, *History of a Voyage to the Land of Brazil*, trans. Janet Whatley (Berkeley: University of California Press, 1990), 246n14.
52. Jean de Léry, *History of a Voyage to the Land of Brazil*, trans. Janet Whatley (Berkeley: University of California Press, 1990), 131–2.
53. Ibid., 132.
54. Ibid., 132.
55. Ibid., 133.
56. David Quint argues that this essay is as much about France as about the New World and does not seek to congratulate Montaigne for his freedom from prejudice: "Des cannibales" "turns out to be at least equally about his own France and that the terms with which it discusses the Brazilian natives are deeply rooted in his own historical and political preoccupations" see Quint, "A Reconsideration of Montaigne's *Des cannibales*," in *America in European Consciousness, 1493–1750*, ed. Karen Ordahl Kupperman (Chapel Hill: University of North Carolina Press, 1995), 168, see 166–91. This view supports my notion of typology between New World and Old.
57. Michel de Montaigne, *Essais de Michel Seignevr de Montaigne* (Paris, 1588); rpt. as *Les Essais de Montaigne: reproduction typographique de l'exemplaire annoté par l'auteur et conservé à la Bibliothèque de Bordeux avec un avertisssement et une*

notice par M. Ernest Courbet (4 vols., Paris: Impr. Nationale, 1906–31), I, 167. Here, I am using the sixth edition of 1588, which involves a number of corrections to the edition of 1580. Courbet's "Advertisement" (v–xv) explains some of the textual complexities of the *Essais*, including the intercalations and the corrections of Pierre de Brach. In Courbet's text, if the readers so choose, they can, on facing pages, see the changes to the text, one reason I used this text rather than the many editions available to me in England, Boston, and Providence. The translation is mine here and below. Having discussed the opposition or ambivalence of humanists, like Erasmus and More, to colonization, it is appropriate to consider their relation to Montaigne; see Aldo Scaglione, "A Note on Montaigne's *Des Cannibales* and the Humanist Tradition," *First Images of America: The Impact of the New World on the Old*, ed. Fredi Chiapelli et al., 2 vols. (Berkeley: University of California Press, 1976), I, 63–70. For a recent and perceptive interpretation of *Des Cannibales*, see David Quint, *Montaigne and the Quality of Mercy: Ethical and Political Themes in The Essais* (Princeton: Princeton University Press, 1998), 75–101.

58. Montaigne's motive was a simple and true narrative of the New World, so that he sought to qualify the use of rhetorical and narrative embellishment and to establish the credentials of his man as a witness. "This man who I had, was a simple and plain man, who was in a proper condition to bear true witness, for refined people are more curious and notice more things, but they gloss them, and [faire valoir leur interpretation & la perſuader] to add to the value of the intrepretation, and to persuade, they cannot prevent themselves from altering the History a little"; Montaigne, *Essais*, I, 169. Perhaps Montaigne mimics the travel literature he discussed. Michel de Certeau thinks of Montaigne's essay on cannibals as having the same structure as a travel account, including the "outbound journey," the depiction of "savage society," and the "return voyage"; see Michel de Certeau, *Heterologies: Discourse on the Other*, trans. Brian Massumi (Minneapolis: University of Minnesota Press, 1986), 69–70.

59. Montaigne, *Essais*, I, 170. For a discussion of Montaigne's thought, see Peter Burke, *Montaigne*. An especially pertinent discussion occurs in chapter 7, "Montaigne as Ethnographer," 44–51, where Burke places Montaigne in the context of Gómara, Benzoni, Thevet, Léry, Ronsard, La Boétie, and others and compares Montaigne to Tacitus who reproached Rome with the description of the courageous German barbarians. This technique Burke aptly calls the "Germania syndrome" (46). For some important works on Montaigne, see Géralde Nakam, *Montaigne et son temps: les événements et les "Essais"* (Paris A. G. Nizet, 1982); Tzvetan Todorov, "L'Etre et l'Autre: Montaigne," *Montaigne: Essays in Reading*, special issue of *Yale French Studies* 64 (1983), 113–44; Olivier Pot, *L'Inquiétude étrangeté: Montaigne: la pierre, le cannibale, la mélancolie* (Paris Honoré Champion, 1993) and *La lecteur, l'auteur et l'écrivain: Montaigne-1592–1992* (Paris: Honoré Champion, 1993); Georges Laffly, *Montaigne; libre et fidèle* (Le Barroux: Editions Sainte-Madeleine, 1997); Gisèle Mathieu-Castellani, *Montaigne, ou, La verité du mensonge* (Genève: Droz, 2000).

60. The translation is "Of Coaches."
61. Montaigne, *Essais*, III, 399–400.
62. Ibid., 399 verso. Florio renders the passage "Oh mechanicall victories, oh base conquest;" see Montaigne, *Essaies*, II, 314. Michel de Montaigne, *Montaigne's Essays: John Florio's Translation* (London: Nonesuch Press, 1931), II. 314; see also Michel de Montaigne, *The essays . . . now done into English by . . . john Florio* (London: Val Simms for Edward Blount, 1603).
63. Montaigne, *Essais*, III, 399 verso. In discussing the French rituals of possession, Patricia Seed says that Montaigne, too, assumed that body language was universal, so that if this assertion were true, his criticism would be qualified and he would resemble Columbus more than I have been saying. I am not sure, none the less, that this is a general position Montaigne took, particularly in his views of Natives; see Montaigne, *Apologie de Raymond Sebond*, ed. Paul Porteau (Paris, 1937), cited in *Ceremonies of Possession in Europe's Conquest of the New World, 1492–1640* (Cambridge: Cambridge University Press, 1995), 55.
64. Montaigne, *Essais*, III, 399 verso. The French "menasses" implies a menacing, but I have used the word "threat" here.
65. Ibid.
66. Ibid., 400–1.
67. Ibid., 401. Florio emphasizes this contrast by applying the epithet "barbarous mindes" to the Spanish torturers; Montaigne *Essais*, II, 317.
68. Montaigne, *Essais*, III, 401.
69. Ibid., 401–2.
70. Ibid., 401–3.
71. Lestringant has an interesting discussion of Hakluyt's mission in Paris; see Frank Lestringant, *Le Huguenot et le sauvage: L'Amérique et la controverse coloniale, en France, au temps des Guerres de Réligion (1555–1589)* (Paris: Aux Amateurs de livres [Klincksieck], 1990), 213–8.
72. Postcolonialism is not something without its own variety, differences, and contradictions, something I have argued elsewhere. For very different post-colonial views, ranging from humanism to a question of humanism, in major studies, particularly in the crucial years of the late 1980s and early 1990s for postcolonial studies, see Edward W. Said, *Orientalism* (New York: Pantheon Books, 1978) and *Culture and Imperialism* (London: Chatto & Windus, 1993); Trinh T. Minh-ha, *Woman, Native, Other: Writing Postcoloniality and Feminism* (Bloomington: University of Indiana Press, 1988); Gayatri Chakravorty Spivak, *In Other Worlds: Essays in Cultural Politics* (New York: Methuen, 1987); Lisa Lowe, *Critical Terrains: French and British Orientalisms* (Ithaca, NY: Cornell University Press, 1991); Homi Bhabha, *The Location of Culture* (London: Routledge, 1994): Benita Parry, "Resistance Theory/ Theorising Resistance or Two Cheers for Nativism," in *Colonial Discourse/ Postcolonial Theory*, ed. Francis Barker, Peter Hulme, Margaret Iversen (Manchester: Manchester University Press, 1994), 172–96. For one of my earlier views, see Jonathan Hart and Terry Goldie, "Postcolonial Theory," *Encyclopedia of Contemporary Literary Theory* (Toronto: University of Toronto Press, 1993), 155–8.

73. Francisco de Vitoria, *Political Writings*, ed. Anthony Pagden and Jeremy Lawrence (Cambridge: Cambridge University Press, 1991). The text is divided according to these questions: I have not put them in quotation marks because the ellipses would be cumbersome but these marks should be understood surrounding these three questions. See. section 6, "On the American Indians," 231–92.

74. Michel Foucault, *Discipline and Punish: The Birth of the Prison*, trans. A. M. Sheridan (Harmondsworth: Allen Lane, 1977); see his *Madness and Civilization*, trans. Richard Howard (New York: Pantheon Books, 1965).

75. C. L. R. James, *The Black Jacobins: Toussaint Louverture and the San Domingo Revolution* (New York: Dial Press, [1938]).

76. Anthony Pagden, "Introduction," Las Casas, *A Short Account*, xiii–xiv.

Chapter 4

1. Miguel de Cervantes Saavedra, *The Adventures of Don Quixote*, trans. J. M. Cohen (Harmondsworth: Penguin, 1950, rpt. 1979), 26.

2. Oviedo is a controversial figure. Todorov describes him as a historian who is a conquistador (148); "a rich source of xenophobic and racist judgments" (*The Conquest of America: The Question of the Other*, Richard Howard ed., 1982 New York: Harper, 1984, rpt. 1992, 151); "already violently anti-Indian" (160); "the racist historian" (166). Elliott (*The Old World and the New 1492–1650*. [Cambridge: Cambridge University Press, 1970, rpt. 1992] represents an Oviedo who thinks Columbus deserves better recognition (11); as a natural historian full of wonder (21); someone who, like Las Casas, emphasizes the wonder and awe of the infinite diversity of America (31); he who respects Pliny too much (32); an advocate of the Christian republic that involved the assimilation of the Amerindians, which the religious most often favored (34); a defender of Amerindian oral sources because Castilians, too, had their own oral history and romances (35); a heroic, admirable, but amateur encyclopedist of the New World (37); a supporter of direct personal observation over traditional authority (40); a historian, like Las Casas, who sometimes used strained analogies (41); a skeptic, like Léry, about Amerindian conversion (43); an admirer of the wealth of the Indies (59, 63); a man proud of Spanish manufacture and accomplishment in the New World (78); a person of intellectual curiosity (*Spain and Its World 1500–1700*. [New Haven: Yale University Press, 1989], 45); someone without a university education (1989, 46). Without belaboring the complexity of Oviedo's work, I want to cite a few of the many references to Oviedo in Pagden's works: Oviedo is an example of a European observer who describes things that looked alike as identical (Anthony Pagden, *The Fall of Natural Man: The American Indian and the Origins of Comparative Ethnography*, [Cambridge: Cambridge University Press, 1982, rev. 1986], 11); a classifier of the Amerindians who compares them to the Ethiopians (24–5); a predecessor to Acosta in the systematic history of America but whom Acosta never mentions (151–52); someone who looks on the Natives of the Antilles with disgust

(Anthony Pagden, *European Encounters with the New World: From Renaissance to Romanticism* [New Haven: Yale University Press, 1993], 17); a natural historian who has a low opinion of the Natives and whom Humboldt calls the Pliny of the New World (56, see 68). For a detailed analysis of Oviedo's *Historia general y natural de las Indias* (published in the nineteenth century, a version of the first part published in 1535), including the nature of accuracy and authority of Oviedo's vision and his relation to the self and to objectivity, see Pagden, *European Encounters*, 56–68, 81–84.

3. Gonzalo Fernández de Oviedo, *Natural History of the West Indies*, trans. Sterling A. Stoudemire (Chapel Hill: University of North Carolina Press, 1959) [*University of North Carolina Studies in Romance Languages and Literatures* 32], 3. In an earlier version of this research, the Spanish appeared in the text and the English translation in the notes and the French original was in the text without translation in the notes; see Jonathan Hart, "Strategies of Promotion: Some Prefatory Matter of Oviedo, Thevet and Hakluyt," *Imagining Culture; Essays in Early Modern History and Culture*, ed. Jonathan Hart (New York and London: Garland, 1996), 73–92.

4. Oviedo, *Historia general* 3.
5. Ibid.
6. Ibid.
7. Ibid., 4.
8. The original reads: *esse testem temporum, vitae magistram, vitam memoriae, veritatis lucen et vestustatis nuntian.*
9. Ibid., 4.
10. Ibid.
11. Ibid., 5.
12. Ibid.
13. Ibid.
14. Roger Schlesinger and Arthur P. Stabler, *André Thevet's North America: A Sixteenth-Century View* (Kingston and Montreal: McGill-Queen's University Press, 1986), xvii–xli. xxxiii, xxxix, see Jean Céard, *La Nature et les prodiges: L'insolite au XVIe siècle, en France* (Geneva: Droz, 1977), 283.
15. Frank Lestringant, "L'Avenir des terres nouvelles," *La Renaissance et le Nouveau Monde*, ed. Alain Parent et al. (Québec, 1984), 45–51. 50–1, cited Schlesinger and Stabler, *Andre Thevet's North America*, xxxix-xl.
16. Schlesinger and Stabler, André Thevet's North America, xl.
17. See Lestringant, *L'Atelier du Cosmographe ou l'image du monde à la Renaissance* (Paris: Albin Michel, 1991), 29.
18. All translations of André Thevet, *Les Singularités de la France antarctique* (Paris: Le Temps, 1982) here and below are mine.
19. Thevet, *Les Singularités*. āij recto.
20. Ibid.
21. Ibid., āij verso- āiij recto.
22. Ibid., āiij recto.
23. Ibid., āiiij recto.
24. See Thevet, 68–71.

25. Here I am applying the first term (W. Jackson Bate's) and the second (Harold Bloom's), which have been used to discuss the struggle of poets for a singular voice in a weighty poetic tradition, to nations, who have built themselves and their empires, in a tradition of empires, so that the translation of empire is like the translation of poetics or the translation of study. See Walter Jackson Bate, *The Burden of the Past and the English Poet* (Cambridge, MA: Belknap Press, 1970) and Harold Bloom, *The Anxiety of Influence: A Theory of Poetry* (New York: Oxford University Press, 1973). The analogy, while imperfect, does, I think, suggest an insight about Hakluyt's self-promotion and the promotion of empire as well as for others in the similar positions in other countries with nationalistic and imperial longings. I am not assuming a seamless personification of nations in which one can overstep the fallacy of composition and equate the part for the whole, the individual for the nation. Such analogies are suggestive but imperfect.

26. See Schlesinger and Stabler, *André Thevet's North America*, xxiii. Hakluyt is described in various terms. For Wayne Franklin, he is someone who appears incidentally, as a collector of narratives and a recipient of letters (*Discoverers, Explorers, Settlers: The Diligent Writers of Early America*. [Chicago: University of Chicago Press, 1979], 135–6, 160–5). Karen Kupperman discusses the Hakluyts as agents for Francis Walsingham and notes their desire for educational reforms at Oxford and Cambridge (moving from a medieval curriculum to one including mathematics and geography) (*Settling with the Indians: The Meeting of English and Indian Cultures in America, 1580–1640*. [Totowa, NJ: Rowan and Littlefield, 1980], 9); observes the international nature of Hakluyt the Younger's material (23, 150); how Hakluyt recommended the robbing of Amerindian graves to achieve riches (125). Greenblatt mentions Hakluyt only twice, once in observing the paradox that the patriotic Hakluyt includes international material (*Marvelous Possessions: The Wonder of the New World*. [Chicago: University of Chicago Press, 1991], 8–9) and then in connection with Mandeville (30–1).

27. Richard Hakluyt, *Voyages*, vol. 1 (London: Dent: Everyman's Library, 1907, rpt. 1967), vol. 1, 6.

28. Ibid., 1. For useful discussions of Hakluyt, see Jack Beeching, "Introduction," Richard Hakluyt, *Voyages and Discoveries*, ed. Jack Beeching (1972; Harmondsworth: Penguin, 1985), 9–29; Mary C. Fuller, *Voyages in Print: English Travel to America, 1576–1624* (Cambridge: Cambridge University Press, 1995), 141–74; David Armitage, "The New World and British Historical Thought From Richard Hakluyt to William Robertson," in *America in European Consciousness, 1493–1750*, ed. Karen Ordahl Kupperman (Chapel Hill: University of North Carolina Press, 1995), 52–75.

29. Hakluyt, *Voyages*, 1.

30. Ibid., 2.

31. Ibid.

32. Ibid.

33. Ibid.

34. See also Lancelot Voisin, sieur de la Popelinière, *L'histoire de France . . .* (n. p. [La Rochelle]: Abraham H., 1581) and his *Les trois mondes . . .*

(Paris Pierre L'Huillier, 1582). I discuss his work in *Representing the New World* (New York and London: Palgrave, 2001).

35. Hakluyt, *Voyages*, vol 1., 2.
36. Ibid. Here I mix translation with paraphrase: "the English, who have the spirit, means & enough valour, to acquire a great honour among all Christians," have not exceeded others in the element of the sea that to them "should be more natural than to other peoples."
37. Ibid., 3.
38. Ibid.
39. Ibid., 4.
40. Ibid.
41. Ibid., 5.
42. Ibid.
43. Ibid.
44. Ibid., 6.
45. Ibid.
46. Walter Bagehot, *Physics and Politics* (London: Kegan Paul, Trench & Co 1887), 2–21, quoted in E. J. Hobsbawn, *Nations and Nationalism Since 1780*, 2nd ed. (Cambridge: Cambridge University Press, 1990, rpt., 1999), 1.
47. Ernest Gellner, *Nations and Nationalism* (Oxford: Blackwell, 1983), 1; Hobsbawn, esp. 1–13; see also Ernest Renan, *Qu'est ce que c'est une nation?* (Paris: C Lévy, 1882); Anthony Smith, *Theories of Nationalism*, 2nd ed. (London: Duckworth, 1983) and *The Ethnic Origins of Nations* (Oxford: Blackwell, 1986). Stalin, like Hobson and Lenin, linked nation, colony, and empire; see Joseph Stalin, *Marxism and the National and Colonial Question* (London: Lawrence and Wishart, 1936).
48. Here I am using Shakespeare's First Folio; these lines are 366–7 (I give this kind of line reference for those who have electronic versions available). *Mr. William Shakespeares' Comedies, Histories, & Tragedies. Published according to the True Originall Copies* (London: Isaac Iaggard, and Ed. Blount, 1623).
49. Shakespeare, First Folio, lines 971–5.
50. Shakespeare, First Folio, lines 1237–51.
51. Hakluyt, *Voyages* 6.
52. Ibid.
53. Ibid., 6–7.
54. Ibid., 7.
55. Ibid., 7–8.
56. Ibid., 9.
57. Ibid.
58. Ibid.
59. Ibid.
60. Ibid.
61. Ibid.
62. Ibid., 10.
63. Ibid.
64. Ibid., 11.

65. Ibid., 12.
66. Ibid.
67. Ibid.
68. Ibid.
69. For my discussion of this sexual element in the representations of the New World, see chapter 5 of *Columbus, Shakespeare and the Interpretation of the New World* (New York and London: Palgrave, 2003).
70. See More, *Utopia* (Cambridge: Cambridge University Press, 1989, rpt. 1999), 57–8, 63, 80, 83, 95; see Logan and Adams, Introduction to this edition, xxvi.

Chapter 5

1. Exodus 1:22, see 1: 11.
2. Exodus 5:1.
3. Matthew 2:13.
4. Charles Verlinden, *The Beginnings of Modern Colonization*, trans. Yvonne Freccero (Ithaca, NY: Cornell University Press, 1970), 33, see esp. 34–76. This essay was published in French as "Esclavage médiévales dans la colonisation de l'Amérique," *Cahiers de l'Institut des Hautes Etudes de l'Amérique Latine* 6 (1961), 29–45.
5. H. V. Livermore, "Portuguese History," Portugal and Brazil: An Introduction, ad. H. V. Livermore (Oxford: The Claredon Press, 1953), 55–62 here and below.
6. G. R. Crone, "Introduction," *The Voyages of Cadamosto and Other Documents on Western Africa in the Second Half of the Fifteenth Century* (London: The Hakluyt Society, 1937), xix
7. Carter G. Woodson, "Attitudes of the Iberian Peninsula," *Journal of Negro History* 20 (1935), 202; Margaret T. Hogden, *Early Anthropology in the Sixteenth and Seventeenth Centuries* (Philadelphia: University of Pennsylvania Press, 1964); Winthrop D. Jordan, *White Over Black: American Attitudes toward the Negro, 1550–1812* (Chapel Hill, NC: University of North Carolina Press, 1968); McAlister, 54–5.
8. Cadamosto, 8, 13.
9. Ibid., 13.
10. Ibid., 13–4.
11. Ibid., 17.
12. Ibid., 17.
13. Ibid., 17.
14. Ibid., 18. See Gomes Eannes de Azurara, *The Chronicle of the Discovery and Conquest of Guinea*, trans. and ed. C. R. Beazley and E. Prestage (London: Hakluyt Society, 1896–99).
15. Cadamosto, 18.
16. Ibid., 49.
17. Ibid., 49; for below, see 50n1.
18. Ibid., 50.
19. Ibid., 54, see 55.

20. Ibid., 55
21. Ibid., 68.
22. Ibid., 69.
23. The bull *Romanus pontifex*, January 8, 1455, in Francis Gardiner Davenport, *European Treaties Bearing on the History of the United States and its Dependences to 1648* (Washington, D.C.: Carnegie Institution of Washington, 1917), 21.
24. Hugh Thomas, *The Slave Trade* (New York: Simon & Schuster, 1997), 46–7, 86, 89. See also Carl Sauer, *The Early Spanish Main* (Berkeley: University of California Press, 1966) for more on Queen Isabella and Columbus.
25. Charles Henry Cunningham, *The Audiencia in the Spanish Colonies: As Illustrated by the Audiencia of Manila (1583–1800)* (Berkeley: University of California Press, 1919), 3, see 1.
26. J. M. Ots y Capdequí, *El estado español en las Indias*, 4th ed. (México: Fondo de Cultura Económica 1965), 45; on Castilian administration, see Mark A. Burkholder and D. S. Chandler, *From Importence to Authority: The Spanish Crown and the American Audiencias, 1687–1808* (Columbia, MO: University of Missouri Press, 1977), 1.
27. Maria Augusta Lima Cruz, "Exiles and Renegades in Early Sixteenth Century Portuguese Asia," in *Historiography of Europeans in Africa and Asia, 1450–1800*, ed. Anthony Disney (Aldershot: Variorum, 1995), 235, 248, see 236–47. The original version, also translated by Sanjay Subrahmanyam, appeared in the *Indian Economic and Social History Review* 23 (1986), 249–62.
28. For an informative survey of European attitudes toward Natives, see David B. Quinn, "European Technology and Preconceptions," in *The Discovery of North America* (London: Elek, 1971), 13–8; on alterity or otherness, see Tzvetan Todorov, *The Conquest of America: The Question of the Other*, trans. Richard Howard (New York: Harper & Row, 1984), *The Conquest*, 42–4, 100–1, 185–6, 195–200 and, more generally, his *Nous et les autres: La réflexion française sur la diversité; humaine* (Paris: Seuil, 1989); Michel de Certeau, "Montaigne's 'Of Cannibals': The Savage 'I,' " in *Heterologies: Discourse on the Other*, trans. Brian Massumi (Minneapolis: University of Minnesota Press, 1986), 79; Stephen Greenblatt, *Marvelous Possessions: The Wonder of the New World* (Chicago: University of Chicago Press, 1991), 135–6; Jonathan Hart, "Mediation in the Exchange between Europeans and Native Americans in the Early Modern Period," *Canadian Review of Comparative Literature: Revue Canadienne de Littérature Comparée* 22 (1995), 321–2. See also Jonathan Hart, "Images of the Native in Renaissance Encounter Narratives," ARIEL 25 (October 1994): 55–76 and *Columbus, Shakespeare and the Interpretation of the New World* (New York and London: Palgrave Macmillan, 2003).
29. Quoted in Anthony Pagden, "Introduction", Bartolomé de Las Casas, *A Short Account of the Destruction of the Indies*, trans. Nigel Griffin (Harmondsworth: Penguin, 1992), xxi; see xxii–xxx for below. For Las Casas's account of Montesino, see Bartolomé de Las Casas, *History of the Indies*, trans. and ed. Andrée Collard (New York: Harper & Row, 1971), chs. 3–5.

30. Jean Alfonse, "*La Cosmographie*. . . . (1545?), ed. Georges Musset (Paris: E. Leroux 1904) and *Les Voyages avantureux du capitaine Ian Alfonse Sainctongeois* (Poitiers: Jan de Marnef 1559). This work was reprinted in Rouen in 1578 and La Rochelle in 1590.

31. Alfonse, *Les Voyages*, quoted in Jean-Paul Duviols, *L' Amérique espagnole vue et rêvée. Les livres de voyages de Christophe Colomb à Bougainville* ([Paris]: Promodis, 1985), 183 n23; my translation. For Duviols's view, see ibid.

32. André Thevet, *La Cosmographie vniverselle*, vol. 2, livre 1, cap. 11, f. 498 verso; see A. C. de C. M. Saunders, *A Social History of Black Slaves and Freedmen in Portugal 1441–1555* (Cambridge: Cambridge University Press, 1982), 11–12, 33.

33. Jean de Léry, *History of a Voyage to the Land of Brazil*, trans. and introduction by Janet Whatley (Berkeley: University of California Press, 1990), 9, see 4.

34. C. R. Boxer. *The Dutch in Brazil, 1624–1654* (Oxford: Clarendon Press, 1957). 106–10.

35. Patricia Seed, *Ceremonies of Possession* (Cambridge: Cambridge University Press, 1995). For a discussion of the *Requerimento*, and the *encomiendas*, which were not feudatories like the lands granted in the French colonies or the quasi-independent occupation in English America, see Pagden, *Lords*, 91.

36. Hugh Thomas, *The Slave Trade: The Story of the Slave Trade: 1440–1870* (New York: Simon & Schuster, 1997), 23, see 74, 79–84, 91–4, 114–45, 180. I am indebted to Thomas here and below. For more on the curse of Ham and slavery, see *The Curse of Ham* (Princeton: Princeton University Press, 2003). See Aristotle, *Politics*, trans. Benjamin Jowett (New York: Dover Publications, 1992), bk. 1, chs. 4–5; G. Zurara (Azurara), *Chronicle of the Discovery of Guinea*, trans. and ed. C. R. Beazley and Edgar Prestage, Hakluyt Society, 1st ser., vols. 95 and 100 (London, 1896 and 1899), esp. vol. 95, 81–3. For secondary sources, see José Antonio Saco, *Historia de la Esclavitud de la Raza Africana en el Nuevo Mundo*, 3 vols. (Barcelona: J. Jépus, [etc.], 1879–93); Charles Verlinden, *L'Esclavage dans l'Europe médiaévale* (Brugge: De Tempel, 1955); Frederic Bowser, *The African Slave in Colonial Peru* (Stanford: Stanford University Press, 1972); Bailey W. Diffie and George Winius, *Foundations of the Portuguese Empire* (Minneapolis: University of Minnesota Press, 1977); Bernard Lewis, *Race and Slavery in the Middle East* (New York: Oxford University Press, 1990); Pierre Bonnassie, *From Slavery to Feudalism in South-Western Europe* (Cambridge: Cambridge University Press, 1991). See also Leo Africanus, *Description of Africa*, ed. R. Brown, Hakluyt Society, vol. 93 (London, 1890); Bartolomé de Las Casas, *A Short Account*. A brief but suggestive discussion of slavery and empire occurs in Anthony Pagden, *Peoples and Empires: Europeans and the Rest of the World, From Antiquity to the Present* (2001; London: Phoenix Press, 2002), 106–18.

37. Boxer 31, *The Dutch in Brazil*, 43–8.

38. Willem Piso, *De Indiae utriusque re naturali et medica libri quatuordecim* (Amsterdam: Lodovicium et Daneilem Elzevirios, 1658).

39. Michael Hemmersam, *West-Indianische Reissbeschreibung* (Nuremburg, 1663). For a helpful catalogue of this and other related books once exhibited at the John Carter Brown Library in 1988, see Dagmar Schäffer, *Portuguese Exploration to the West and the Formation of Brazil 1450–1800* (Providence, RI: The John Carter Brown Library, 1988), esp. 65–6. A key study remains important; see Boxer, *The Dutch in Brazil.*

40. *Oroonoko: Or, The Royal Slave. A True Story. By Mrs A. Behn* (London: Will. Canning, 1688).

41. Behn, Ibid., A3 verso-A4 recto.

42. Ibid., A 4 recto-verso.

43. Ibid., A4verso.

44. Ibid., A 4 verso-A5 recto.

45. Ibid., A5 recto.

46. Ibid., A6 verso.

47. Ibid., A7 recto.

48. Ibid., A6 verso-A7 recto.

49. Ibid., A7recto-verso.

50. Ibid., A7 verso.

51. Ibid., A7 verso.

52. Ibid., A7 verso-A8 recto.

53. Ibid., A8 recto.

54. Ibid., 1.

55. Ibid., 2–3.

56. Ibid., 3.

57. Ibid., 4.

58. Ibid., 7.

59. Ibid., 8.

60. Ibid., 10.

61. Ibid., 10.

62. Ibid., 11.

63. Ibid., 12.

64. Ibid., 13.

65. Ibid., 14, see 13.

66. Ibid., 15–6.

67. Ibid., 16.

68. Ibid., 17.

69. Ibid., 18–19.

70. Ibid., 19.

71. Ibid., 20–1.

72. Ibid., 23.

73. Ibid., 23.

74. Ibid., 24.

75. Ibid., 25.

76. Ibid., 25.

77. Ibid., 32.

78. Ibid., 33.

79. Ibid., 34.
80. Ibid., 43.
81. Ibid., 62.
82. Ibid., 67.
83. Ibid., 67.
84. "Code Noir . . . *Mars* 1685" *Receuils de Réglemens, Édits, Déclarations et Arrêts, Concernant le Commerce, l'Administration de la Justice, & la Police des Colonies Françaises de l'Amerique, & les Engagés. Avec Le Code Noir, Et l'Addition audit Code. Nouvelle Édition* (Paris: Libraires Associés, M.DCC.LXV.), 67; see 67–83 [supplements of the changes to the *Code Noir* appear on 84–174]; Baldwin Room copy, Toronto Reference Library. The phrase is "les peuples que la Divine Providence a mis sous notre obéissance." In consulting the *Dictionnaire de L'Académie française*, 1st ed. (1694) the word in this context is glossed as being put under a king's domination: "On dit, *Vivre sous l'obeïssance d'un Prince*, pour dire, Estre sous sa domination: & on dit dans le mesme sens. *Les Peuples qui sont sous l'obeïssance, dans l'obeïssance du Roy. il a reduit, rangé cette Province sous son obeïssance. dans tous les pays, dans toutes les terres de l'obeïssance du Roy. se soustraire de l'obeïssance d'un Prince. rentrer dans l'obeïssance de son Prince*" (135). This dictionary is now online: see *Dictionnaire de l'Académie Française Database Project* directed by R. Wooldridge and I. Leroy Turcan, the ARTFL Project and The University of Chicagoat http://www.lib.uchicago.edu/efts/ARTFL/projects/dicos/ACADEMIE/PREMIERE/ . I chose "obeisance" in the sense of definitions 2 and 2b in the OED, which, when taken together, combines authority and dominion, both senses of the word having long histories in the English language and being related to "obedience." See *Oxford English Dictionary Online* (second edition 1989). Using the same dictionaries with their access to etymologies and historical contexts, I have chosen "memorandum" for the original term: "Memoire. s. m. Escrit pour instruire, pour faire ressouvenir de quelque chose. *J'oublieray vostre affaire, si vous ne m'en donnez un memoire. memoire instructif*" (38).
85. "Code Noir . . . Mars 1685", 67–77. "S'attrouper. v. n. p. S'assembler en troupe. Il est deffendu par les Ordonnances de s'attrouper. il s'attroupa une quantité de gens. au son du tocsin les paysans des environs s'attrouperent"; see *Dictionnaire de L'Académie française*, 1st edition (1694), 602; for "fouet", see the same source: "Foüet, se dit aussi Des coups de verges dont on chastie les enfants. Donner le foüet. meriter le foüet. avoir le foüet. sujet au foüet. craindre le foüet. menacer du foüet. Il se dit aussi Des coups de verges dont la Justice fait chastier quelques criminels; & dans ce sens on dit, Condamné au foüet. avoir le foüet par les carrefours. avoir le foüet sous la custode" (481); children and criminals receive this corporal punishment. Whip or whisk are usual translations for "foüet". The Code referred to "le jarret," which also could have been translated as hock or ham. The fleur-de-lys was a royal emblem of France, which still appears on the flag of Quebec. For more on the *Code Noir*, see 6531.- Documents Historiques: Le Code Noir at http://www.haiti-reference.com/; Louis Sala-Molins, *Le Code noir, ou Le calvaire de Canaan,*

4th. ed. (Paris: Presses universitaires de France, 1987); *Le code noir / introduction et notes de Robert Chesnais* (Paris : L'esprit frappeur, 1998).

86. Hety Shepard, *A Puritan Maiden's Diary*, ed. Adeline E. H. Slicer, *New England Magazine*, n.s. 11:20–25 (1894), 23; I have listed the references to books for easier access; but these sources in this chapter and in chapter 6 on women's views on slavery are available at the excellent *North American Women's Letters and Diaries*, Alexander Street Press, L.L.C., 2001. PhiloLogic Software, 2001 The University of Chicago, 2001.

87. Letter from Sarah Kemble Knight, October 2, 1704, in *Journal of Madam Knight*, ed. Malcolm Freiberg (New York, NY: Wilder & Campbell, 1825), 34.

88. Ibid., 34–5.

89. Ibid., 35.

90. *Oxford English Dictionary*, 2nd ed., 1989, online.

91. Knight, *Letter*, 35.

92. Ibid., 35–6.

93. *The Lee Max Friedman Collection of American Jewish Colonial Correspondence: Letters of the Franks Family, 1733–1748*, ed. Leo Hershkowitz and Isidore S. Meyer (Waltham, MA: American Jewish Historical Society, 1968).

94. Diary of Patience Greene Brayton, November, 1771, in *A Short Account of the Life and Religious Labors of Patience Brayton: Late of Swansey, in the State of Massachusetts* (New York: William Phillips, 1802), 27.

95. Letter from Isabella Marshall Graham to John Graham, January 16, 1773, in *The Unpublished Letters and Correspondence of Mrs. Isabella Graham, From the Year 1767 to 1814: Exhibiting Her Religious Character in the Different Relations of Life*, ed. Joanna Bethune (New York: John S. Taylor, 1838), 74, see 73.

96. Letter from Abigail Smith Adams to John Adams, July 31, 1775, in *Letters of Mrs. Adams, The Wife of John Adams*, 3rd ed., vol.1, ed. Charles Francis Adams (Boston: Little, Brown, 1841), 64.

97. Leonard Guelke, "Freehold Farmers and Frontier Settlers, 1657–1780," in *Historiography*, 174–7, see 175–216; for an earlier version, see *The Shaping of South African Society, 1652–1840* (Middletown CT: Wesleyan University Press, 1989), 66–108.

98. Paul Kennedy, *The Rise and Fall of the Great Powers: Economic Change and Military Conflict From 1500 to 2000* (New York: Random House, 1987), 79–84; see P. G. M. Dickson, *The Financial Revolution in England: A Study in the Development of Public Credit 1688–1756* (London: St. Martin's Press, 1967); C. H. Wilson, *Anglo-Dutch Commerce and Finance in the Eighteenth Century* (Cambridge: Cambridge University Press, 1966); J. C. Riley, *International Government Finance and the Amsterdam Capital Market 1740–1815* (Cambridge: Cambridge University Press, 1980); and J. F. Bosher, *French Finances, 1770–1795* (Cambridge: Cambridge University Press, 1970); R. Davis, *The Rise of the Atlantic Economies* (London: Weidenfeld and Niedson, 1975); J. G. Clark, *La Rochelle and the Atlantic Economy During the Eighteenth Century* (Baltimore: Johns Hopkins University Press, 1981);

A. Calder, *Revolutionary Empire: The Rise of the English-Speaking Empires from the Fifteenth Century to the 1780s* (London: J. Cape, 1981); Carolyn Webber and Aaron Wildavsky, *A History of Taxation and Expenditure in the Western World* (New York: Simon and Schuster, 1986).

99. Kennedy, *Great Powers*, 97, see 94–115. I am once more indebted to Kennedy. See also Paul Kennedy, *The Rise and Fall of British Naval Mastery* (London: A. Lane, 1976).

100. Henry Folmer, *Franco-Spanish Rivalry in North America 1524–1763* (Glendale, CA: Arthur H Clark Company, 1953), 309–10.

101. Martin Kitchen, *The British Empire and Commonwealth: A Short History* (1994; London: Macmillan, 1996), 16.

102. Thomas, *The Slave Trade*, 153–61, 170–82, 197–203, 231, 247–61, 270–8; see Elizabeth Donnan, *Documents Illustrative of the Slave Trade to America*, 4 vols. (Washington, 1935); see I: 97; UNESCO, *The Slave Trade from the Fifteenth to Nineteenth Century* (Paris, 1979); Moses Finlay, *Ancient Slavery and Modern Ideology* (London: Chatto & Windus, 1981); Robin Blackburn, *The Making of New World Slavery: From the Baroque to the Modern 1492–1800* (London: Verso, 1997).

103. H. M. Feinburg, "New data on European Mortality in West Africa: The Dutch on the Gold Coast, 1719–1760," in *Historiography*, ed. Anthony Disney, 70, 7,283, see 69–82; see the earlier version in *Journal of African History* 15 (1974), 357–71.

104. Robin Hallett, "The European Approach to the Interior of Africa in the Eighteenth Century," in *Historiography*, 68, see 53–67; for the first appearance of this article, see *Journal of African History* 4 (1963), 191–206.

105. See, e.g., Alfred W. Crosby, *Ecological Imperialism : The Biological Expansion of Europe, 900–1900* (Cambridge: Cambridge University Press, 1986, rpt. 2000) and. David E. Stannard, *American Holocaust: The Conquest of the New World* (Oxford: Oxford University Press, 1992, rpt. 1993).

106. Montesquieu, *Spirit of Laws*, bk. 15, ch. 1, *The Founders' Constitution*, Vol. 1, Ch. 15, doc. 4, The University of Chicago Press at http://presspubs. uchicago.edu/founders/documents/v1ch15s4.html.

107. Ibid., bk. 15, CH. 5.

108. Ibid., bk. 15, CH. 7.

109. Benjamin Franklin, *A Conversation on Slavery. To the Printer of the Public Advertiser. SIR, Broad-Street Buildings, Jan. 26, 1770. The Writings of Benjamin Franklin: London, 1757–1775;* http://www.historycarper.com/ resources/twobf3/slavery.htm; see also http://www.assumption.edu/ahc/ 1770s/pexpandfound.html.

110. Letter from Abigail Smith Adams to John Adams, September 22, 1774, in *Letters of Mrs. Adams*, 3rd ed., vol.1. (1841), 24.

111. Abigail Adams, Letter to John Adams, September 22, 1774. Massachusetts Historical Society. Africans in America. Revolution at http://www.pbs. org/wgbh/aia/part2/2h23.html.

112. Phillis Wheatley, *Poems on Various Subjects, Religious and Moral* (London: Archibald Bell, 1773). This text can also be seen online electronically: the

Renascence Editions text was transcribed from the 1786 edition of J. Crukshank, Philadelphia.

113. Aristotle, *Politics*, VII.14.21–22 (1333b–1334a, 290).

114. Ibid., VII.2.14. (1324b, 262). Ernest Barker's translation uses a slightly different and more direct idiom, yet the same point comes through: "But when it comes to politics most people appear to believe that mastery is the true statesmanship; and men are not ashamed of behaving to others in ways which they would refuse to acknowledge as just, or even expedient, among themselves. For their own affairs, and among themselves, they want an authority based on justice; but when other men are in question, their interest in justice stops"; see *The Politics of Aristotle*, trans. Ernest Barker (1946; London: Oxford University Press, 1958), VII.ii.14 (1324b, 285–6).

115. Benjamin Franklin to Peter Collinson, May 9, 1753, in ed. *Papers of Benjamin Franklin* Leonard W. Labaree, (New Haven: Yale University Press, 1959), 36 vols., vol. 4:481–2. See also J. Norman Heard, *White into Red: A Study of the Assimilation of White Persons Captured by Indians* (Methuchen, NJ: Scarecrow Press, 1973) and James Axtell, "The White Indians," in *The Invasion Within: The Contest of Cultures in Colonial North America* (New York: Oxford University Press, 1985), 302–27.

116. THE DECLARATION OF INDEPENDENCE. *The omission*. As is, except I have corrected typographical errors. The website makes the following claim: "Spurred by his conviction that natural rights accrued to all men, Thomas Jefferson, decided that slavery had a destructive conditioning effect which stamped Africans with 'odious peculiarities.' When he was assigned with drafting a declaration calling for separation from Great Britain, he included this short attack of King George III's indulgence of the slave trade. But, pressure from South Carolina and Georgia and from Northern delegates whose ports housed and profited from slave ships, led to the clause omission from the final version. The omission of the above clause has led some historians to believe the Declaration of Independence never meant for Africans in America to share in the fruits of independence and equally in their adopted homeland." See *Afro-American Almanac*. Historical Documents at http://www.toptags.com/aama/.

117. On Adams and other founders and their views of slavery, see The E Pluribus Unum Project at http://www.assumption.edu/ahc/1770s/pexpandfound. html. "Slavery in Early America:What the Founders Wrote, Said, and Did."

118. Thomas, *The Slave Trade*, 481–2, 523, 577, 611–3.

Chapter 6

1. Eliza Yonge Wilkinson, Letter from Eliza Yonge Wilkinson, 1782, in *Letters of Eliza Wilkinson, during the Invasion and Possession of Charleston, SC, by the British in the Revolutionary War*, ed. Caroline Gilman (New York, NY: S. Colman, 1839), 67–8; this and other documents by women I use here and below can also be found at *North American Women's Letters and Diaries*, Alexander Street Press and the University of Chicago, 2001.

2. Ibid., 68.
3. Ibid., 68.
4. Ibid., 68–9.
5. Ibid., 69.
6. Ibid., 69–70.
7. Ibid., 70.
8. Ibid., 70–1.
9. Ibid., 71.
10. Ibid., 60.
11. Ibid., 60–1.
12. Ibid., 61–2.
13. Abigail Smith Adams, Letter from Abigail Smith Adams to John Quincy Adams, December 26, 1783, in *Letters of Mrs. Adams, The Wife of John Adams*, 3rd ed., vol.1. Charles Francis Adams (Boston, MA: Little, Brown, & Co., 1841), 204.
14. Patience Greene Brayton, Diary of Patience Greene Brayton, July, 1787, in *A Short Account of the Life and Religious Labors of Patience Brayton: Late of Swansey, in the State of Massachusetts* (New York, NY: William Phillips, 1802), 123.
15. Elizabeth Sandwith Drinker, Diary of Elizabeth Sandwith Drinker, January 30, 1794, in *Extracts from the Journal of Elizabeth Drinker, from 1759 to 1807, A.D.*, ed. Henry D. Biddle (Philadelphia, PA: J.B. Lippincott & Co., 1889), 220.
16. Charlotte Sheldon, Diary of Charlotte Sheldon, May 29, 1796, in *Chronicles of a Pioneer School from 1792 to 1833, Being the History of Miss Sarah Pierce and Her Litchfield School*, ed. Emily Noyes Vanderpoel and Elizabeth C. Barney Buel (Cambridge, MA: Harvard University Press, 1903), 12.
17. Isabella Marshall Graham, Letter from Isabella Marshall Graham, July 4, 1797, in *The Unpublished Letters and Correspondence of Mrs. Isabella Graham, From the Year 1767 to 1814: Exhibiting Her Religious Character in the Different Relations of Life*, ed. Joanna Bethune (New York: John S. Taylor, 1838),
18. Drinker, Diary of Elizabeth Sandwith Drinker, July 22, 1799.
19. Editor's Note, Olaudah Equiano, *The Life of Olaudah Equiano, or Gustavus Vassa, the African* (London, 1789; rpt. Leeds, 1814; New York: Dover, 1999), iv.
20. An address to the public, from the Pennsylvania Society for promoting the abolition of slavery, and the relief of free negroes, unlawfully held in bondage . . . *Signed by order of the Society, B. Franklin, President. Philadelphia, 9th of November, 1789*. Pennsylvania Society for promoting the abolition of slavery. Philadelphia, 1789. Library of Congress. American Memory. An American Time Capsule: Three Centuries of Broadsides and Other Printed Ephemera. Library of Congress, Rare Book and Special Collections Division. Printed Ephemera Collection; portfolio 147, folder 10.
21. Jeremy Belknap, *A Discourse, Intended to Commemorate the Discovery of America by Christopher Columbus; Delivered at the Request of the Historical Society in Massachusetts, on the 23rd Day of October 1792, Being the Completion of the Third Century Since that Memorable Event* (Boston: Belknap and Hall, 1792), 19.
22. Ibid., 46–7.

23. For this painting, see Hugh Honour, *The New Golden Land* (New York: Pantheon Books, 1975), plate 150.

24. C. R. Boxer, *The Golden Age of Brazil 1695–1750: Growing Pains of a Colonial Society* (Berkeley: University of California Press, 1962, rpt.1964), 1.

25. Equiano, *The Life*. The American edition appeared in 1791, the German edition in 1790, and the Dutch edition in 1791. By 1837, there were nine more editions; see Note (1999), iv. The Dover edition uses the Leeds edition of 1814, which is corrected, as does Henry Louis Gates, Jr. in *The Classic Slave Narratives*, ed. H. L. Gates, Jr. (1987; New York: Signet, 2002).

26. Ibid., 2.

27. Ibid., 2.

28. Ibid., 3.

29. Ibid., 38–9.

30. Ibid., 184.

31. Ibid., 183–4.

32. Ibid., 184.

33. Ibid., 184.

34. Ibid., 9–10.

35. Ibid., 23.

36. Ibid., 28.

37. Ibid., 31.

38. Ibid., 31.

39. Ibid., 32.

40. Ibid., 32.

41. Ibid., 32.

42. Ibid., 32.

43. Ibid., 34.

44. Ibid., 34.

45. Ibid., 40.

46. Ibid., 40, 52.

47. Ibid., 46.

48. Ibid., 50–1.

49. Ibid., 50–1.

50. Ibid., 63, see 54–5, 65.

51. Ibid., 74.

52. Ibid., 74.

53. Ibid., 74.

54. Ibid., 74–5.

55. Ibid., 76.

56. Ibid., 77. For an appreciation of Equiano's use of chiasmus and the double voice of the innocent and sophisticate, see Gates, Jr., Introduction, *The Classic Slave Narratives*, 7–8. See also Sidney Kaplan, "Olaudah Equiano," in the *Black Presence in the Era of the American Revolution, 1770–1800* (Washington, DC: New York Graphic Society and the Smithsonian Institution Press, 1973), 193–207 and Houston A. Baker, Jr. "Figurations for

a New American Literary History," in *Blues, Ideology, and Afro-American Literature: A Vernacular Theory* (Chicago: University of Chicago Press, 1984).

57. Equiano, *The Life*, 77.
58. Ibid., 77.
59. Ibid., 81.
60. Ibid., 81.
61. Ibid., 82.
62. Ibid., 87, 89.
63. Ibid., 90–102.
64. Ibid., 103.
65. Ibid., 107.
66. Ibid., 121.
67. Ibid., 123–4.
68. Ibid., 125, see 126–7.
69. Ibid., 129.
70. Ibid., 137–50.
71. Ibid., 153.
72. Ibid., 155, see 156.
73. Ibid., 161–2.
74. Ibid., 167.
75. Ibid., 169–70.
76. Ibid., 172.
77. Ibid., 176.
78. Ibid., 177.
79. Ibid., 179.
80. Ibid., 179.
81. Ibid., 179.
82. Ibid., 180.
83. See, e.g., Hugh Thomas, *The Slave Trade* (New York: Simon and Schuster, 1997), 516, 541, 619.
84. Ibid., 470–3.
85. Thomas Jefferson to Antoine Louis Claude Destutt de Tracy, January 26, 1811—*Thomas Jefferson Papers Series 1. General Correspondence. 1651–1827*, American Memory, Library of Congress. Rather than insert' "sic" after "it's," I think it is fair to say that this was a literate equivalent as a possessive as the form we use today: "its." See Simone Goyard Fabre, "Avant Propos," Antoine-Louis-Claude Destutt de Tracy, *Commentaire sur "L'esprit des lois" de Montesquieu* (Caen: Centre de philosophie politique et juridique, 1992), [1–3], Bibliothèque Nationale de France [BNF]. For Jefferson's English translation, see Destutt de Tracy, see *A commentary and review of Montesquieu's Spirit of laws* (Philadelphia: printed by William Duane, 1811).
86. See M. de Bovis, *Essais sur l'esprit des lois colonials* (Paris: impr. de Everat, 1820), 6; BNF; my translation. This book discusses other aspects of slavery in the colonies; see esp. 5–7, 35–6.
87. Philip Schofield, "Editorial Introduction," Jeremy Bentham, *Colonies, Commerce, and Constitutional Law: Rid Yourselves of Ultramaria and Other*

Writings on Spain and Spanish America, ed. Philip Schofield (Oxford: Clarendon Press, 1995), xv–xvi.

88. Bentham, Letter 15, Part 1, *Colonies*, 126–7.

89. Ibid., Letter 16, Part 1, 130.

90. *General Treaty signed in Congress at Vienna* (London, 1816), 132, quoted in Thomas, *The Slave Trade: The Story of the Slave Trade: 1440–1870* (New York: Simon & Schuster, 1997), 585. See Thomas, 291–302, 315, 370–1, 414, 423–4, 449–63, 482–4, 499–510, 526–85.

91. Ibid., 592, see 587–91. On slavery more generally, see John Wesley, *Thoughts Upon Slavery* (London: R. Hawe 1774); Thomas Day, *A Fragment of a Letter on the Slavery of Negroes* (London: J. Stockdale, 1785); James Stephen, *The Crisis in the Sugar Colonies* (London: Printed for J. Hatchard, 1802); William E. Channing, *Remarks on Slavery* (Boston: J. H. Eastburn, 1836); R. I. and S. Wilberforce, *The Life of William Wilberforce* (London: J. Murray, 1838); Mariano Torrente, *La cuestión importante sobre la esclavitud* (Madrid: Jordané Hijos, 1841); T. Nelson, *Remarks on Slavery and the Slave Trade* (London, 1846); Joseph Denman, *West India Interests, African Emigration and the Slave Trade* (London: James Bigg & Son, 1848); Theodore Canot, *Memoirs of a Slave Trader* (New York, 1850); Frederick Law Omstead, *A Journey in the Southern Slave States* (New York, 1856); Andrew H. Foote, *Africa and the American Flag* (New York: D. Appleton & Co., 1862); Rafael Labra, *La abolición de la esclavitud en el orden económico* (Madrid: J. Noguera á Cargo de m. martinez, 1873); W. E. B. Dubois, *The Suppression of the African Trade to the United States of America* (New York: Longmans, Green, 1896); Thesis (Ph.D) Harvard University, 1895; Harvard Archives.

92. For a black and white reproduction of this painting, see Hugh Honour, *The European Vision of America* (Cleveland: The Cleveland Museum of Art, 1975), plate 316.

93. See this connection on the website of the United States National Park Service at http://www.nps.gov/wori/ugrrexhibit.htm and http://www.nps.gov/wori/ugrrpanel%205.htm.

94. Douglass, quoted in James M'Cune Smith, "Introduction," Frederick Douglass, *My Bondage and my Freedom* (New York, Miller, Orton & Mulligan, 1855), 8–9. For an online version of this text, see Avalon Project: *My Bondage and Freedom* by Frederick Douglass; 1855 at http://www.yale.edu/lawweb/avalon/treatise/douglas/douglas01.htm.

95. Second Inaugural Address of Abraham Lincoln, Saturday, March 4, 1865, Avalon Project, here and above.

96. Abraham Lincoln, January 4, 1855 (Notes on the history of the African slave trade), *The Abraham Lincoln Papers at the Library of Congress, Series 1. General Correspondence. 1833–1916*, ms. 2pp. [431 marked on first page], here and below.

97. THE CONSTITUTION OF THE COMMONWEALTH OF LIBERIA, Afro-American Almanac, Historical Documents.

98. From Abraham Lincoln to James N. Brown [Fragment of a Draft or Copy], October 18, 1858; the complete text of Lincoln's letter to Brown is in *Collected Works*, III, 327–8.

99. Orlando Figes, *Natasha's Dance: A Cultural History of Russia* (2002; London, Penguin, 2003), 143–6.
100. See Thomas, *The Slave Trade*, 793–8.
101. First Inaugural Address of Abraham Lincoln, Monday, Monday, March 4, 1861, Avalon Project, Yale Law School, here and below at http://www.yale.edu/lawweb/avalon/presiden/inaug/lincoln1.htm.
102. Abraham Lincoln, Emancipation Proclamation; September 22, 1862, the Avalon Project, at http://www.yale.edu/lawweb/avalon/emancipa.htm.
103. Gettysburg Address, November 19, 1863, Avalon Project at http://www.yale.edu/lawweb/avalon/gettyb.htm.
104. Second Inaugural Address of Abraham Lincoln, Saturday, March 4, 1865, Avalon Project, here and below.
105. Lincoln, "Second Inaugural."
106. Paul Kennedy: *The Rise and Fall of the Great Powers: Economic Change and Military Conflict From 1500 to 2000* (New York: Random House, 1987), 158–82 here and above. See A. J. P. Taylor, *The Struggle for Mastery in Europe 1848–1918* (Oxford: Clarendon Press, 1954); K. Bourne, *Britain and the Balance of Power in North America 1815–1908* (London: Longmans, 1967); K. Bourne, *Victorian Foreign Policy 1830–1902* (Oxford: Clarendon Press, 1970); H. Hattaway and A. Jones, *How the North Won: A Military History of the Civil War* (Urbana, IL: University of Illinois Press, 1983); A. R. Millett and P. Maslowski, *For the Common Defense: A Military History of the United States of America* (New York: Free Press, 1984).
107. For an interesting discussion of race and empire, see Allison Blakely, *Blacks in the Dutch World: The Evolution of Racial Imagery in Modern Society* (Bloomington: Indiana University Press, 1993). See Lynn Hunt et al., *The Making of the West: People and Cultures* (Boston, New York: Bedford St. Martins, 2001), 904–09, 922.
108. *Great Speeches*, 169; see James Creelman, *On the Great Highway: The Wanderings and Adventures of a Special Correspondent* (Boston: Lothrop Publishing, 1901), 299–302. Textual production and delays affect many works, such as those by Columbus, Jean de Léry, Shakespeare, James Joyce, and others, so that this transmission and delay are reminiscent of Marco Polo dictated his story to Rusticello, a French writer of romance, while he was in prison. I have discussed some aspects textual transmission and authorship in earlier works like *Columbus, Shakespeare and the Interpretation of the New World* (New York and London: Palgrave Macmillan, 2003).
109. Mary Morton Dexter, Letter from Mary Morton Dexter, September 8, 1811, in *Memoirs and Letters of Mrs. Mary Dexter, Late Consort of Rev. Elijah Dexter*, ed. William T. Torrey (Plymouth, MA: A. Danforth, 1823), 141. See *North American Women Letters and Diaries*, Alexander Street Press with The University of Chicago, 2001; the texts here and below are also available electronically.
110. Ibid., 142.

111. Anne Mott, Letter from Anne Mott to James Mott, 1819, in *James and Lucretia Mott: Life and Letters*, ed. Anna Davis Hallowell (Boston, MA: Houghton, Mifflin & Co., 1884), 70–1.

112. Angelina Emily Grimké Weld, Diary of Angelina Emily Grimké Weld, 1829, in *The Grimké Sisters: Sarah and Angelina Grimké, The First American Women Advocates of Abolition and Woman's Rights*, ed. Catherine H. Birney (Boston, MA: Lee & Shepard Publishers, 1885), 92.

113. On this biography, see North American Women's Letters and Diaries as well as James, and Boyer's *Notable American Women 1607–1950: A Biographical Dictionary* (Cambridge MA: Belknap Press, 1971); Lynda G. Adamson's *Notable Women in American History* (Westport: Greenwood Press, 1999); Kathryn Cullen-DuPont's *The Encyclopedia of Women's History in America* (New York: Facts on File, 1996); Frank N. Magill, ed., *Great Lives from History: American Women Series* (Pasadena: Salem Press, 1998).

114. Lydia Maria Francis Child, Letter from Lydia Maria Child to E. Carpenter, September 4, 1836, in *Letters of Lydia Maria Child with a Biographical Introduction by John G. Whittier and Appendix by Wendall Phillips*, ed. John G. Whittier, Wendall Phillips (Boston, MA: Houghton, Mifflin & Co., 1883), 20.

115. Ibid., 21.

116. Ibid., 21.

117. On this biography, see *North American Letters and Diaries* and James's, and Boyer's *Notable American Women 1607–1950: A Biographical Dictionary*; Adamson's *Notable Women in American History*; Lina Mainiero, ed., *American Women Writers: A Critical Reference Guide from Colonial Times to Present* (New York: Ungar, 1979–94).

118. Sarah Pugh, Letter from Sarah Pugh, May 8, 1837, in *Memorial of Sarah Pugh: A Tribute of Respect from Her Cousins* (Philadelphia: J.B. Lippincott & Co., 1888), 16. For this biographical information, see *North American Women's Letters and Diaries* and James's, and Boyer's *Notable American Women 1607–1950: A Biographical Dictionary*.

119. Pugh, 17.

120. Sarah Moore Grimké, Letter from Sarah Moore Grimké to Mary S. Parker, October 20, 1837, in *Letters on the Equality of the Sexes, and the Condition of Woman. Addressed to Mary S. Parker* (Boston: I. Knapp, 1838), 124–5.

121. Ibid., 125.

122. Frances Kemble, Letter from Frances Kemble to Elizabeth Dwight Sedgwick Rackemann, Febuary 14, 1839, in *Journal of a Residence on a Georgian Plantation in 1838–1839* (London, England: Longmans & Co., 1863), 183–4.

123. For Kemble's biography, see *North American Women's Letters and Diaries*; Jonathan Yardley, *Washington Post Book World*. September. 17–23, 2000; *Notable American Women 1607–1950: A Biographical Dictionary American Women Writers: A Critical Reference Guide from Colonial Times to Present*, ed. Lina Mainiero.

124. Lucretia Coffin Mott, Letter from Lucretia Coffin Mott to Richard D. Webb, May 14, 1849, in *James and Lucretia Mott: Life and Letters*, ed. Anna Davis Hallowell. (Boston, MA: Houghton, Mifflin & Co., 1884), 321. For Mott's biography, see *North American Women's Letters and Diaries* and *James and Lucretia Mott: Life and Letters*.

125. Ella Gertrude Clanton Thomas, Diary of Ella Gertrude Thomas, January 2, 1859, in *Secret Eye: The Journal of Ella Gertrude Clanton Thomas, 1848–1889*, ed. Virginia Ingraham Burr (Chapel Hill, NC: University of North Carolina Press, 1990), 168–9.

126. Elizabeth Leslie Rous Wright Comstock, Letter from Elizabeth Leslie Rous Comstock, February 8, 1860, in *Life and Letters of Elizabeth L. Comstock*, ed. Catherine Hare (Philadelphia: John C. Winston & Co., 1895), 81; on her life, see Elizabeth Comstock, *Life and Letters of Elizabeth L. Comstock* (Philadelphia: John C. Winston & Co., 1895); "Comstock, Elizabeth Leslie Rous," *Encyclopedia Britannica*, 1999–2000.

127. Catharine Maria, Sedgwick, 1789–1867, Letter from Catharine Maria Sedgwick to Lucy Russell, January 5, 1861, in *Life and Letters of Catherine M. Sedgwick*, ed. Mary E. Dewey (New York, Harper & Row, 1871), 389.

128. Letter from Lydia Maria Child to Sarah Blake Sturgis Shaw, May 05, 1861, in *Letters of Lydia Maria Child*, 151.

129. On slave narratives and African American writing, see Federal Writers' Project, Slave narratives, a folk history of slavery in the United States from interviews with former slaves. Typewritten records prepared by the Federal Writers' project, 1936–38, assembled by the Library of Congress project, Work Projects Administration, for the District of Columbia, sponsored by the Library of Congress, illustrated with photographs (Washington, 1941); Charles H. Nichols, *Many Thousand Gone: The Ex-Slaves' Account of Their Bondage and Freedom* (Bloomington: Indiana University Press, 1963); Paul D. Escott, *Slavery Remembered: A Record of Twentieth-Century Slave Narratives* (Chapel Hill: University of North Carolina Press, 1979); Robert B. Stepto, *From Behind the Veil: A Study of Afro-American Narrative* (Urbana: University of Illinois Press, 1979); Houston A. Baker, Jr., *The Journey Back: Issues in Black Literature and Criticism* (Chicago: University of Chicago Press, 1980); Marion Wilson Starling, *The Slave Narrative: Its Place in American History* (Boston: G. K. Hall, 1982); Henry Louis Gates, Jr., *The Signifying Monkey: A Theory of Afro-American Literary* Criticism (New York: Oxford University Press, 1988); Paul Q. Tilden, *African-American Literature: An Overview and Bibliography* (New York: Nova Science Publishers, 2003).

130. See, e.g., Valerie Smith, *Self-Discovery and Authority in Afro-American Narrative* (Cambridge, MA: Harvard University Press, 1987) and her *Not Just Race, Not Just Gender: Black Feminist Readings* (New York: Routledge, 1998).

131. Gates, Introduction, *Classic Slave Narratives*, 9; see William Andrews, "Six Women's Slave Narratives, 1831–1909," in *Black Women's Slave Narratives*, ed. W. L. Andrews (New York: Oxford University Press, 1987).

132. Mary Prince, "The History of Mary Prince, A West Indian Slave. (Related by Herself)," in *The Classic Slave Narratives*, ed. Henry Louis Gates, Jr. (1987; New York: New American Library, 2002), 255, see 253–4.
133. Ibid., 260–1.
134. Ibid., 262.
135. Ibid., 266, see 262–5.
136. Ibid., 269, see 267–8.
137. Ibid., 269.
138. Ariel's words at line 348 of Shakespeare's *First Folio* captures yet another instance of the vexation of slavery in a place where Prince was born. Ariel alludes to Bermuda even though Shakespeare's play, having as its one of its source a manuscript about a shipwreck there en route to Virginia, takes place on an island between Italy and North Africa in the Mediterranean. See William Shakespeare, *The Tempest*, *The First Folio of Shakespeare*, The Norton Facsimile, ed. Charlton Hinman (New York, W.W. Norton & Company, 1968).
139. Prince, "The History of Mary Prince," 270.
140. Ibid., 278.
141. Ibid., 279.
142. Ibid., 284–6.
143. Ibid., 287.
144. Ibid., 288.
145. Ibid., 288.
146. Ibid., 288.
147. William Lloyd Garrison, Preface, Frederick Douglass, *The Narrative of the Life of Frederick Douglass* in *The Classic Slave Narratives*, ed. Henry Louis Gates, Jr., 325.
148. Ibid., 326.
149. Ibid., 326–7.
150. Ibid., 327.
151. Ibid., 328.
152. Ibid., 328, see 329.
153. Ibid., 329.
154. Ibid., 330.
155. Ibid., 331.
156. Ibid., 333, see 332.
157. Ibid., 333.
158. Ibid., 333–4.
159. Phillips, in Douglass, *Narrative, Classic Slave Narratives*, ed. Gates, 335.
160. Ibid., 335.
161. Ibid., 335.
162. Ibid., 336.
163. Ibid., 336–7.
164. Frederick Douglass, *Narrative, Classic Slave Narratives*, ed. Gates, 339.
165. Ibid., 341.
166. Ibid., 341.

167. Ibid., 347.
168. Ibid., 349.
169. Ibid., 353.
170. Ibid., 354.
171. Ibid., 363.
172. Ibid., 365.
173. Ibid., 373, see 366–72.
174. Ibid., 376, see 375.
175. Ibid., 379.
176. Ibid., 388, see 385–7.
177. Ibid., 394, see 393, 395.
178. Ibid., 397, see 398.
179. Ibid., 412.
180. Ibid., 421.
181. Ibid., 423.
182. Ibid., 427.
183. Ibid., 427.
184. Ibid., 429.
185. Ibid., 431.
186. Ibid., 433.
187. Ibid., 436.
188. William Kaufman, Introduction, Sojourner Truth, *Narrative of Sojourner Truth* (Mineola, NY: Dover Publications, 1997), iv–vi.
189. Ibid., *Narrative of Sojourner* Truth, 2.
190. Ibid., 16.
191. Ibid., 22, see 21, 23.
192. Ibid., 45–6.
193. Ibid., 62.
194. Ibid., 73.
195. Harriet Jacobs, Preface by the Author, *Incidents in the Life of a Slave Girl* (Mineola, NY: Dover, 2001), 2.
196. L. Maria Child, Introduction by the Editor, Harriet Jacobs, *Incidents in the Life of a Slave Girl*, 4.
197. Ibid., 4.
198. Ibid., 5.
199. Ibid., 5.
200. Jacobs, *Incidents in the Life of a Slave Girl*, 8.
201. Ibid., 8.
202. Ibid., 8–12.
203. Ibid., 34.
204. Ibid., 34.
205. Ibid., 36.
206. Ibid., 68.
207. Ibid., 64.
208. Ibid., 64.
209. Ibid., 103–5.

210. Ibid., 105–9.
211. Ibid., 114.
212. Ibid., 118.
213. Ibid., 122.
214. Ibid., 137.
215. Ibid., 138.
216. Ibid., 138–45.
217. Ibid., 147.
218. Ibid., 149.
219. Ibid., 149.
220. Ibid., 150.
221. Ibid., 150.
222. Ibid., 151.
223. Ibid., 153.
224. Ibid., 155–69.
225. Ibid., 164.
226. Ibid., 164.
227. Ibid., 165–7.
228. W. E. B. Du Bois, *The Suppression of the African Slave-Trade to the United States of America, 1638–1870* (1896; Mineola, NY: Dover, 1999), 199.
229. W. E. B. Du Bois, The Forethought, *The Souls of Black Folk* (1903; Mineola, NY: Dover, 1994), v.
230. W. E. B. Du Bois, *Darkwater: Voices from Within the Veil* (1920; Mineola, NY: Dover, 1999), 17.
231. Ibid., 18.
232. Ibid., 29.
233. James Weldon Johnson, *The Autobiography of an Ex-Colored Man* (1912; Mineola, NY: Dover, 1995), 99.
234. Ibid., 100.
235. Mary Anderson, interviewed at age eighty-six, *When I Was a Slave: Memoirs from the Slave Narrative Collection*, ed. Norman R. Yetman (Minneola, NY: Dover, 2002), 3; the interviews were conducted from 1936 to 1938 and compiled as a manuscript collection in the Library of Congress in 1941.
236. Ibid., 4.
237. Ibid., 4.
238. Boston Blackwell, interviewed at age ninety-eight, *When I Was a Slave*, 13.
239. Ibid., 13.
240. Ibid., 13.
241. Ibid., 13–4.
242. Tines Kendricks, interviewed age one hundred and four, *When I Was a Slave*, 82–3.
243. Ibid., 84.
244. Ibid., 85–6.
245. Ibid., 86.
246. Ibid., 87.

247. Ibid., 87.
248. Fannie Moore, interviewed at age eighty-eight, *When I Was a Slave*, 91.
249. Ibid., 93.
250. Bill Simms, interviewed at age ninety-seven, *When I Was a Slave*, 123.
251. Ibid., 124.
252. Ibid., 124.
253. Ibid., 126.
254. See Gates, Introduction, *Classic Slave Narratives*, 1.
255. Thomas, *The Slave* Trade, 804–5. I am using Thomas's estimated statistics as the basis of my analysis here.
256. These estimates are based on those in various sources, but most recently, Hugh Thomas's *Appendix Three*, 804–5. See also Philip Curtin, *The Slave Trade, A Census* (Madison: University of Wisconsin Press, 1969); Leslie Rout, *The African Experience in Spanish America* (Cambridge: Cambridge University Press, 1976); Joseph Inikori, *Forced Migration* (London: Hutchinson University Library for Africa, 1982) and Jean-Michel Déveaux, *France au temps des négriers* (Paris: France-Empire, 1994).
257. See, e.g., R. Law, ed., *From Slave Trade to Legitimate Commerce* (Cambridge: Cambridge University Press, 1995).
258. Martin Luther King, Stride, *Toward Freedom:The Montgomery Story* (New York: Harper & Brothers, 1958).
259. M. K. [Mahatma] Gandhi, *Hind Swaraj and Other Writings*, ed. Anthony J. Parel (Cambridge: Cambridge University Press, 1997) xiv–xvii.
260. Ibid., 72–3.
261. 'The Atlantic Conference: Joint Statement by President Roosevelt and Prime Minister Churchill, August 14, 1941, Avalon Project, at http://www.yale.edu/lawweb/avalon/wwii/atlantic/at10.htm#2.
262. PROCEEDINGS IN THE SENATE, MONDAY, DECEMBER 8, 1941, DECLARATION OF STATE OF WAR WITH JAPAN; Declarations of a State of War with Japan, Germany, and Italy: Part 4, Avalon Project.
263. On British economic decline, see E. J. Hobsbawm, *Industry and Empire* (Harmondsworth: Penguin, 1969); and C. Barnett, *The Audit of War* (London: Macmillan, 1986) and Hunt et. al, 1073. On decolonization, see, e.g., L. von Albertini, *Decolonization* (New York, 1971); C. Barnett, *The Collapse of British Power* (New York: Morrow, 1972); R. F. Holland, *European Decolonization: The British, French, Dutch and Belgian Empires 1919–63* (London, 1978); T. Smith, *The Pattern of Imperialism: The United States, Great Britain and the Late-Industrializing World Since 1915* (Cambridge: Cambridge University Press, 1981); D. A. Low, *Eclipse of Empire* (1991; Cambridge: Cambridge University Press, 1993); Frances Gouda, *Dutch Culture Overseas: Colonial Practice in the Netherlands Indies, 1900–1942* (Amsterdam: Amsterdam University Press, 1995). On Churchill, Eisenhower, and general ideas about the beginnings of the Cold War, see Robert Dallek, *The American Style of Foreign Policy* (New York: Knopf, 1983), 170; M. Balfour, *The Adversaries: America, Russia and the Open World, 1941–1962* (London: Routledge & Kegan Paul, 1981), 71; Kennedy, *Great Powers* 366–72; on the

nuclear issue, see B. Brody, *The Absolute Weapon* (New York: Harcourt, Brace, 1946); J. Prados, *The Soviet Estimate: U. S. Intelligence Analysis and Russian Military Strength* (New York: Dial Press, 1982); W. Kohl, *French Nuclear Diplomacy* (Princeton, NJ: Princeton University Press, 1971); L. Freeman, *Britain and Nuclear Weapons* (London: Royal Institute of International Affiars, 1980); J. Baylis, *Anglo-American Defense Relations, 1939–80* (London: Macmillan, 1981); D. Holloway, *The Soviet Union and the Arms Race* (New Haven CT: Yale University Press, 1983).

264. Universal Declaration of Human Rights Written at the U.N. in 1948, at http://www.yale.edu/lawweb/avalon/un/unrights.htm.

265. Bunche paid tribute to his grandmother in *Reader's Digest*, "My Most Unforgettable Character"; see "Ralph Bunche—Biography," Nobel e-museum, at http://www.nobel.se/peace/laureates/1950/bunche-bio.html.

266. *Ralph Bunche—Nobel Lecture,December 11, 1950, "Some Reflections on Peace in Our Time,"* here and below at http://www.nobel.se/peace/laureates/1950/bunche-lecture.html.

267. Hunt, *The Making of the West*, 1177.

268. Top Secret, Foreign Office telegram No. 2938 to Washington, 2; see page 76 of Public Record Office Reference, PREM 11/2880.

269. *Souvenir of the Visit of the Rt.Hon. Harold Macmillan Prime Minister of the United Kingdom to the Houses of Parliament, Cape Town, Wednesday, 3rd February, 1960, Printed on the Authority of Mr. Speaker* (Parow: Cape Times Limited [n.d., 1960?]), 5; see [ms 11], Public Record Office Reference, PREM 11/4937.

270. Macmillan, 7 [ms. 12].

271. Ibid., 7 [ms. 12].

272. Ibid., 8 [ms. 13].

273. Ibid., 8 [ms. 13].

274. Ibid., 9 [ms. 14].

275. Ibid., 9 [ms. 14].

276. Ibid., 10 [ms. 15].

277. "Martin Luther King's Letter from Birmingham Jail," April 16, 1963, at http://almaz.com/nobel/peace/MLK-jail.html. This version keeps all original typographical errors. Possibly, "stiff" is "still".

278. "The I Have a Dream Speech," The United States Constitution Online, at http://www.usconstitution.net/dream.html.

279. "Martin Luther King's Nobel Prize Acceptance Speech," December 10, 1964, Oslo, Norway at http://www.nobelprizes.com/nobel/peace/MLK-nobel.html for quotations from this speech here and below.

280. Martin Luther King, "I've Been to the Mountaintop," at http://www.afscme.org/about/kingspch.htm, © American Federation of State, County and Municipal Employees, 2002.

281. Nelson Mandela – Nobel Lecture, Acceptance and Nobel Lecture, Norway, 1994 at http://www.nobel.se/peace/laureates/1993/mandela-lecture.html.

282. F. W. de Klerk, Acceptance and Nobel Lecture, Norway, 1994, at http://www.nobel.se/peace/laureates/1993/mandela-lecture.html.

283. Thomas, 593–623, 629, 656–5, 672–3, 712, 726–45, 774–85, 790–3, 861–62. On China, the Exhibition of 1851, and economic and political imperialism, see Hunt et. al, 823–5, 841. See also Jonathan Sperber, *The European Revolutions, 1848–1851* (Cambridge: Cambridge University Press, 1994). On slavery and economic contexts, see also W. L. Mathieson, *Great Britain and the Slave Trade* (London: Longmans, 1929); H. G. Soulsby, *The Right of Search and the Slave Trade in Anglo-American Relations* (Baltimore: The Johns Hopkins Press, 1933); C. Lloyd, *The Navy and the Slave Trade* (London: Longmans, 1949); C. L. R. Boxer, *The Portuguese Seaborne Empire* (New York: A. A. Knopf, 1969); Arthur P. Corwin, *Spain and the Abolition of Slavery in Cuba* (Austin: University of Texas Press, 1967); Philip Curtain, *The Slave Trade, A Census* (Madison: University of Wisconsin Press, 1969); W. E. F. Ward, *The Royal Navy and the Slavers* (London: Allen & Unwin, 1969); Leslie Bethell, *The Abolition of the Brazilian Slave Trade* (Cambridge: Cambridge University Press, 1970); Seymour Dreschler, *Econocide, British Slavery in the Era of Abolition* (Pittsburgh: University of Pittsburgh Press, 1977); Enriqueta Vila Vilar, *Hispanoamerica y el comercio de esclavos* (Seville: Escuela de Estudios Hispano-Americanos, 1977); Joseph Inikori, *Forced Migration* (London: Hutchinson University Library for Africa, 1982); David Brion Davis, *Slavery and Human Progress* (New York: Oxford University Press, 1984); Stuart Schwartz, *Sugar Plantations in the Formation of Brazilian Society* (Cambridge: Cambridge University Press, 1985); John Lynch, *The Spanish American Revolutions* (London: Weidenfeld & Nicolson, 1986); David Eltis, *Economic Growth and the Ending of the Slave Trade* (New York: Oxford University Press, 1987); Jean-Michel Déveaux, *France au temps des négriers* (Paris, 1994); Robin Blackburn, *The Overthrow of Colonial Slavery 1776–1848* (London: Verso, 1998).

Chapter 7

1. R. A. Skelton, Introduction, Antonio Pigafetta, *Magellan's Voyage: A Narrative Account of the First Circumnavigation*, trans and ed. R. A. Skelton (1969; New York: Dover, 1994), 5–6.

2. Pigafetta, *Magellan's Voyage*, 148, see 181n24, 27, 28.

3. "Pedro de Castañeda's Narrative," in Pedro de Castañeda et al., *The Journey of Coronado*, trans. and ed. George Parker Winship (1904; 1933; New York: Dover, 1990), 5.

4. Ibid., 5.

5. William Apes, "Eulogy on King Philip," *Great Speeches by Native Americans*, ed. Bob Blaisdell (Mineola, NY: Dover, 2000), 93–4.

6. Ibid., 112.

7. Ibid., 114.

8. Ibid., 114–5.

9. Ibid., 115.

10. See Ibid., 95–6.

11. Mary Reynolds, interviewed at age hundred+, *When I Was a Slave: Memoirs from the Slave Narrative Collection*, ed. Norman R. Yetman (Minneola, NY: Dover, 2002), 104.

12. Richard Hakluyt, *Voyages and Discoveries: The Principal Navigations [,] Voyages, Traffiques and Discoveries of the English Nation*, ed. Jack Beeching (Harmondsworth: Penguin, 1972, rpt. 1985), 105–16. Beechings's selection is taken from the second edition of Hakluyt's *Principal Navigations* brought out between 1598 and 1600.

13. Ibid., 106–7.

14. N. A. Worden, "Rural Slavery in the Western Districts of Cape Colony During the Eighteenth Century," Ph.D. thesis (University of Cambridge, 1982), 14, 408.

15. Professor G. Graham, "Slave Traders in the Indian Ocean," Library Talk, Royal Commonwealth Society, May 2, 1961; Royal Commonwealth Library in Cambridge University Library (Manuscript Room), 1, 6, see 2–5, 7–8.

16. Le Sr. de Cussy au Cap Coste de St Domingue, October 18, 1685, Archive d'Outre Mer, France, page 1 of 4 pp. ms.

17. Mr. C. H. Fyfe, Library Talk on Sierra Leone, Royal Commonwealth Society, November 4, 1958; Royal Commonwealth Library in Cambridge University Library (Manuscript Room), 4, see 1–3, 5 for the general discussion of Sierra Leone and the figures here discussed.

18. In the question period following Fyfe's talk, (among others) Sir Alan Burns and Dr. M C F. Easmon, who has written on doctors from Sierra Leone and who said that he was descended from a Maroon and a Nova Scotian from that group. See Fyfe, 6–7.

19. See Alan Stewart, *Philip Sidney: A Double Life* (2000; London: Pimlico, 2001), 265–76.

20. Richard Price, *Two Tracts* (1778), in *Political Writings*, ed. D. O. Thomas (Cambridge: Cambridge University Press, 1991), 72.

21. Ibid., 30.

22. William Lloyd Garrison, *The Liberator* (Boston), January 1, 1831, in *The Declaration of Independence and Other Great Documents of American History 1775–1865*, ed. John Grafton (Mineola, NY: Dover, 2000), 70.

23. Niccolò Machiavelli, *The Prince*, trans. N. H. Thomson (1910; New York: Dover, 1992), 44.

24. Rabindranath Tagore, *Gitanjali (Song Offerings)* (1912), in *Empire Writing: An Anthology of Colonial Literature 1870–1918*, ed. Elleke Boehmer (Oxford: Oxford University Press, 1998), 379. W. B. Yeats seems to have a hand in the translation and editing of this and other poems in this volume.

Index ~

abolition/abolitionist(s), *see* slavery, 3, 91, 117–18, 122, 127, 135–8, 144–54, 157, 159–75, 181–2, 201, 236n20

Acosta, José de, 73, 215n142, 224n2

Acuera, 100

Adam, 101, 204n3; Adam and Eve, 110

Adams, Abigail Smith, 118, 123, 134

Adams, John, 118, 123, 127, 235n117

Adams, John Quincy, 134, 164

Adams, Robert M., 219n31, 220n32, n34

Africa/African, *see also* South Africa, 3, 6–7, 9, 13–4, 17, 19, 28, 32, 43–4, 52, 85, 91–167, 177, 182–3, 186–200, 217n6, 235, n116, 242n129, 243n138; Angola, 101; Ashanti, 146; Azanaghi, 95; Barbazini (Barbacenes), 96; Barbary, 27, 93, 95; Ceuta, 93; Congo, 44, 101; Gambra, 96; Ghana, 97, 188, 191; Guinea, 93, 152, 172; Ibos, 199; languages—Joloff, Mende, Yorubas, 199; Mauritania, 7, 193; Liberia, 152; Marrakesh, 103; Morocco, 92–3, 103; Mozambique, 199; Nigeria, 138, 186, 188; Scramble for Africa, 156, 183; Sereri (Serer), 96; Sierra Leone, 19, 153, 198–200, 249n17; Somalis, 199

African Americans, 7, 89, 129, 131–2, 134–5, 149–50, 152, 155–6, 189–90, 195, 198

agon/agony, 1, 9, 178, 194–5, 201

Ailly, Pierre d', 52

Alfonse (Alphonse), Jean (João Affonso), 102–3

Alfonso the Wise, 43

allegorical/allegory, 58–9, 72, 77

Alexander the Great, 77, 82, 197

Alexander II, (czar [tsar] of Russia), 153

Álvares, Jorge, 44

ambivalence/ambivalent, 3, 5, 9, 11, 14, 16, 21, 33, 44–7, 49, 52, 56, 59, 62, 65, 73, 85, 88, 96, 100, 103, 104–6, 114, 118, 122, 136, 173, 181, 193, 199, 208n26, 222n57

Ammonio, Andrea, 53

Anderson, Mary, 179

Ango, Jean, 103

anthropologists/anthropology, 7, 60, 72, 74, 208n226, 221n50

Antwerp, 14, 53, 55, 93, 214n137

anxiety/anxieties/anxious, 14, 17–18, 31, 55, 79, 155, 159, 187; sexual anxiety, 88

Apes, William, 197–8

Arab(s)/Arabia/Araby/Arab States, 3, 6–7, 77, 95, 121, 146, 186, 193, 199

archive(s), 14, 18, 20, 22, 24, 32, 69, 206n15

Aristotle, 2, 6, 68, 73, 77, 93, 100–1, 106, 121, 125–7, 164, 201

art of persuasion, *see* rhetoric, 6, 68, 173

Asia, 17, 29, 43–5, 65, 82, 86, 97, 99, 102–3, 105, 118–9, 145, 187–9, 198–9; Ceylon (Sri Lanka), 55, 188; Malacca, 100; Malaya, 188; Pakistan, 188; Philippines, 98; Singapore, 148, 186

Azurara, Gomes Eannes de (also Zurara), 6, 95

Atlantic, 1–2, 15, 27–8, 38, 44, 65, 67, 70, 77, 89, 92, 94–5, 97–9, 103–4, 119, 121, 127–8, 139, 147, 152, 157, 167, 182, 184, 195–6, 198, 218n9; Atlantic islands—Azores, 182; Canarians (Guanche), Canaries (Canary Islands), 92, 94–5, 101; Madeira (the Madeiras), 7, 39, 92, 94, 101, 182, 206n15; Atlantic charter, 184; Atlantic world, 2, 94
Auratus, Johannes, 76
Australia, 145, 157, 186
Austria, 7, 24–6, 147–8, 153
Avilés, Pedro Menéndez de, 38, 40, 205n15, 208n30

Bainton, Roland, 219n21
Baker, Richard, 140
Banneker, Benjamin, 125
barbarian(s)/barbaric/barbarism/ barbarity/barbarous, 2, 11, 20, 27, 37, 45, 51, 60–2, 65, 75–6, 97, 111, 124, 126, 134–5, 144, 168, 170, 185, 222n59, 224n67
Barker, Ernest, 235n114
Barros, João de, 99
Basanier, Martin, 34–5, 213n126
Bate, W. Jackson, 226n25
Batimaussa, Lord, 96
Baxter, Richard, 105
Behn, Aphra, 6, 105–15, 138; *Oronooko*, 6, 105–15, 138
Belgium, 183
Belknap, Jeremy, 136–7
Belleforest, François de, 17, 19, 73, 76–9, 209n34, n36
Bengorion, Joseph, 85
Bentham, Jeremy, 7, 146
Benzoni, Girolamo, 21, 28, 32, 60, 209n45, 212n113, 222n59
Berardi, Juanotto, 98
Bermuda, 165, 186, 205n15; Juan Bermudez, 206n15
Biard, Auguste-François, 148

biblical authors/figures, Aaron, Herod, Isaiah, Jesus, Joseph, Matthew, Moses, 92
Black Legend, 16, 19, 28, 36–7, 40, 46, 50–1, 53, 64, 136, 207n22, 214n137, 218n17
Blackstone, William, 93, 145
Blackwell, Boston, 179
Blake, William, 125, 193
Bloom, Harold, 226n25
Bodin, Jean, 215n142
Bolívar, Simon, 146
Bonaparte, Napoleon (born Napoleone Buonaparte), 119, 145–7, 195
Boston (Massachusetts), 116, 123–4, 160, 168, 176–7, 197–8, 222n57
Bourdieu, Pierre, 7–8, 203n8–n9
Bovis, Monsieur de, 145
Boxer, C. R., 137
Brach, Pierre de, 222n57
Brayton, Patience Greene, 117, 134
Brayton, Preserved, 117
Brazil, 146, 148–50, 153–4, 182, 186, 193, 207n25, 209n42, 215n142, 221n56
Brent, Linda, 173
Britain, see England, xvii, 12–13, 31, 85, 89, 118–22, 127, 129, 134, 136, 138, 145–50, 153, 155–6, 182–4, 186–8, 192–3, 199–201, 235n116; Royal Navy, 118, 145, 147, 199–200; Scotland, 25, 161, 199; United Kingdom, 188; Wales, 83, 86
British Empire, xvi, 3, 24, 31, 146, 150, 182, 186, 188, 195, 200–1, 218
British North America, xvi, 7, 120–3, 136, 156–7, 182
Brown, James N., 152
Brown, John, 161
Bruès, Guy de, 47
Bruges, 93, 204n5
Buchanan, James, 153
Bunche, Ralph, 182, 185–6, 247n265
Bunyan, John, 29, 212n101
Burgundy, 13, 26, 57

Burke, Peter, 47, 60, 222n59
Burleigh, Lord, 87
Burns, Alan, 249n18
Burrowgh, William, 87
Butler, Pierce, 163

Cabot, John (Giovanni Caboto), 14,
    33, 41, 43–5, 56, 67, 86, 213n121
Cabot, Sebastian, 14, 18, 213n121
Cabral, Pedro Álvares (Alvarez or
    Pedralvarez), 44, 54
Cadamosto, Alvise, 94–6
Calvin, Jean, 215n138; Calvinist(s),
    17, 199
Camelo, Hernandéz, 206n15
Camillus, 92
Canada, 7, 12, 16–17, 73, 119, 148,
    156–7, 163, 171, 176–7, 181, 184,
    186, 192, 208n26, 215n142;
    Montreal, 118, Nova Scotia, 13, 200,
    249n18; Quebec, 118, 232n85
Candish, Thomas, 87
Canning, George, 147
Canny, Nicholas, 213n125
Canzo, Gonzálo Méndez de, 40
Capdequí, J. M. Ots y, 99
Cape Breton, 44; Cape Cod, 206n15;
    Cape of Good Hope, 43–4; Cape
    Verde islands, 43
capital/capitalism, 12, 91, 93, 101
Cardinal Morton, 56; Cardinal
    Riario, 53
Caribbean, *see also* West Indies, 7,
    18–19, 48, 99, 101, 114, 120, 127,
    138, 143, 145, 154, 173, 186;
    Barbadoes, 141; Guadeloupe and
    Martinique, 7; Jamaica, 127, 137,
    143, 200; Santo Domingo (Sainte-
    Domingue), 98–9, 119, 199; Taino
    Indians, 98
Carlisle, Thomas, 109
Carpenter, E., 160
Carpio, Lope de Vega, 49
Cartier, Jacques, 16, 18, 33, 67
Castanheda, Fernão de, 99

Castañheda, Pedro de, 196
Castile/Castilian, *see* Spain, 12, 49,
    54–5, 57, 59, 63, 72, 93, 98–9,
    224n2, 229n6
Castlereagh, Lord (Robert Stewart), 147
Catalan(s), 44, 92; *Catalan Atlas*, 93
Cathay (China), 71, 81–2
Catholic(s)/Catholicism, 1, 15–19,
    29–31, 35, 37, 62, 69, 71, 97, 104,
    115, 143, 152, 170, 190, 200,
    209n42, 214n137, 215n138;
    Catholic Church, 1, 30, 120;
    Catholic emancipation, 170;
    Jesuit(s), 17, 44
Certa, Don Luis de la, 43
Certeau, Michel de, 222n58
Cervantes (Miguel de Cervantes
    Saavedra), 68
Champlain, Samuel de, 37
Charles I, 99; Charles V, Holy Roman
    Emperor, 2, 13, 52, 54, 69, 71, 101,
    152, 196, 207n18
Charles III (Spain), 120
Chateaubriand, François-René de, 147
Chaucer, Geoffrey, 78, 81
Chauveton, Urbain, 21, 32, 212n113
Child, David Lee, 160
Child, Lydia Maria Francis (also known
    as Francis), 160–1, 172–4
China, 44, 81–2, 99–100, 148–9, 186,
    191, 248n283
Christ, Jesus, 18–9, 52–4, 158,
    171, 182; Christendom, 19, 24,
    28–9, 52, 63, 86, 210n57
Christian/Christianity, 2, 4–5, 13–5,
    23, 29, 32, 37, 40, 43, 46–53, 58–9,
    61, 82, 86, 88, 91, 93–7, 100, 103,
    113, 124–5, 127, 137, 141, 143–4,
    151, 156, 158–9, 168, 171, 183,
    188, 190, 196, 210n57, 224n2,
    227n36; Christian, 5, 46; humanist
    critique, 46; critique of empire, 15;
    republicanism, 37; Judeo-Christian, 1;
    hypocrisy of Christianity, 171;
    non-Christians, 2

Churchill, Winston, 184, 186–7, 246n263
Cicero/Ciceronian, 47, 55–6, 71, 75, 77, 93
Cieza, Pedro de, 36
class, 7, 56, 95–6, 100, 107–8, 111, 128–9, 156, 160, 163–4, 181
Classical world, see Greece and Rome, 12, 47, 52, 62–3, 73, 85, 87–8, 123; Carthage, 57; classical allusions/ myths, 46, 61, 73; antecedents, 91–2; authority/tradition, 73; inheritance, 1, 6; knowledge/ learning, 64, 69; past, 13, 46, 73, 85; classicism, 62; Hannibal, 201; Syria, 57
Clayton, George, 149
close attention/reading, 6, 68
Cobden, William, 150
Code Noir, 6, 114, 127, 145, 232n85
Cohinto, Diègue, 44
Colbert, Jean-Baptiste, 114
Cole, Christien, 199
Colet, John, 53
Coligny, François de, 21; Coligny, Gaspar de, 16–18, 21, 24, 35, 209n42
collection(s), 16, 32, 68–9, 85, 94, 179, 214n137, 245n235
Colletet, Guillaume, 214n138
colonial/colonies/colonists/colonization/ colonizer/colony, xvii, 2–9, 13–14, 16–23, 29–40, 46, 49–51, 59–60, 62–9, 73, 75, 86, 88, 92, 97–100, 102–7, 114, 117–20, 122–3, 126–7, 129–30, 135–7, 145–50, 152–3, 156–7, 181, 188–90, 195–201, 205n15, 208n26, 212n111, 213n125, 215n142, 230n35, 238n86; decolonization, 181, 183, 186–7, 190, 193, 195, 246n263; postcolonial/postcolonialism, 64, 217n8, 222n57, 223n72, 227n47
Columbus, Christopher (Colón), 1, 4–6, 12, 15, 24, 32, 35, 41, 43–8, 53–4, 56, 58–9, 67–8, 71–3, 86, 88,

95, 97–100, 105, 108, 111, 136–7, 157, 195–7, 205n8, 209n40, 217n7, 223n63, 224n2, 229n24, 224n108
Columbus, Diego (Colón), 48–9
companies, 86, 120; British East India Company, 148; Companie of Muscovy Marchants, 86; Company of Senegal, 199; Dutch East India Company (VOC), 105, 198; Netherlands or Dutch West India Company, 104, 120; Royal Africa Company, 121
comparative context, 201; comparative method, 3; comparative cultures and empires, 8; comparative discussions, 5; comparative ethnology, 72; comparative European context, 66; comparative study of empires, 9
Comstock, Elizabeth Leslie Rous Wright, 163
conquer/conqueror(s)/conquest, 1, 4, 12, 16, 21, 23–4, 26–7, 33, 36, 38, 57, 63–4, 82, 86, 93, 96, 99, 105, 112–3, 123, 136, 184, 207n22, 224n2
conscience/conscientious, 12, 104, 168, 173, 180, 185, 194–5
contest(s)/contestation/contestatory/ contesting, see agon, xv–xvii, 1–4, 7–9, 67, 84, 88, 102, 107, 118, 131, 164, 178, 184, 193–7, 200–1
contesting empires, xv, 1, 3–4, 194
contradiction(s)/contradictory, 3, 7, 9, 11, 16, 47, 49, 64, 69, 88, 103, 122, 148, 155, 166, 173, 181, 193, 195, 199, 200, 223n72
Cope, William, 87
Córdoba, Pedro de, 49
Coronado, Francisco Vásquez de, 196–7
Correia, Gaspar, 99
Corte Real, Gaspar and Miguel (brothers), 44
Cortés, Hernán (Cortez),, 23, 28, 60, 211n92

cosmographer/cosmography, 14–15, 17–20, 55, 67, 73–4, 76, 78–9, 85–6, 88, 102, 208n26

Courbet, Ernest, 222n57

Couto, Diogo do, 99

Creelman, James, 156

Crignon, Pierre, 102

critique, 19, 32, 46, 51, 56, 59, 62–3, 76, 81, 116, 140, 183, 220n34; alternative/oppositional, 48, 51, 64

Cromwell, Oliver, 47

Crone, G. R., 93

Crowther, Bishop Adjai, 200

cruel/cruelty, 41, 46, 51, 61–3, 139–40, 174, 201, 209n37, 220n34; cruel blessedness, 41; cruelty as a word or term, 139, 174; cruelty of Americans, 151, 158, 197; of the British, 127, 130, 139; of Christians, 158; of Europeans, 139, 174, 197; of the Spaniards, 5, 12, 19, 22–4, 28, 30–2, 37–8, 46, 48, 50–1, 60–1, 63, 100, 136, 139, 195, 201, 209n45, 214n137, 218n17; of the Natives, 20, 23, 61, 96, 123; of slaveowners/ slavery, 138, 140, 141–3, 151, 158, 165–6, 169–74, 180, 201; of whites, 140, 197; drama of cruelty, 140; papal cruelties, 143; theme of cruelty, 140, 165

Cuba, 120, 137, 146, 148–9, 153, 182

Cullen, James and Ann, 144; Miss Cullen, 144

culture(s), xv, 1–9, 29, 60, 64, 67, 83, 91–4, 99, 108, 113, 120, 130, 156, 198–9, 201; cultural and economic practice, 91; cultural capital, 91; cultural comparison, 143; cultural difference, 116; cultural domination, 1; cultural exchange, 94; cultural framework(s), 48, 111; cultural history, 64; cultural imposition, 156; cultural relativism, 49, 185; cultural studies, 6; culture of truth and fiction, 218n8; ethnological and

cultural glass, 76; high culture, 4; interpretation of cultures, 7; meeting of cultures, 9; metropolitan culture, 8; multicultural states/democracy, 186, 192; transcultural translation, 8

Dances with Wolves, 157

Davies, William, 199

Davis, John, 86

Davis, Natalie Zemon, 217–18n8

De Bry, Theodor (Theodore), 36, 51

Declaration of Independence, 122, 124–7, 152, 169, 185, 190, 192, 197, 201, 235n116

democracy/democracies/democratic, 3, 89, 146, 183, 185, 192–3

De Monts, Pierre du Gua, sieur, 37

Dexter, Mary Morton, 158; Mrs. N. N. (her sister), 158

Dias, Bartolomeo, 43

Diaz, Pedro (Pero), 39–40

Diderot, Denis, 66, 122

Dier, Edward, 87

discover/discover, *see* recognition/ misrecognition, 1, 8, 13, 16–18, 20, 23, 25, 32–3, 35–7, 39, 47, 57, 62, 68, 71, 76, 78–80, 85–7, 102, 106, 123, 136, 176, 178, 191, 206n15

displace/displacement, xvi, 4, 11, 16–17, 28, 65, 73, 79, 103, 151, 154, 178

donation(s) (bulls), papal, 2, 15, 32, 35, 43–5, 88, 96–7, 100, 127, 205n12, 207n19

Douglass, Frederick, 150–1, 166–71, 175–6; figures in narrative, Mr. Covey, 170; Mr. Gore, 170; Mr. Severe, 170

Drake, Francis, 24, 28, 35, 38, 40, 85–7

Drinker, Elizabeth Sandwith, 134–5

Du Bellay, Joachim, 18, 73

Du Bois, W. E. B., 157, 177–8, 198; *Souls of Black Folk*, 177–8; *Suppression of the African Slave-Trade*, 177

Dudley, John (earl of Warwick and
duke of Northumberland), 15
Dulcanquellín, 49
Duplessis-Mornay, Philippe (Philippe
du Mornay, seigneur du Plessis-
Mornay), 23–31, 80, 210n57
Duviols, Jean-Paul, 102

early modern, 12, 47, 68, 78, 92, 196
Easmon, M. C. F., 249n18
East Indies, 24, 28
Eccles, W. J., 207n19
economic(s)/economy, 8, 17, 56, 65,
91, 93–5, 97–9, 104, 119–20, 137,
144–7, 150, 155–6, 168, 174, 182,
186, 188, 192–3, 197–8, 208n32,
248n283; Atlantic economy, 98;
British economy, 119, 137, 144,
246n263; economic analysis, 193;
economic and political imperialism,
248n283; economic dependence, 89;
economic and political restraints, 34;
economic development, 186–7, 193;
economic growth, 193; economic
models and trade patterns, 28;
economics of slavery/bondage, 3, 7,
103; economic opportunity and
safety, 186; economic servitude, 186;
European economy, 118–19; market
economy, 12; world economy, 146
Eden, Richard, 14–16, 33, 85, 205n12
Eisenhower, Dwight, 184, 186,
246n263
El Dorado, 59, 214n136
Elizabeth I (England), 18, 23, 25, 29,
34, 81–2, 101, 103, 147, 157
Elliott, J. H., 1
emancipation, *see* slavery, 127,
153–4, 164–8, 170, 175, 177,
180, 189, 198
empire(s), xv–xvii, 1, 3–5, 7, 9, 11,
12–17, 23, 26, 29, 33–4, 36, 41,
44–7, 50, 53, 59, 64, 66–7, 70,
72–5, 78–9, 82–3, 88, 91–2, 94–5,
100–2, 105, 113, 118, 126, 144,

146–7, 149–50, 156–7, 178, 181–8,
193–201, 207n22, 208n26, 211n92,
226n25, 227n47, 240n107
Empiricus, Sextus, 47
emulate/emulation, 4–5, 11–12, 16, 31,
65, 119; imitate/imitation, 17, 20,
33, 35, 53, 75, 77, 88, 132, 210n54,
215n142
England, xv–xvi, 3–6, 11–18, 22–5, 27,
29–39, 44–6, 50–1, 53–7, 62–6,
79–85, 87–9, 97, 101, 120–1,
134–6, 138, 142–3, 146–7, 162–3,
165–6, 176, 183, 201, 205n8, n15,
213n121, 219n22, 222n57; Church
of England, 17
English America, 92, 117, 123,
230n35; British America, 2, 121–2,
125, 129, 133–4, 136
English Commissioners, list of (Peace
of 1604), x
English Empire, 24, 31, 65
Enlightenment, 12, 65–6, 83, 115,
122, 129, 145
envy, 11, 17, 37, 162
Equiano, Olaudah (Gustavus Vassa),
122, 137–44, 158, 165, 237n56;
The Life of Olaudah Equiano, 137–44
Erasmus, Desiderius, 4–5, 46–7, 51–4,
59, 64, 201, 219n2–22, n25,
220n32, n34, 222n57
Erondelle, Pierre, 37
ethnography/ethnographic, 8, 73–4,
208n26; ethnographical description,
94; ethnographical estrangement, 60;
ethnographer, 60; ethnographic
writing, 8
ethnology/ethnological, 6, 9, 56;
comparative ethnology, 72;
ethnological lens/glass, 61, 76
example of Spain (instance or model of
Spain), 3, 14, 16, 21, 34–8, 44, 59,
65, 101, 123, 219n22; after Spain, 4,
11, 41, 65, 201
eyewitness, 50, 54, 61, 69–70, 73–4, 76,
86–7, 109, 172, 208n26, 215n142

Feinburg, H. M., 120
Fenton, Edward, 86
Ferdinand II of Aragon (V of Castile), 45, 70–1, 98–100
Ferdinand VII, 146
Ferguson, Stephen, 212n110
Fichet, Guillaume, 52
Fisher, M., 8, 203n8
Flanders, 13, 22, 26–7, 39, 54, 57, 93
Flemish, xv–xvi, 39, 55, 93, 206n15, 208n32, 214n137; Flemish Commissioners, list of (Peace of 1604), xvi
Flores (Florius), Lucius, 81–2
Florida, 16–21, 31, 35–6, 38–41, 64, 80, 86, 100, 120, 196, 198, 200, 205n15, n22–n23, 208n27, 213n125 n130
Florio, John, 34, 223n62, n67
Foster, Abby Kelley, 150
France, 3–6, 11–44, 46, 48, 50–8, 60–8, 73–7, 80, 84, 88, 97, 102–3, 118–21, 127, 145, 147–8, 153, 157, 182–3, 186, 196, 199, 205n8, n15, 207n18, n22–n23, 209n42, 215n139, n142, 219n22, 221n56, 232n85
François Ier (king of France), 13, 16, 45, 52, 157, 196, 204n3, 205n6
Franklin, Benjamin, 122, 126, 136
Franklin, Wayne, 226n26
Franks, Bihah Abigail Levy, 117
freedom, 53, 89, 92, 96, 106, 122–3, 125, 129, 134, 138–9, 141–2, 150, 152, 154–6, 159, 162–3, 166–7, 169, 171–3, 175, 177–91, 195, 200, 202, 221n56; freedom of worship/conscience, 30, 104, 169
French Empire, 114, 119
Frobisher, Martin, 23, 32, 34, 86
Froude, James, 206n17
Fugger (merchants), 101
Fumée, Martin, 22
Fyfe, C. H., 200

Gage, Thomas, 123
Gama, Vasco da, 43
Gandhi, Mahatma (M. K.), 7, 182–3, 190, 192; *Hind Swaraj*, 183
Garrison, William Lloyd, 159, 166–8, 171, 201
Garthe, Richard, 87
Gates, Henry Louis, Jr., 237n25, n56
Gaugin, Robert, 52
Geertz, Clifford, 8
gender, 7, 107, 112, 128–9, 132–3, 149
Genoa/Genoese, 29, 86, 92, 97
geographer(s)/geographical/geography, 14, 16, 27, 54, 73, 77, 79, 226n26
George II, king of Britain, xvi
George III, king of Britain, xvi, 122, 127, 235n116
German Empire, 26
Germania syndrome, 222n59
Germany (German states), 25–6, 65, 119, 183–4, 186, 219n28, 222n59; Brandenburg, 120
Gerrard, Thomas, 200
Gilbert, Humphrey, 32, 34, 86, 200
Gilbert, Olive, 172
Giles, Peter, 53–6
Giovio, Paolo, 99
Gladstone, William, 156
glorify/glorious/glory, 12, 14–15, 17, 23, 33, 37, 52, 59, 70, 72, 77, 81–5, 112, 124, 133, 135, 138, 150, 178, 192; la gloire, 37
Gómara, Francisco López de, 21–3, 60, 222n59
Gonneville, Binot Paulmier de, 41, 44–5
Gordon, Nathaniel, 153
Goropius, Joannes, 82
Gossan, Stephen, 210n54
Gourges, Dominique de, 35
Graham, G., 199
Graham, John, 117
Graham, Isabella Marshall, 117–18
Grant, W. L., 214n138

Greece, 17, 62, 77, 88; Greek(s), 12,
    55, 62–3, 78, 80, 92, 116, 184, 199
Greenblatt, Stephen, 220n32, 226n26
Grenville, Richard, (Grinfil), 34–5,
    38–9
Grey, Lady Jane, 15
Grey Owl (Archie Belaney), 157
Grimké, John Faucheraud, 159
Grimké, Mary Smith, 159
Grimké, Sarah Moore, 161
Grotius, Hugo, 84
Guaynacapa (emperor of Peru),
    214n136
Guiana, 36, 106, 110, 112, 154,
    214n136
Guzman, Nuño de, 196–7

Habsburgs (House of, Spain and
    Austria), 13, 24, 51; Bourbon
    (House of), 31
Hacket, Thomas, 18, 20, 208n31
Hakluyt, Richard the Elder, 79,
    213n126
Hakluyt, Richard the Younger, 3–4, 6,
    12–13, 16, 20–4, 28–34, 36–7,
    64–9, 78–88, 200–1, 204n6,
    206n17, 210n55, 212n111,
    213n126, 215n142, 223n71,
    226n25–n26, n28, 249n12; Hakluyt
    Society, 216n150, 217n7
Hallett, Robin, 120
Hancock, John, 124
Hawkins, John, 6, 18–19, 86–7,
    103, 198
Hegel, Georg Wilhelm Friedrich, 196
Hemmersam, Michael, 104
Henri de Navarre/Henry IV (France), 3,
    23; Henri II (Henry II, France), 16,
    21; Henri III (Henry III France),
    23–8
Henry, Patrick, 167
Henry VII (England), 11, 82, 86;
    Henry VIII (England), 82, 86
Henry the Navigator (Prince Henry of
    Portugal), 93

Herodotus, 60, 214n138
Herrara, Alfonso de, 206n15
Hill, Christopher, 29
Hispaniola, 48, 86, 99–100
historiography, 37, 67, 75; the
    historiography of expansion, 20, 78
history, 6, 9, 13, 16–17, 19, 21, 24, 34,
    48, 50, 52, 60, 68–74, 81–2, 99,
    106–7, 109, 121–2, 127, 167–8,
    184, 187, 189, 191, 214n136,
    215n142, 217n8, 218n18, 221n50,
    222n58; chauvinistic history, 52;
    Ciceronian history, 71; critical
    history of race, 178, 184; cultural
    history, 64, *see* culture, 64; history as
    event or writing, 21; as memory and
    glory, 23; as mirror, 213n128; as
    representation of the heroic, 77; as
    representation or observation, 69–70;
    as story and inquiry, 78; as story
    and/or truth, 106, 109–10; history
    of Bermuda, 205n15; history of
    conquest, 23; history of discourse,
    20, 35; history of slavery/the slave
    trade, 152, 167; history plays, 23,
    210n50; natural history, 16, 69–74,
    77, 208n26; official history, 75, 154;
    oral history, 224n2; political, legal,
    constitutional history, 189–90;
    school history, 154; scientific history,
    78; systematic history, 224n2; textual
    history, 20, 94, 210n57, 214n131;
    universal history, 50; world
    history, 43
Hitler, Adolf, 184
Hobson, John A., 227n47
Homer/Homeric, 56, 77–8, 133,
    211n92
Horace/Horatian, 46, 77, 138
Horton, James Africanus, 199–200
Huguenot(s), 3, 16–21, 23–4, 28–31,
    34–5, 64, 80, 118, 200, 205n15,
    208,n32
humanism/humanist(s), 14–15, 17,
    37, 46–7, 51–6, 59, 64, 99,

183, 222n57, 223n72; humanist
critique, 46
human rights, 3, 7, 65, 129, 149–50,
159–60, 162, 168, 181–2, 184, 189,
201; Universal Declaration of
Human Rights, 185
Hutchinson, Thomas, 124
Hythlodaeus, Raphael, 54–9

ideological/ideology, 1, 131, 145;
ideological Cold War, 184; editor,
49; voice, 68
imperial/imperialism, 68–9, 73, 79,
88, 103, 105, 120, 145, 148–9,
156, 178, 182–4, 186, 188, 195–6,
214n136, 226n25, 248n283
India, 3, 43–4, 85, 99, 148, 156, 183,
186, 188, 190–3
Inquisition, 30, 48, 143
interpret/interpretation/interpreter(s), 3,
7, 8, 13–14, 21, 43, 46, 49, 59, 61,
65, 69, 81, 96, 99, 127, 135, 155,
168, 174, 198, 203n9, 222n57–n58
Iodelle, Estienne, Seigneur du Limodin,
75–6
Ireland, 83, 213n125
ironic/ironies/irony, 9, 46–8, 52, 54,
56, 64, 96, 106, 108, 112–3, 123,
125, 138, 151, 164, 171, 220n32
Isabella I of Castile (and Aragon), 45,
70–1, 98, 229n24
Italy, *see* Rome, 13, 26–7, 52–3, 57,
59, 61, 65, 77, 93, 183, 221n28,
243n138; Florence/Florentine, 13,
97–8, 121, 204n5; Genoa/Genoese,
29, 86, 92, 97; Milan, xvi, 13, 27,
57, 94; Naples, 27, 57; Sicily, 26–7,
95; Venice/Venetian, 28, 52–3,
57, 105
ivory, 93, 104, 150

Jackson, Andrew, 160
Jackson, Isaac, 161
Jacobs, Harriet, 160, 172–7; *Incidents in
the Life of a Slave Girl*, 160, 172–7;

figures in narrative, Benny, 176–7;
Dr. Flint, 175–7; Ellen, 176–7;
Mr. and Mrs. Bruce, 176–7;
Mr. Sands, 175–6
James, Daniel, 166
James I (England, James VI of
Scotland), 29, 36, 83
Jane, Cecil, 217n7
Japan, 44, 82, 184
Jeannin, Pierre, 215n143
Jefferson, Thomas, 122, 125, 127, 145,
173, 201, 235n116, 238n85
Jenkinson, Anthonie (Anthony), 86–7
Jew(s)/Jewish, 62, 92, 99, 104, 115,
117, 119, 121, 151, 185, 190, 201
João III (John III of Portugal), 54,
99–100, 196
Johnson, James Weldon, 178;
*Autobiography of a Ex-Colored
Man*, 178
Johnson, Lyndon, 186
Joyce, James, 240n108
Juvenal/Juvenalian, 46, 76, 139

Keats, John, 28, 191, 211n92
Kemble, Charles, 162
Kemble, Frances Anne (Fanny), 162–3
Kemble, Maria Theresa de Camp, 162
Kendricks, Tine, 180; figures in the
interview, Arch Kendricks, 180;
Reverend Dickey, 180; interviewer,
Watt McKinney, 180
Kennedy, John, 186
Kennedy, Paul, 119
Kennett, White, 31
kidnap/kidnapper/kidnapping, 99, 101,
103, 113, 121, 123, 138–9, 144,
156, 193
Kilham, Hannah, 119
King, Martin Luther, 7, 164, 177,
182–3, 189–92, 195
King Philip (Metacom or Metacomet),
115, 197–8
Knight, Sarah Kemble, 116–17
Kupperman, Karen, 226n26

La Boétie, Estienne de (Étienne),
222n59
Lafayette, marquis de (Marie Joseph
Paul Yves Roche Gilbert du
Motier), 148
Lafitau, Joseph-François, 215n142
Lane, Ralph, 34
La Popelinière, Lancelot Voisin, sieur
de, 22, 80–2, 209n46, 215n142
Las Casas, Bartolomé de, 3, 5–6, 19,
21–3, 32, 40, 41, 46, 48–53, 58–66,
100–3, 108, 110, 128, 136, 138–40,
142, 157, 164–5, 174, 197, 200,
209n45, 217n7, 218n16, n18,
224n2, 229n29
Latin, 12, 20, 36, 47, 52–3, 75–6,
80–3, 87, 94, 116, 204n1, 210n54,
213n121; Latin America, 16, 146–7,
217n8
Laudonnière, René de Goulaine de,
18–19, 35
law, 13, 19, 32–3, 37, 43–4, 57, 91–2,
98–9, 116, 121, 127, 142, 145,
152–4, 160, 162, 169, 174–6, 180,
185–6, 193; antislavery laws, 147–8;
Athenian Constitution, 126; canon
law, 96; civil law, 30, 145; Civil
Rights Act (US), 190; constitution,
146, 152, 189; Constitution of
Liberia, 152; divine/holy law, 13,
18; Fugitive Slave Law, 177;
illegitimate/outlawed, 7, 89, 127,
182, 236n20; international law, 2;
Jim Crow law, 180; private law, 2;
law of nations, 84, 145, 164; law of
nature (natural law), 2, 84, 93, 145;
lawmakers/lawyer(s), 37, 45, 50, 56,
146, 159–60; Laws of Burgos, 101;
legitimacy/legitimate, 32, 97, 101,
187; New Laws of, 1542, 101;
Roman-Dutch law, 104; Roman law,
92, 98; rule of law, 188; *terra nullius*,
13, 157; U.S. Constitution, 126,
137, 146, 153–4, 164, 189–90,
192, 198

Le Challeux, Nicolas, 18, 18–21, 28,
208n30
Ledesma, Martín de, 101
Lenin, Vladimir Ilyich, 193, 227n47
Leon, Ponce de, 100
Léry, Jean de, 11, 17, 20–1, 60–2, 66,
73, 102, 240n108
Lescarbot, Marc, 17, 37, 60,
214n137–n138, 215n139,
n142–n143
Lestringant, Frank, 73, 207n24,
208n26, 209n46, 213n126,
215n142, 223n71
liberty, *see* freedom, 7, 28, 32, 88, 118,
122–3, 126–30, 133–7, 142, 144,
146, 150, 154–6, 160, 166–7, 177,
184, 190–2, 195, 197, 200–1
life-writing, autobiographies, 109,
122, 137, 139, 157, 173, 178;
biographies, 109, 159–60, 214n138,
241n117–n118, n123, 242n124,
247n265; diaries, 7, 115, 117, 129,
134–5, 138, 157, 159; memoirs, 105,
139, 163, 175, 178, 210n57, 232n84
literary/literature, 6, 64, 76, 80, 137,
148; Latin literature, 47; literary
and cultural studies, 6; literary and
historical representations, 5; literary
fame, 124; literary/literature, 6;
literary representations, 5, 12; literary
studies, 9; literature of expansion, 78;
literature of the Black Legend, 36;
literatures, histories and politics, 9;
promotional literature, *see*
promotion, 34; travel literature, 83,
222n58; Western literature, 124
Lincoln, Abraham, 7, 151–5, 172, 182,
189–90
Lisbon, 44, 93, 97, 100–1, 121, 182
Liverpool, Lord (Jenkinson), 147
Lloyd, Selwyn, 189
Logan, George, 219n31, 220n32
Lok (Locke), Michael, 23, 34
London, xv–xvi, xviii, 3, 15, 22, 23,
33, 52, 54, 117, 119, 123, 137,

143–4, 148–9, 161–2, 165, 176, 199, 204n5; Royal Academy, 137, 148
Lopez, Aaron, 119
Lopez, Francisco, 36, 214n136
Loring, E. G., 160
Lorraine, Cardinal de, 209n42
Louise of Savoy, 196
Louis XIV (France), 31, 37, 114, 119
Louisiana, 118–20
Lowther, George W., 177
Lucian/Lucianic, 46, 52, 55, 58, 220n32
Lynum, Edward, 217n7

Mabo case, 157, *see* law (*terra nullius*)
Macarthy, Charles, 199
Machiavelli, Niccolò, 201
Macmillan, Harold, 182, 186–9, 191
Magellan, Ferdinand (Fernão de Magalhães), 22, 44, 81, 196–7
Maitland, Lord and Lady, 106–8
Mandela, Nelson, 182–3, 188–9, 192
Mandeville, John, 59–60, 226n26
Manifest Destiny, 19
Manuel (king of Portugal), 44; Manuel I, 54
Marchionni, Bartolommeo, 97; Marchionni merchants, 98
Marcus, G., 8, 203n8–n9
Marivaux, Pierre Carlet de Chamblain de, 122
Marquand, Allan, xvi
Marqués, Pedro Menéndez, 38–40
Martyr, Peter (Pietro Martire d"Anghiera), 15, 58, 217n7
Marx, Karl, 168, 193
Mary I (England), 14–15, 22, 31, 33
Massachusetts, 118, 123, 159, 161, 163–4, 171, 177
Maurits, Johan, 104
mediate/mediation/mediator(s) (go-between[s]), *see* interpret, 16, 30, 36, 41, 96, 131, 177, 229n28
Medici, Lorenzo Pietro di, 59

Mediterranean, 27–8, 94, 101, 119, 143, 196, 243n138; Malta, 148
Mendoza, Bernardino de, 38
Mercer, General, xvi
Mexico, 20, 31, 63, 86, 101, 154, 186, 196
Middle Ages, 1, 48, 84, 92–3, 95, 97, 178
Middle East/Near East, Egypt/Egyptian, 77, 92; Gulf of Arabia, 28; Iran, 186; Israel/Israelites, 45, 92; Levant, 76–8; Saudi Arabia, 186; Suez, 28, Suez Canal, 183, Suez Crisis, 186
military-clerical complex, 41
Milton, John, 142
Mirandola, Gianfrancesco Pico della, 47
Molucca(e)(s) (Indonesia), 28, 81
Montaigne, Michel de, 4–5, 11, 34, 46–7, 56, 59–64, 76, 108, 110, 113, 138, 201, 217–18n8, 218n10, 220n34, 221n56, 222n57–n59, 223n63
Montesino, Antón (Antonio Montesinos), 2, 48–9, 64, 100, 229n29
Montesquieu, Charles de Secondat, Baron de, 121–2, 145, 201
Montúfar, Alonso de, 101
Moor(s), 6, 49, 91, 93, 95, 99, 105
More, Thomas, 4–5, 11, 14, 46–7, 52–9, 76, 88, 201, 219n25, n30, 220n32, n34, 222n57; *Utopia*, 5, 46–7, 51, 53–9, 76, 88, 219n25, n30–1, 220n32, n34, 222n57
Morland, George, 137
Motive(s), 4, 15, 39, 88, 108, 121, 131, 188, 222n58; synecdochic motive, 15
Mott, Anne, 159
Mott, James, 159
Mott, Lucretia Coffin, 163, 242n124
Moura, Bastiam, 44
Muslim (culture, empire, traditions, slavers), 91, 94, 97–8, 103, 146, 156; Islam/Islamic, 94

Münster, Sebastian, 14
Musquito, 143
Muthos (mythos), 23;
  mythology/myths, xvi, 13, 20, 46,
  83, 94, 154, 198

nation/national/nationalities/nationalis
  m, 4–5, 9, 11, 14, 16–17, 21–2, 24,
  28–9, 31, 35, 38, 43–7, 51–3, 57,
  61, 63, 66, 68–9, 71, 73, 76–7,
  80–9, 97, 102–3, 112, 119–20, 123,
  138, 141, 143, 145, 149, 151, 153,
  155, 158, 161, 164, 177–8, 181–4,
  186–99, 201, 205n15, 208n26,
  214n136, 226n25, 227n47;
  multinational, 101, 105; League of
  Nations, 147; nation above race, 189;
  National Assembly of France, 137;
  National Maritime Museum
  (Greenwich), ix; National Portrait
  Gallery (London), xvi;
  self-determination, 188, *see* United
  Nations
Native(s), 1, 2, 5–6, 12–13, 15–16,
  18, 20–4, 32–4, 36, 40–1, 45–51,
  56, 58–65, 89, 97–103, 110,
  116, 122–3, 126, 136, 138, 143,
  148, 156–7, 160, 181, 195–8,
  207n25, 221n56, 223n63, 224n2,
  229n28
natural historians/history, 5, 16, 68–71,
  73–4, 77, 208n26, 224n2
Netherlands, xvi, 5, 11–12, 16, 23–32,
  35, 38, 50–3, 64–5, 89, 97, 102–5,
  120, 127, 147, 182, 195, 200,
  207n18, n22, 246n263
Nettesheim, Agrippa of, 47
New England, 37, 115, 119, 123, 137,
  158, 160
Newfoundland, 44, 198
New Zealand, 148
Nicholas, Thomas, 22–3, 210n54
Nobel, Alfred, 191; Nobel Prize, 185,
  190, 192
Northwest Passage, 13, 44, 86

object/objectivation/objectivism/
  objectivity, 8, 71, 87, 110, 225n2
oceans, *see* Atlantic; Indian, 198–9;
  Pacific, 28, 189, 211n92
Ockham, William of, 47
Oliveira, Fernão de, 101
opposition/opposition-from-within (to
  expansion, empire, slavery), 1–5, 9,
  34, 36, 41, 43–67, 100–1, 105, 110,
  115, 135–7, 147–8, 152, 154, 158,
  163, 166–7, 181, 183–4, 195, 199,
  201, 222n57; self-criticism, 11, 65
Oré, Luis Jerónimo de, 40
origins, 14, 32, 35, 53, 71, 118–19,
  162, 206n15
Oviedo, Gonzalo Fernández de, 4–5,
  17, 50, 66–75, 79–80, 87–8,
  206n16, 208n26, 224–5n2
Oxnam, John, 86

Pagden, Anthony, 66, 214n137, 224n2
Paris, xviii, 13, 19, 23, 38, 52, 64, 80,
  94, 120, 127, 148, 153; Convention
  of Paris, 127; Peace of Paris, 153
Parker, John, 18
Parker, Mary S., 161
Parmentier, Jean, 102
Peale, Charles Willson, xvi
Peale, James, xv, xvi, xviii
Peckham, George, 200
Peru, 28, 31, 35, 36, 63, 81, 98,
  101–2, 105, 214n136
Peters, John, 125
Philip II (prince then king of Spain), 4,
  14–15, 22–3, 25–6, 33, 37–8, 102,
  205n16, 206n16, 207n18, 213n22
Philip III, 40
Phillips, Wendell, 168–9
Pigafetta, Antonio, 196
Piso, Willem, 104
Pitt, William, xvi, 122, 137
Plato, 46, 54–7, 59, 62, 75, 77–8,
  183, 185
Plautus, 58
Pliny, 69–70, 73, 81, 224n2

Plutarch, 109
politics/political, 3, 7–9, 17, 27, 34, 46,
    57, 65, 73, 76, 83, 91–3, 96–7, 99,
    104, 119–22, 126, 133, 136–7,
    144–6, 151, 156, 162, 168, 174,
    183, 187–9, 192, 195, 197, 200–1,
    208n26, 235n114, 248n283;
    European politics, xvi, 41; political
    independence, 189; political
    persecution, 186; political
    philosophy, 185; politics of the
    British Empire, 218n9, 221n56;
    politics of racism, 181; religious
    politics, 96; triangulation of Spain,
    England and the Netherlands, xvi
Polo, Marco, 46, 60, 196, 240n108;
    Rusticello, 240n108
Pope/papacy/papal, 1–2, 5, 7, 12, 15,
    17, 32, 35, 43–5, 47, 51–3, 63,
    88, 97, 100, 127, 143, 207n19,
    215n139; Papal Inquisition, 48; Pope
    Alexander VI, 15; Benedict, 143;
    Julius II, 53; Leo X, 100; Nicholas V,
    43, 96; Urban VIII, 105
Portugal, 2, 5, 12–13, 15–18, 21–4,
    27–8, 32–3, 35, 43–5, 48, 54–5, 65,
    87–8, 91, 93–9, 101–3, 120, 122,
    127, 137, 147–8, 157, 182–3,
    195–6, 200
Portuguese Empire, 102, 118, 217n6
Post, Amy, 177
practice(s), 3, 7, 9, 16, 22, 41, 49, 77,
    89, 91–3, 95, 97, 99, 103–4, 114,
    127, 129, 134, 137, 139, 143–6,
    148, 162, 169, 173, 181, 186,
    189–90, 193, 198, 208n5
Pratt, Mary Louise, 8
Price, Richard, 200–1; *Two Tracts*, 200
Prince, Mary, 165–6, 172, 243n138;
    figures in her narrative, Daniel James,
    166; Hetty, 165; Mash, 166; Mr. and
    Mrs. Williams, 165; Mrs. Pruden,
    165; the Woods, 166
Princeton (New Jersey), ix–xii,
    212n110

promotion (of expansion, empire,
    slavery), xvii, 1, 3, 6, 11, 15, 23, 34,
    41, 45, 67–89, 167, 195, 199,
    226n25; promotional tracts/
    literature/tactics, 6, 34, 45, 67;
    self-promotion, 68, 226n25
Protestant(s), 12, 14, 16–21, 24–5,
    29–31, 34–5, 37–8, 50, 62, 64–5,
    80, 83, 190, 196, 200, 207n25,
    214n137; Calvinist(s), 117; Calvinist
    certainty, 198
Prussia, 7, 147–8, 153
Ptolemy, 76–7, 79, 85
Pugh, Catherine, 161
Pugh, Jesse, 161
Pugh, Sarah, 161
Purchas, Samuel, 16, 21, 37

Quaker(s) (Society of Friends), 117,
    121, 127, 134–6, 143, 152, 160–1,
    163, 172, 177, 199
Quincy, Justice, 123
Quinn, David and Alison, 210n55;
    David, 216n150
Quint, David, 220n34, 221n56,
    222n57

Rabelais, François, 52, 63
race/racial/racism, 6, 94, 100, 106–7,
    111–2, 118, 124–5, 129, 133, 140,
    143, 149–51, 156, 162, 167, 169,
    173, 177–8, 180–2, 184, 186–7,
    189–90, 193, 197–8, 224n2,
    240n107; Klu Klux Klan, 178–80;
    Nazi(s), 178, 181, 184–6, 201
Ralegh, Walter, 24, 29, 34–6, 38, 87,
    213n126, 214n136
Ramusio, Giovanni Battista, 33, 204n6,
    213n121
Rastell, John, 14, 53, 219n30
Raynal, Abbé Guillaume, 66
razzias/raids (seizures of slaves), 6, 97
recognition/misrecognition, 1, 8, 168,
    176, 185, 224n4
Reed, Ishmael, 181

religion, 4, 12, 15–17, 19, 22, 25, 29,
  31, 33, 35, 45–6, 48–50, 53–4,
  59–65, 80, 83, 92, 94, 96, 108,
  115–17, 120–3, 135, 137–8, 141–52,
  158, 166, 168–76, 183, 190, 192,
  196–201, 207n25, 213n125, 224n2
Remond, Charles Lenox, 167
Renaissance, 1, 12, 16, 23, 68–9, 74,
  122, 185, 208n26
Republican/Republicanism, 37, 47,
  154, 215n143
Requerimento (Requirement), 100, 103
revolt, 22; Revolt of/in the Netherlands,
  5, 12, 16, 30–1, 35, 38, 64, 146,
  207n18, n22; Dutch Revolt,
  103, 200
revolution/revolutionary, 125, 127,
  151, 167, 174, 177; American
  Revolution (War of Independence),
  ix, 2, 6, 7, 47, 89–137, 148, 150,
  157, 167, 177; English Revolution,
  7, 129, 134, 136, 146; French
  Revolution, 7, 65, 128–9; Glorious
  Revolution, 128; Revolutions of
  1848, 149
Reynolds, Mary, 198; figures in her
  narrative, Master, 198; Miss
  Sarah, 198
rhetoric, 3–4, 6, 8, 12, 15–17, 34, 41,
  52, 58, 65, 67–8, 70–3, 77, 81, 85,
  127, 166, 174; outsized rhetoric, 166;
  rhetorical analysis, 8, 68; rhetorical
  and narrative embellishment,
  222n58; rhetorical flourish, 166;
  rhetorical heritage, 88; rhetorical
  history, 78; rhetorical magpie, 85;
  rhetorical means and motives, 88;
  rhetorical moves, 72, 74; rhetorical
  proofs (exempla), 78; rhetorical
  squint, 72; rhetorical strategy, 70;
  rhetoric of freedom, 167; rhetoric of
  seduction and/or exploitation, 88,
  112; rhetoric of texts, 17
Ribault, Jean (also Ribaut), 18–21,
  28, 33

Ríos, José de los, 105
rival(s)/rivalry/rivalries, 4–5, 11–14, 17,
  20, 22, 25, 31, 34, 44–6, 50–1, 65,
  71, 81, 102, 119, 196, 201, 209n40
Roberval, Jean-François de la Rocque,
  16, 18, 102, 196
Rocha, Frei Manuel Ribeiro da, 122
Roman(s), 12–13, 28, 49, 75, 86, 88,
  92, 111, 215n139; dictator,
  Camillus, emperors, Titus and
  Vespasian, 85; Holy Roman
  emperor/Empire, 13, 24, 26;
  Roman-Dutch law, 104; Roman
  emperor/Empire, 25, 73, 85, 187,
  191; Roman law, 92, 98; Rome, 6,
  12, 17, 47, 52–3, 57, 70, 73, 81–2,
  92, 99, 185, 222n59
romance, 74, 105, 107–8, 112, 144,
  208n26, 224n2, 240n108
Ronsard, Pierre de, 18, 73, 76, 222n59
Roosevelt, Franklin Delano, 184
Rousseau, Jean-Jacques, 110, 122
Ruggles, David, 171
Russell-Wood, A. J. R., 44
Russia/Russian, 7, 86, 91, 147–8, 153,
  191; Kiev, 86; Moscow, 86; Soviet
  Union (USSR), 184

Saint Augustine, 55–6, 93, 107, 174;
  Saint Thomas Aquinas, 93
Saint Bartholomew's Day/Massacre
  (La Charité-sur-Loire), 11, 19–21,
  60; Sancerre (famine/siege), 20, 60–1
Santa Cruz, Pedro de, 38
satire/satirical, 4, 9, 11, 46, 51–2, 54,
  56–8, 60, 64, 76, 125, 138, 178,
  219n25, 220n34
Scandinavia, Denmark, xv, 25, 120,
  137, 182; Norway, 190; Sweden, 25,
  120, 147, 186
Schlesinger, Roger, 73–4, 208n26
science/scientific, 8, 14, 47, 52, 75,
  77–8, 111, 125, 138, 144, 173, 188,
  205n8; human sciences, 8; natural
  philosophy, 8

Sedgwick, Catherine Maria, 164
Seed, Patricia, 223n63
self-government, 157, 184, 188
Seneca, 58, 87
Sens, Cardinal de, 74
Sepúlveda, Juan Ginés de, 2, 23, 50, 100–1
serf(s)/serfdom, 7, 153, 157; servitude, 6, 89, 92, 100, 152, 186, 197
Seville, 33, 51, 97–8, 100, 121
Seward, William, 153
sex/sexual, 6, 88, 107, 112–13, 126, 133, 141, 161, 193, 228n169; sexing of America, 88; sexual and racial equality, 150
Shakespeare, William, xvii, 39, 58, 83–4, 105, 107, 112, 204n11, 210n50, 227n48, 228n69, 229n28, 240n108, 243n138; *As You Like It*, 107; *Othello*, 105
Sheldon, Charlotte, 134–5
Shepard, Hety, 115
Sidney, Henry, 32
Sidney, Philip, 4, 29–30, 33, 106, 200
Simms, Bill, 180–1; interviewer Leta Gray, 180
Sitting Bull (Tatanka Yotanka), 156–7
Skelton, R. A., 196
slave ports, Amsterdam, 149; Bahia, 101, 121, 149; Bristol, 149; Florence, 121; Glasgow, 118; Havana, 119, 149, 206n16; La Rochelle, 118; Lisbon, 93, 110, 121; Liverpool, 118–19, 147, 149; London, 119; Nantes, 119, 149; New Orleans, 149, 160; Newport (Rhode Island), 119, 123; New York, 117–19, 130, 134, 149; Pernambuco, 101, 104, 149; Rio de Janeiro, 149; Salem, 119; Seville, 97–8, 100, 121; New York/abolitionists/antislavery courts/women's rights, 153, 159, 161, 171–2, 176–7
slavery, 2, 3, 6–7, 9, 58, 88, 91–194; antislavery, 105, 137, 148, 152, 156, 159–63, 166–72, 177, 184;

antislavery cities, 103–4; antislavery laws, 147–8; antislavery societies, American and Foreign Anti-Slavery Society, 150; American Anti-Slavery Society, 160–1; American Colonization Society (antislavery), 152; American Women's Anti-Slavery Convention, 161; antislavery petition, 159; Anti-Slavery Society (New York), 159; British and Foreign Anti-Slavery Society, 161, Pennsylvania Society for Promoting the Abolition of Slavery, 136; Philadelphia Female Anti-Slavery Society, 159, 161; curse of Ham, 103; Slave Narrative Collection (Federal Writers' Project), 179; theory of natural slavery (Aristotle), 2, 6, 23, 100–1, 126, 164; Underground Railroad, 161; West India code, 142
slave trade, 2, 6, 9, 18, 89, 91–195, 198, 235n116; *asiento*, 119
Smith, Adam, 193
Smith, John, 60
Smith, Valerie, 242n130
social, 6, 8, 46, 56, 61, 95, 107–8, 120, 149, 151, 154, 191, 197; Social Darwinism, 186; social change/reform, 149, 213n125; social movement/mobility— emigrant(s)/emigration, 150; immigrant(s)/immigration, 156, 186; migrant(s)/migration, 7, 186; social myth, 154; social strife/unrest, 56, 198; sociology, 7
Somerset House, xv–xvi, xviii
sovereign/sovereignty, 2, 30–1, 45, 70–1, 74, 84, 119, 157, 184, 188, 208n26
Soto, Domingo de, 101
South Africa, 118, 183, 186–93, 198; Bishop Desmond Tutu, 192; Boers, 156; Cape Town, 153, 187, 198; Chief Albert Luthuli, 191; F. W. de Klerk, 192; Xhosa, 156; Zulu, 156

Spain, xv–xvi, 2–5, 11–46, 48–55, 58–9,
    62–7, 70–2, 84, 88, 91, 94–103,
    119–20, 123, 127, 136, 146–7,
    152–3, 157, 182, 195–6, 198,
    200–1, 205–6n15, 207n22–n23,
    208n32, 214n136–n137, 219n22;
    Madrid, 43; Spanish Armada, 20,
    35; Spanish Commissioners, list
    of (peace of 1604), xv1; Spanish-
    Flemish-English Peace Conference
    (1604), xv–xvi
Spanish Empire, 23, 64, 86, 102,
    146, 182
spice trade, 43, 102; Carreira da
    India, 43
Stabler, Arthur P., 73–4, 208n26
Staël, Madame de (Germaine de Staël-
    Holstein), 148
Stafford, Edward and Lady, 23, 80
Stalin, Joseph, 227n47
Steele, Ian K., 206n16
Stowe, Harriet Beecher, 153, 163,
    172; *Uncle Tom's Cabin*, 153,
    163–4
Stanton, Elizabeth Cady, 163
Staper, Richard, 87
Strabo, 76
Stukely, Thomas (Stucley), 18,
    213n125
subjective/subjectivity, intersubjectivity, 8
sugar, 7, 97–9, 101–2, 104, 110,
    119–20, 137, 145–50, 154, 169,
    182, 195
Surinam, 105, 113, 182
Swift, Jonathan, 113, 138; *Gulliver's
    Travels*, 54, 141
symbol/symbolism, 125, 189

Tacitus, 222n59
Tagore, Rabindranath, 201; *Gitanjali*,
    200–2
Tarquin; 47, 92, 185; Lucretia
    (Lucrece), 47, 185
Tejo, 196
Terence, 124

theory/theoretical/theorists, 2, 6–7, 22,
    64, 93, 97, 100–1, 127, 129, 164,
    189, 198, 208n5, 217n8; racial
    theories, 167, 181; theory of
    empire, 126
Thevet, André, 4, 6, 16–17, 19–20, 60,
    62, 66–9, 73–82, 87–8, 102, 201,
    207n25, 208n26, 209n36–n38 n40,
    215n142, 222n59
Thomas, Ella Gertrude Clanton, 163
Thomas, Hugh, 103, 147, 230n36,
    246n255–n256
Thompson, George, 161
Thoreau, Henry David, 183
Thorne, Robert, 33
Thorpe, John, 119
Todorov, Tzvetan, 224n2
Toscanelli, Paolo, 43
Tracy, Antoine Louis Claude Destutt
    de, 145, 238n85
trade, 5, 16, 19–22, 27–9, 34, 36,
    43–5, 82, 92–8, 101–6, 111, 114,
    118–22, 127, 144–52, 159, 194,
    208n32; foreign merchants, 204n5
translation/translator, xvi, xvii, 4, 8,
    14–16, 18, 20–3, 28, 33–7, 59,
    64–5, 81, 83, 85, 87–8, 94, 145,
    153, 160, 172, 183, 196, 204n6,
    205n12, 208n30–n31, 209n41,
    n48, 210n54, n57, 212n114,
    213n128, 214n136, n138,
    215n142, 218n14, 220n40,
    221n44, 222n57, 223n60, 225n3,
    226n25, 227n36, 230n31, 232n85,
    235n114, 238n86, 249n24;
    translation of empire (*translatio
    imperii*), 11–12, 17, 28, 47, 62, 70,
    73, 88, 144, 211n92, 226n25; of
    faith, 88; of poetics, 226n25; of
    study, 17, 73, 211n92, 226n25
treaties, 147, 153, 184, 206n16;
    Quintuple Treaty, 148; Treaty of
    Paris, 120
trope(s), 12, 69, 74, 78–9; of God
    and gold, 45; of translation of

empire (*translatio imperii*), 17, 47, 70, 85, 94
Trowbridge, Caleb, 116
Trudel, Marcel, 207n19
Truth, Sojurner (Isabella Baumfree), 172; figures in her narrative, the Wagenens, 172
Tupinamba, 44, 60; Tupinikin, 44
Turgenev, Ivan Sergeyevich, 153
Turk(s)/Turkey, 26, 28, 49, 77, 87, 98, 105, 143, 196
typological/typology, 1, 5, 12, 21, 29, 38, 46, 61, 92, 95, 107, 138, 166, 169, 176, 187, 221n56; typological comparison, 60, paradigm, 46, urge, 1
tyrannical/tyranny/tyrant, 2, 13, 23–4, 30–1, 47–8, 61–2, 92, 122, 133, 135, 138–42, 175, 185

United Nations, 89, 91, 147, 182, 184, 186, 189, 193; Charter (U.N. and League of Nations), 147; Universal Declaration of Human Rights, 185
United States, xvi–xvii, 3, 7, 19, 89, 92, 119, 122, 126–7, 134–7, 145–57, 163–5, 167, 169, 171, 177, 181–2, 184, 186, 189–91, 193, 195, 197, 199–200, 242n129
Usselincx, Willem, 104–5
utopia/utopian, 5, 6, 46, 51, 53–60, 68, 76, 88, 190, 219n31, 220n32; utopian descriptions of America, 6

Valladoid, Juan de, 97
Valverde, Francisco, 38
Venezuela, 51, 127, 146
Venice, 52–3, 57, 105
Verlinden, Charles, 92
Verrazzano, Giovanni de (also Verrazano), 5, 13, 18, 33, 45–6, 102, 204n5–n6
Vespucci, Amerigo, 14, 53, 55–6, 58–9, 205n8, 219n30–n31

Victoria (queen of Britain), 156
Villegagnon, Nicolas Durand de (also Villegaignon), 16, 20–1, 61–2, 102, 207n25, 209n42
Virgil/Virgilian, 47, 56, 77–8
Virginia, 36–7, 40, 86, 104, 127, 153, 161, 206n15, 243n138
Vitoria, Francisco de, 2, 65, 84
Vives, Juan Luis de, 52, 219n22
Voltaire, François Marie Arouet de, 122, 185

Walsingham, Francis, 23, 34, 79, 82, 200, 226n26
war, xv, 1, 3–4, 6, 12, 22–7, 37–9, 47–8, 51–3, 56–60, 88–9, 92, 98, 101–2, 110–2, 119–23, 126–7, 130–1, 134, 136, 147, 151, 154–6, 164, 180–1, 183–8, 193, 195–201, 206n16, 209n45, 220n34; American Civil War, 127, 144, 151, 153–5, 161, 164, 168, 177, 181; Cold War, 184, 193; Crimean War, 153; Eighty-Years War, 214n137; English Civil War, 47; First and Second Opium Wars, 149; First World War, 183, 187; French Civil War, 21, 24, 35, 64; hegemony, 31, 60, 220n34; King Philip's War, 115; Napoleonic wars, 146, 199; propaganda war(s), 12–13, 65; Second World War, 178, 184–8; Seven Years' War, 119; War of 1812, 148; War of Spanish Succession, 16, 31; Wars of Religion, 18, 35, 60–1; world wars, 181, 187; war with the Turks, 105
Washington (DC), 155, 189–90
Washington, George, xvi, 197
Weld, Angelina Emily Grimké, 159
Weld, Theodore, 159
Wellington, duke of (Arthur Wellesley), 147
West, Benjamin, xvi
West India/West Indian/West Indies, 6, 13, 18, 32, 36–8, 68–70, 86, 97–8,

West India—*continued*
104, 118–20, 122, 136, 138, 141–3,
145, 148, 150, 159, 166, 182,
198–9, 208n32
Wheatley, John, 123–4
Wheatley, Phillis, 123–5
White Indians, 126, 156, 178
White, John, 1, 35–6
Whittier, John Greenleaf, 170
Wilberforce, William, 7, 137, 147–8
Wilkinson, Eliza Yonge, 130–4
Wilson, Charles, 207n18
Withrington, Robert, 86
Wolfe, James, 140
women, 114–5, 117, 128, 133–5,
149, 157, 163, 165, 186, 197,

201, 235n1; and the exotic, 110;
First
Women's Rights Convention, 149–50;
slavery, 118, 142, 158–9, 163, 165,
169–73, 179, 233n86; rights, 7, 94,
149–50, 159, 161–3, 172; Native
women, 111; women's suffrage, 161,
182; writing about slaves/slavery,
129–35, 157–66, 201
Worden, N. A., 198
Wordsworth, William, 191, 193

Xenophon, 220n34

Yearsley, Mrs., 135
Yeats, W. B., 249